Defending the Community College Equity Agenda

Defending the Community College
Equity Agenda

Edited by

THOMAS BAILEY

VANESSA SMITH MOREST

The Johns Hopkins University Press

Baltimore

The Johns Hopkins University Press
2715 North Charles Street
Baltimore, Maryland 21218-4363
www.press.jhu.edu

Library of Congress Cataloging-in-Publication Data
Defending the community college equity agenda /
edited by Thomas Bailey and Vanessa Smith Morest.
p.   cm.
Includes bibliographical references and index.
ISBN 0-8018-8447-0 (hardcover : alk. paper)
1. Community colleges—United States—Administration. 2. Community colleges—
Curricula—United States. 3. Educational equalization—United States.
I. Bailey, Thomas R., 1950– II. Morest, Vanessa Smith, 1969–
LB2341.D39 2006
378.1′01—dc22
2006008099

A catalog record for this book is available from the British Library.

For C. Lloyd Bailey and David J. T. Smith
our fathers

CONTENTS

Thomas Bailey is the George and Abby O'Neill Professor of Economics and Education in the Department of International and Transcultural Studies at Teachers College, Columbia University. He is the founder and director of the Community College Research Center at Teachers College, Columbia University. He is a labor economist, and his current research is focused on the institutional and individual determinants of student success in higher education.

Vanessa Smith Morest is Assistant Director of the Community College Research Center. Dr. Morest's research uses sociological perspectives to analyze organizational change in education and is currently working on institutional research at community colleges.

Kevin J. Dougherty is Associate Professor of higher education and a Senior Research Associate at the Community College Research Center, Teachers College, Columbia University. Dr. Dougherty is currently researching the origins and consequences of performance accountability policies, the content and origins of state policies shaping access to and success in community colleges for minority and low-income students, and the impacts of business financing of university research.

Esther Hong is a doctoral student in sociology and education at Teachers College, Columbia University. She also works on collegiate learning assessment at the Council for Aid to Education, a national initiative focused on assessing higher education institutions' value added to undergraduate student learning.

Rebecca D. Cox is Assistant Professor in the Department of Education Leadership, Management, and Policy at Seton Hall University. Her research interests include the organizational and institutional contexts of faculty work and the realities of teaching and learning inside community college classrooms.

Jim Jacobs is the Associate Director for Community College Operations at the Community College Research Center and the Director of the Center for Workforce Development and Policy at Macomb Community College. He was the past president of the National Council for Workforce Education, a national postsecondary organization of occupational education and workforce development specialists.

W. Norton Grubb is the David Gardner Chair in Higher Education in the Graduate School of Education at the University of California, Berkeley, where he is also faculty coordinator of the Principals Leadership Institute. In addition to community colleges, his interests span the economic and occupational effects of education, the "improved" school finance, high school reforms, equity and inequality, and comparative dimensions of education.

Dolores Perin is Associate Professor of psychology and education at Teachers College, Columbia University, where she also directs the Reading Specialist Program and is a Senior Researcher at the Community College Research Center. Her research interests include learning difficulties in adults, cognitive processes underlying literacy acquisition, and curriculum and policy in developmental and adult literacy education.

Kerry Charron is a Doctor of Education candidate in the Higher and Postsecondary Education program at Teachers College, Columbia University.

Melinda Mechur Karp is a Research Associate at the Community College Research Center, Teachers College, Columbia University. Her work focuses on the transition from high school to college and work.

First and foremost, we must thank the Alfred P. Sloan Foundation, and particularly Jesse Ausubel, our program officer at the foundation. In 1996, on behalf of the foundation, Jesse asked Teachers College to submit a proposal for a community college research center. This led to the founding of the Community College Research Center (CCRC) at Teachers College. As a project of CCRC, this book, and indeed all of our work, would not have been started or completed without the encouragement and support of the foundation.

During the past several years, community colleges have attracted a great deal of attention from the press, policy makers, private foundations, the U.S. Departments of Education and Labor, other public-sector agencies and funders, and academic researchers. Several foundations—such as the Lumina Foundation for Education, the Ford Foundation, the Mott Foundation, and the Gates Foundation—have initiated high-profile, multimillion-dollar initiatives to strengthen community colleges. But that situation was very different ten years ago, when only a handful of academics specialized in community colleges. The overwhelming majority of research on higher education focused on four-year institutions. A trickle of research funding flowed from a small number of foundations, and, despite some ambitious programs such as the National Science Foundation's Advanced Technological Education program, the colleges were not a priority at the federal level.

The Sloan Foundation realized that community colleges enrolled almost half of all undergraduates, and among them were concentrated many low-income, first-generation, and minority students who faced particular barriers to achieving their higher education goals. Moreover, the institutions played a crucial role in many labor markets in preparing the country's workforce. In light of the significant role that the institutions played, the dearth of research on them made little sense. The foundation set out to correct that deficiency. Events of the last decade have shown that many others subsequently played a fundamental role in raising awareness about community colleges, and shedding light on these important institutions.

Second, we want to thank the community college staff, administrators, faculty, and students who generously gave their time and answered our questions. Setting up the field work is time consuming for staff members involved, and in many cases we continued to ask for information and data long after we left the campuses. We are indebted to the dedicated staff at the colleges, who embraced our research and assisted us at every step of the way so we could conduct the field research. Our experiences during the course of this study have shown us the amount of work and responsibility taken on by community college staff, administrators, and faculty and their deep commitment to supporting the missions of their colleges. As a result, we are much more appreciative of the time that they devoted to talking with us and providing information and insights. Over the course of these visits, and many more for other projects, we have come to respect and admire the work and dedication of community college faculty, administrators, and staff.

It was also a great pleasure working with our team of authors. Although this is an edited volume, it is also very much a collective work. We met several times during the project and jointly designed the protocols, selected the sample of states and colleges, discussed early drafts, and developed general themes. All of the authors participated in the field work and cooperatively responded to our many requests for revisions and updates. We learned a great deal from out work with them.

We also want to thank the many research assistants, associates, and staff who participated in the field work. These include Norena Badway, Debra Bragg, Kerry Charron, Terry Orr, Kathleen Keane, Jennifer Kim, Moonhee Kim, and Erika Rasch. Tim Leinbach cheerfully responded to our many requests for data and updates of data (as the length of the project grew). No project at CCRC is possible without the help and guidance of Lisa Rothman, the associate director for finance, administration, and communications. The project required a tremendous amount of travel, logistics, organization, and coordination, and Lisa deftly managed these. Excellent clerical support was provided by many of our project assistants, including Tia Dole, Annika Fasnacht, Alexandra Gribovskaya, Kathleen Keane, Gretchen Koball, Lauren Koch, Agnes Kwong, Lauren O'Gara, and Nikki Thompson. Mort Inger edited earlier drafts of the chapters. As the manuscript was being completed, many of our colleagues and coauthors at CCRC helped read drafts and correct errors. These included Peter Crosta, Katherine Hughes, Analia Ivanier, Melinda Mechur Karp, Lauren Koch, Tim Leinbach, Dolores Perin, Lauren O'Gara, Monica Reid, Lisa Rothman, and Andrea Soonachan. We particularly want to thank Brooke Mahl, who took charge of managing the manuscript in its last stages, a tedious and complex task she carried out with skill and good humor.

Although this book is the result of a discrete project and was funded by resources from the Sloan Foundation, the thinking and insights that underlie it have all been influenced by our work on other projects, and reports and publication based on those projects are cited throughout the book. We particularly want to acknowledge the following funders and projects: the U.S. Department of Education, though both the National Assessment of Vocational Education and various projects funded through the Office of Vocational and Adult Education; the National Science Foundation, through its Advanced Technological Education Program; the Ford Foundation, through the Bridges to Opportunities project; and the Lumina Foundation (and other funders) through the Achieving the Dream: Community Colleges Count initiative. But just as important as the funders are the numerous friends and colleagues we have met and worked with in the course of our activities on all of these projects. We are sure that many of them will see the influence that they have had on this work.

We are particularly indebted to two of our close colleagues at the CCRC who were not directly involved in this project but have had a profound influence on our thinking—Katherine Hughes and Davis Jenkins. Two CCRC alumni have also been helpful—Greg Kienzl and Mariana Alfonso.

Finally, we must thank our spouses and children—Claude and Henry Morest, Carmenza Gallo, and Erika and Daniela Bailey—who have put up with the interminable travel, meetings, and weekends at the computer.

We dedicate this book to C. Lloyd Bailey and David J. T. Smith, our fathers. We lost both of them during this project, and we are constantly reminded of the void their loss has left in our lives. This work owes a great deal to the goals and values they taught us.

Defending the Community College Equity Agenda

CHAPTER ONE

Introduction

Defending the Community College Equity Agenda

THOMAS BAILEY AND VANESSA SMITH MOREST

During the past two decades, access to higher education has become increasingly important. Individuals without education beyond high school have limited access to good jobs. At least some college education has become the minimal entry requirement to the middle class. College access has therefore become fundamental to economic opportunity in the United States. Young people perceive that reality, and when high school students are asked about their ultimate educational goals, the vast majority states that they want at least an associate degree (Alfonso, 2004; Bailey, Jenkins, and Leinbach, 2005).

In light of the growing importance of a college education, in the past several decades public policy has sought to open access to higher education to students from all income levels. In 2001, the (Congressional) Advisory Committee on Student Financial Aid stated that "three decades ago, there was unanimous agreement on the nation's access goal: low-income students who were academically prepared must have the same educational opportunity as their middle- and upper-income peers" (p. vi). By the beginning of the twenty-first century, the federal government made available more than $8 billion a year in direct grants, most of which were need-based, and about $33 billion in loans (U.S. Department of Education, 2003b, Indicator 42). In the 2003–2004 academic year, states provided another $6 billion in grant aid, about three-quarters of which was need-based (National Association of State Student Grant and Aid Programs [NASSGAP], 2005). Of course, a much more substantial public investment comes from direct state subsidies to colleges. In 2000 this totaled $63 billion (U.S. Department of Education 2005b, Table 335). Although these state resources go to students of all income levels, the lower tuition made possible by these subsidies has been crucial to providing access to higher education for lower-income students.

Recently, the discussion of equity in higher education has expanded beyond the concept of equal access articulated by the Congressional Advisory Committee. In addition to access, equity in higher education depends on both strengthening every student's opportunity to become "academically prepared" and enhancing their chances of achieving success once they are enrolled. Getting students into college (access) is not enough if they face financial, social, or educational barriers to achieving their postsecondary educational goals.

The overall concept of higher education equity involves three parts: equity in college preparation, access to college, and success in reaching college goals. These three components form a framework for thinking about the higher education equity agenda. For several reasons, higher education remains inequitable for each of these three components. Low-income and many minority students have less access to high-quality secondary education that would prepare them for college; once prepared, they are less likely to enroll in college; and once in college, they are likely to accumulate fewer credits and less likely to complete their degrees. When they do complete their degrees, they are likely to be lower-level degrees, such as certificates and associate degrees rather than baccalaureate degrees.

Many factors influence eventual college outcomes, and some students secure relatively good jobs or meet their personal goals without completing a college degree. Nevertheless, outcomes that are highly correlated with income or race and ethnicity are strongly suggestive of inequalities at some level. It is the premise of this book, and of our overall work, that a student's income or race should not be a significant determinant of his or her educational achievements. Public and institutional policy should be designed to break that relationship. Data on educational attainment by race and income indicate that we are far from achieving that goal.

Political, fiscal, demographic, and technological trends over the past fifteen years have introduced new barriers to the postsecondary equity agenda. One trend is the long-term decline in the share of the cost of higher education borne by the public sector, often referred to as the privatization of higher education (St. John and Parsons, 2004). As a result of this trend toward privatization, tuition has risen significantly, even at public institutions, and financial aid—especially need-based financial aid—has not kept up (College Entrance Examination Board, 2004; NASSGAP, 2005). From the point of view of the colleges, however, increased tuition has not been able to compensate for the loss of state support. In any case, colleges and states are reluctant to raise tuition at community colleges because doing so conflicts with their mission of providing access to all.

Other trends that complicate the college equity mission include demographic growth, increasing demand for college education, taxpayer resistance, the growth of outcome-based accountability, growing competition among higher education institutions, including the strong growth of a for-profit sector, technological and pedagogical developments, and growing demands and expectations among employers. In many cases, these developments appear to have created strong incentives for colleges to weaken their focus on the equity agenda, complicating a mission that was already daunting.

These are challenges that face all of postsecondary education. The contributors to this volume focus on the role of community colleges both because they play such a large role in educating low-income and minority students and because, in the past, the overwhelming majority of research on higher education has been focused on baccalaureate-granting institutions (Bailey and Alfonso, 2005).

Four-year colleges face many of the same challenges addressed in this book, and the analysis presented here also has lessons for the four-year sector. For example, the economic value of the bachelor degree relative to a high school degree has grown dramatically over the past two decades. The premium associated with the bachelor degree has grown faster than it has for the associate degree. Equity in educational attainment at the four-year level is increasingly important. Four-year colleges also must confront problems associated with restricted state funding and students with inadequate academic preparation.

Nevertheless, community colleges play a particular role in the higher education equity agenda. Although they enroll just under half of all credit-earning undergraduates (U.S. Department of Education, 2003a, p. 117), community colleges serve a disproportionate share of low-income students.[1] Community colleges have built their activities around their open-door mission—providing access to college for a wide range of students. To provide this access, community colleges are expected to offer education for almost any student who comes in the door. Community colleges are also playing an increasingly important role in preparing students for college through their vast developmental education programs and growing relationships with high schools. Four-year colleges certainly have many students with weak academic skills, but the problem is much more severe at community colleges.

Although community colleges provide greater accessibility to higher education than four-year colleges, their role in increasing a student's ultimate educational attainment and their contribution to promoting overall educational equity is more difficult and more controversial. As we shall see, fewer than half of students who start at a community college earn a certificate or degree within eight years of their initial enrollment. Within community colleges, low-income and minority students are much less likely than white and middle-income students to earn credentials or transfer to a baccalaureate-granting institution. Finally, as the value and importance of the baccalaureate degree increase, the effectiveness with which community colleges can prepare students for transfer and eventual completion of a four-year college diploma will become more salient and more controversial.

Community colleges face an especially difficult task. They enroll those students who have the most daunting educational, economic, and social barriers to their education, yet they have the fewest resources per student to serve those students. Community college instructional expenditures in 2000 averaged $3,979 per full-time-equivalent student (FTE), compared to $7,149 at four-year public colleges and $8,654 at four-year public universities (U.S. Department of Education, 2005c, Tables 349–351). At the same time, as public community institutions, they are asked to carry out a variety of different functions, some of which conflict with their access and equity missions (Bailey and Morest, 2004). Furthermore, in an environment of shrinking public support for higher education, the challenges to the equity agenda may be particularly difficult for community colleges, because they are much more dependent on public resources than other sectors of higher education.

Thus, although community colleges share many equity-related issues and problems with their four-year counterparts, they also stand apart from those institutions because of their lower funding levels, their enrollment of students who tend to face greater academic, social, and economic problems, and their particular place within the higher education sector. In light of these circumstances, they deserve much more concentrated attention than they have so far received.

With this background, the goal of this book is to assess the role played by community colleges in promoting student success and equity in higher education, analyze the strength and implications of emerging challenges to the equity mission, and make suggestions that could be used to strengthen that role. We offer a reassessment of the higher education equity agenda in the context of trends that threaten the success of that agenda. We do so through a fine-grained look at the institutional predicament of a sample of community colleges as they struggle with the tension of upholding the ideal of equality of opportunity in American society while confronting growing challenges in their political, economic, and social environments that threaten that ideal. How serious are the challenges to that ideal? Have community colleges lived up to the goal of equal opportunity? Does it appear that these threats are indeed weakening the community college equity mission? How have community colleges reacted to them? What can community college administrators, faculty members, and policy makers do to maintain quality and standards, to meet the varied expectations of their communities, while they continue to enroll and effectively serve a broad range of students?

Finding answers to these questions is particularly important at this time. Pressure on state budgets will create strong incentives to promote lower-cost postsecondary education, and some states and many families have already turned to their community colleges as a less-expensive alternative to baccalaureate-granting colleges, at least for lower-division education. Will such a trend increase or weaken educational equity and, if this happens, what can colleges and policy makers do to ensure that the trend benefits all students?

The book draws on information from a variety of sources, but most of the analysis is based on information collected from fieldwork at fifteen colleges in six states. We refer to this as the National Field Study.

In the remainder of this introduction, we first assess the role that community colleges can play in promoting overall educational equity, separately discussing their roles in providing access, preparing students for college, and promoting overall educational attainment. We then review the current challenges and developments that threaten the community college equity agenda. The subsequent sections of the chapter describe the National Field Study and summarize the chapters of the book.

Community College and the Educational Equity Agenda

We identified three components over the overall equity outcomes for higher education, which we label preparation, access, and college success. We will consider the role of community colleges in each of these three areas.

College Preparation

Preparing students for college is the role of the K–12 system, and there is ample evidence that, in many cases, that system fails to carry out its role. As a result, community colleges have been forced to get involved, either through providing developmental education services to students who arrive at college with inadequate academic skills or, more recently, by working directly with high schools to improve secondary education.

Problems with the K–12 system are particularly severe for low-income students who have limited access to high-quality elementary and secondary education and therefore are less likely to be prepared for college. In the past decade, a tremendous amount of effort has been devoted to high school reform aimed at providing better preparation for college. In the early years of the twenty-first century, for example, the Gates Foundation invested hundreds of millions of dollars in this type of high school reform, and the federal government has increasingly sought to encourage better alignment between high school education and college preparation. This alignment problem is much more concentrated in high schools attended by lower-income students.

At many community colleges, more than half of the entering students are judged to be unprepared for college-level work (Perin and Charron, this volume), so community colleges have come to play an extensive role in preparing students for college. Thus, in addition to offering an open door to students who are prepared for college, they also admit students who are not prepared for college. In most states, community colleges are committed to providing supplemental instruction and services that will bring the academic skills of those students up to that standard. It is by providing students a second chance to get a high school education (in some cases, developmental students enter with no more than middle-school-level academic skills), community colleges are directly engaged in addressing the inequities in college preparation.

More recently, community colleges have begun to work with secondary schools to help strengthen college preparation in those institutions. The 1990 reauthorization of the Carl D. Perkins Vocational and Technical Education Act (commonly referred to as the Perkins Act) funded the Tech Prep program, which encouraged cooperation between high schools and community colleges and articulation between their programs, particularly occupationally oriented programs. Thus, students would take a program of courses in high school specifically designed to prepare them for the analogous program at a community college. Since the early 1990s, high school–college collaboration has broadened to encourage students to earn college credit in high school (Morest and Karp, this volume). Unlike the Advanced Placement program, which is aimed at well-prepared students clearly on a college-bound trajectory, dual or concurrent enrollment is being developed as a strategy to strengthen the academic, social, and psychological preparation of a much wider range of students. It remains to be seen whether this approach has a positive influence on students who would not otherwise have been prepared for college. Nevertheless, by the middle of the first decade of the twenty-first century, it has attracted abundant attention and enthusiasm as a strategy by which community colleges can be directly involved with strengthening the nation's college preparation system.

Access

There is strong evidence that the presence of community colleges promotes access to higher education. Lower tuition results in higher college enrollments (St. John, 2003; Kane, 2004)—an increase in average tuition of $1,000 (in 1990 dollars) would result in a 5% decline in college enrollments. Research over the past twenty years has concluded that this effect is strongest for low-income students (McPherson and

TABLE 1.1
Undergraduate Student Characteristics, Percent by Institution Type
(2003–2004 School Year)

Characteristic	All Students		
	Community College (Public Two-Year)	Public Four-Year	Private Four-Year (Not-for-Profit)
Income[1]			
Less than $20,000	29.2	22.7	20.7
Less than $30,000	42.9	33.6	31.9
Less than $50,000	63.5	51.7	49.9
Received Pell Grant	22.6	25.7	27.1
Age (on 12/31/03)			
Under 24	47.0	71.0	66.9
24–29	18.2	15.6	12.2
30 or over	34.8	13.4	20.9
Has dependent children	32.5	13.2	18.3
Enrollment			
Part-time	66.1	30.2	26.7
Part-year	46.9	23.2	27.9

SOURCE: U.S. Department of Education, National Center for Education Statistics: National Postsecondary Student Aid Study, 2004 (Data Analysis System).
1. Parents' income for dependent students; student's (and spouse's) income for independent students.

Shapiro, 1991; Kane, 1994, 1995), though some more recent research has found no statistically significant difference in the responsiveness to tuition changes by income (Cameron and Heckman, 1998; Ellwood and Kane, 2000; Dynarski, 2002). In any case, lower tuition results in higher enrollments, and the median in-state community college tuition was $1,671 in the 2003-2004 academic year, compared to $4,260 for public four-year institutions (NCES, 2005a, Table 315).

Proximity also promotes access. With more than 1,000 community colleges in the United States, at least one is located within driving distance of the vast majority of Americans. Rather than seeking prestige through the number of applicants they turn away, as four-year colleges do, community colleges anchor their social mission to inclusion with the pledge to accept any high school graduate: in many states even a high school diploma is not a requirement.

Enrollment data clearly show that community colleges play an important role in educating students from lower socioeconomic backgrounds and those who face various barriers to higher education. As Table 1.1 indicates, when compared to students at public and private not-for-profit four-year colleges, community college students are more likely to come from lower-income households, to be first-generation college students, to attend part-time or part-year, to have dependent children, and to be older. Community college students are also much more likely to have lower academic skills and to enroll in developmental or remedial education.[2] Thus, community colleges serve a disproportionate number of older, working, part-time students whose purposes, goals, and support-service needs may differ substantially from those of more typical 18–22-year-old college students.

The data on part-time enrollments are particularly interesting and illustrate a stark contrast between community colleges and four-year institutions. During the 2003–2004 academic year, only about one-third of community college students attended full time and almost half attended part year. Students at four-year colleges are much more likely to be full-year, full-time students. Thus, community colleges make postsecondary enrollment possible for many students who would otherwise have no education beyond high school (Rouse, 1995; Alfonso, 2004), though many low-income students, in particular, still have limited access to higher education.[3]

Success in College

What about college success beyond access? Do equally prepared students enrolling in college have the same opportunity to complete a degree or achieve some other postsecondary outcome? Researchers have long been preoccupied with college retention and completion and, in general, find that low-income students have lower retention and completion rates, even after controlling for measures of academic preparedness (Alfonso, 2004; Alfonso, Bailey, and Scott, 2005). College success, however, has not been prominent in the public policy discussion until recently. Graduation rates, for example, are still not widely known by the public or policy makers. Accreditation systems were traditionally focused on college inputs, such as minimum qualifications for professors, rather than outputs, such as student graduation or retention rates, and federal and state regulation of colleges was, in turn, built on the accreditation system. During the past decade, accreditation agencies and state and federal agencies have increased their focus on graduation and other student outcomes. Some states are developing accountability systems with a stronger focus on outcomes (Dougherty and Hong, this volume), and, since the late 1990s, the federal government has made available data on graduation rates for all colleges whose students are eligible to receive federal financial aid.

We have argued that low tuition and open-door policies at community colleges do promote access to higher education, but what happens to students once they enter? As tuition rises, and if that increase is not matched by additional financial aid, we might expect to see relatively more low-income students, and even middle-income students, enrolling in community colleges than in four-year institutions because community colleges cost less. Such a shift might dampen the negative access effects of

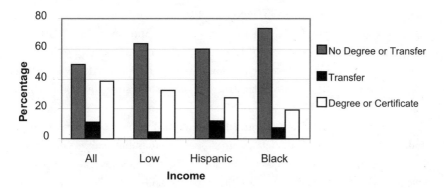

Figure 1.1. Educational (Highest) Outcomes for Community College Students with Eight Years of Initial Enrollment.

Source: National Educational Longitudinal Survey (NELS); author's calculation.
Note: Outcomes are for the highest credential earned. A student is labeled as a transfer only if he or she does not earn a degree or certificate. Socioeconomic status defined by NCES; quartiles computed among all NELS students in postsecondary education.

increased tuition, but its effect on overall equity of educational attainment would depend on the success that those students have once they have enrolled.

Seventeen percent of starting community college students never complete ten credits within eight years of high school graduation. Another 33% complete ten credits or more but never earn a certificate or degree or transfer to a four-year college. Within those eight years, 18% of those who started college in a community college earn a bachelor degree, 15% an associate, and 6% a certificate, and an additional 11% had transferred to a four-year college but had not earned any degree.[4]

Furthermore, low-income and minority students complete degrees and transfer at lower rates than white and higher income students. Figure 1–1 compares outcomes for low-income (lowest SES quartile), black, and Hispanic students to those of all students. After eight years, only 29% of low-income and 20% of black community college students have completed a degree or certificate.

These are simple single-variable comparisons. Nevertheless, more comprehensive analyses that control for other background characteristics likewise find that blacks, Hispanics, and low-income students are less likely to complete degrees or transfer than their upper-income and white community college counterparts (Alfonso, Bailey, and Scott, 2005).

There is no question that the characteristics of community college students thwart their success in college. Students who delay enrollment in college, attend part time, or interrupt their studies are less likely to complete degrees (Horn and Carroll, 1996; Adelman, 1999; Alfonso, Bailey, and Scott, 2005). Significantly, as we have seen, these are typical characteristics of community college students. Community college students also face a complex of academic, family, work, and personal problems that make it difficult for them to succeed in college (Cohen and Brawer, 2003; Gooden and Matus-Grossman, 2002).

Community college advocates and staff often argue that many community college students do not intend to complete a degree. Because community colleges have many focused programs designed to teach practical skills, it is possible that students enrolled in the colleges are there to learn those specific skills rather than earn degrees. Evidence does suggest that modest economic benefits do accrue to students who earn credits in community colleges, even without obtaining a degree (Kane and Rouse, 1995, 1999; Grubb 2002a; Marcotte, Bailey, Borkoski, and Kienzl, 2005), though the strongest earnings gains go to degree completers. Subdegree goals could account for the low graduation rate. As one community college president said in response to criticisms of colleges for low graduation rates, "I continue to be discouraged that these articles do not ever account for the students who come to the community colleges with different goals. . . . I think this continues to be one of our challenges: to remind university researchers of the multiple missions of the community colleges and define success by the students who meet their personal goals. Then we would be in a better position to talk about how much more community colleges need to do."

Initial college goals do influence student outcomes. Students who start college stating that they are there to learn a specific skill are less likely to persist and complete than those who state that they want to earn a degree. One of the strongest effects of social class on college attendance is that lower-income students end high school with less-ambitious goals than middle- and upper-class students. These expectations and goals do influence their eventual achievement (Alfonso, 2004). Nevertheless, the large majority of community college students state that they want at least an associate degree, and indeed, among the traditional students in the NELS sample, 80% say that they expect to earn a bachelor degree. After eight years of initial college enrollment, fewer than half of those in this group have earned a baccalaureate degree or transferred to a four-year college. Expectations and goals do influence community college persistence and attainment, but, even when these factors are taken into account, many community college students are not attaining their goals (for a more detailed discussion of this issue, see Bailey, Jenkins, and Leinbach, 2005).

One long-standing controversy in community college research involves the contention that students who want a bachelor degree are less likely, if they start in a community college, to complete a baccalaureate than if they enroll directly in a four-year college. Critics have argued that community colleges appear to offer an open door to the bachelor degree, through enrollment and eventual transfer, but that, as we have seen, very few students ever complete this trajectory. Students either end up in vocational programs that do not transfer or have difficulties navigating the complicated transfer process (Brint and Karabel, 1989; Dougherty, 1994). Thus, although community colleges may promote equality of access to some postsecondary institution, they may exacerbate educational outcome inequality. Empirical tests of this contention suggest that otherwise-similar students who want to earn bachelor degrees are less likely to achieve that goal if they start their postsecondary education in a community college (Rouse, 1995; Alfonso, 2004; Pascarella and Terenzini, 2005). One implication of this argument is that it might make sense for community colleges to be merged with four-year institutions, perhaps as branch campuses (Dougherty, 1994). This is an interesting possibility to consider, and a growing number of community colleges are seeking the authority to grant bachelor degrees through so-called applied baccalaureates. (Floyd, Skolnik, and Walker, 2005). In the private sector, for-profit institutions are more likely than public universities to grant both associate and bachelor degrees (Bailey, this volume). In light of the existence of more than a thousand community colleges nationwide that are independent from four-year institutions, working toward bringing the two types of colleges closer together institutionally is a long-term project. One problem is that shifting community college students to lower divisions in four-year colleges would be much more expensive. Moreover, although starting in a community college may lower a student's chances of earning a bachelor degree, research also shows that the availability of community colleges does increase the total years of schooling attained by U.S. students (Rouse, 1995, Leigh and Gill, 2003). In any case, community and four-year colleges and state policy makers need to work to improve the process through which community college students can complete a baccalaureate degree.

In summary, community colleges play a positive role in promoting access to higher education. Their low cost and proximity are particularly important for low-income students, who indeed are overrepresented in these institutions with respect to their presence in higher education. Still, about a quarter of high school graduates do not enroll in college and low-income students are particularly concentrated in that group.

The open-door policy of community colleges is made more difficult by the low levels of academic preparation of many of their students. The colleges, however, are working to address that problem both through their developmental education programs and, more recently, by reaching back into the high schools and working directly with students while they are there.

The community college contribution to overall educational equality is more complex. There is evidence that they promote overall years of educational attainment, and many community college students do transfer and eventually earn baccalaureates. Still, that process remains difficult for many students. Moreover, by any reasonable standard, degree completion and transfer rates at community colleges remain low. Community college students do have ambitious goals, but the majority of community college students do not achieve those goals. Furthermore, low-income, African-American, and Hispanic students are overrepresented among those students who leave community college without having completed a degree or transferred.

To be sure, community colleges operate in a particularly difficult environment, especially as they try to develop their equity agenda. Within the system of public higher education, they have the least money and the students with the most difficult problems. As if this were not enough, the turn of the new millennium brought with it new challenges for community colleges. These challenges were often perceived as such by community college insiders and outsiders, because they make achievement of greater educational equity that much more difficult. How serious are these threats and how are community colleges responding? Are there new opportunities to strengthen the institutions and their equity mission, and what public and institutional policies could help achieve that goal?

Emerging Challenges

The factors described so far have created deeply rooted challenges for the community college equity agenda, and developments during the past few years have the potential to reinforce and expand these barriers to opportunity. One important development is a general reassessment of the role of the public sector in higher education. Among these factors is the decline in the share of higher education funding borne by the states, strong resistance to tax increases, and the declining share of state budgets accounted for by higher education. All of this has resulted in rising tuition and a growth in the share of higher education funding coming from tuition. At the same time, publicly funded financial aid, especially need-based aid, has failed to keep pace (College Entrance Examination Board, 2004). Moreover, there has been a general growth in competition among institutions of higher education, including the growth of a strong for-profit sector. This increased competition could threaten high-cost, low-revenue functions such as serving low-income students who face many academic and social barriers (Newman, Couturier, and Scurry, 2004). Other developments that have caused concern among community college personnel include the outcomes-accountability movement, the popularity of industry-based certifications, and advances in on-line distance education. In some instances, community college personnel and proponents have acknowledged potential threats to the preservation of the open-door role of community colleges, but in others potential problems remain unexamined. In this section, we will take a closer look at some of these perceived challenges to the community college equity mission.

Declining State Funding:
The Privatization of College Financing at a Time of Growing Enrollments

Community colleges are unusually dependent on state revenues. Direct state subsidies to institutions account for 33% of revenues for public four-year colleges and 44% for public community colleges (U.S. Department of Education, 2005b, Table 333). The recession of the early 2000s hit state higher education budgets particularly hard. Between 2000 and 2002, annual state appropriations per student declined by 15%, from $3,711 to $3,226 (in constant 2001 dollars). In the same period, state appropriations for community colleges—which had increased during the 1990s—declined 13% in constant dollars. Some states experienced particularly severe cuts. In 2003 alone, state appropriations for community colleges dropped by 13.6% in Massachusetts and by 10% in Colorado (Evelyn, 2004).[5] Although community college finances in some states improved with a stronger economy, these cyclical changes have taken place at a time of growing debate about the public role in higher education (St. John 2003; Newman, Couturier, and Scurry 2004; St. John and Parsons, 2004). As a result, the share of state funding going to higher education has been dropping steadily throughout the past fifteen years as other priorities, particularly corrections and medical care, have grown (Kane, Orszag and Gunter, 2003). Because few states are prepared to increase taxes, increases in state appropriations for community colleges will be difficult to come by.

State funding cuts also came at a time of significant growth in community college enrollment. Driven by the baby boom echo, continued immigration, a soft job market, and bleak employment prospects for those without a college education, community college enrollment, which was relatively flat during the 1990s, increased by 20%, from 3.1 million in 2000 to 3.7 million in 2003. Some states such as California, Florida, and Virginia expect enrollment growth of more than 50% between 2004 and 2014 (Evelyn, 2004).

One result of these trends has been an increase in tuition at community colleges (College Entrance Examination Board, 2004). Tuition increases are more likely to create barriers for community college students because, as we have seen, they are more likely than students at four-year colleges to come from lower-income families.

Trends in publicly funded financial aid have also created more barriers to community college students, first, as overall funding has not kept up with rising tuition and, second, as the emphasis has shifted from need-based to merit-based aid.[6]

From the point of view of the colleges, tuition increases are not going to make up for declines in state funding. College administrators are reluctant to raise tuition, precisely because they want to preserve access, but in many states state regulations or laws constrain them from doing so. Faced with this landscape, colleges have very strong incentives to turn away from or at least weaken their access role.

Confronting growing enrollments and falling funding, one response would be to cut expenditures per student. Student counseling, efforts to recruit high school students and other student services are easier to cut than faculty. For example, in response to dramatic growth in enrollments and severe cuts in state expenditures in 2003, community colleges in Colorado drastically cut their student services staffs. Because low-income students often require more services and assistance than affluent students, this strategy is likely to affect disadvantaged students disproportionately.

Limiting enrollments is another possible approach, and press reports suggest that in 2003 California, Florida, and North Carolina turned away tens of thousands of students (Hayward, Jones, McGuinness, and Timar, 2004). Although students are not selected for limited spaces on the basis of academic records, enrollment is closed when classes are filled. This favors the better-organized and informed students and is a de facto form of selectivity. Indeed, several forces are giving colleges at least the opportunity and incentives to seek out and enroll more middle-class students. Tuition at four-year colleges has risen faster than at community colleges, and four-year colleges have been less willing to increase enrollments. This is leading to an increase in demand for community college places among middle-class students who previously would have enrolled directly in four-year colleges. Such students are also less likely to need extensive student services and developmental education.

Several developments suggest that community college leaders are interested in attracting more middle-class students. During the last decade, many community colleges have sought the authority to grant baccalaureate degrees. Although this so-called community college baccalaureate movement remains controversial, it is clearly growing (Floyd, Skolnik, and Walker, 2005). Critics of the development worry that it will dilute the traditional community college access mission (see Townsend, 2005, for discussion). Community colleges have expanded their honors program, also in an attempt to attract students who would otherwise probably go directly to four-year colleges. Finally, community college presidents are often proud to point out that many of their students already have bachelor degrees. These students are presumably enrolling in community colleges to learn more practical skills. This trend is evident in the changing demographic characteristics of community college students. Between 1991 and 2001, the median age of community college students dropped from 26.5 to 23.5 years, and the proportion of community college students under the age of 22 rose from 32% to 42% (Adelman, 2005, Table 1). Other evidence also suggests that community colleges have increased their enrollments of more middle-class and traditional college students (Astin and Oseguera, 2004).

A final complication for the equity agenda resulting from the decline in state funding is that colleges must work hard to find alternative sources of revenue. To some extent they have been able to find federal and some state support for their work with low-income and disadvantaged students, but they have also looked to continuing education and local employers to generate income. These activities are not necessarily in conflict with the colleges' access role, but at the same time they do not reinforce it. Thus, the search for new revenue further restricts the colleges' abilities to prioritize the equity mission.

To summarize, the financial situation of community colleges currently poses a threat to the educational equity mission. This is occurring because colleges are seeking to supplement declining state and federal funds with tuition increases, programs that take advantage of increasing tuitions at four-year institutions by enrolling would-be four-year students, and programs that focus on the needs of business and industry. Disadvantaged students are not well positioned to take advantage of these programs because, among other reasons, they may be unable to pass placement exams, they may require intensive counseling to provide adequate information about educational options, or they may not be employed, which prevents them from taking advantage of employer-reimbursed training. Cuts in funding may also threaten the types of services that low-income students in particular need to persist and graduate, such as student services and developmental education.

Accountability

Institutions of higher education have traditionally been evaluated, accredited, and even paid on the basis of enrollments and the characteristics of inputs (i.e., teacher credentials) rather than on outputs and results. The accountability movement has sought to shift attention to student outcomes. Accountability based on performance reporting has so far been much more influential in the public K–12 sector, as indicated by the passage of the No Child Left Behind Act. The idea of funding and comparing institutions on the basis of performance measures is increasingly taking hold in higher education as well. The federal government, many state governments, and accreditation agencies have introduced accountability systems based at least partly on measuring student outcomes (Burke and Minassians, 2002).

The impact of these developments on community colleges is complex. On the one hand, the ability to help colleges identify weak programs and practices should provide a mechanism for change and improvement. On the other hand, these policies may have unintended consequences that threaten the equity mission. Motivations for "creaming," or selecting and enrolling easier-to-educate students, can result from public sector accountability programs when the accountability measures are based on outcomes such as program completion, job placement, or graduation. For example, graduation rates can be made to rise by discouraging enrollment of students who face many economic, social, and academic barriers to their education. Also, programs can be shortened and reduced in academic content and rigor to aid students in completing their programs of study. The incentives to do this are only strengthened by declining state funding, and the opportunities to be more selective are enhanced by the growing college age population (Dougherty and Hong, this volume).

Recent discussions of accountability have moved the focus beyond the individual institutions. The influential report card published by the National Center for Public Policy and Higher Education (2004) grades each state system of higher education on six measures. Policy makers and analysts have increasingly sought to promote and, in particular, to measure the transitions between institutions that ultimately influence postsecondary attainment. For example, reformers have sought to better align high school graduation and college entrance assessments (Conley, 2004) and promote better transitions from high school to college through dual or concurrent enrollment systems (Morest and Karp, in this volume). Policy makers have also turned their attention to transitions between noncredit programs, such as those that offer adult basic education, and regular credit programs in community colleges (Council for Advancement of Adult Literacy, 2005; Prince and Jenkins, 2005). Traditional transfer from community college to four-year colleges and universities continues to be an important policy issue (Wellman, 2002; AACC and American Association of State Colleges and Universities, 2004)

Thus, policy makers and educators have increasingly taken a system focus, working to develop a more integrated K–16 pathway (Ewell, 2004). So far, incorporating this into an accountability system has been difficult, because typical data systems simply are not capable of tracking students across educational levels or within the postsecondary system. As a result, policy makers have sought to strengthen and integrate their statewide data systems, to provide a better understanding of a student's overall educational trajectory.[7] At this point, only a handful of states have systems that allow analysis of student movement from high school and through the public postsecondary system (Ewell, Schild, and Paulson, 2003). Even the best state systems, however, would not take account of cross-state student movements. Efforts in 2005 by the U.S. Department of Education to develop a national unit-record system that would allow analysis of a student's full postsecondary trajectory were blocked in Congress in 2005 but discussions continued in 2006. (Field, 2005).

On balance, a greater understanding of the full K–16 system will be helpful to community colleges. More than for any other postsecondary institutions, data from single institutions give only a partial and misleading picture of community college performance and the experience of community college students. By contrast, managing transitions among institutions is particularly difficult for community college students, who commonly face many financial, academic, and social problems. Greater scrutiny of these difficult processes could also create incentives for the colleges to avoid the students with the most serious barriers to college success.

Industry-Based Certifications

In the late 1990s, the use of industry-based skill certifications grew rapidly. The most notable of these were in information technology. Certifications are created by individual companies, such as Microsoft or Cisco, or by industry associations, such as the National Automotive Technicians Education Foundation, not by educational institutions. Students earn certifications by passing assessment tests administered by organizations that are selected by the relevant companies. Students can sit for these certifications without having taken any courses. Information-technology education has been an important market for community colleges, and, if industry-based certifications catch on as a mainstream approach to workforce development, an important community college market would be threatened. During the late 1990s, certifications appeared to be growing so rapidly that one influential analyst argued they represented a "parallel universe" (Adelman, 2000). The certification movement seemed to resonate with the accountability movement, because it focused on measured outcomes. The important feature of this movement, however, is that accreditation role is assumed by business and industry as opposed to the traditional national and regional accrediting boards.

The certification movement poses a potential threat to the access mission of community colleges for several reasons. First, the movement has the potential to weaken the colleges in general by moving some of the higher-profile and fastest-growing occupational programs to other institutions. It could also weaken important relationships between the colleges and local businesses by creating incentives to emphasize generic training rather than responding to the articulated needs of local businesses. A second threat to the equity agenda involves the cost of the courses that most students take to prepare for the certification assessments. Many of these courses are taught by private companies and are much more expensive than typical community college for-credit courses. Low-income students could be blocked from gaining access to those workforce areas where certifications catch on.

For-Profit Higher Education

The growth of the for-profit higher education sector has also been perceived as a potential threat to traditional institutions of higher education, including community colleges. Since the early 1990s, high-profile for-profit colleges such as the University of Phoenix and DeVry Institutes attracted a great deal of attention and investor interest. Although they were more expensive, they had a reputation for effectively tapping public financial aid for their students. Rapid growth of these institutions, especially in high-profile occupational areas, presents a challenge to the enrollments in community colleges. One president asked, "Will our students be their students?" (Zeiss, 1998) One possibility is that public educational institutions may have problems similar to those experienced by public hospitals. The argument is that, as for-profit institutions gather momentum, they may "cherry pick" the best students and the best programs, further concentrating the poorest and least-prepared students in the community colleges while robbing those institutions of a market for the most remunerative programs such as information technology and business. Although, in this case, the community colleges would not necessarily turn away from low-income students, these developments might weaken the colleges' ability to work effectively with those students.

Distance Education

Will the rapid growth of distance education pose problems for less-advantaged students in community colleges? Distance education, especially its on-line variety, presents potential challenges to the community college access mission for several reasons. One is associated with the growth of the for-profit sector. From this point of view, for-profit institutions were believed to be particularly adept at on-line education, thus creating another competitive threat to traditional, presumably slow-moving, educational institutions (Levine, 1997). Because on-line education could potentially be mounted from anywhere in the world, community colleges could lose their geographic advantages—their convenience and proximity to so many students. Access to computers, or the so-called digital divide, was another potential problem for low-income students. Many households still do not have computers, and certainly the poorest would be the least likely. Finally, the text-heavy on-line teaching modalities and the need for a higher level of organization and self-motivation for students might be most challenging for those students who were already facing academic problems. Thus, introducing on-line courses into the basic curriculum of community colleges may pose a threat to students who benefit from the support and structure enabled by frequent face-to-face contact with professors and peers.

"Vocationalization" of Community Colleges

The discussion of "vocationalization" of the community college as a threat to higher education equity has a long history (Brint and Karabel, 1989; Dougherty, 1994). This discussion has resulted from a very influential critique of community colleges and is based on the contention that most students enter community colleges aspiring to earn bachelor's degrees. Almost four-fifths of those who enter community colleges state that their long-term goal is to earn a bachelor's degree or higher (Bailey, Jenkins, and Leinbach, 2005) and, indeed, the strongest income benefits from higher education do accrue to those who reach those levels (Marcotte, Bailey, Borkosky, and Kienzl, 2005). We have also discussed many of the problems that community college students who want to transfer must face. Furthermore, credits from many vocational programs at community colleges are difficult or impossible to transfer to four-year programs. Therefore, although vocational degrees and certificates may lead to jobs immediately after graduation, they may limit the future educational opportunities of students who enroll in them. We have already pointed out that research suggests that starting college in a community college lowers the probability of bachelor's degree completion for those students who state that this is their goal. The vocationalization of the community college is one of the explanations advanced for why starting in a community college diverts students away from their BA goals.

Moreover, proponents of the vocationalization thesis suggest that higher education and community colleges in particular are increasingly oriented toward job preparation. Widespread efforts by community colleges to court local businesses and even the growth of industry-based certifications indicate a close tie to the workplace. This focus on close ties to the workplace, according to this perspective, weakens the colleges' commitment to serving the bachelor's degree aspirations of their students. Moreover, it is not surprising that lower-income students are concentrated in short-term certificate and associate occupational programs in community colleges, since these programs are designed to lead to immediate employment and low-income students are most in need of immediate income. Therefore, to the extent that there is an increasing emphasis on these programs, it is these groups who are most likely to be diverted.

Challenges to the community college equity mission certainly go well beyond the purview of individual colleges. We have already emphasized the extreme inequities in preparation for college. Community colleges have limited control and influence over public resources, state policy, the structure of higher education, the education of high school students, and the overall distribution of income in the country, all of which are factors shaping their ability to ensure educational equity. Financial aid, day care funding, and health care and employment policy can all have profound effects on the experience and success of community college students. A comprehensive policy to promote educational equity will have to take all of these factors into account (Grubb and Lazerson, 2004).

Nevertheless, colleges do have some control over the success of their students. For example, graduation rates vary dramatically among colleges, even after taking account of variables that might influence those rates, including location, college size, demographic variables, and the percentage of students who attend part time (Bailey, Calcagno, Jenkins, Kienzl, and Leinbach, 2005). Although colleges can argue that they face many problems that are beyond their control, they can still make progress within the current environment.

Our book has several goals. First, we will assess the extent to which these developments threaten the community college equity agenda, taking into consideration equity as a three-part formula consisting of preparation, access, and success. Second, we will analyze how the colleges in our sample have responded to both the long-standing and the newer challenges. Finally, each chapter contributes to suggestions for institutional-level practice and policy that would strengthen the college's equity agenda.

The National Field Study

We are primarily concerned with how colleges have tried to improve their performance in view of the environment and nature of the students they enroll. The discussion in the book is based on extensive fieldwork at fifteen community colleges carried out between 2000 and 2002. In our analysis, we take into account the characteristics of students and the policy environments in which the colleges operate. The colleges are located in six diverse states: California, Washington, Texas, Illinois, Florida, and New York. We chose states on the basis of two criteria. First, we wanted states

TABLE 1.2
Colleges in the Study

College	State	Location	Decade Established	Number of Campuses	Fall 2000 Enrollment (rounded)	Percent Nonwhite
WUCC	California	Urban	1910s	1	14,400	61.0
WSCC	California	Suburban	1960s	1	13,200	34.9
WRCC	California	Rural	1940s	3	4,300	58.7
SMCC	Florida	Mixed	1960s	5	13,200	20.0
SUCC	Florida	Mixed	1960s	4	27,600	42.1
MWUCC	Illinois	Urban	1960s	1	8,100	81.3
MWSCC	Illinois	Suburban	1960s	1	28,900	27.7
MWRCC	Illinois	Rural	1960s	1	7,700	10.2
NESCC	New York	Suburban	1950s	1	9,300	12.0
NEUCC	New York	Urban	1950s	1	6,900	96.0
NERCC	New York	Rural	1960s	1	4,500	4.8
SWUCC	Texas	Urban	1970s	3	25,700	35.2
SWSCC	Texas	Suburban	1980s	3	13,000	24.6
NWRCC	Washington	Rural	1960s	1	1,900	25.5
NWSCC	Washington	Suburban	1960s	1	11,200	30.2

with large community college enrollments. Second, we wanted a sample of states that varied with respect to the balance between state and local control.

In each of these states, we studied combinations of urban, rural, and suburban colleges. The colleges were therefore selected, first, on the basis of geography and second, because, they possessed unique programs or characteristics that made them interesting to the researchers. Several of the colleges in the study are well known within their own state systems as successful community colleges on one or more dimensions. For example, one of the colleges had gained a national reputation for its industry relations in high technology, several of the colleges were known for high transfer rates, and another for its innovative practices in student services. Access was obtained through initial contacts with the college presidents. Once presidents had agreed to participate in the case studies, we established liaisons at the colleges who would assist us in scheduling visits.

Table 1.2 includes important background information on the colleges, including geographic locations, the decades during which they were established, their credit headcounts, and percent nonwhite (African American, Hispanic, Native American, and Asian). Nine of the colleges in the study were established during the 1960s. Overall, 457 community colleges were established during this decade, which was approximately 43% of the colleges in operation in 2000 (American Association of Community Colleges, 2002a). Because community college missions are thought to have evolved over the past century, the age of a college may have important implications for its mission focus (Deegan and Tillery, 1985; Bogart, 1993). From our standpoint, it is important that these colleges were drawn from all the periods of community college development.

Most of the colleges in this study were single-campus institutions. Community colleges typically distinguish between campuses and centers. The counts included in Table 1.2 do not include centers, which generally consist of only classrooms and a few staff. An important caveat is that some of the colleges studied were also part of community college districts or systems operating within states. For example, California groups community college campuses into districts. Two of the colleges in this study were part of community college districts that included three separate campuses. At the time of our study, the third California college was evolving from a single college to a multicollege district. Two of the other urban colleges (MWUCC and NEUCC) are part of major urban systems.

The enrollments shown in Table 1–2 are headcounts taken during the fall 2000 semester. Enrollments at the fifteen colleges ranged from just under 2,000 to nearly 30,000 credit students. It is not surprising that the rural colleges were the smallest of this group. Four of five suburban colleges occupied a relatively narrow range of 9,000 to 13,000 students. The fifth suburban college was uncharacteristically large. The urban colleges ranged greatly in size, from 7,000 to nearly 26,000 students. This broad range reflects the organizational structure of the colleges as either operating alone or as part of state subsystems. The dynamics of enrollment change during the 1990s will be discussed later in the book, but it is worth noting here that most of these colleges were growing. Enrollment change at the fifteen sites between 1990 and 2000 ranged from a 3% decline at SWUCC to a 75% increase at WRCC. Four of the colleges had enrollment declines (WUCC, MWUCC, MWSCC, and NESCC), whereas six of the colleges increased in size by more than 25% (WSCC, NERCC, SWSCC, MWRCC, SUCC, and WRCC).

The National Center for Education Statistics reports institutional graduation rates for each college through *Integrated Postsecondary Education Data System*. These rates are referred to as the Student Right to Know data. They are computed by tracking a cohort of all first-time, full-time students who enter at a particular time. The graduation rate is the percentage of that cohort that earned an associate degree or certificate within 150% of the time required to complete the credential for the program in which the student was initially enrolled (for example, three years for a two-year associate degree). In our sample of colleges, the graduation rates for the cohort that entered in the fall of 2000 ranged from 42% for SMCC to 3% for SWUCC. Although this measure does not reveal anything about the experience of part-time students, who make up a majority of community college students, it does suggest that there is wide variation in the graduation rates of the colleges in our sample.

Universities and four-year colleges are perceived as highly diversified in their structures and missions, leading to the many categories used in the Carnegie classification. No such system exists for identifying differences among community colleges. Our fifteen colleges provide examples of the many shapes and forms of community colleges. We included large, comprehensive suburban colleges and metropolitan colleges (serving both urban and suburban communities). For comparison, we also included several very small and isolated rural colleges. WRCC and NWRCC are both notable because they are located more than four hours by car from the nearest major airports. Both of these colleges served agricultural communities, whereas other colleges served local economies dominated by high-tech and service industries.

The project was carried out jointly by the contributors to this volume under the auspices of the Community College Research Center at Teachers College, Columbia University (CCRC). Most of the authors are at Teachers College and work directly with CCRC: Thomas Bailey, Vanessa Smith Morest, Melinda Mechur Karp, Dolores Perin, and Kevin Dougherty. Esther Hong and Kerry Charron were research assistants at Teachers College. Norton Grubb and Rebecca Cox have worked closely with the team on this and other projects. The team met four times over the course of the project. They jointly designed the protocols, selected the sample, discussed the results and implications, and read each others' drafts. Therefore, although the authors are ultimately responsible for the content of their chapters, the book is the result of a collective process and reflects a collective perspective.

We used a multiple case study design (Yin, 1984). The primary source of data collected from the colleges was intensive semistructured interviews conducted at each of the sites. From October 2000 to July 2002, teams of three to five researchers conducted visits to each of the fifteen colleges. Each visit lasted three or four days and involved approximately thirty-five group and individual interviews. Interviews were tape recorded and transcribed for analysis by each of the project's researchers. In total, more than 400 interviews were conducted with 658 administrators (42.4%), faculty and counselors (42.5%), and students and clients (12.2%) at the colleges. This distribution allowed for triangulation across a variety of college stakeholders. All senior administrators at the colleges were interviewed (eighty-two individuals) as well as a selection of administrators with managerial responsibilities that were representative of all college missions (defined as general/academic, occupational/applied, remedial, continuing, contract, and adult basic education). All of the interviews were taped and transcribed. Analysis of the transcripts was carried out independently by the authors of each of the chapters. Each author developed his or her own coding and employed his or her own methodology to the analysis.

Thus, our study examines the internal responses of fifteen community colleges by looking intensively at eight different topics. These topics correspond to the focus of chapters 2 through 9 in this volume. These issues were chosen either because they were considered significant threats to the equity function—accountability, the for-profits, vocationalization, certification—or because they represented crucial features of the equity function of community colleges—remediation, dual enrollment, and student services. Distance education could be considered both a potential threat and a crucial feature of the equity mission. These issues interact, but they are also independent because they involve distinct programs and activities managed or taught by different college personnel. The goal of these chapters is to generate analysis and suggestions for reform both at the micro level—innovations within the particular functions and areas that we examine—and at the macro or structural level. Here we describe the central issues raised in the chapters. The concluding chapter summarizes the main findings.

The first section of the book looks at the emerging challenges to the community college equity agenda, including the balance between occupational and vocational education (the possible "vocationalization" of the community college), the growth of accountability, the emergence of industry-based certifications, the for-profit phenomenon, and the spread of distance education. The second part analyzes college activity in three areas—developmental education, student services, and dual enrollment. These are all programs or policies that colleges use, at least in part, to increase the chances that low-income and minority students will be prepared for and have access to community colleges and will experience success once they are there.

In chapter 2, Vanessa Smith Morest looks at developments in the balance between occupational and academic instruction at community colleges. In the past, sociologists have argued that the curricula of community colleges was "vocationalizing." As opposed to serving as one prong of the dual academic/vocational mission of community colleges, however, today's vocational education is highly diversified. Community college students can enroll in credit-bearing or noncredit courses, programs of varying lengths, and those that lead to degrees, certificates, transfer, or no degree or credential. A central question shaping community colleges today is the balance of credit and noncredit and the relationship between them. Morest uses the material from the field study to analyze trends in the balance between academic and vocational, between credit and noncredit, and between transferable and nontransferable instruction and to examine the implications of those trends for the equity agenda.

The growing accountability movement is the focus of Kevin Dougherty and Esther Hong's chapter. All public-sector educational institutions are increasingly being asked to provide data showing evidence of success. Although this pressure has the most traction at the K–12 level with respect to standardized testing, community colleges and public universities are also being asked to respond by reporting on a variety of measures including graduation rates, student racial characteristics, transfer rates, and job placements. Accountability has the potential to weaken the access mission by creating incentives for colleges to "cream." There have also been growing calls to develop an integrated or at least coordinated K–16 accountability structure. Dougherty and Hong describe the trajectory of the accountability movement in community colleges and assesses its impact on college performance and the educational opportunities of community college students.

In chapter 4, Thomas Bailey describes the growth of for-profit institutions in both the two- and four-year sectors and assesses the extent to which they compete directly with community colleges. He also suggests that community colleges may be able to learn some useful lessons from the for-profit experience. This is the one chapter that is not based on material from the National Field Study.

Rebecca Cox examines the growth of Internet-based distance education, in chapter 5. On-line education is widely promoted as a means to expand access to postsecondary education, yet it is possible that this approach could increase access for students in general while limiting it for low-income and poorly prepared students. She assesses the forces that encourage and thwart the growth of on-line education at community colleges and examines the equity implications of those trends. She is particularly interested in the extent to which colleges have focused on the special pedagogic issues related to this approach to education.

Industry certifications were believed to have the potential to threaten the enrollments of community colleges by creating an alternate route to valuable industry-recognized credentials. This might also thwart the equity agenda by shifting high-demand courses and programs out of community colleges to higher-cost institutions. Jim Jacobs and Norton Grubb's chapter describes the community college response to the growth, and subsequent decline, of industry-based certifications, particularly those in information technology fields, and assesses the equity implications of these developments. Their chapter also has broader implications concerning the relationship between credit and noncredit courses and programs in community colleges.

The next section of the book deals with three key functions of community colleges that relate directly to sustaining the ideal of access and student success. Dolores Perin and Kerry Charron analyze the remediation programs of the fifteen National Field Study colleges. There is no question that many entering community college students are not prepared for college-level work. Developmental education is one of the most important elements of the community college equity agenda and one of the least well understood. Perin and Charron describe the large variety of formal and informal approaches taken in these colleges to working with students who are not prepared for college-level work. They are particularly interested in the nature of the evidence about the effectiveness of developmental education and the many different approaches and strategies that are in use.

Grubb's chapter on student services echoes some of the themes articulated in Perin's chapter. Counseling and advising are clearly crucial for many low-income and first-generation community college students who lack the social networks that affluent students can draw on for advice, guidance, and psychological support. Grubb examines the structure and underlying philosophy of students services at the National Field Study colleges and studies the manner in which those services are measured and assessed on the campuses.

Dual enrollment of high school students in community colleges is a practice that has expanded within the past decade from local partnerships into statewide policy. Community colleges have been at the center of this reform because they are geographically dispersed to maximize access and because they have been willing to enroll high school students in large numbers. Currently, many community colleges not only allow high schools students to enroll in college classes on campus but also conduct classes at the high schools. In some cases, high school teachers teach these classes. Our chapter on dual enrollment, by Morest and Melinda Mechur Karp, explores the perceived benefits of these programs to community colleges, high schools, and students and assesses the extent to which colleges and high schools are using the programs to move beyond the typical high achieving college-bound students to serve a broader range of lower- and middle-achieving students. In other words, do these programs promote equity in higher education or do they reinforce existing stratification?

It is clear that the colleges are enrolling a diverse population of students, many of whom experience significant barriers to educational success. To that extent, they are fulfilling their role of providing wide access to higher education, though more progress still needs to be made. Moreover, colleges are carrying out this function in a challenging context characterized by restricted (and probably shrinking) resources combined with complex and heterogeneous public demands and expectations. In this context, how can community colleges strengthen their role in promoting equity and student achievement? This question is at the heart of this book and the National Field Study on which it is based.

NOTES

1. U.S. Department of Education (2003e [NELS], 2003f [BPS 96/01]). Authors' calculation.
2. U.S. Department of Education (2003f [NELS]). Authors' calculation.

3. Although community colleges do, on average, enroll greater numbers of lower-income students than four-year institutions, students from families in the lowest income quartile often do not attend any college. Data from NELS (U.S. Department of Education, 2003e) show that, within twelve years of entering the eighth grade, 7% of all students had not finished high school or earned a GED. An additional 15% had earned a high school diploma or earned a GED but had not attended college, so 22% had never attended college. More than 60% of the high school dropouts and 42% of the high school graduates who did not attend college come from the lowest socioeconomic status (SES) quartile, a composite measure that combines family income and parental income and occupation. Slightly more than 50% of all students from the lowest SES quartile attend any college at all, compared to 97% of students from families in the highest SES quartile. Thus, although community colleges provide access for many low-income and nontraditional students, we are still a long way from universal or equal access to higher education. The large majority of community college students come from the center (middle two quartiles) of the income distribution, whereas 50% of all students attending four-year colleges are from the top quartile of the SES distribution. The stratification of the U.S. system of higher education mirrors that of family income.

4. U. S. Department of Education, (2003e [NELS]). Authors' calculations.

5. Figures in Evelyn (2004) were provided by JBL Associates.

6. For example, according to figures from the National Association of State Student Aid and Grant Programs (2005), the proportion of state grant aid that was need-based dropped from 90% of all states' totals in 1993–1994 to only 74% in 2003–2004 (Table 4 and 7).

7. See Ewell (2004) and L'Orange (2004) for more extensive discussions of the data needs for accountability systems that take a K–16 perspective.

CHAPTER TWO

Double Vision

How the Attempt to Balance Multiple Missions Is
Shaping the Future of Community Colleges

VANESSA SMITH MOREST

Community colleges have been balancing multiple missions for more than half a century. The Truman Commission's recommendation that community colleges should serve "the total post–high school needs of the community" (President Truman's Commission on Higher Education, cited in Bogart, 1994, p. 62) paved the way to massive expansion and endless controversy. There are two important parts to this controversy. First is the potential problem of offering so many educational services that it is impossible to do any of them well. Although this has been a concern of a number of authors, the comprehensive model is now widespread (Bailey and Averianova, 2001; Bailey and Morest, 2004). At least as an organizational strategy, comprehensiveness has been highly resilient.

The second part of the controversy is an underlying problem of the first: how much emphasis should community colleges put on vocational as opposed to academic transfer-oriented education? This debate has a very long history, not only for community colleges but for all sectors of U.S. public education. Our economy requires well-trained workers, and individuals certainly must be prepared for work. In fact, vocational education arguably occurs in all sectors of the educational system (Grubb and Lazerson, 2004). At the same time, however, we value delayed entry into the workforce because each additional year of education returns a higher salary and greater opportunity for advancement. In recent years, the baccalaureate degree has acquired increasing importance partly because of the growing gap between the earnings of those with bachelor degrees and those with no more than a high school degree (Bailey, Kienzl, and Marcotte, 2004). Furthermore, although today's high school graduates lack firm conceptualizations about their career choices or how to attain their educational goals, the vast majority claim baccalaureate degrees as their aspiration (Schneider and Stevenson, 1999; Bailey, Jenkins, and Leinbach, 2005).

This chapter focuses on two aspects of the missions and roles of community colleges. On one side is the concern that community colleges are becoming vocationalized, to the detriment of other missions, particularly transfer. This perception emerged early on, with the development of comprehensiveness. Today's version of the vocationalization debate has to be expanded to include contract and continuing education. Continuing education is often noncredit and is aimed at students seeking to learn or upgrade specific job-related skills. Many community colleges have established special departments that market or repackage continuing education and other college programs to business and industry clients. These services are described as contract training, and the departments that offer them have such names as "business training institute" or "center for business and industry." The perceived threat against community colleges in the late 1990s was that contract and continuing education would take over the focus of community colleges, diverting attention and resources away from college credit programs (Dougherty and Bakia, 2000).

The second aspect of the mission debate discussed here is a concern that only recently has gained attention. This is the potential for community colleges to shift their attention away from an important constituency: low-income and disadvantaged students. With college tuitions rising sharply and increasing numbers of students seeking baccalaureate degrees, community colleges are well situated to move up the ladder in our highly stratified postsecondary system. Whereas enrollments at public four-year institutions grew by 3.5% from 1990 to 2000 (9% at all four years), public two-year enrollments increased by 14% (U.S. Department of Education [USDOE], 2003c, Table 173). Not only are more students beginning their postsecondary experiences at community colleges, but a larger proportion of these students are recent high school graduates. Community colleges are not growing at the expense of four-year colleges, but they are attracting larger numbers of young students whose parents did not attend college and who are from the middle and lower socioeconomic quintiles (Adelman, 2005).

Because bachelor degrees are the educational ambition of the majority of this growing number of traditional students, community colleges have an increasing responsibility to provide postsecondary access through transfer. At the same time this is happening, tuition at both the two- and four-year levels is increasing. Although there is considerable variation across the country, state subsidies to community colleges are not keeping pace with tuition increases. This reflects the ongoing trend toward privatization in higher education, in which the cost for public education is shifting from the states to student tuition and fees. The implications of these developments are that, although community colleges need to increase their emphasis on transfer, they may be thwarted by the inability of students to afford the rapidly increasing costs of attending a four-year college during the junior and senior years.

Altogether, these developments create an increasing motivation to shift institutional missions and activities toward better prepared students with more resources, resulting in relatively less emphasis on low-income and more poorly prepared students. Evidence of this is to be found in the community college baccalaureate movement, which has gained momentum in certain states over the past few years. Community colleges have also established and expanded honors programs, which focus on transfer to selective colleges. This developing image is reflected in the media, which provides evidence that the public is taking a broader view of the potential of community colleges. For example, *Rolling Stone* told its readers that "community colleges give you small classes and an affordable head start on some of the top universities in the country" (Featherstone, 1998, p. 87). In December, 2002, the *New York Times* ran a front-page article with a similar theme: "Junior Colleges Try Niche as Cheap Path to Top Universities" (winter, 2002). And, in 2003, *USA Today* ran an article about articulation agreements between Miami Dade Community College and a number of public and private institutions, reporting that "more and more, two-year institutions are serving as launching pads for the best and brightest, luring students . . . with merit scholarships, intensive academic programs and the potential to be discovered by a big-name school" (Marklein, 2003, p. 10D).

Evidence of this shift is found in the increasing proportion of traditional students attending community colleges. Between just 1993 and 2001, the proportion of public two-year students between the ages of 18 and 24 grew by 7%, so that now more than half (54%) of the students fall into this age range. In addition to traditional college students, community colleges are also increasing their share of high school students. During the same period, the proportion of students younger than 18 grew from 2.4% to 5.5%. Although the size of this population of students remains relatively small, it is considerably larger at community colleges than any other sector (1.5% of public four-year students were under 18 in 2001; USDOE, 1995, Table 171; USDOE, 2003c, Table 178).

These developments increase the importance of the role of community colleges in the educational pipeline. Although at the national level we are learning about how this pipeline works (Adelman, 2005), much less is known at the institutional level. The colleges in this study collect some data about the destinations of their transfer students, but none of the colleges pursued information about what happened to their youngest students—those who started as high school students. So, to a large extent, a community college education is a private affair. Not only are students paying for it increasingly out of their own pockets, but they also take full responsibility for determining how they will use the institutions.

The National Field Study indicates two major trends in community college missions. The first is the expansion and institutionalization of contract and continuing education. Although discussion about vocational education at community college often treats it as monolithic, in reality vocational education is highly diversified. Community colleges are clearly strengthening their position as service providers to business and industry, though not without some internal growing pains. The second trend involves academic education and the growing importance to community colleges of transfer. Evidence of this is found not in the rhetoric of administrators, but in student enrollment patterns and organizational structures of the colleges. The chapter concludes with a discussion about how these conflicting trends can be occurring simultaneously within the institutions and the implications for the future of community colleges.

Social and Economic Pressures Shaping Community College Missions

The controversies about the missions of community colleges have focused particularly on the role and purposes of vocational education. The concurrent democratization of postsecondary education and emergence of the vocational mission of community colleges occurring during the 1960s is reminiscent of the Progressive Era expansion of comprehensive high schools. One can argue that high schools and community colleges adopted new curricular programs as a method of appealing to a broader cross-section of society (Powell, Farrar, and Cohen, 1985). In this way, expansion and diversification of missions go hand in hand.

Sociologists have argued that the role of the colleges is to reproduce economic and class distinctions in society (Bowles and Gintis, 1976). The process by which this occurs is one of "cooling out" or diverting the ambitions of students into occupational programs. Students arrive at the colleges with long-term plans of obtaining bachelor degrees, but their college experiences lead them to shift their goals toward shorter-term vocational degrees and certificates. The end result is that, by choosing to attend a community college, students secure for themselves positions on the same low-status social rungs as their parents. According to this formulation, vocational education serves the interests of businesses and the social elite rather than community college students.

The colleges have lived under the shadow of these conclusions for decades and argue strongly that their popularity and growth, as well as individual examples of success with disadvantaged students, provide evidence that they play a key role in promoting social mobility. Research on community colleges has also failed to support the social reproduction perspective, primarily because it is not clear that businesses and community colleges historically maintained strong direct ties to one another (Brint and Karabel, 1989; Dougherty, 1994). Furthermore, students arrive at community colleges with a diversity of goals, and many do not seek bachelor degrees from the outset.

Instead, researchers recently have been asking, what are the benefits of multiple missions to the institutions themselves, or even to the college officials who are responsible for setting their visions? Posed this way, the question takes a different perspective from earlier discussions, because it understands community colleges as self-interested. Brint and Karabel's (1989) examination of the development of community colleges resulted in the finding that the colleges were encouraged to expand their missions to include vocational education by community college leaders such as the American Association of Community Colleges and other community college advocates who sought a unique niche for the colleges, particularly in light of the relatively greater power of the public four-years universities. Dougherty (1994) concluded that state officials and school principals seeking to establish themselves as college presidents contributed to the rapid growth of the sector.

In recent years, researchers interested in public universities and community colleges have attributed mission expansion into contract training to reductions in state and federal funding. The context for this expansion is one of a gradual shift toward privatization of higher education. As a result of declining state funding, colleges and universities are supplementing their budgets by developing private enterprises. In the case of public universities, this takes the form of increasing reliance on private contracts for research, particularly in the physical sciences (Slaughter and Leslie, 1997). Further, students are being asked to bear a greater part of the financial burden of postsecondary education by taking out loans to cover increasing college tuitions. These developments reflect a changing educational policy environment in which market mechanisms are presumed to encourage reform.

John Levin (2001) analyzed community colleges in the United States and Canada to find out how they had been affected by these broad environmental changes. His study concluded that community colleges have also become more privately focused. The community colleges in his study were increasingly focusing their efforts on contract training, continuing education, and other entrepreneurial programs that would be capable of attracting private funds to the colleges to diversify away from public funds. Levin argues that, during the past decade, community colleges increasingly saw themselves as part of a global marketplace, in which they could compete effectively for the right to provide skills training. In his view, today's community colleges are adopting corporate, rather than collegiate, structures.

One of the problems with drawing conclusions about community colleges as a sector is that the colleges are considerably more diverse in form and function than the research perspectives described here might suggest. There are currently more than 1,200 community colleges in the United States. Some of these colleges enroll more than 20,000 students, but many are very small, with fewer than 1,500 students, and located in rural places where few Americans, let alone researchers, have been. Dealing with this diversity was at the core of the National Field Study.

The findings from our study show that community colleges continue to expand their missions. Often, the problem faced by community colleges is not the variety of student goals but the fact that each individual student may arrive at the college with multiple goals. In other words, a student may have the long-term goal of a bachelor degree and the short-term goal of finding better employment. The solution has been to spread vocational education across all departments of the college. In fact, non-credit vocational education has been expanding over the past decade at the same time as academic education and vocational education for transfer. Under these circumstances, the old argument that community colleges are at risk of vocationalization no longer holds much weight, and instead we need to be concerned with the stratification of programs within the colleges.

An important impediment to studying community college missions is that there are many different ways to measure the relative importance of each mission, depending on which data sources are selected. Enrollments are obviously one way to think about missions. It is difficult, however, to analyze enrollments for this purpose, because colleges often do not have easy access to student data categorized by mission or function and generally cannot provide data going back a decade or more. This situation may change with developments in technology. A second source would be interview data. College administrators and faculty often hold strong perspectives about missions, but there can be conflicting viewpoints even within the same institution. Furthermore, people often do not remember historical change accurately unless it is dramatic. Rapid turnover or expansion at a college can also contribute to skewed, misleading, or missing information about mission developments. Institutional mission statements can serve as another source. Community college mission statements often identify five or six roles played by the colleges, and, if one assumes that they are listed in order of priority, conclusions about the institutional focus can be drawn. These findings, however, are vague and not strongly based on evidence from the actual practices of the colleges.

A lesson of this study is that college catalogs can serve as a rich source of information about missions. They are generally available at the colleges from most years, often dating back to a school's first year of operation. Catalogs list not only mission statements but also information about programs, degrees, curriculum, and personnel. Therefore, in addition to our extensive interviews with faculty, administrators, and students, this chapter draws on college catalogs and data from the Integrated Postsecondary Education Data System (IPEDS).

College catalogs were obtained during visits to the colleges. To the extent that they were available, they were collected from 1970, 1980, 1990, and 2000. Information on college structures was obtained from the sections of the catalogs that list college administration and faculty. These sections include a wealth of historical information about the colleges, including their faculties' disciplines and educational backgrounds. Information on curriculum was drawn from the descriptions of general education requirements and degree programs provided in the catalogs. This chapter focuses primarily on catalogs from 1990 and 2000.

College and state documents and data from IPEDS were used to triangulate on the information obtained through catalogs and interviews. IPEDS data were used to gather information on the enrollments and demography of the colleges. These data were cross-checked against college and state data. The advantages of IPEDS are that it improves comparability across institutions and that these data can be readily obtained from 1990. Nevertheless, triangulation was essential, because educational programs can vary from state to state.

Enrollment Growth and Organizational Change

Vocational education at community colleges is typically offered through three departments: contract education, continuing education, and college credit. Although this three-pronged approach is now institutionalized, it is not necessarily accepted by college faculty, who see some of its fundamental characteristics as misaligned with college goals and who believe that it creates internal competition for enrollments. The development of contract and continuing education suggests an increased acceptance of adjunct faculty, greater control of business and industry over curriculum, and the widespread use of noncredit education that does not need to adhere to the many rules and regulations to which credit education is subject. A result of these differences has been the inability of colleges to integrate their contract and continuing education departments with the preexisting credit-bearing departments (Bailey and Morest, 2004).

Nonetheless, contract and continuing education were areas of expansion for the colleges in our study. Increases in the enrollments of contract and continuing education were estimated by the colleges and supplemented with information from state institutional research offices. Two of the colleges had no, or almost no, contract and continuing education programs. In both of these instances, the colleges were part of community college districts in which some other institution held primary responsibility for providing these types of programs. For example, one of these colleges was part of a district that runs a separate employee-training institute serving students district-wide that has 100–150 contracts per year totaling more than a million dollars.

Other colleges had large and growing contract and continuing education enrollments. For example, SUCC grew from 8,875 duplicated students in 1994–1995 to 12,907 in 2000–2001. SMCC, with less growth, expanded from 6,785 to 7,995 duplicated students during the same period. NERCC, serving a rural area with many small businesses, brings in about $80,000–$90,000 per year by serving around 2,000 students. MWSCC served 7,458 duplicated students in 2001. MWRCC, another Illinois college, served 4,946 through contracts and 2,519 in continuing education. The two Texas colleges had some of the larger programs. SWUCC enrolled 9,111 duplicated students in 2000–2001 and SWSCC served 21,457 duplicated.[1] SWUCC enrollments had increased 84% since 1996 and SWSCC's enrollments were up about 24%. Finally, the suburban Washington college had contract and continuing education enrollments of 9,937 in 1999, which was up about 44% since 1995. The very rural Washington college, NWRCC, served fewer than 1,000 students through its business development center.

Although the growth of noncredit education and the institutionalization of contract training are striking, their effects on college structure can easily be exaggerated. In fact, only one college employed a full-time faculty member with responsibility for teaching in customized training. Furthermore, the share of staff devoted to customized and continuing education ranged from 0% to 16% and was, at most, 18% of the administrators at any of the National Field Study colleges. Most of the colleges, however, fell into the 2%–4% administrator range for these missions combined.

Concurrent with the developments in noncredit education, credit enrollments at many community colleges have been growing rapidly. Table 2.1 below shows the increase in the fall headcount at each of the colleges in the study. Enrollments at half the colleges, including WUCC, NESCC, MWSCC, SMCC, and MWUCC remained stable or declined. Seven of these colleges, however, grew considerably. Some of these colleges—including WSCC, NERCC, and NWSCC—increased their size by about a quarter in the past decade. WRCC, SUCC, MSRCC, and SWSCC grew by nearly half

TABLE 2.1
Credit Enrollment Growth at the NFS Sites

College	State	2000 Unduplicated Headcount (rounded)	2000 Full-Time-Equivalent Students (rounded)	Change in Upduplicated Headcount, 1990–2000 (%)
MWRCC	Illinois	7,700	4,300	47
MWSCC	Illinois	28,900	15,500	−1
MWUCC	Illinois	8,100	4,500	−2
NERCC	New York	4,500	2,900	27
NESCC	New York	9,300	6,300	−1
NEUCC	New York	6,900	5,300	8
NWRCC	Washington	1,900	1,400	6
NWSCC	Washington	11,200	7,000	19
SMCC	Florida	13,200	6,100	3
SUCC	Florida	27,600	15,800	50
SWSCC	Texas	13,000	7,500	43
SWUCC	Texas	25,700	12,800	6
WRCC	California	4,300	2,400	75
WSCC	California	13,200	7,800	26
WUCC	California	15,100	8,300	10

SOURCE: U.S. Department of Education, IPEDS (1990, 2000b).

or more. We can see in these results some variation across colleges, with overall community college credit enrollments growing and enrollment growth that is quite dramatic at certain institutions.

Two features of this enrollment growth are of interest in this chapter. First is that growth in credit and noncredit were not in conflict. Those colleges that were growing rapidly in noncredit were some of the ones with the large credit enrollment expansion. Second, increases in faculty and administrators in the colleges did not necessarily follow the patterns of enrollment growth shown in Table 2.1. The evidence suggests that all of these colleges were very much invested in expanding their role in credit-based academic and vocational education.

As enrollments increased during the 1990s, the organizational structures of administrators and faculty to serve these students expanded and developed. Understanding these changes can be challenging because college personnel rarely remember with accuracy the developments at their institutions over the course of ten years. In fact, because many positions were added during the past decade, relatively few administrators had more than a few years of experience with any given college. In several cases, colleges had undergone multiple reorganizations during this period. Nonetheless, analyzing the size, disciplinary focuses, and backgrounds of full-time community college faculties and the characteristics of college administrations can provide important insights into organizational change.

During the 1990s, most of the National Field Study colleges increased their numbers of full-time faculty. Table 2.2 shows the number of full-time faculty by college

TABLE 2.2
Full-Time Faculty, by College and Year

College	Total Full-Time Faculty			Ratio of Students to Faculty[1]	
	1990	2000	% change	1990	2000
MWRCC	76	109	43	69	70
MWSCC	245	323	32	119	89
MWUCC	153	89	−42	54	92
NERCC	74	61	−18	48	74
NESCC	292	279	−4	32	33
NEUCC	300	183	−39	21	38
NWRCC	43	48	12	41	39
NWSCC	104	143	38	91	79
SMCC	135	163	21	95	81
SUCC	202	231	14	91	119
SWSCC	81	204	152	112	64
SWUCC	208	336	62	117	77
WRCC	45	57	27	55	76
WSCC	122	142	16	86	93
WUCC	121	151	25	114	95

SOURCE: U.S. Department of Education, IPEDS (1990, 2000b).
  1. Based on fall credit headcount from IPEDS.

and the number of faculty per student headcount. Only four colleges reduced the sizes of their full-time faculties during the past decade, while ten others increased by 12% to 62%. One college (SWSCC) tripled the size of its faculty, but the 1990s was the first full decade of operation for this college.

Because we know that enrollments were also increasing during the 1990s, it is useful to compare the number of full-time faculty to the size of the colleges. The last two columns of the table show these ratios. This measure is not the most precise, because it uses fall headcounts as opposed to full-time equivalent (FTE) enrollments; however, because none of these colleges underwent a major shift in the balance of full-time to part-time students, the ratios offer a useful method of comparison. Overall, eight of the colleges either maintained or reduced their faculty-to-student ratios during the course of the 1990s.

The colleges that increased their faculty-to-student ratios were concentrated in the states of New York, California, and Florida. In New York, interviews revealed that there was significant retrenchment in the early 1990s, which was consistent with the data. In Florida, rapid increases in student enrollments are at least part of the story. Interviews at both colleges focused on expansion and the development of new campuses. For the California schools, the explanations are less clear. Certainly the rural college was expanding rapidly and reported some difficulty attracting full-time faculty to the area.

These results are surprisingly consistent with regard to adjunct faculty. As Table 2.3 shows, only four of the colleges reduced their proportions of adjunct faculty.

TABLE 2.3
Part-Time Faculty, by College and Year

	Total Part-Time Faculty			Ratio of Students to Part-Time Faculty[1]	
College	1993	2001	% change	1993	2001
MWRCC	193	144	−25.4	28	45
MWSCC	835	806	−3.5	37	37
MWUCC	465	181	−61.1	24	44
NERCC	200	170	−15.0	22	28
NESCC	259	275	6.2	39	37
NEUCC	423	447	5.7	19	16
NWRCC	36	73	102.8	53	26
NWSCC	304	444	46.1	33	27
SMCC	617	813	31.8	20	17
SUCC	851	739	−13.2	27	40
SWSCC	401	659	64.3	25	22
SWUCC	1,105	1,058	−4.3	22	28
WRCC	75	169	125.3	32	28
WSCC	193	443	129.5	55	32
WUCC	225	382	69.8	58	72

SOURCE: U.S. Department of Education, IPEDS (1993, 2001).
1. Based on fall credit headcount from IPEDS.

Nevertheless, the ratios of adjunct faculty-to-student headcounts indicate that nine of the colleges maintained or reduced their ratios of adjunct faculty-to-students and six of the colleges increased them.[2] The strategy of employing adjuncts varied in scope at these colleges. Combining the information on full-time and part-time faculty, only two of the colleges (both in California) showed evidence of shifting resources from full-time to part-time faculty. Two additional colleges, MWUCC and SUCC, increased their faculty-to-student ratios for both full-time and part-time faculty, which indicates an overall reduction in faculty resources.

Remarkably, even as the number of full-time faculty increased, the balance of vocational to academic, full-time faculty remained relatively stable. These results are shown in Table 2.4. For the purposes of this study, academic faculty were defined as those teaching in English, global languages and speech, math, the physical and social sciences, developmental education, the arts and humanities, and physical education. Vocational faculty were all those teaching in business, education, engineering, computer science and computer graphics, nursing and allied health fields, hospitality, and the trades.

The table shows that MWRCC increased its full-time faculty by 43% yet retained exactly the same ratio of academic to vocational faculty during the past decade. Similarly, MWSCC added 78 faculty while retaining the same balance. SWSCC, the newest of the colleges, more than doubled its full-time faculty but changed the balance of academic to occupational faculty a mere 2%. On the basis of increases in

TABLE 2.4
Full-Time Faculty, by College and Year

	Percent of Faculty Teaching in Academic Subjects		
College	1990	2000	% Change
SMCC	No data	No data	No data
NESCC	44	45	1
NWRCC	44	47	3
SWUCC	43	49	6
MWRCC	50	50	0
WRCC	51	58	7
NERCC	57	60	3
MWSCC	62	62	0
WUCC	60	66	6
SWSCC	65	67	2
NWSCC	66	67	1
SUCC	70	72	2
MWUCC	76	75	−1
NEUCC[1]	60	77	17
WSCC	80	77	−3

SOURCE: College catalogs.

1. This college housed a nursing program in 1990 that increased the nursing faculty by sixty-seven from its size in 1980. Omitting these faculty, there was still a reduction of the full-time faculty by about 16.7%. In 1970, 73% of the faculty were teaching in academic subjects and 79% in 1980.

the importance of applied programs such as business, education, and the health fields, as well as the literature on community college vocationalization, one would expect that any change in the structure of community colleges would be in favor of expansion of occupational faculty. This was not the case at the colleges in the study, where in almost all instances any shift was toward increased academic full-time faculty.

Not only did the colleges increase full-time faculty to meet the demands of expanding enrollments, they also added administrative lines. In fact, the growth of full-time faculty paled by comparison to the growth of college administrations. Table 2.5 shows the number of administrators at each of the National Field Study colleges and how the ratio of administrators to students changed during the past decade. Although only about half of the colleges expanded their full-time faculties to outpace student enrollments, the number of students to each administrator declined at all but three colleges in the study. MWRCC, for example had one administrator for every 127 students in 1990 compared with one for every 96 in 2000 (31 fewer students per administrator).

The question that is important for understanding the development of community college missions is to know how these new administrators were distributed across college functions. Table 2.6 shows the number of administrators added by each college according to eight categories of college operations. This table shows that most new administrators were added in regular college programs rather than the spe-

TABLE 2.5
Ratio of Student Headcount to Faculty and Administration, by Year

College	Students to Faculty 2000	Change since 1990	Students to Administrators 2000	Change since 1990
MWRCC	70	1	96	−31
MWSCC	89	−30	704	108
MWUCC	92	38	370	−46
NERCC	74	26	50	0
NESCC	33	1	258	−104
NEUCC	38	17	89	−100
NWRCC	39	−2	66	−59
NWSCC	79	−12	225	−102
SMCC	81	−14	356	−9
SUCC	119	28	263	−129
SWSCC	64	−48	81	−145
SWUCC	77	−40	161	−162
WRCC	76	21	197	−114
WSCC	93	7	882	383
WUCC	95	−19	626	−290

SOURCE: U.S. Department of Education, IPEDS (1990, 2000b) and college catalogs.

cialized areas of contract or continuing education and grant-funded programs. Some areas seemed to have lost support during the 1990s. For example, adult education, which is also noncredit, had a net gain of three administrators added across all fifteen colleges. Institutional research departments did not expand much, despite new reporting and accountability requirements. Most of the growth was focused in general college functions and student services.

The types of positions added at each of the colleges are difficult to capture. Drawing on one of the smaller college administrations as an example, Table 2.7 below identifies changes that occurred at NWSCC during the period from 1990 to 2000.

This college created new positions for a variety of college services, such as child care, printing, and food services. They also added positions to accommodate the rapidly changing computer technology. This school was located in a region that was particularly affected by the "dot-com" boom of the late 1990s, which is reflected in their emphasis on technology.

At the time of our study, NWSCC was adding a new vice presidential position to cope with the diversification of vocational programs. Although most of the National Field Study colleges employed directors or deans of workforce development and continuing education, several were considering converting these positions to vice presidential positions that would bring together the functions of credit vocational education, continuing education, and contract education. At NWSCC, an instructional dean explained to us how this was developing at his college:

TABLE 2.6
Positions Added, by College and Role

College	General Administration	Recruit-ment	Student Services	Grant Programs	Entre-preneurial	Finance	Institutional Research	Adult Education	Total
MWRCC	22	1	8	−1	11	0	1	−3	39
MWSCC	−10	0	3	−1	0	0	0	0	−8
MWUCC	0	−1	−1	4	2	−2	0	0	2
NERCC	7	1	1	1	0	0	0	0	10
NESCC	10	4	2	3	−1	−1	1	0	18
NEUCC	11	1	10	11	3	5	0	2	43
NWRCC	3	1	2	2	2	2	0	2	14
NWSCC	10	2	−3	11	1	0	0	0	21
SMCC	1	0	−1	0	1	0	1	0	2
SUCC	26	3	10	0	12	5	2	0	58
SWSCC	71	6	15	1	14	8	5	0	120
SWUCC	37	2	14	8	9	13	0	2	85
WRCC	5	0	2	4.5	1.5	0	1	0	14
WSCC	−4	1	−2	1	−1	0	−1	0	−6
WUCC	4	1	2	2	−1	1	−1	0	8

SOURCE: College catalogs.

NOTE: *General administration*—Everything related to academic and occupational education. Includes co-op education and tutoring centers, unless they are explicitly grant funded. *Recruitment*—Admissions, registrar, marketing. *Student Services*—Counseling and advising, financial aid, student activities. *Grant Programs*—Individuals responsible for grant-funded programs, public services, and administrators running grants offices. *Entrepreneurial*—Contract and continuing education, small business incubation, foundation and money raising departments. *Institutional Research*—Individuals with explicit responsibility for collecting and analyzing institutional data. *Adult Education*—GED, Adult Basic, Federally funded adult education programs. Does not include remediation.

When you asked about reorganization, I said 5 years ago, but I am overlooking the fact that we are undergoing the results of not a full reorganization but a rethinking of how to best coordinate and offer workforce education so that a number of entities that have been a part of the institution have been reorganized somewhat with the concept that we will now have a V.P. for Workforce Development education. A part of continuing education, all of our workforce and Work First, and those programs that have come on the last 4 or 5 years to speak to welfare reform. All of the professional/technical training programs and so forth will all be consolidated under a V.P. for Workforce Development. So that hasn't fully formed but that is a position that is still open.

By following up with this college, we learned that they did indeed create this position. This college had a fairly well-integrated notion of how credit and noncredit could work together and at the time of our study sought to "creditize" some of its noncredit continuing education programs.

In light of the current complexity of community college missions, administrative roles that bring together multiple workforce and economic development programs may develop at larger institutions over the next decade. There is, however, a caution in this: elevating the status of this position institutionalizes the colleges' involvement

TABLE 2.7
Administrative Changes at NWSCC, 1990–2000

General College Administration, 1990	General College Administration, 2000
a. President	President (a)
b. Executive Dean, Educational Services	VP, Human Resources (c)
c. Dean, Human Resources	VP, Institutional Advancement (i)
d. Dean, Instructional Services	Executive Dean, Instructional Services (b)
e. Dean, Instructional Services	Dean, Instruction (d)
f. Associate Dean, Library Media	Dean, Instruction and Special Assistant to the President (e)
g. Director, Campus Operations	Dean, Workforce Development (new)
h. Director, Fitness Assessment Center	Associate Dean, Telecommunications (half position, new)
i. Director, Planning and Capital Projects	Director, Academic Computing (new)
	Director, Athletics (new)
	Director, Bookstore (new)
	Director, Campus Operations (g)
	Director, Food Services (new)
	Director, Library Media Center (f)
	Director, Printing Services (new)
	Director, Radio Station (new)
	Director, Student Childcare and Early Learning Center (new)
	Director, Technology Services (new)
	Division Chair, Telecommunications (half position, new)
	Human Resources Representative (new)

SOURCE: College catalogs.

in programs that are not considered sufficiently collegiate by some. At another college in our study, a vice president was hired on the basis of her ability to bring together the credit and noncredit "cultures." This vice president was given an academic title, though she was hired explicitly on the basis of her willingness to work with and even promote noncredit programs: "In '94 we had taken what was basically two colleges here and made them into one administratively, culturally it didn't take . . . and [the college president] asked me if I could help close the schism. But that I'd have to be very patient—acquire institutional patience, he said. So I see myself having become a paradigm broker actually. And caught—positioning myself between two paradigms" (MWSCC, Associate Vice President of Academic Affairs). For most of the colleges in the study however, the idea of a position that would bring together credit and noncredit was far from consideration. These departments were perceived as differing in ways so fundamental that they could not be combined. Differences included, for example, the types of students served, faculty, funding sources, and facilities. But there are internal issues that community colleges need to resolve that go deeper than these logistics because they have to do with curriculum and its implications for the social role of the colleges.

What Should Be the Curriculum of Vocational Education?

Although there is considerable excitement at community colleges about the growth of contract and continuing education, its development also raises significant questions. College personnel distinguished a difference between credit-bearing vocational programs and those in contract and continuing education. As one faculty member observed, "Continuing education has done some of it (Microsoft and Cisco certifications), but we really believe that there needs to be a balance between education and skill-level training. And a lot of the certifications, they are teaching to the test. They are not teaching them the overall concepts" (SWUCC, Distance Education Faculty). Faculty did not view programs offering only skills as necessarily consistent with the overarching mission of the colleges. A director of contract training described this tension to us as follows:

> I think the real question for community colleges is deeper, because do you provide the specialized training that the client wants, or do you take the higher road and say "we're an educational institution, we do not believe that's the problem" and we choose not to play? And, I don't know. I don't know the answer to that, because in a lot of colleges— ours is not entrepreneurial, yet, but certainly other community colleges are extremely entrepreneurial, and they're you know, totally self-sustaining. They would never turn down a contract, you know? But it gets to be an issue in education. (NERCC, Director of Workforce Development).

This tension was cited as getting in the way of the development of contract and continuing education at the college. Many faculty still see the fundamental role of these institutions as academic. The contract education administrator above went on to comment that "the college has always prided itself on being a two-year transfer college, and I think that that needs to change a bit" (NERCC, Director of Workforce Development). Similarly, a dean at another college observed that "there's probably been some concern by our traditional faculty that we are getting away from our traditions, but I believe that the professional technical programs that we offer are solid professional technical programs. And to me, the integrity of the institution and the curriculum and the faculty that we hire are the issue" (NWSCC, Associate Dean of Enrollment). At this college, the president had sought ways of bringing local businesses into partnerships with the college. The response, she told us, was "we had kind of a revolt of the liberal arts faculty saying I was dramatically changing the mission of the college" (NWSCC, President).

One official described the tension at a college in Texas: "In a community college, I think that one of the things that we are continually dealing with is the issue of the classroom—integrity of the classroom, academic freedom. We're a very high tech, innovative campus, and sometimes there's pressure to be innovative in a way in which some faculty members are not comfortable with. Or they think it compromises academic standards, so that's sort of a trade-off" (SWCC, Chair of Faculty Senate).

Underlying the faculty resistance to the curriculum of contract and continuing education courses is that in their areas curriculum is headed in the opposite direction. As degrees in business, health, education, and technical areas such as engineering and computer science have become increasingly popular at four-year institutions, community colleges are adding transferable vocational programs to their catalogs. In fact, every college in the National Field Study was involved in developing vocational programs for transfer students. Faculty and administrators described these developments to us:

> And what we have done recently, we have really changed our curriculum a lot and wanted to make it a lot more flexible . . . this is my first time to actually teach at a community college. I came from the university and so I wasn't really used to that, you know. A student going on to get a bachelor degree, how do we create that link? And now that it's more and more important in our industry to do that, we know that we needed at a community college level to be able to do that as well. So SWUCC has really supported a lot of the programs that want to jump on that bandwagon, and one of the angles that we've taken with it is to create a specialized degree that is totally transferable. (SWUCC, Hospitality Management Faculty)

> Criminal justice has evolved. You can't teach the same skills to change spark plugs as you do to carry an M-16 and police a society. We're getting ripped off, the taxpayers are getting ripped off, and students are getting ripped off. They don't care. They just think "go for it" and when we go up and say we have to evolve. Criminal justice has to evolve into an academic program and has to be transferable, [the college administration] turns a blind ear. They're not interested in those kinds of problems or solutions. You keep it vocational; if it makes money, then go do it. (NWSCC, Criminal Justice Faculty)

Both of these professors perceived the development of vocational transfer as motivated by changes in the requirements of work. Where state policy is allowing or even encouraging articulation between community colleges and four-year universities in occupational areas, policy may also be serving as an impetus:

> *Interviewer (I):* Would you say that the larger percentage (of articulation agreements) is in workforce transfer?
> *Articulation Officer (AO):* Of what I'm doing?
> *I:* Let's say as compared to liberal arts transfer.

AO: It has been recently, I really believe that is because of the development of the core curriculum, the "fields of study." The state has really kind of taken care of a lot of transfer issues with nonacademic courses; they're prescribing it. (Articulation Officer, SWUCC)

The state of Texas has not only established a general education curriculum for transfer but has also added to it ten "fields of study," most of which are in traditionally vocational areas: business, communications, computer science, criminal justice, nursing, and engineering technology.

Discussion and Conclusions

The findings of this study show that community colleges are expanding their vocational and academic enrollments, though the growth of contract and continuing education remains minor in comparison to changes in the credit-bearing departments of the colleges. Evidence from interviews suggests that little consensus exists within the colleges about the direction in which these institutions are headed. On the one hand, we see a growing emphasis on noncredit training, and, on the other, we see an increasing demand for transfer programs.

The pressures that are shaping these developments are not likely to diminish in the near future. First are the aspirations of high school students. According to Schneider and Stevenson, in 1955—when community colleges were being established at a rapid pace—only about 30% of high school seniors expected to complete a bachelor degree (1999, p. 74). By 1992, this share had increased to 70% (p. 72). This represents a complete reversal of the proportions that formed the context of community colleges' earlier expansion. The importance of this cannot be understated. Whereas community colleges had to invent a niche for themselves fifty years ago to enroll some of those 70% of students who were not pursuing four-year college degrees, today they find themselves in the mainstream of postsecondary education.

Second, a rapid increase in college tuition has made attending a less-expensive college a necessity for a broader cross-section of students. According to an informal survey conducted by the *Chronicle of Higher Education,* most tuition increases fell in the range of 7%–12% for public four-year universities and 4%–9% for community colleges during the 2004–2005 school year (Fleming, 2004, p. A22). So, although low cost was an advantage of community colleges in the past, its primary motivation was to provide access to low-income students. Now, community colleges need to provide access to middle-class students as well.

A final important pressure shaping the developments described in this chapter is the emergence of new technologies in the 1990s. Widespread use of microcomputers put community colleges under pressure to develop "high-tech" programs and services. The training required to bring the workforce up to date on how to install and operate computer systems created a niche in vocational education that elevated the importance of community colleges in economic development. The downside for community colleges has been the shortage of state support for capital investment. Community colleges have pursued grants and funds from private sources such as Cisco and Microsoft to support their high-technology training.

These trends are contributing to developments at community colleges that are in direct conflict with one another. On one hand, there is a growth in noncredit occupational training, and, on the other, there is an expansion of academic education and transfer. Whereas in the past some argued that vocationalization of the community college curriculum posed a threat to equity and access, those involved with the colleges today see the vocational/academic dichotomy as an oversimplification of the programs offered by community colleges. In reality, vocational education is diversified into noncredit training with and without certification, credit training with certification, and two-year training with and without the prospect of transfer. Each of these possibilities consists of some blend of academic and vocational education. Furthermore, with universities and graduate programs offering degrees in business, nursing, education, hospitality, engineering, and so on, it is no longer possible to make the argument that vocational training represents a dead end to students.

On the other hand, the development of noncredit vocational education and certification presents community colleges with new challenges to their mission. The extent to which contract and continuing education divert resources away from other programs is unknown. These departments tend to be described by college personnel as "self-sustaining" and do not receive state funds (there are exceptions, including Texas, which funds noncredit vocational programs). Unlike the research endeavors carried out at universities, the community colleges that we studied do not charge their contract and continuing education department overhead costs. This suggests that some subsidization is occurring. It is quite possible that, in exchange for operating costs, contract and continuing education return other dividends to the colleges, for example, positive publicity and strengthened relationships with business and industry. Unfortunately, we did not find sufficient institutional research at the colleges in our study to fully elaborate the relationship between credit and noncredit education. Worse yet, the lack of information about institutional benefits of contract and continuing education contributes to the lack of coordination between credit and noncredit "sides of the house" that we heard about in interviews.

In addition to drawing on college resources, the curriculum of contract and continuing education needs to be scrutinized for the reasons described earlier in this chapter. If the skills learned in noncredit programs are not transportable, and they do not aid students in acquiring college degrees, it is questionable whether they support the equity and access roles of community colleges. Stratification and diversification often go hand in hand, so to assume that the diversification of vocational options at community colleges is merely horizontal and does not represent a hierarchy of options may be naïve. Stratification does not have to pose a problem to students, but the key to overcoming its negative effects is to create strong connections between levels so that students may follow coherent pathways.

At the same time, the conclusion that expanding the transfer mission of the colleges is equated with ensuring equity is not without its own problems. Each year, thousands of students embarking on college education fail to complete even a semester. Around one-sixth of first-time college students starting out at community colleges complete no more than ten credit hours (Bailey and Alfonso, 2005). Large numbers of entering community college students are placed in remediation (more than 50% at some institutions in our study), and, as Dolores Perin and Kerry Charron show in their chapter, completion rates of remediation are low. The pathway to a four-year degree can prove to be a decade-long pursuit for some students, which suggests that the opportunity costs are high.

The motivations for community colleges to expand their role as transfer institutions are currently strong. More that 70% of high school students aspire to one day earn a bachelor degree (Schneider and Stevenson, 1999), and the four-year sector has not kept pace with this increased demand. Furthermore the tuition of community colleges is lower than that of four-years. Because many people live only a few miles from their local community college they can integrate college education into their current lifestyles, avoiding the cost of moving and/or seeking a new job. Community colleges are likely to continue to absorb this plethora of students and enroll them with the promise of transfer; however, the details of transfer remain inconsistent within states and are largely based on institutional agreements, and the actual outcomes of students seeking transfer are not well understood. With regard to credit programs, community colleges may be focusing too much on expansion and not enough on completion.

These threats to equity and access are more acute in the face of current policy developments. President Bush's Skills for the 21st Century initiative provides an example of this. Various aspects of this initiative emphasized exactly the types of programs that are leading to the contradictory developments described in this chapter. The initiative included funds for dual-enrollment or early-college programs, support for community college partnerships with business and industry, and loans to pay for short-term training that leads to an industry-recognized credential or certificate. In addition, the president proposed expanding student aid to support students in "competency-based programs, as an alternative to traditional credit-hour programs" (White House, 2004).

The picture that emerges from these initiatives is a fairly accurate portrait of the developments identified in our field study. Community college access grants can help to solidify many colleges' position in their communities as transfer institutions for traditionally aged students, while the other initiatives are helping to fund the expansion of noncredit vocational training. The danger is a new schism in community college programs, whereby credit programs are for younger students with bachelor degree aspirations, and noncredit programs are for older, working adult students. These working adults were historically an important constituency served by college credit programs. The question this raises is about the qualitative differences in the types of education obtained through various types of vocational education. For example, what happens to students enrolled in credit certificate programs versus noncredit certificate programs? Developing an understanding of this problem returns to the debate of the best balance of academic and vocational education, which is as yet unresolved and continues to adopt new forms.

In light of the growth in credit education and transfer, there is little threat that community colleges could be transformed into vocational-technical schools. The new challenge that the colleges face is to manage and integrate noncredit services with their credit departments in ways that promote access for all populations of students: young or old, rich or poor. This calls for insisting on curricular coherence across entire colleges (and even systems) rather than encouraging contract and continuing education to continue to develop in their own silos. Designing explicit pathways from noncredit into credit and on to the bachelor degree may be one method of doing this.

In addition, policy makers should be keenly aware of the implications of policies that encourage industry certifications and the growth of noncredit education. An example of this can be found in the Cisco certification programs. Most colleges run these programs through their noncredit departments. The primary objective of students and teachers involved in the programs is to pass the Cisco certification test. As Jim Jacobs and Norton Grubb show in their chapter, taking these courses at community colleges can be expensive for students—much more so than taking credit courses.

A number of colleges in California, Tennessee, Washington, and elsewhere, however, are demonstrating that Cisco training can not only be integrated into credit courses, but can also become part of a broader preparation for information technology (IT) jobs. Through the National Science Foundation's Advanced Technological Education (ATE) program, full-time community college faculty are learning how to integrate IT skills needed to pass Cisco certification with business and "soft" skills. These are full- and part-time faculty in regular credit programs who are finding ways not only to keep pace with industry, but also to be leaders in understanding how disadvantaged students can master the complex technical curriculum allowing them to prepare for stable and well-paid employment after graduation. At least two of the sites we are familiar with are also developing transferable IT degree programs that articulate to public universities. Unlike the pared-down curriculum of noncredit Cisco training, these credit-bearing IT programs allow students to test for multiple certifications, which make them more marketable.

These developments relate to a fundamental question in education: how much and what types of education are taxpayers willing to fund? As state funding is reduced, colleges are turning to two resources: students willing to pay higher tuition and fees and businesses interested in outsourcing training. It is interesting to note that, although these sources are generally considered private, they too receive public subsidies. Students receive public funds through federal and state financial aid. Businesses receive government subsidies for education through tax incentives, the continuing education tax deduction taken by individuals, and public training grants to name a few. Nonetheless, pursuing these funds implies new priorities for community colleges when compared with the relatively undiversified resources in the form of state FTE reimbursements.

The implications of privatization are consistent with the findings of our field study. Colleges are willingly accepting their expanded role in postsecondary education by absorbing large numbers of new students and by shifting the focus of credit occupational programs toward transfer. At the same time, privatization would suggest that the colleges are going to become increasingly entrepreneurial in their attempts to diversify their resources. This is happening through contract and continuing education, which sell deregulated or industry-regulated skills training. Both of these efforts focus on the students who can pay.

If the burden for paying for education is shifted from the state to the individual, educational policy needs to recognize the implications for equity. As we discussed in chapter 1, equity can be thought of as consisting of preparation for college, access to college, and successful outcomes for students. Much money could be saved by both individuals and states if community college students were better prepared for college. Similarly, money could be saved if students moved more swiftly and successfully through the college system. In this context, community colleges must think of themselves as transitional institutions. Although the outlook for low-income students in an increasingly privatized system is not good, finding ways to streamline transitions would be one way to support equity.

Community college institutional decisions are strongly shaped by social and economic pressures that are external to the colleges. A century ago, universities called for junior colleges, and the transfer mission was established. A half century later, President Truman called for comprehensive community colleges, and we have them today. Currently, we have students and parents asking for transfer and businesses and policy makers calling for continuing education. It will be up to the community colleges to figure out how to integrate these distinct institutional missions into a coherent vision for education.

NOTES

1. It is important to note that enrollments for noncredit courses are often duplicated. This means that students may be counted more than once, for example, if they took multiple workshops through a particular college.

2. Data on adjuncts are less reliable than those reporting on full-time faculty. There are greater fluctuations from year to year. It is also impossible to discern the number of credit hours taught by adjuncts. Colleges collect data on faculty workload, but comparable historical data were not available.

CHAPTER THREE

Performance Accountability as Imperfect Panacea

The Community College Experience

KEVIN J. DOUGHERTY AND ESTHER HONG

In the 1990s, performance accountability burst into the awareness of higher education policy makers. The theme was to make higher education institutions demonstrate how well they were performing by citing not enrollment growth but, instead, gains in student learning, graduation, and placement in good jobs. The hope was that performance accountability—particularly if an institution's funding was tied to it—would lead colleges and universities to become more effective and efficient, doing better despite lagging or even dropping state funding. This idea had already been in operation since 1979 in Tennessee (Bogue, 2002), but what produced an explosion in public awareness and debate was 1996 legislation in South Carolina, putting 100% of state appropriations for its public higher education institutions on a performance basis (Burke, 2002). The main proponent of the bill, State Senator Nikki Setzler, said it was the most meaningful piece of legislation in higher education in South Carolina in thirty years: "It will move us to a level of excellence and it makes us a leader in the nation" (quoted in Fix, 1996).

Despite these grandiose expectations for performance funding and other forms of performance accountability, there is surprisingly little analysis of its impact. To be sure, many excellent studies of performance accountability are available (Banta and Associates, 1993, 2002; Gaither, Nedwek, and Neal, 1994; Ruppert, 1995; Ewell and Wellman, 1997; Albright, 1998; Layzell, 1999; Alexander, 2000; McKeown-Moak, 2000; Laanan, 2001; Zumeta, 2001; Burke and Associates, 2002, 2004; Longanecker, 2004; National Commission on Accountability in Higher Education, 2005). These analyses, however, focus on why performance accountability has arisen or why it would be desirable, what is its temporal and geographical distribution, what forms it has taken, how it should be implemented, and (to a lesser extent) how it has been implemented. What is largely missing—in good part because of the relatively recent vintage of performance accountability—is in-depth analysis of its impact on institutions and their students. This is a vitally important question. Performance accountability in higher education—like the standards movement in K–12 education (Fuhrman, 2001)—has the potential of substantial both positive and negative impacts on how institutions work. It could make them sharply improve their performance by focusing their attention on outcomes rather than simply on inputs and processes. If badly designed, however, performance accountability can simply fail or—more worrisome—cause institutions to shift their behavior in socially deleterious directions. A key concern is that these standards, while putting great emphasis on higher rates of retention, graduation, and job placement, put much less emphasis on the role of community colleges in providing greater access to higher education and a general education. Another concern is that performance accountability has not taken enough account of obstacles to good institutional performance—such as depressed local labor markets or lack of organizational resources—so as to give all community colleges a fair shot at successfully meeting state standards.

This chapter analyzes three aspects of the impact of performance accountability systems on community colleges: to what degree have performance accountability systems had the desired impacts; what are the main problems community colleges have encountered in meeting performance accountability demands; and what have been the negative unintended impacts that have occurred as a result of performance accountability?

Before describing our research questions and research design in greater detail, we should further clarify the meaning and dimensions of performance accountability.

The Nature of Performance Accountability

Public institutions have long been subject to accountability, justifying how they have spent funds and reporting on their enrollments, staffing, and plant and equipment holdings. The current excitement over accountability, by contrast, is focused on *performance:* how well institutions do in such things as effectively teaching students, graduating them, and placing them in jobs. That is, the focus has moved beyond inputs or processes to include outputs (Gaither, Nedwek, and Neal, 1994; Ruppert, 1995; Burke and Serban, 1998; Carnevale, Johnson, and Edwards, 1998; Layzell, 1999; Alexander, 2000; Zumeta, 2001; Burke and Associates, 2002, 2004; Laanan, 2001; Longanecker, 2004; National Commission on Accountability in Higher Education, 2005).

Forms of Accountability

Joseph Burke and his colleagues have developed a useful typology of performance accountability systems: performance funding, performance budgeting, and performance reporting (Burke and Associates, 2002, pp. 8–23). These three forms differ in their theory of action: that is, the means by which institutional responses are meant to be catalyzed.

Both performance funding and performance budgeting focus on variations in funding as the prod to institutional change. Where they differ is in the tightness of connection between funding and performance. Performance funding connects state funding directly and tightly to institutional performance on individual indicators. A formula is created in which specific institutional outcomes such as graduation rates are translated into discrete amounts of funding. As of 2003, fifteen states had performance funding (Burke and Minassians, 2003, p. 5). In the case of performance budgeting, the connection between institutional performance and funding is more contingent. State government bodies (such as governors, legislators, and coordinating or system boards) announce that they will consider institutional achievements on performance indicators as one factor in determining their allocations to those institutions.[1]

The third form of performance accountability, performance reporting, depends on a different theory of action. It involves little or no explicit connection between performance and funding. The indicators used may be the same, but funders do not commit themselves to basing funding on that performance. In fact, the main spur to institutional improvement is not so much threatened shifts in government funding but rather changes in institutional self-awareness and public reputation. The acquisition and dissemination of performance data may compel institutional change by making institutions more aware of their performance or of state priorities or by fostering status competition among institutions desirous of being seen publicly as effective organizations.[2]

Sources of Performance Accountability Demands

Community colleges encounter performance accountability pressures from several different directions: state governments, the federal government, accrediting associations (both regional and professional), and other actors. In this chapter, we focus on state accountability systems.

State governments have actively joined the performance accountability movement. As of 2003, forty-seven states had some form of performance accountability: fifteen had performance funding, twenty-one had performance budgeting, and forty-six had performance reporting (Burke and Minassians, 2003). In addition to college-wide systems, there are specialized performance accountability systems attached to particular programs. For example, states may provide financial rewards to community colleges for every graduate coming out of a remediation or English as a second language program.

Although states vary greatly in the content of their performance accountability systems for community colleges, certain standards have been fairly common: persistence and retention rates; rate of transfer to four-year colleges; graduation or completion rate; degree of success in placing students in jobs; student performance on licensing exams; and success in workforce development (Burke and Serban, 1998, pp. 51–55, 98; American Association of Community Colleges, 1999b; Laanan, 2001, pp. 62–63). These measures, however, may change if states pursue the recent call for performance accountability systems that encompass not just higher education, but the entire K–16 or K–20 system (State Higher Education Executive Officers, 2003; Florida Department of Education, 2004a; Kazis, Vargas, and Hoffman, 2004).

Research Design

To keep its analysis within bounds, this chapter will concentrate on state performance accountability systems. The focus will be on the impact of performance accountability on community colleges.

Research Questions

This chapter will focus on the impacts of state performance accountability in three areas:

- To what extent have state performance accountability systems had the impacts intended by policy makers?
- What are the main obstacles community colleges have encountered in meeting state performance accountability demands? Whatever policy makers' intents, has performance accountability run into obstacles—whether in the design of performance accountability or in the nature of community colleges it is applied to—that hamper colleges in performing effectively?
- What have been the unintended, often negative, impacts of state performance accountability? For example, have community colleges—in a quest for high

retention and graduation rates—pressured faculty members to not fail students or even tried to avoid admitting less-prepared students who are more likely to drop out?

Research Methods

The analysis reported here is based on data collected by the National Field Study conducted by the Community College Research Center at Teachers College, Columbia University. The National Field Study involved intensive analysis of fifteen community colleges in six states. These states and localities and our general research methods are described in chapter 1. In addition, for the purpose of this chapter, we have drawn on additional material concerning community colleges in the six states.

To ascertain the impact of performance accountability, we interviewed community college officials and faculty and state and federal government officials. At the community colleges, we spoke with presidents; vice presidents or deans of finance, instruction or academic affairs, and occupational or workforce development; directors of institutional research; heads of faculty senates or unions; and faculty members and students from various divisions. At the state level, we interviewed staff of state community college or higher education boards, legislative staff, and gubernatorial education advisers. Beyond these interviews, this chapter draws on policy documents issued by the states and community colleges in our sample. In addition, we reviewed the research literature on performance accountability in higher education.

The interviews were analyzed using the QSR N'Vivo qualitative data analysis system. We coded interviews for references to the forms of accountability, their intended and unintended impacts, obstacles community colleges faced in responding to accountability demands, and suggestions for what form performance accountability should best take.

The Accountability Systems in Our Six States

The six states in our sample vary greatly in the nature and strength of their performance accountability systems. As can be seen in Table 3.1 below, all six states have had performance reporting.[3] Not all of those states, however, publicly report the performance of the community colleges. Moreover, their accountability systems can be differentiated in strength according to whether they have included performance funding and, if so, how long that performance funding was in place and what percentage of total community college revenues were at risk. In pulling this information together, we have rated the strength of the state performance accountability systems

TABLE 3.1
The State Performance Accountability Systems in the NFS States

	Florida[1]	Illinois[2]	Washington[3]	Texas[4]	California[5]	New York
General Strength of State System of Accountability as of 2000	High	Medium	Medium	Low	Low	None
Performance funding (asterisk indicates if one was once in place)	Yes PBB (1996–) WDEF (1996–2000)	Yes* PBIS 1998–2002	Yes* AIP 1997–1999	Yes* Developmental Education 1998–2003	No	No
Proportion of total community college revenues	5.0%	0.2%	0.3% (1999)	NA	NA	NA
Performance budgeting	No	No	Yes POG 2004–	Yes LBB	No	No
Performance reporting	Yes PR 1991–	Yes PR 2003–	Yes PRP 1999–	Yes SLIEP 1997–	Yes PfE 1998–2002 PBA 1996–	—
Input Measures						
Proportion of local population served	—	PF[7]	—	—	—	—
Access rates for minority students	PR[7]	—	—	PR	—	—
Outcome measures in 2000						
Retention (one semester or year)	—	—	—	PR	—	—
Remediation success	PF,PR	PF	PR	PF,PB,[7] PR	PR	—
Course completion rate	—	—	PF	PB,PR	PR	—
Student learning outcomes	PR (CLAST)	—	—	—	—	—
Prepared for work	—	—	PR	—	—	—
Prepared to transfer	—	—	PR	—	PR	—
Transfer to four-year colleges	PF	PF	PF	PB,PR	PR	—
Transfer success at university	PR	—	—	—	—	—
Graduation rate	PF,PR	PF	—	PB,PR	PR	—
Time to degree	PF	—	PF	—	—	—
Prepared for work	—	—	PR	—	PR	—
Professional licensing passage rate	PF,PR	—	—	PB,PR	—	—
Job placement rate	PF,PR	PF	—	PR	PR	—
Public assistance use	—	—	—	—	PR	—
Earnings	PF	—	PF	—	PR	—
Student satisfaction	—	PF	—	—	—	—

1. Florida: The state has had a small performance funding system (Performance Based Budgeting or PBB) since 1996. It overlapped for a while with a larger performance funding system—Workforce Education Development Fund (WDEF). Since 1991, there has been a performance reporting system (Florida Community College System, 1998, 2000; Wright, Dallet, and Copa, 2002).

2. Washington: A performance funding system was in place for fiscal years 1998 and 1999. It was replaced by a performance reporting system beginning in fiscal year 2000. And in 2004, the state enacted a performance budgeting system (Washington State Board for Community and Technical Colleges, 1997, 1998, 2000b, 2004a).

3. Illinois: Illinois had a performance funding system—the Performance-Based Incentive System (PBIS)—until 2002, when it failed to

in 2000. We picked 2000 because it would allow some time for possible policy effects to demonstrate themselves in the performance data reported by the states in subsequent years and in the interviews we conducted in 2001 and 2002. It should be noted, however, that the performance accountability systems have changed somewhat in the states since then. For the most part, the changes have been relatively minor. They have involved not changes in structure (such as a performance reporting system giving way to a performance funding system) but rather in content, involving changes in the outcome measures being used. Nevertheless, even these changes in measures have not been large. With this in mind, we categorize the National Field Study states by degree of strength of their performance accountability system in 2000 as follows:

- Strong state performance accountability system: In addition to the performance reporting that continues to this day (2006), Florida has had a performance funding system since 1996. At the peak of that system in the years 1996–2000, performance funding amounted to as much as 5.0% of the total community college educational and general revenues (Florida Community College System, 2002, p. 80; Wright, Dallet, and Copa, 2002, p. 163).

- Middling strength state performance accountability systems: Both Illinois and Washington had performance reporting and, for a number of years, performance funding systems. Those performance funding systems, however, were shorter lived than in Florida and applied to much smaller proportions of total community college revenues. For example, at its apogee, the Illinois Performance Based Incentive System only accounted for 0.2% of total community college revenues (Illinois Community College Board, 2002b, pp. 91, 98). And in

---

TABLE 3.1
notes continued

get further funding. It was replaced by a performance reporting system—the Performance Report (formerly known as the Results Report)—that uses some of the same measures, though it adds several more (Illinois Community College Board, 1998, 2000a, 2003, 2004d).

4. Texas: The state performance reporting system—State Level Institutional Effectiveness Process (SLIEP)—was legislatively enacted in 1997. It was joined by a performance budgeting system that provides data to the Legislative Budget Bureau. For a few years, there was a very limited performance funding system rewarding successful completion of remediation (Texas Higher Education Coordinating Board, 2000b, 2000c, 2002d, 2002e).

5. California: In 2000, the state had two performance reporting systems in place: the Partnership for Excellence (PfE) and an additional system for workforce programs specifically, the Performance-Based Assessment (PBA) (California Community Colleges, 1999d, 2000; California Workforce Development Board, 2002). In 2005, the state enacted a new performance reporting system to replace the Partnership for Excellence (Chancellor's Office, California Community Colleges, 2005).

6. New York: The state does not have a performance reporting system, though it does collect outcomes data from the SUNY community colleges.

7. PF indicates that measure was used in performance funding system; PB that measure was used in performance budgeting system; and PR that measure was used in performance reporting system.

the case of Washington, the $2 million allocated for performance funding in fiscal year 1998–1999 accounted for only 0.3% of the sum of community college tuition and state appropriation revenues (Washington State Board for Community and Technical Colleges, 1997, 1998a; Education Commission of the States, 2000; Washington State Higher Education Coordinating Board, 2001, p. 75).

- Weak state performance accountability systems: Both Texas and California had state performance reporting systems involving publicly reported data but no performance funding of any consequence. (Texas had a small performance funding system for a few years that applied only to developmental education.)
- No state performance accountability system: New York does not have a sate performance reporting system (Burke and Minassians, 2003; interviews we conducted with state and local community college officials). The state does collect some performance data, but they are not issued in the form of a performance report and are not used—except perhaps informally and individually—to push changes on the part of the community colleges.

Assessing the Intended Impacts of Performance Accountability

The intended impacts of performance accountability on community colleges involve immediate, mediated, and ultimate changes. The immediate impacts of performance accountability involve changes in state funding of colleges, self-awareness, awareness of state priorities, or concern about how well they compare with peer colleges. These immediate changes are intended to catalyze modifications of institutional behavior—the mediated changes—that will result in the changes of ultimate interest to policy makers, such as improved rates of retention, successful remediation, graduation, or job placement.

As we assess whether performance accountability realizes its intended impacts on the community colleges in our study, we find that the strength of this impact steadily declines and becomes harder to determine as we move down the causal chain. Moreover, it is not clear that stronger systems, involving performance funding, generate significantly stronger effects than systems involving only performance reporting.

Immediate Impacts

In assessing the immediate impacts of performance funding, we begin by looking at its impact on funding and then move to its impacts on knowledge, whether in the form of greater awareness of state priorities, self-knowledge, or status competition.

Changes in Funding

State performance accountability appears to have had relatively little financial impact on community colleges, whether we look at performance funding or performance budgeting.

Performance Funding. In our interviews with local community college officials in the three National Field Study states with performance funding systems (Florida, Illinois, and Washington) in place in 2000, two state officials and officials at six of the eight community colleges that we studied in those states expressed an opinion on the question of the impact of performance funding. One of the two state officials and officials at five of the six community colleges stated that the amount of money the colleges received through performance funding had little impact on the colleges.[4] A typical expression of this perception was the following from a Florida college: "There is a tiny amount of money . . . you're talking about, in an institution this size. . . . So Florida talks a lot about being performance based. And the governor pats us on the back. 'It's the only system that's performance based. We love you guys.' Yes, but they're not funding us. So it hasn't worked as an advocacy tool to say we'll be accountable if you'll keep our end of the covenant and fund us for it. And furthermore, it doesn't have the impact on practice that they anticipated it would have."

This perception that performance funding has little financial impact is not surprising. For the most part, little money is involved. In Illinois, when the Performance Based Incentive System was in operation, it accounted for only 0.2% of total community college revenues (Illinois Community College Board, 2002b, pp. 88, 91, 102). And even in Florida, where performance funding accounted for 5% of total community college revenues in 1999–2000, the financial impact of that performance funding, while greater, was still only moderate.[5] Year-to-year fluctuations in their state appropriations due to performance funding amounted to a smaller share of their total revenues. For example, in 1999–2000, the three Florida colleges we studied experienced the following shifts in their performance funding from the state: one experienced a gain of $817,000 over the previous year (1.9% of total expenditures), another a gain of $325,000 (0.4% of the college's total expenditures), and the third a loss of $485,000, 3.6% of the college's total expenditures (Florida Community College System, 2001, p. 85; Windham, 2003).[6] It should be noted, however, that the Florida college that we quoted above as stating that performance funding had little impact was the one that experienced a shift of only 0.4% of its total revenues; the colleges experiencing greater shifts did not express clear opinions about the impact.

Performance Budgeting. Performance budgeting also does not seem to have had a marked impact on the finances of community colleges. To be sure, some studies indicate that performance budgeting has a moderate impact on state funding decisions. For example, in a survey of sixty legislative leaders in the fifty states, Ruppert (2001) found that 62% rated performance results as an important and increasing factor in state appropriations for public higher education institutions.

At the same time, a nationwide survey in 2003 of state higher education finance officers (who are mostly located in state boards for higher education) found that none reported that performance indicators had a considerable influence on state funding, and only 19% reported even a moderate influence (Burke and Minassians, 2003, p. 11).[7] Our interviews with state and local community college officials also paint a picture of little influence. Only one high-level community college official (in Texas) and officials of three of eight community colleges studied in Texas, Florida, and Illinois stated that they saw performance data as having much influence on the budgetary decisions of the legislatures and state coordinating bodies.

Changes in Knowledge

Nevertheless, if the mode of action operating through funding has not been all that strong, it is important to remember that another mode of action has been operative: the dissemination of information and its consequence of enhanced institutional awareness of state priorities and their own performance and of increased competition for status. As it happens, this mode of action has had a rather significant impact.

Increased Awareness of State Priorities. Performance accountability is a means of focusing the attention of community college officials on the priorities of state government. This greater awareness can be generated only if the implementation of performance accountability systems requires state officials to enunciate formally and more clearly their priorities, rather than if officials of higher education institutions must glean them from budget documents or the comments of governors, legislators, and system officials (Burke and Associates, 2002, p. 268). In fact, there is evidence that performance accountability does lead campus officials to become more aware of state priorities. In a survey of officials of community colleges and four-year colleges in five states with performance funding systems, 33% said that performance funding had increased campus responsiveness to state needs (Burke and Associates, 2002, pp. 74–76).[8] This conclusion finds some resonance in our interviews with state and local community college officials. State officials in Washington and Texas and officials at four community colleges (two in Washington and one each in Florida and Illinois) did say that performance accountability led faculty and administrators at the colleges to become more aware of state goals.

At the same time, we should not exaggerate the degree of community college awareness of state priorities. In a survey of administrators of two-year and four-year colleges in five states with performance funding, Burke and Associates found that academic deans and department chairs were much less familiar with their state's performance funding system than were higher level college administrators (presidents, chief academic officers, and senior business officials). Whereas 88% of the top administrators were "very familiar" or "familiar" with their state's performance funding system, only 58% of the academic deans and 40% of the department chairs were familiar (Burke and Associates, 2002, pp. 63–64).

Increased Self-Awareness. A second important channel by which the collection and dissemination of information can affect community colleges is by increasing their awareness of their own performance, thus setting the stage for corrective action if needed. Indeed, a state official in Illinois and two community colleges in Washington said that the state accountability systems in their states had led community colleges to become significantly more aware of their own performance, and officials at another two colleges in Illinois and California said there was some, but less significant, influence.

At the same time, we need to acknowledge the limits of self-awareness. Officials at three other colleges noted that the state performance accountability requirements had little impact on their self awareness, either because the college was already collecting such data or because they simply disregarded the data the state required them to collect.

Increased Status Competition

The publication of data that allow community colleges to compare themselves to each other raises the possibility that poor performance will be taken as an embarrassment requiring corrective action and good performance will reinforce the actions the college is already taking. At two community colleges in Florida and Illinois, we found some evidence of such a mechanism at work.

As can be seen above, there is evidence that performance accountability does have some impact—though it is moderate at best—on community colleges, operating through shifts in funding, changes in awareness of state priorities and self-knowledge, and status competition. The next question is whether we also see mediated impacts, whereby those shifts in funding or knowledge result in behavioral changes that could produce the ultimate impacts that state officials seek.

Mediated and Ultimate Impacts

Performance accountability does seem to have moderate impacts on actions of community colleges that might yield the ultimate outcomes that state officials seek. Burke and Associates (2002, pp. 72–74) asked local community college officials (ranging from presidents to department chairs) in five states with performance funding to rate their use of performance results in various areas on a five-point scale: 1 (very extensively), 2 (extensively), 3 (moderately), 4 (minimally), or 5 (not at all). The average ratings for various areas of institutional action ranged between moderate and extensive: institutional planning (2.46), curriculum planning (2.77), and student outcomes assessment (2.79).[9]

We asked state and local community college officials to detail what actions the colleges took in response to state accountability requirements in the areas of improved remediation, retention and graduation, transfer, and job placement. The patterns can be seen in Table 3.2.[10]

We will explore the specific outcomes below. We should note at the outset that those outcomes data leave much to be desired. All too often, it is difficult to find comparable measures across the states. Moreover, in this analysis, we have not been able to control for key differences between the states in their demographic, educational, and economic characteristics, which have been confounded with the impact of their performance accountability systems. Hence, any statement about the ultimate effect of those systems has to be treated with considerable caution.

Remediation

Officials of five community colleges (three in Florida and one each in Washington and Texas) stated that their state accountability system had led them to take actions to improve the performance of their remedial education students.[11] As the director of developmental education at a Washington community college noted, "One of our initiatives is underprepared students at this college, and it is coming a lot from the legislature. They want to count the students, they want to know how many developmental education students there are, what is not working in the system. All that kind of data. I think the college is definitely looking at that; it is one of our initiatives that we are working on over the next three years. I think we chose that, and the board has

TABLE 3.2
Reports of Community Colleges Responding to State Accountability Demands

	Florida	Illinois	Washington	Texas	California
Number of community colleges studied in state	3	3	2	2	3
1. Remediation					
State had PA measure	PF,PR[1]	PF	PR	PF,PB,PR	PR
Reports of response	3 CCs		1 CC	1 CC	
2. Graduation			—		
State had PA measure	PF,PR	PF		PB,PR	PR
Reports of response	3 CCs	1 CC		1 state official	
	1 state official	1 state official			
3. Transfer to four-year					
State had PA measure	PF	PF	PF	PB,PR	PR
Reports of response	1 CC		1 CC		1 CC
			1 state official		1 state official
4. Job placement			—		
State had PA measure	PF,PR	PF		PR	PR
Reports of response	2 CCs	1 CC			1 CC
	1 state official				

1. PF indicates that measure was used in performance funding system in 2000; PB that used in performance budgeting system; and PR that used in performance reporting system.

chosen that as one of our initiatives. We should be getting more information over the next couple years on this very area." Beyond examining themselves in greater detail, the five community colleges involved took a variety of actions to improve their performance in the area of remediation. First, they worked with high schools to improve the academic preparation of students before they arrived at the community college.[12] They also mandated remediation if students tested as needing remediation at entrance to the community college. Finally, they provided intensive counseling during remediation.[13]

Has Remedial Success Increased? As Table 3.3 shows, four of five of our states that had measures for remediation performance improved their rates of remedial success. It is not clear, however, that those with stronger accountability systems improved more than those with weaker ones. Part of the problem is that the states use rather different measures of remediation success. Even when the measures are roughly comparable—as is the case with Illinois and California—the stronger system is not clearly producing stronger results. Although it has the stronger accountability system, Illinois has had slower yearly growth in remediation success than has California (0.33 percentage points a year versus 0.6).

TABLE 3.3
Change in Remediation Rate

	Florida	Texas	Illinois	Washington	California
Did state have remediation success measure as part of its PA system in 2000?	Yes	Yes	Yes	Yes	Yes
Strength of state accountability system for this measure	High (PF,PR)	High (PF,PB,PR)	Medium (PF,PR)	Low (PR only)	Low (PR only)
Measures					
Remedial course completion: Remedial credits earned as % of remedial credits attempted: % point change (Illinois Community College Board, 2004a; California Community Colleges, 1999c, 2004).	—	—	+1.0 1999/00–2002/03 (0.33 per year)	—	+3.0 1997/98–2002/03 (0.6 per year)
Passage of exit exam: % of those in remedial education who pass Texas Academic Skills Program (TASP) test in FY: % point change (Texas Higher Education Coordinating Board, 1999a, 2004b)	—	−8.2 1996/97–2002/03	—	—	—
Completion of highest remedial course: % passing highest remedial course within 2 years: % points change (Windham, 2003)	+5.5 R +5.7 M +4.4 W 1995/6–1999/00	—	—	—	—
Gain in skill: Percentage of ESL, ABE, and GED who gain one competency level in at least one subject area during the year: % points change (Washington State Board for Community and Technical Colleges, 2000a–2003a)	—	—	—	+14 1998/99–2002/03	—
Gain in skill: Completion of coursework with C or higher within 2 years of entrance in course at least one level above prior basic skills enrollment: % points change (California Community Colleges, 2000–2004)	—	—	—	—	+0.5 Eng. +4.3 math +2.0 total 1997/8–2002/3

Retention and Graduation

A major thrust of state and federal performance accountability systems has been to improve the retention and graduation of students. As Table 3.2 shows, state officials in three states and four community colleges (three of them in Florida) stated that community colleges responded to state demands for improved retention and graduation rates. For example, an academic faculty member at a Florida community college

TABLE 3.4
Change in Graduation Rate

	Florida	Illinois	Texas	California	Washington[1]	New York[2]
Did state have graduation measure as part of its PA system in 2000?	Yes	Yes	Yes	Yes	No	No
Strength of state accountability system for this measure	High (PF,PR)	Medium (PF)	Low (PB,PR)	Low (PR)	None	None
Measure: % change in number of associate's and certificates awarded	+19% 1996/7– 2002/3 (3.2%/yr)	+32% 1997/8– 2002/3 (6.4%/hr)	+14% 1997/8– 2002/3 (2.8%/hr)	+14% 1997/8– 2002/3 (2.9%/hr)	+38% 1996/7– 2003/4 (5.4%/hr)	+3.5% 1997/8– 2003/4 (0.6%/hr)

SOURCES: California Community Colleges (2000–2004); Florida Department of Education (2004a); Illinois Community College Board (2004c, 2004e); Texas Higher Education Coordinating Board (1999a, 2000c, 2001a, 2002a, 2004a, 2004b); State University of New York (2004); Washington State Board for Community and Technical Colleges (1998c, 2004a).
1. Washington collected data on graduation rates but did not make them part of its performance reporting system.
2. New York state does not have a performance reporting system, though it does collect data on graduation rates.

noted, "The topics of discussion in our faculty meetings have an awful lot to do with retention and we've had workshops for different teaching and learning styles like this. . . . We're better than the average in the state but you want higher and higher because we're starting to get paid on how we teach students. And one thing where all the emphasis is on doing things with faculty."

Colleges have used several different means to improve their retention and graduation rates. One is improving precollege preparation and college remediation. Others are improving orientation programs, removing graduation obstacles, defining intermediate completion points on the way to a degree or certificate, and dropping courses and programs with low completion rates.

How Much Have Graduation Rates Been Raised? As we look across the states, the association between the strength of a state's performance accountability systems and its graduation rate is moderate at best. This can be seen in Table 3.4, which arrays the states by the strength of their performance accountability system and provides data on graduation rates.[14]

Although states that have stronger performance accountability systems with respect to graduation do tend to have greater increases in graduation rates, the relationship is still not very strong. To be sure, Florida and Illinois do show greater increases in graduation rates than most of the other National Field Study states. It is still striking, however, that Washington, which did not include graduation rates in its performance funding or performance reporting systems in 2000, has nearly as good a record of rising graduation rates. Moreover, Florida's record is weaker than that of Illinois, which had a considerably weaker performance funding system.[15]

Transfer Rates

We found some evidence—though it is of modest strength at best—that community college officials have been made more aware of and responsive to the push by state governments for higher transfer rates. State officials and three community colleges in three states stated that community colleges were responding to state demands for higher transfer rates. For example, a California community college official told us, "There is a master plan of ensuring that we have more transfer students who go on. . . . [T]he state chancellor's office for the community colleges and I believe the UC [and] CSU systems are all wondering how come there are not a lot more people transferring. Then the legislature is also looking at that, so we're getting a lot of what's coming down. In our district, our chancellor was asking us to establish the goal of increasing transfers by X amount."

Transfer Rates across States. As Table 3.5 shows, there is little evidence that differences in the strength of state performance accountability systems are strongly associated with differences in transfer rates. Florida has had far smaller increases in numbers transferring than states with weaker accountability systems. It is interesting, however, that the states with performance accountability systems addressing transfer generally demonstrated greater increases in the number of transfers than did New York, which has not had a state performance reporting or funding system.[16]

Job Placement

As seen in Table 3.2, one state official and officials of four community colleges in three states attested to the responsiveness of their community colleges to state demands for higher job placement rates. For example, an official of a Florida community college stated, "See, what we've aimed at here is we've aimed at programs that will produce high wage jobs. . . . We've really geared away from low-wage jobs. [Interviewer: How much of that has been in response to the state accountability rules, the workforce development accountability pot?] Well, you're going to be rewarded more for high wage students. Our funding is going to be based on right now, a piece of that funding is based on my placement. . . . I get more points if I put them in a higher wage job than I do if I put them in a lower wage job."

TABLE 3.5
Change in Transfer Rate

	Florida	Illinois	Washington	Texas[1]	California	New York
Did state have transfer to public universities measure as part of its PA system in 2000?	Yes	Yes	Yes	Yes	Yes	No
Strength of account-ability system for this measure	High (PF)	Medium (PF)	Medium (PF)	Low (PB,PR)	Low (PR)	None
Measures						
Number of com-munity college students trans-ferring into public four-year colleges in given year (% change)	+2% 1996/7– 2002/3 (fall only) (0.33%/yr)		−1.2% 1996/7– 2002/3 (annual) (−0.2%/yr)	+16% 1996/7– 2001/2 (fall only) (3.2%/yr)	+14% 1997/8– 2002/3 (annual) (2.8%/yr)	+2.9% 1997/8– 1999/00 (fall only) (1.4%/yr)
Proportion of entering cohort who transfer (% change)		+0.8% 1995/6– 1998/9 (0.2/yr)				

SOURCES: California Community Colleges (1999a, 2000–2004); Florida Division of Colleges and Universities (2001); Illinois Community College Board (2004b); Texas Higher Education Coordinating Board (1999a, 2002a); Washington State Board for Community and Technical Colleges (1998b, 2004a).

1. Texas uses a somewhat different measure of transfer numbers than other states. It is the number of those at university who had taken more than 15 credits at a community college or technical college in the last 3 years.

Our interviewees described several different means their colleges use to improve their colleges' job training success. These included revamping course content and job placement efforts and, if need be, canceling courses and programs with poor place-ment records.

Job Placement Rates across the States. As Table 3.6 shows, over the course of the late 1990s, three National Field Study states showed improvements in job placement rates.[17] The states, however, use quite varied measures of success in job placement, so it is impossible to examine how differences in the strength of accountability systems are associated with differences in job placement rates. Data for federally funded Perkins and Workforce Investment Act programs should allow for comparison across the states. Unfortunately, these data do not seem to be broken down by training provider, which would enable us to look at the job placement rates for community colleges specifically.

TABLE 3.6
Change in Job Placement Rate

	Florida	Illinois	California
Did state have job placement measure as part of its PA system in 2000?	Yes	Yes	Yes
Strength of state accountability system for this measure	High (PF,PR)	Medium (PF)	Low (PR)
Measures			
Placement in jobs related to training, in continuing education, or in military: % change (Florida State Department of Education, 2003a–e):	1996/97– 1999/2000	—	—
Associate of Science degree	+2		
Postsecondary vocational certificate	−15		
Postsecondary adult vocational	−2		
Placement in job or further schooling in year after graduation of degree and certificate recipients: % change (Illinois Community College Board, 2004d)	—	+1.2 1997/98– 1999/00	—
Job placement any time during year after graduation: % change (California Workforce Development Board, 2002)	—	—	+0.6 1996/97– 1998/99

Summary of Intended Impacts

We certainly have found clear—though not overwhelming—evidence that community colleges have responded to state demands for improved remediation, higher rates of retention, graduation, and transfer, and improved job training. At the same time, however, we have at best moderately strong evidence that states with seemingly stronger accountability systems have indeed produced stronger student outcomes. Four of five of the National Field Study states with performance accountability systems addressing remediation exhibited improvements in remedial success, but it is not clear that those with stronger accountability systems showed greater improvements than those with weaker ones. Second, in the case of retention and graduation, the association between strength of a state's performance accountability systems and its retention and graduation rates has been only moderate. Although the states with stronger systems (Florida and Illinois) clearly show greater increases in degree production than do states with weaker systems, the relationship between the two variables is by no means monotonic and smooth. Third, there is no apparent association between the strength of state performance accountability systems and changes in transfer rates. Finally, it is impossible to determine how the strength of an accountability system is associated with job placement rates because the states have such different measures of job placement and are located in distinctive labor markets experiencing different economic trajectories.

If the Intended Impacts Are Small, Why Is This?

The data we have reviewed above do not conclusively demonstrate that stronger performance accountability systems have greater impacts on community college performance. The association between the strength of a state's performance accountability system and the size of its performance outcomes is rather weak. One can argue, however, that these data do not definitely disprove that stronger forms of accountability have a greater impact. As we have noted, the data do not control for differences between states—in their student bodies, labor market conditions, and other factors shaping student success—that might be swamping any program effects. Second, the performance funding systems we have examined are not all that strong. Although in Florida performance funds amounted to as much as 5% of the total community college budget, in Illinois the figure was only 0.2%. Furthermore, these funds have not been provided for a long time on a stable basis. Whereas, by 2006, Florida's performance accountability system has been around for ten years, Illinois' lasted only four years before being defunded and Washington's two years before being repealed. And during those eight years, Florida's system has shifted considerably in the outcomes being used, how they have been weighted, and the amount of funding involved.

In addition, as we will explore in the next section, states may not be realizing outcomes as great as they intend because their performance accountability systems place considerable obstacles in the way of community colleges attempting to meet accountability demands.

Obstacles to Meeting Accountability Demands

Although the community colleges in our sample have responded to accountability demands, they have done so with difficulty. Four obstacles stand out: inappropriate measures of success; unclear funding; funding that does not rise with enrollments; and inequalities in institutional capacity to meet the standards. We will explore each of these in turn below. Table 3.7 reports the number of state officials and colleges in our sample reporting these problems.

Inappropriate Measures

Many of our community college respondents (at ten different colleges) argue that state performance measures fail to fully capture successful performance by community colleges. Here the issue is not that important missions of community colleges are

TABLE 3.7
Reports of Problems in Meeting Accountability Demands

	5 States Total	Florida	Illinois	Washington	Texas	California
General strength of state accountability system		High	Medium	Medium	Low	Low
Number of community colleges studied in state	13	3	3	2	2	3
Problems						
Inappropriate measures:						
Retention	6 CCs	1 CC	3 CCs	—	1 CC	1 CC
Job and wage placement	6 CCs	2 CCs	1 CC	3 CCs[1]	—	—
Funding instability	4 CCs	3 CCs 1 state official	1 CC	—	—	—
Funding does not keep pace with enrollments	3 CCs	3 CCs	—	—	—	—
Inequality of institutional capacity	2 CCs 1 state official	1 state official	2 CCs	—	—	—

1. We are drawing not only on the two community colleges we studied in Washington but also a community college that was the subject of the dissertation by Nissenson (2003).

not backed by standards, though this is a problem that we will return to below. Rather, the problem is that, even when there is such backing, the measures of success make community colleges seem to perform more poorly than they really are. These problems of mismeasure fall into two areas: retention and graduation, and job and wage placement.

In the case of retention and graduation, community college leaders nationally complain that state accountability measures apply far less well to community colleges than four-year colleges. They argue that many two-year students enter college as an experiment, to see whether they are really interested in college, and they leave when they decide it is not to their taste (Grubb, 1996, p. 62; Burke and Serban, 1998, p. 26). Moreover, other students enter community colleges wanting to acquire certain skills but not a credential. Once they achieve those skills, they often leave the community college without a credential, making it seem as if the institution failed to do its job (Hudgins and Mahaffey, 1997, p. 26). For example, an official at an Illinois community college argued,

> Defining completion is so hard. What is completion? Because it can be that two to three courses or it could be in the associate degree, could be the certificate . . . some of the accountability factors they're so interested in completions but they look at completions not from a standpoint of what the student need is. For example, I do an EMT [Emergency Medical Training] program, and we run 375 students through EMT every year. From an accountability standpoint, if you look at our graduation rate or certificates, out

of these 375, we may give, from the college, 10 certificates. . . . . But, we have three hundred . . . [that] get their state certification and licensure. . . . The certificate from here actually means zero. It's the state licensure that counts.

Finally, graduation measures typically do not include students who transfer from the community college to another college without a degree in hand (Hudgins and Mahaffey, 1997, p. 25).

There is some merit in this complaint about the limitations of simple measures of retention and graduation. What this would suggest is a need for measures that take into account students' initial aspirations at college entrance. At the same time, such measures must address the fact that community colleges do have distressingly high rates of students leaving without earning degrees. For example, in the Beginning Postsecondary Student survey of first-time students entering college in fall 1995, 47% of those entering public two-year colleges had left higher education by June 2001 without a degree (Berkner, He, and Cataldi, 2002, p. 12).[18]

This problem of low retention and graduation is founded in good part on the fact that community college students are significantly less advantaged socially and prepared academically than are students at four-year colleges, and these differences affect retention rates.[19] It also reflects community colleges' lesser ability than four-year colleges to integrate their students academically and socially. As commuter institutions attracting many part-time students, community colleges are less able to provide students with extensive contact with faculty and fellow students—whether through dormitories, clubs, or other means—that help bind them to the college and prevent dropout (Dougherty, 1994, pp. 85–92; Deil-Amen, 2005).

Job and wage placement was another issue for our respondents at six colleges. The validity of job and wage placement measures as indicators of college performance is weakened because these measures are greatly affected by factors outside the control of colleges, in particular the general state of the economy (Zumeta, 2001, p. 185). Several of our respondents noted that state demands for placement in high-wage, high-skill jobs sometimes fail to acknowledge that weak local labor markets rather than poor college performance may account for low placement rates. A Washington community college official felt that the state's accountability measures were quite unfair to community colleges located in rural, often depressed, economies: "They were so ridiculous it became obvious. I mean one of them was a wage-level, a certain dollar amount per hour that every college had to average in their programs [that graduates attained]. Well, [her college] is always at the top because we have a lot of high-wage programs but Yakima and Walla Walla [rural community colleges], those places, no, they're never going to get there probably. And it doesn't make any sense."

Funding Instability

Local community college officials often complain that performance-funding formulas are unstable, making it very hard for them to plan. In a survey of community college and four-year college campus officials in five states with performance funding, 40.1% rated budget instability as an extensive or very extensive problem of performance funding in their state (Burke and Associates, 2000 and 2002, p. 77). In our study, this criticism was particularly strong in Florida, where performance funding had applied to a relatively large portion of the community college budget and the funding formula has been changed almost every year (Wright, Dallet, and Copa, 2002, p. 161). Community college officials argued that this made it difficult for them to plan effectively because they could not easily predict how much their college would receive.

Lagging State Funding

A frequent complaint by community college officials in Florida was that performance funding formulas do not take into account rising enrollments. Moreover, performance funding may provide a cover for governors and legislators to keep down the base budgets of higher education institutions either by providing the illusion that institutions can receive more money if they improve their performance or by making institutions seem unworthy of increases because they have not performed well enough (Burke and Minassians, 2001, p. 3; Moden and Williford, 2002, p. 191). In fact, if funding does not go up sufficiently, community colleges can greatly improve their performance and yet receive no additional funding. For example, between 2000–2001 and 2001–2002, the Florida community colleges increased the number of workforce education points they produced by 21%, but funding rose only 0.7% (Wright, Dallet, and Copa, 2002, p. 164). As a result, it was quite possible for a community college to improve its performance and still lose money, because it simply did not improve as much as the other community colleges. A Florida community college president lamented this fact:

> We have had no increase in that pot of money for four to five years and it's very, very discouraging to all of us. . . . We've spent enormous energy and funds to do what we thought the legislature was asking us [only] to find no reward. In fact, it got so discouraging the second year those of us that had done a lot better actually lost money because with a finite pot of money and more people learning how to do the reporting better they had more points every year and they divided the points into the same

finite number of dollars to figure out how much the points would get. So, we could do a lot better and still lose money.

Inequality of Institutional Capacity

A question that has been raised is whether performance funding will create a vicious cycle for poorly performing, often underresourced community colleges. Will overburdened urban community colleges and small, rural community colleges that have less-advantaged students and fewer institutional resources experience difficulty meeting state standards and hence lose funding, further compounding their lack of resources and imperiling their future performance (Laanan, 2001, p. 72; Burke and Associates, 2002, p. 275)? This was the specter raised by a state official in Florida and officials at two community colleges in Illinois. For example, when asked whether there have been instances in which a community college may fail to really pursue enhanced performance for lack of technical or other resources, an official of the Florida state community college system replied, "I think some of the smaller colleges have certainly the potential for that problem. Florida has spent a lot of money trying to get all 28 of its institutions with good technical systems and good computer systems. But some of our smaller colleges, X and Y [names two], come to mind, where there's just so few people in some of these [institutional research] programs, I know this is causing them a lot of problems trying to keep up with things."

Publicly Unintended Impacts

As with any policy intervention, performance accountability is subject to un-intended consequences. These can be beneficial or, if negative, of minor consequence. Performance accountability, though, has already generated some important publicly unintended,[20] negative consequences: lowering academic standards, narrowing open-door admissions, restricting college missions, and increasing compliance costs. The reported incidence of these problems across the community colleges, as evidenced by our interviews, is indicated in Table 3.8.

Lower Academic Standards

An unintended consequence of accountability pressures can be a weakening of academic standards at community colleges (Zumeta, 2001, p. 185). To raise their graduation rates, several community colleges in our study made an effort to remove various hindrances to their students easily achieving a degree. If these hindrances

TABLE 3.8
Reports of Negative Unanticipated Consequences

	5 States Total	Florida	Illinois	Washington	Texas	California
General strength of state accountability system	—	High	Medium	Medium	Low	Low
Number of community colleges studied in state	13	3	3	2	2	3
Negative consequences						
Lower standards (grading, graduation)	3 CCs	2 CCs	—	—	1 CC	—
Narrowed open door	4 CCs	2 CCs[1]	—	—	2 CCs[1,2]	—
Mission restriction	0 CCs	—	—	—	—	—
Compliance costs	7 CCs	3 CCs	1 CC	2 CCs[1]	—	1 CC

1. Includes data from additional college that were not part of the original National Field Study (NFS) sample. The Texas and Florida data were part of a precursor study of community college missions. The Washington community college was the subject of a dissertation by Nissenson (2003).

2. At one of the Texas community colleges, the respondent made it clear that his college was not restricting its admissions. It was a matter more that he thought that other colleges might begin to become more selective in their admissions if the state moved to a much tighter accountability system.

were simply matters of organizational rigidity, this clearing of obstacles would be desirable, but this is not always the case. The obstacle clearing can end in eliminating difficult, yet important, intellectual requirements. An official of a Florida community college spoke about this danger: "What it [performance accountability] could produce, if you say to me that I'm going to be totally driven in this direction [is that] I may think, 'Well, one of the reasons why my students do so terribly is they can't get through the English comp.' So now what I'm going to do is maybe I'm going to give them a much lower-level course if I need to have students that are going to finish. So it could truly have an impact on the academics and the preparedness of students if I am so driven by a formula of dollars."

There is also reason to fear that community colleges are being pushed by accountability demands for higher retention and graduation rates to pressure faculty to avoid giving failing grades. Faculty members at a Texas community college reported that they are required to submit, for every student who has dropped out from their course, a written report specifying what steps they took to prevent the withdrawal. In a focus-group interview, several faculty members indicated that this led them to be loath to give students bad grades for fear of causing student to drop out, which would then trigger the requirement to explain what the faculty member did to prevent that. This report was echoed by the president of the American Association of University Professors chapter at a Florida community college:

> There's a lot of pressure to retain every single student no matter what it takes. [So implicitly does this then push the faculty towards grade inflation and that sort of thing?] Well, every meeting and every discussion this comes up. They begin by saying, "Do not

misunderstand us; we are not talking about lowering your standards." But from that point in the meeting, we don't know any other way to interpret it. And so it's like you can't say it out loud and in fact if you say anything it's going to be the reverse, but in reality there's no other way to achieve what their goals are. . . . And we're evaluated based on that. We have to report every conference we've had, the outcome, if the student wasn't retained, why, how many efforts were made.

Restricting the Open Door?

If it is problematic that community colleges may buoy their retention and graduation rates by grade inflation and looser graduation standards, there is a far more disturbing possibility: keeping up retention and graduation rates by limiting the intake of less prepared and less advantaged students, thus undercutting the community college's commitment to open-door admissions (Ruppert, 1995, p. 13; Zumeta, 2001, p. 185). It is likely that this tactic is more a danger than a reality, for it would be anathema to community college officials, for whom open-door admissions are a touchstone. Yet there are signs that some community colleges have restricted admission to certain occupational programs in order to raise eventual graduation rates. An official at a Florida college noted, "There are people who may need to take a course in a program and we would not necessarily want to attract those people because you're going to be working for performance-based funding. . . . But, in the health sciences, this is a major concern because it's not who you start with, it's who completes that matters." Similarly, an administrator at a Texas community college stated he was restricting admissions to some training programs because of accountability requirements attached to state workforce training aid.

Such barriers to entry to specific programs raise worrisome issues of denial of opportunity. To be sure, it is understandable that certain programs may have more difficult content and may require selective admissions to prevent students (and the institutions) from wasting their efforts by failing to graduate. At the same time, admissions selectivity can be a way of avoiding the effort to bring students up to speed and, in the case of programs with high payoffs, reserving scarce and valuable goods for more-advantaged students. Fortunately, we have not seen evidence that performance accountability is leading community colleges to raise barriers to entry to colleges as a whole. Nevertheless, one wonders whether such concerns about quality and failure to aggressively pursue a wide range of students will become more common if accountability bites deeper into higher education. Will we see outreach efforts focusing more on high school with advantaged students because they have a higher likelihood of graduating from a community college and securing better-paying jobs, outcomes rewarded by state and federal accountability systems? Such a quiet shift of outreach efforts would effectively undermine the open-door commitment, but it would be very difficult to spot.

Mission Restriction?

A danger with performance accountability is that it may cause community colleges to weaken their long-standing commitment to a comprehensive mission. Some of this mission restriction may come from the contradictory pressures on community colleges to, on the one hand, maintain an open-door admissions policy and, on the other hand, graduate a high proportion of their students. For example, a major area of concern is the relative dearth of performance funding measures targeting minority access and graduation (Burke and Associates, 2002, p. 43).

Other aspects of mission restriction may come from the fact that key missions of the community college are not backed with performance measures, which might lead community colleges to deemphasize them. Rarely, if ever, do performance accountability systems reward community college efforts in the important areas of general education and community services (except in the form of contract training and workforce development). If these missions are to continue thriving under a performance accountability regime, it is important that they be backed by indicators (especially well-tailored ones).

High Compliance Costs

A final unintended impact of performance accountability is that it often imposes considerable compliance costs on community colleges, for which they are not fully reimbursed (if at all). As officials at seven colleges indicated, the data-reporting requirements of state performance accountability programs can require large outlays of money and time to collect and report required data. A Florida state community college official noted, "I think part of the problem with the workforce [program] is the formula itself is so cumbersome in trying to set up just the processing of it. Some of the colleges are almost spending as much money on collecting the data and turning the information in as they're getting back."

Policy Recommendations

The overall worth of performance accountability will depend on the relative balance that emerges between, on the one hand, the degree of responsiveness it elicits from community colleges and, on the other hand, the institutional costs performance accountability imposes on community colleges and the socially problematic choices it leads colleges to make in pursuit of what is considered acceptable performance. The question is whether the benefits can be maximized and the costs minimized by judicious modification of extant performance accountability systems.

Achieving Greater Impact on Outcomes

If states wish to secure greater (or at least clearer) results from their accountability systems, there are a number of things they should consider. Although there is no certainty it will make a huge difference, it is certainly worth continuing to explore tying more funding to performance outcomes. It is important, however, to keep the funding and the measures stable over several years so that colleges can effectively plan on the basis of anticipated revenue streams. Frequent change in the performance indicators and their weight in performance funding systems hampers colleges in their attempt to pursue organizational change consistently.

It should be kept in mind that much of the impact of performance accountability may lie in its mobilization of information and the status strivings of community colleges rather than its funding outcomes. This leads to other recommendations. It is important that states build up the institutional research capacity both of state government and of the colleges. The colleges need funding and technical assistance to acquire new equipment and train their administrators and faculty in how to analyze and interpret data and develop strategies to address the performance shortfalls those data might uncover (Petrides, 2002, pp. 78–79; Grubb and Badway, 2004, p. 25).[21] In addition, Joseph Burke and his associates have suggested that states further encourage internal reflection on performance data by adding as a performance indicator whether colleges have developed a system of internal performance accountability for institutional subunits. Moreover, states could financially reward colleges that use state indicators as a basis of their internal budgetary allocations (Burke and Associates, 2002, p. 272; Burke and Minassians, 2002, pp. 123–24).

Similarly, state governments also face the problem that data are gathered but not acted upon. One proposal is that state officials be required to sign off that they have read and responded to state accountability information. In fact, state officials could be asked to detail precisely how they have taken performance indicators into account in improving policy (Burke and Minassians, 2002, p. 124).

Reducing Obstacles to Meeting Performance Standards

As we have seen, existing performance accountability systems impose significant obstacles on community colleges, including poorly designed measures of success, funding that is unstable and does not keep pace with increasing enrollments, and inequalities in institutional capacity.

States can address the criticism that performance accountability systems do not accurately gauge the actual successes of community colleges by giving them partial credit for partial completions, in a manner akin to Florida's system of Occupational Completion Points. In Florida, occupational programs have been divided into several course clusters, so colleges can get partial credit for students who complete a definable cluster of courses that has vocational meaning but is less than a degree. Another device would be to set retention and graduation targets for colleges that vary according to student composition in terms of degree aspirations at the time of entry. Colleges with larger proportions of students with no degree aspirations or very weak ones would have lower targets set than those with fewer such students.

We must, however, be very cautious with this. We should not assume that most community college entrants do not want a degree. The 1996 Beginning Postsecondary Student survey found that 90% of first-time community college entrants wanted at least a certificate, with 63% wanting at least a baccalaureate degree (Hoachlander, Sikora, and Horn, 2003, pp. 10–11).[22] Moreover, even if many community college students were to have only weak degree aspirations, community colleges should still have as one of their central missions "warming up" and strengthening the aspirations of less-advantaged students. Therefore, redesigned retention and graduation measures must not let low credential aspirations on the part of many community college entrants become an excuse for tolerating high rates of dropout. One way of preventing this is to gradually increase retention and graduation targets from year to year, spurring colleges to warm up their students' aspirations.

The difficulties of some colleges—particularly those in rural areas,—in meeting demands for placement in well-paying jobs need to be addressed by accountability policies that acknowledge local labor market differences. Job placement standards should explicitly build into job and wage placement measures corrections for differing labor market conditions.

State performance accountability systems need to address the frequent criticism that those systems are often subject to considerable instability of funding and failure to keep up with rising enrollments and emerging needs. With regard to funding instability, states need to provide community colleges with a greater sense of security and ability to effectively plan. The formulas governing fund allocation under performance funding systems should remain in place for four or five years, and changes should be made on the basis of carefully considered evaluation and deliberation by state leaders (Burke and Associates, 2002, p. 280). Moreover, state performance funding budgets need to take into account growing enrollments so that colleges are not put in the position where improved performance can actually result in lower state funding because the funding pot has not grown as fast as enrollments or other demands on colleges.

Finally, to help colleges with fewer institutional resources, fiscal and human, state performance accountability systems need to provide funds to meet the costs of acquiring new data management systems and training institutional research staff. Moreover, resource-poor colleges need more extensive help in developing their capacity to devise solutions to performance problems (Grubb and Badway, 2004, pp. 13, 25, 28). This not only means the provision of state funds, but also entails providing extensive technical assistance. Otherwise, a performance funding system may create a vicious cycle for resource-poor colleges in which their lack of organizational capacity generates poor performance, leading to declining state aid and in turn further weakening of their performance.

Reducing or Eliminating Unintended Negative Effects

Even if performance accountability is made more effective, it still does produce unintended negative effects that need to be actively mitigated and even eliminated. The pressure on colleges to resort to grade inflation and lower standards in order to retain and graduate students is not easily relieved. One expedient historically has been to use exams external to the institution to determine graduation. A variety of states already have such exams, but establishing such tests in other states will prove a contentious process, particularly when questions remain about the content validity of such tests, especially when applied to disadvantaged groups.

The temptation to improve institutional performance by reducing the admissions of less-prepared students needs to be forcefully resisted. One way to avoid penalizing colleges that enroll many disadvantaged students is to allow performance targets to vary across colleges according to their student characteristics (Zumeta, 2001, p. 187). Regression analysis can be used to develop predicted performance targets for colleges on the basis of student composition (Bailey, Calcagno, Jenkins, Kienzle, and Leinbach, 2005; Scott, Bailey, and Kienzl, 2006), though this system is not foolproof. Regression-adjusted performance targets were used to set standards for service delivery areas (SDAs) under the Job Training Partnership Act.[23] The system, however, enshrined already existing selective admissions on the part of the SDAs and still did not provide a strong incentive for SDAs to serve disadvantaged clients (Bailey, 1988). Thus, it is important to also think of providing more direct incentives for outreach to students who are less likely to persist in and graduate from college. Performance accountability systems can include measures of the enrollment, retention, and gradu- ation of minority and low-income students (Dowd, 2003, pp. 109–116). For example, Florida requires community colleges to report the enrollment composition of their student bodies, and the state makes degree of fit between the racial-ethnic makeup of the student body and the surrounding district an indicator in its Performance Based Budgeting performance funding system.[24]

The danger of a narrowing of the community college's missions can be combated by providing measures addressing all important missions. States should emulate the successful efforts of Florida, Texas, Washington, and California of using remedial education as a performance indicator (Texas Legislative Budget Board, 2002; Wash- ington State Board for Community and Technical Colleges, 2002b, 2003b; Wright, Dallet, and Copa, 2002, p. 148; California Community Colleges, 2004). States, how- ever, also need to include measures pertaining to general education and continuing education, important community college missions that have been ignored by perfor- mance accountability systems and thus face the danger of being neglected by institu- tional leaders.

Summary and Conclusions

Performance accountability for community colleges is still in its infancy. There is much to discover about its impacts. Nevertheless, we already have substantial indica- tions that it is in need of improvement if it is to have a positive effect on the commu- nity college's role in promoting student access and success in college.

As we have seen, performance accountability has not had significant financial impacts on community colleges. The funds devoted to performance funding have been quite limited, except in Florida. Whatever the funding impact, though, there is fairly substantial evidence that performance accountability has succeeded in rai- sing local community college officials' awareness of state priorities and interest in their own college's performance. In turn, these immediate impacts—whether funding fluctuations or changed awareness—have led community colleges in turn to make changes in their structure and operations to achieve such state goals as more student retention, improved remediation, greater numbers of graduates, and better job place- ment rates.

The evidence, however, is only moderate at best that states with apparently stron- ger accountability systems (indexed by the presence and strength of a performance funding system and performance reporting involving public reporting) have indeed produced better student outcomes. We certainly see evidence of colleges taking actions to improve their remedial success and of rates of remedial success rising. Yet, because of incompatible measures of remediation success across the states, it is impossible to tell whether states with stronger accountability systems involving remediation, such as Florida, show greater improvement in remedial success than do states with weaker systems. There is considerable evidence that the rising state emphasis on retention and graduation has led community colleges to move to improve both. Despite these efforts, the association between the strength of state accountability systems and changes in state retention and graduation rates is moderate at best. Higher rates of transfer between community colleges and four-year colleges are a frequent goal of performance accountability systems, but there is no evident relationship between the strength of a state's accountability system with respect to transfer and increases in the number of transfers. Finally, the states showed improvements on various measures of job placement. As with remediation, however, the indices the states use are not comparable, preventing any comparison between strength of a state's accountability system and their degree of success in job placement.

As can be seen, the association between the strength of a state's performance accountability system and degree of change in its performance outcomes is only moderately strong at best. Among our six states, those with both performance funding and performance reporting systems do not clearly outperform those with performance reporting only. To be sure, the data we have reviewed do not control for demographic, educational, and economic differences between states that might be swamping any program effects. Moreover, with the exception of Florida, the performance funding systems we examined have not involved much money or operated long. Even if one were to control for the factors discussed above, there is the distinct possibility that performance *funding* may simply not prove important. There is reason to believe that community colleges are already responsive to performance accountability in the form of performance *reporting* so that fiscal incentives may not add much impact, unless very large funds are at risk.

Although the community colleges in our sample have responded to accountability demands, several obstacles stand out: poorly designed measures of success; funding that is unstable and does not keep pace with increasing enrollments; and inequalities in institutional capacity. Our community college respondents were especially critical of measures of retention and graduation and job placement that do not reflect the particularities of community colleges' mission and context and thus make them seem to perform less well than they actually do. They argue, for example, that measures of student success that focus on the attainment of degrees often fail to acknowledge that many students enter community college without any intention—and perhaps even need—to receive a degree. There is some validity to this criticism, but it is also important to reaffirm that the vast majority of community college entrants indicate a desire for a degree and, in any case, an important mission of the community college is to "warm up" the aspirations of disadvantaged students who are not thinking of getting a degree but are capable of it and would certainly benefit from it. Another obstacle community college officials note is that performance funding formulas are often unstable, making it difficult for community college officials to predict accurately how much money they will receive and plan their curricular offerings accordingly. Furthermore, community college officials, especially in Florida, complain that performance funding does not keep pace with enrollment increases and provides a cover for keeping down state appropriations in the name of greater efficiency. Finally, some of our interviewees raised the concern that performance funding may create a vicious cycle where urban community colleges and small, rural community colleges with more disadvantaged students and fewer institutional resources will find it difficult to meet state standards and, hence, will lose funding, further compounding their lack of resources and imperiling their future performance. This would create a strong disincentive for colleges to reach out vigorously to disadvantaged students.

The intended impacts of performance accountability are not the only ones at issue. Effects not publicly intended by policy makers occur as well, and they are often negative. They include a weakening of academic standards, constriction of open-door admissions, narrowing of institutional missions, and significant costs of complying with accountability demands. The weakening of academic standards has taken the form of pressing faculty to avoid giving out failing grades and eliminating courses and course content that, while barriers to graduation, are also important elements of the preparation of educated people. So far, the constriction of the open door has involved instances of making some programs more selective in order to elevate their retention and graduation rates by limiting the enrollment of less-prepared students. The possibility remains of community colleges being tempted, if performance demands tighten, to become more selective in their admissions to wider swaths of their programs, weakening the access mission of the community college. Mission restriction, however, may also occur because key missions of the community college—for example, general education and community services—are not encouraged by performance measures and thus may receive less attention from community colleges. The final unintended impact of performance accountability is that it often imposes considerable compliance costs on community colleges in the form of large outlays to collect and report required data.

In the face of the problems encountered by performance accountability for community colleges, we reviewed various ways of strengthening its intended impacts and reducing its costs and unintended negative impacts. To improve its effects, we discussed instituting or strengthening performance funding and, more important, building up the capacities both of state government and of the colleges to conduct research on institutional performance, analyze the results, and devise appropriate policy responses. Performance accountability, however, also suffers from obstacles it puts in the way of community colleges wishing to perform well. Therefore, various means were suggested for improving inadequate measures of success, providing more stable funding, and reducing inequalities in institutional capacity. Finally, this chapter analyzed ways of reducing or eliminating the unintended negative consequences of performance accountability by sustaining academic standards, providing incentives to enroll and graduate disadvantaged students, and safeguarding the mission of the community college as more than just a place to acquire skills.

At present, performance accountability remains an enigma. We should certainly not discard it. It has demonstrated some potential to realize important public goals. Nevertheless, we need to ponder carefully the evidence that its impact is uneven and at best moderately strong, in part because performance accountability programs are of fairly recent vintage, inadequately funded, and unsteadily implemented. Moreover, we need to think about how to guard against the distinct possibility that performance accountability produces some significant negative unintended outcomes. All this argues not for abandoning performance accountability, but certainly for carefully designing and redesigning it to maximize its benefits and minimize its costs. This careful crafting of policy will become particularly important as states experiment with performance accountability systems that try to encompass not just higher education, but the entire K–16 system.

NOTES

1. The theory of action behind performance funding and performance budgeting is that higher-education institutions are resource seeking organizations that wish to maximize their revenues or, at least, minimize revenue loss. This theory of organizational behavior resembles resource dependence theory in organizational sociology, which portrays organizations as centrally concerned with the acquisition of resources and the survival of the organization, as well as the stabilization of relationships with environmental elements (Aldrich and Pfeffer, 1976, p. 83).

2. Two of these logics of action for performance reporting (alignment with state priorities and status competition) fit institutional theory in sociology. In this analysis, organizations are driven to behave in certain ways in order to maintain their legitimacy in the eyes of relevant audiences, whether peer organizations, government officials, or the public. To be sure, this

quest for legitimacy is directed in part by a desire to maintain, ultimately, an adequate flow of resources. It is also directed by the goals of preserving organizational powers and responsibilities, maintaining ties to powerful external supporters, and enhancing organizational prestige, seen as a good in and of itself (Meyer and Rowan, 1977 [1991], pp. 50–52; DiMaggio and Powell, 1991).

3. The data in the table refer to the contents of the states' performance accountability systems in 2000.

4. Of these five colleges, three were in Illinois, one in Washington, and one in Florida. At the sixth college, which was in Washington, the officials stated that performance funding did have a monetary impact on their college, but their statements did not make clear how significant this impact was.

5. This was the last year that the Workforce Education Development Fund operated in tandem with the smaller Performance Based Budgeting program. After 2000, Workforce Education Development Fund was not funded, so the performance funding share of total community college revenues dropped to less than 1%.

6. The state annual data book does not report revenues by individual college, so we are using expenditures as a proxy.

7. It should be noted that state higher education finance officers had rated the impact of performance indictors on state budgeting higher in previous years. In 2002 4% had rated the impact as considerable and 35% as moderate, and in 2001 the two percentages had been 11% and 37%, respectively. It is clear that this drop reflected the financial straits of state governments in 2003, which had left them much less room for discretionary spending on higher education (Burke and Minassians, 2003, pp. 10–11).

8. The officials ranged from presidents to department chairs. The five states had performance funding at the time: Florida, South Carolina, Tennessee, Ohio, and Missouri (Burke and Associates, 2002, pp. 74–76).

9. It is interesting that the community college officials indicated significantly more use of performance data than did their four-year college counterparts, whose ratings for the three categories above were 2.80, 3.32, and 3.13, respectively (Burke and Associates, 2002, pp. 72–74).

10. We should emphasize that the counts given in Table 3.2 should be treated as tentative. Personnel with insights into the responses to accountability policies differ from college to college, so we cannot be sure that we captured all relevant responses.

11. For an extended analysis of what our National Field Study colleges have been doing in the area of remediation, see the work of my CCRC colleague, Dolores Perin (Perin and Charron, in this volume; Perin, 2006).

12. This work with the high schools is going to be an important part of any emerging P–16 system of accountability. Many states such as Florida and Texas are trying to create a closer alignment between their high school exit requirements and their college entrance requirements (Texas Higher Education Coordinating Board, 2000a; Florida Department of Education, 2004c). For more on the development of such P–16 systems, see State Higher Education Executive Officers (2003) and Kazis, Vargas, and Hoffman (2004).

13. For more on these steps taken to improve remediation, see Perin and Charron (in this volume).

14. Similarly disappointing results have occurred in other states with performance funding.

In Tennessee, the rates of persistence to graduation for community colleges dropped from 26% in 1988–1994 to 22% in 1992–1998 (Bogue, 2002, p. 96). And in Missouri, the community colleges failed to meet a state goal of having 55% of full-time freshmen complete twenty-four credits with a grade point average of 2.0 or higher by the end of their freshman year and the number of certificates and degrees conferred by public two-year colleges decreased 3% between fiscal year 1993 and fiscal year 1999 (Stein, 2002, pp. 122, 124).

15. It is interesting, however, that the number of certificate graduates rose sharply while the number of associate graduates remained flat (Florida Community College System, 1998, pp. 28–32; Wright, Dallet, and Copa, 2002, pp. 154–55, 165). This might reflect the impact of the Workforce Education Development Fund component of Florida's performance funding system, which was much larger than the Performance Based Budgeting System that targeted associate degrees.

16. Moreover, Missouri, a state with a strong performance funding system, experienced a 25% increase between fiscal year 1995 and fiscal year 1999 in the number of students transferring from community college and completing a bachelor degree (Stein, 2002, p. 123).

17. The trend data reported in Table 3.6 go up only to 1999–2000 to eliminate the effect of the recession beginning in 2000. If the trend data are taken through the next year or two, all the states show declines in job placement rates. In Missouri, the rate for successful job placement of two-year college graduates in technical areas increased from 64% to 76% between fiscal years 1993 and 1998 (Stein, 2002, p. 124). In Tennessee, by contrast, the job placement rates for community colleges stayed flat, at 90% in 1993–1994 and 91% in 1997–1998 (Bogue, 2002, p. 96).

18. Of the remainder, 36% had attained a degree (anywhere from a certificate to a bachelor degree) and 17% were still enrolled. Meanwhile, for four-year colleges, the rate of leaving college without a degree was 23%, and for for-profit less than four-year colleges, it was 37% (Berkner, He, and Cataldi, 2002, p. 12).

19. Bailey, Calcagno, Jenkins, Kienzl, and Leinbach (2005) find that the size, location, and gender and racial-ethnic composition of community colleges explains 60% of the variance in the percentage of first-time, full-time students in 1999–2000 who completed a certificate or degree program in that same institution by 2002–2003.

20. The reason for this somewhat clumsy wording is that certain impacts may be intended, but are not publicly stated. For example, some community college officials charge that performance funding is intended to keep down or even reduce state expenditures on higher education by turning heretofore stable base budget allocations into contingent performance funding allocations.

21. A notable effort along these lines is the Achieving the Dream initiative founded by the Lumina Foundation and other funders. In 2004 it was working with twenty-seven community colleges with high proportions of minority and low-income students to improve their capacity to gather, analyze, and act on performance data (Lumina Foundation for Higher Education, 2004 and http://www.Achievingthedream.org).

22. This figure, however, overstates their more immediate expectations. In the same survey, only 37% of the students entering a community college reported that their primary purpose for enrolling was to transfer to a four-year college (Hoachlander, Sikora, and Horn, 2003, p. 13).

23. Service delivery areas were the local administrative units responsible for administering and contracting with providers of training funded by the Job Training Partnership Act.

24. The Texas Higher Education Coordinating Board requires all colleges to report the racial and gender composition of their workforce education enrollment in comparison to that for all community college enrollments (IE 2–1) (Texas Higher Education Coordinating Board, 2004a). Illinois, meanwhile, allows community colleges to choose whether to report enrollment by race-ethnicity, gender, or disability status. It does, however, require all colleges to report completions by the same characteristics (Illinois Board of Higher Education, 2003; Illinois Community College Board, 2003).

CHAPTER FOUR

Increasing Competition and Growth of the For-Profits

THOMAS BAILEY

Throughout the 1990s and into the early years of the twenty-first century, the growth of for-profit education providers was one of the most closely watched trends in higher education (Burd, 1998; Strosnider, 1998; Selingo, 1999; Blumenstyk, 2000). Influential analysts foresaw a much more competitive higher education landscape in which the traditional established institutions were threatened by burgeoning new educational providers and new forms of educational technologies. Frank Newman, former president of the Education Commission of the States argued, "Competition is forcing a hard reexamination of the purpose and effectiveness of every activity—from how well and often faculty interact with students, to whether expenditures on student life actually create a learning community, to the issue of costs and wise use of re-sources" (Newman, 2001, p. 9).

The for-profit sector was not the only source of new competition in higher educa-tion. Growing competition for research funding and the fierce battles for *U.S. News and World Report* rankings were indications of competition among the public and traditional not-for-profit private institutions. New technologies were also expected to play a pivotal role. Nevertheless, the highly publicized growth of some for-profit institutions was an integral part of the discussions of the new educational environ-ment and indeed generated growing anxiety among both private not-for-profit and public colleges and universities. For-profit institutions comprised a growing and robust sector of higher education. Many for-profit corporations maintained impres-sive profit margins and stock valuations despite the three-year-long stock market slump starting in 2000. A Public Agenda report, *Meeting the Competition*, argued that higher education officials "have a strong sense of mounting pressures from for-profit and virtual institutions, new technologies, and the expansion of competition from existing institutions" (Immerwahr, 2002, p. 3). Public Agenda's informants also expressed anxiety "about the convergence of two factors: limited public revenues and a growing number of new competitors, especially the for-profits. The main concern was that new competitors would 'cherry pick' the most profitable programs, leaving important but less-profitable programs and functions 'naked and alone' " (p. 3).

Community colleges appeared to be particularly vulnerable to this competition. Many for-profit institutions focused on the technical fields that had been mainstays of community college enrollments. The for-profits also appealed to older, nontraditional, working students, another crucial market for community colleges. Some prominent community college representatives voiced this concern. For example, Tony Zeiss (1998), the president of Piedmont Community College, in Charlotte, North Carolina, and former president of the American Association of Community Colleges, asked, "Will our students become theirs?" He warned with some urgency that proprietary colleges "already have the jump" on meeting the needs and expectations of a broad cross-section of community college students.

Some analysts, though, feared that competing head on with the for-profits may have negative social consequences. Community colleges and other public or not-for-profit institutions may successfully respond to the emerging environment, but at the expense of the broader public purposes of education (Newman, Couturier, and Scurry, 2004).

At the end of the 1990s and beginning of the new century, a new set of concerns have influenced the thinking about the role of the for-profits in higher education. As pointed out in the first chapter, many states have had to confront growing student enrollments with dwindling resources for higher education. The growth in enrollments results from several factors including the baby boom echo, continued high levels of immigration, and a growing consensus about the economic value of some postsecondary education. Resource constraints have resulted from increased taxpayer resistance, the politically supported growth of other claims on state resources including Medicaid, corrections, and K–12 education, and the recession of the early years of the decade. State encouragement for private higher education may offer some advantages to states as they search for solutions to this fiscal vice. William Zumeta (2004) has argued that the expansion of private capacity accompanied by state financial aid, which is designed to encourage access for low-income students, may be a lower cost alternative to the expansion of the public sector itself. The for-profits may offer particularly good opportunities for this, in light of their apparently aggressive growth strategies, assuming that they maintain high educational quality.

This chapter examines how community colleges perceived this potential threat, how they responded, whether states can turn to the for-profits as lower-cost alternatives to the expansion of the public sector, and the implications of these developments for the community college equity agenda. Was Zeiss's view widespread? How have community colleges been shaped by the new, more competitive environment? Did colleges lose students to the new competitors? In trying to respond to the competition, did they change their structures and purposes in undesirable ways? Has the for-profit phenomenon led to a more or a less equitable higher education system?

To provide context, this chapter first presents some background information on the characteristics, size, and growth of for-profits in the two-year sector. The following section compares the for-profits to public community colleges. That section is followed by a discussion of how colleges perceived the potential competition from the for-profits and other educational institutions. Unlike other chapters in this book, this discussion is not based on the fieldwork for the National Field Study, but rather on fieldwork carried out at eight colleges for a study on the missions of community colleges (Bailey and Morest, 2004). The chapter then discusses how competition from the for-profits shaped community colleges, differentiating between the credit and noncredit operations of the colleges. The subsequent section describes the community college reaction to the growth of the importance of vendor-developed certifications discussed by Jacobs and Grubb in this volume; for-profit firms often provided the preparation for the assessments on which these certifications are based. The chapter ends with conclusions.

Size, Growth, and Characteristics

This section presents national data on enrollments, degrees, and tuition to provide some baseline comparison among three sectors—public, private not-for-profit, and for-profit institutions. Each of these sectors is in turn divided among two- and four-year institutions, though the focus of the analysis is on the two-year sector. A two-year institution is one in which the associate degree is the highest degree granted. Institutions granting both a baccalaureate and an associate degree would be categorized as a four-year institution. The data are from the 2002–2003 Integrated Postsecondary Educational Data System (IPEDS) file, which is collected and maintained by the National Center for Education Statistics (NCES).[1] This was the last year for which NCES had provided "final" data at the time of publication of this book.

Institutional characteristics are displayed in Table 4.1. Several characteristics revealed in these data are worth emphasizing. First, minorities, especially blacks, account for a somewhat larger share of enrollments in two-year for-profit institutions than they do in either of the other two two-year sectors. Second, among two-year institutions, the for-profits enroll the smallest percentage of students 25 years or older. In contrast, among the four-year institutions, the for-profits enroll the highest

TABLE 4.1
Mean Enrollment, Demographics, and Tuition, by Sector, 2002–2003[1]

	Two-Year			Four-Year		
	Public	Private Not-for-Profit	Private For-Profit	Public	Private Not-for-Profit	Private For-Profit
Total Number of Institutions[1]	1,177	313	781	624	1,702	295
Fall enrollment						
Mean total undergraduates (headcount)	5,552	248	337	8,588	1,725	1,198
Mean full-time undergraduates	2,078	183	299	6,821	1,411	939
Mean FTE undergraduates	3,243	208	314	7,521	1,527	1,040
Part-time undergraduates (%) (headcount)	63	27	12	21	19	22
Female undergraduates (%) (headcount)	58	61	56	55	58	48
Undergraduates 25 or older (%) (headcount)	40	31	23	17	14	23
Student demographics (% FTE)						
Black	13	13	20	11	11	14
Hispanic	13	10	14	7	5	10
Asian	6	7	4	6	5	5
Minority[2]	33	33	38	25	21	29
Tuition for full-time undergraduates						
In-state	$1,790	$6,724	$9,891	$3,074	$13,821	$11,457
Out-of-state	$4,417	$6,796	$9,866	$9,134	$13,830	$11,457

SOURCE: U.S. Department of Education, 2002b, IPEDS 2002–2003 institutional characteristics and fall enrollment files.
1. Number of institutions used in calculations of means and percents may be less due to missing values for some institutions.
2. Includes Native Americans.

percentage of older students. Within their level (two year or four year), however, the for-profits are serving different types of students than the public or not-for-profit sectors. Third, in four-year for-profit institutions women are in the minority—the only sector in which this occurs. Fourth, most students at the for-profits, particularly at the two-year institutions, attend full-time. Indeed, the public two-year colleges are by far the most important providers of education for part-time students. Finally, in general, the for-profit two-year institutions are tiny compared to public community colleges, averaging only 337 students compared to more than 5,500 for community colleges. It is not surprising that the for-profits are much more expensive than community colleges. These data suggest that the for-profit two-year schools are fundamentally different institutions and that they serve very different populations than public community colleges.

Table 4.2 presents data on enrollments in institutions across all levels and sectors during the 1992–1993 and 2002–2003 academic years. These data show that the two-year for-profit sector does not offer significant competition for community colleges. The for-profit institutions remained minor players among the two-year institutions; they account for only 4% of all enrollments at that level. Moreover, the for-profits

TABLE 4.2

Total Fall Enrollment (headcount), by Sector and Regional Accreditation, 1992–1993 and 2002–2003

	Two-Year				Four-Year			
	Public	Private Not-for-Profit	Private For-Profit	Total	Public	Private Not-for-Profit	Private For-Profit	Total
1992–1993								
All institutions	5,635,124	125,032	247,602	6,007,758	4,731,794	2,075,858	72,253	6,879,905
Row % within level	94	2	4	100	69	30	1	100
Regionally accredited	5,556,102	71,066	35,579	5,662,747	4,731,783	1,980,445	45,211	6,757,439
Row % within level	98	1	1	100	70	29	1	100
2002–2003								
All institutions	6,323,772	64,855	249,559	6,638,186	5,152,578	2,294,321	304,207	7,751,106
Row % within level	95	1	4	100	66	30	4	100
Regionally accredited	6,208,128	36,884	33,263	6,278,275	5,152,009	2,243,491	203,039	7,598,539
Row % within level	99	1	1	100	68	30	3	100

SOURCE: U.S. Department of Education, 1992 and 2002b; IPEDS 1992–93 and 2002–3 institutional characteristics and fall enrollment files.

TABLE 4.3

Credentials Awarded, by Sector and Regional Accreditation, 2002–2003

	Two-Year				Four-Year			
	Public	Private Not-for-Profit	Private For-Profit	Total	Public	Private Not-for-Profit	Private For-Profit	Total
Less than one-year certificates								
All institutions	172,764	8,849	24,848	206,461	5,777	2,976	2,104	10,857
Row % within level	84	4	12	100	53	27	19	100
Regionally accredited	146,524	633	804	147,961	5,777	2,429	698	8,904
Row % within level	99	0	1	100	65	27	8	100
Less than two-year certificates								
All institutions	119,907	2,143	39,527	161,577	4,778	5,622	4,136	14,536
Row % within level	74	1	24	100	33	39	28	100
Regionally accredited	103,934	821	1,414	106,169	4,710	4,144	528	9,382
Row % within level	98	1	1	100	50	44	6	100
Associate degrees								
All institutions	466,220	12,259	55,358	533,837	46,151	36,430	34,408	116,989
Row % within level	87	2	10	100	39	31	29	100
Regionally accredited	463,318	9,690	9,010	482,018	46,050	34,568	12,600	93,218
Row % within level	96	2	2	100	49	37	14	100
Bachelor's degrees:								
All institutions	—	—	—	—	875,420	446,622	31,189	1,353,231
Row % within level	—	—	—	—	65	33	2	100
Regionally accredited	—	—	—	—	875,408	441,501	24,702	1,341,611
Row % within level	—	—	—	—	65	33	2	100
Total								
All institutions	758,891	23,251	119,733	901,875	932,126	491,650	71,837	1,495,613
Row % within level	84	3	13	100	62	33	5	100
Regionally accredited	713,776	11,144	11,228	736,148	931,945	482,642	38,528	1,453,115
Row % within level	97	2	2	100	64	33	3	100

SOURCE: U.S. Department of Education, 2002b, IPEDS 2002–03 institutional characteristics and completions files.

have a negligible 1% share of all enrollments in regionally accredited two-year institutions, and their enrollment totals actually dropped during the decade among accredited institutions. In contrast, overall enrollments and enrollments in regionally accredited institutions in the four-year, for-profit sector more than quadrupled during the decade, though they still accounted for no more than 4% of all four-year college enrollments.

Table 4.3 presents data on degrees and certificates awarded by institutions in each of the sectors. For example, it shows that two-year public institutions account for 87% of all associate degrees and 84% of the sum of associate degrees and all certificates conferred by all two-year institutions. Furthermore, those rates increase to 96% and 97%, respectively, among regionally accredited two-year institutions. The table reveals that certificates are a more important credential to for-profit schools than they are to community colleges. Certificates account for about 39% of all credentials awarded by public two-year colleges, whereas they represent 54% of all credentials awarded by the two-year for-profits (percentages calculated from the sum of all certificates divided by credential totals).[2] Although IPEDS does not provide data on enrollments by degree objective, it is still useful to consider the enrollment data from Table 4.2 in light of the degree data in Table 4.3. As shown in Table 4.2, the for-profits account for 4% of the total enrollments in two-year institutions in 2002–2003, but we know from Table 4.3 that the for-profits emphasize certificates more than associate degrees. Therefore, we can conclude that the 4% for-profit enrollment share is an overestimate of the for-profit share of all students pursuing an associate degree.

A comparison of data from Tables 4.2 and 4.3 can also provide a rough sense of the percentage of students enrolled in the different types of institutions who earn a credential—the completion rate. Table 4.2 shows that the for-profits accounted for 4% of the 6 million students enrolled in all two-year institutions in the 2002–2003 school year. Table 4.3, however, indicates that the for-profits accounted for 13% of the total degrees and certificates awarded by all two-year institutions. The for-profits accounted for 10% of the associate degrees, even though for-profits accounted for less than 4% of the students who were enrolled with the goal of earning an associate degree. This suggests that completion rates for the for-profits are higher than they are for public community colleges. One reason may be that, as we saw in Table 4.1, students in community colleges are much more likely to be attending part-time, and part-time students are less likely to complete degrees. Data based on the Beginning Postsecondary Students Longitudinal Study presented in the Futures Project (2000) report on the for-profits also suggest a higher, or at least a more rapid, completion rate for both associate degrees and certificates for the for-profits. On the other hand, institutions that are not regionally accredited grant the large majority of degrees conferred by the for-profits. This raises the possibility that the quality of those degrees is suspect.

One interesting point about four-year institutions reported in Table 4.3 is that four-year for-profits are much more likely to confer both certificates and associate degrees than their four-year public counterparts. Indeed, the four-year for-profits granted far *more* associate degrees and certificates (combined) than bachelor degrees, while certificates and associate degrees accounted for only 6% of all credentials granted by public four-year institutions.

In sum, enrollments in the for-profits remain marginal in the two-year sector. The enrollment share of the for-profits actually shrank between the 1992–1993 and 2002–2003 academic years. Minorities and younger students were somewhat more concentrated in the two-year for-profits, and there is some tentative evidence that degree completion rates are higher in the for-profits. In sharp contrast to the public sector, four-year schools grant more than one-third of all of the associate degrees granted by for-profit institutions. On the other hand, regionally accredited institutions account for a small minority of enrollments in the two-year, for-profit sector.

Public and Private Institutions Compared

So far I have focused on enrollments and degrees, but how do the content of the education and the student services at the public and for-profit schools compare? Critics of the for-profits have argued that at best they "train" rather than "educate," while advocates point out that they provide a more flexible, responsive education that is particularly suited for nontraditional students.[3] Despite the interest in the for-profits, there is still little empirical research that compares the two types of schools. Here, conclusions are summarized from two research projects based on interviews with students, staff, and faculty and the examination of available documents in the two different types of institutions. One, by Bailey, Badway, and Gumport (2001), compared a national for-profit chain to three community colleges located near branches of that chain. That study compared a variety of characteristics of the two types of institutions. These included the missions, curriculum development, pedagogy, student services, flexibility of scheduling, selectivity, course sequencing, and transfer. The second, by Deil-Amen and Rosenbaum (2003a, 2003b) compared seven community colleges to seven for-profit institutions in urban and suburban Chicago. Deil-Amen and Rosenbaum's study focused on student services and the relationships to employers, especially for the purpose of placing students and graduates in jobs. All of the for-profit institutions studied in both projects were regionally accredited, so they are not typical of two-year for-profit institutions. Bailey, Badway, and Gumport (2001) came to six broad conclusions relating to the comparison:

1. The most important distinction had to do with the goals and mission of the different types of colleges. The for-profit college conceptualized its mission in much narrower terms than any community college. Its goal is to prepare students for careers in a very limited number of technical areas. This goal is only one among dozens of objectives and functions of community colleges. In general, the for-profits use a much more focused strategy, whereas community college missions continue to proliferate.

2. A second fundamental difference concerned the nature of an academic culture. Community college faculty tend to have a "collegiate" view of their institutions and to think of themselves as more or less traditional college faculty. At the for-profit college, the tradition of shared governance and faculty professional prerogatives was much weaker.

3. The curriculum development process at the for-profit was centralized. Community college departments and individual faculty members have much more responsibility for program and course development.

4. The for-profit placed much greater emphasis on degrees. Faculty and administrators emphasize that they have programs that lead to degrees and that the various parts of those programs fit together. In contrast, community college degree programs tend to be much less structured, and community colleges are much more likely to argue that many of their students do not want degrees and instead seek specific skills that can be learned in one or a small number of either credit-bearing or noncredit courses.

5. In terms of instruction, the technical training, and even some of the academic courses, the for-profit made more use of labs and tended to tie their academic courses to practical applications and to the occupational curriculum. At the for-profit, the professors worked to relate the academic to the technical learning. Some of these things were also happening at the community colleges, though, consistent with the more decentralized structure, there was much more variation.

6. Finally, student services such as admissions, counseling, and career placement were more integrated and better developed at the for-profit than at the comparison community colleges. The for-profit placed more emphasis on job placement and tracking students after they had graduated or left.

Many of these overall conclusions were supported by the views of one community college faculty member who had previously worked at the for-profit. He believed that the quality of education at the community college was just as good as the for-profits's but that the for-profit institution had four specific advantages. First, it could be more responsive in the event of academic program change, whereas bureaucracy hampered the community college. Second, the for-profit provided access to a more extensive program-specific career network. Third, in the specific substantive areas, the for-profit provided focused training that was widely recognized by industry as meeting their needs. The community college where he worked was actively trying to strengthen its collaboration with industry. And, fourth, the for-profit simply had more advanced computers and technology in general, giving students better access to computers and facilitating the most up-to-date technical training.

The Deil-Amen and Rosenbaum (2003b) study confirmed some of these conclusions. Their work, published in two papers, makes two broad points. In one paper, they argue that counseling and student services are much more structured in the for-profits. Students have much fewer choices, are required to see counselors, and student progress is tracked carefully. In broad terms, this is consistent with the findings of the Bailey, Badway, and Gumport (2001) report. The plethora of choices and the difficulty of seeking information and obtaining guidance at community colleges are not serious problems for students whose families, social networks, and other resources can provide information and guidance and can help them navigate the confusing environment. According to Deil-Amen and Rosenbaum, however, the more structured system with much fewer choices works better for first-generation college students with few social and financial resources.

Deil-Amen and Rosenbaum (2003a) also argue that public community colleges rely on their reputation as colleges (their "charter") to communicate the skills of their graduates to prospective employers. In contrast, the for-profits work assiduously to build relationships with employers to facilitate graduate placement. Bailey, Badway, and Gumport (2001) also found that the for-profit college focused more effort on job placement than the comparison colleges.

These enhanced services ought to lead to higher graduation and employment rates for graduates of the for-profit schools. In principle, these conclusions can be tested empirically. Suggestive data on the relative numbers of students and degrees are at least consistent with these hypotheses. Minority students are somewhat more concentrated in the for-profits, and the degree-to-enrollment ratio is higher for the for-profits. Bailey, Badway, and Gumport (2001) report that the for-profit institutions in their study did publish data on their web sites on the employment experience of its graduates, and these data suggest that the large majority of graduates secured jobs with good salaries. Indeed, in some programs 99% of graduates who looked for work found jobs in areas related to their education within six months of leaving the college. Data on persistence to graduation, however, was not presented, so the graduates may be a highly select group. Moreover, no similar data were available for the comparison community colleges. Therefore, these data are only suggestive of higher graduation and placement rates. A more definitive test would require longitudinal unit record data. Although there are some data from the National Center for Education Statistics, the sample sizes are not large enough to discern a for-profit effect on completion or subsequent employment and earnings.

Perceptions and Reactions

What are the perceptions of community college administrators about potential competition from the for-profit sector? In this section, we draw on two sources of information. The first comes from the comparison colleges in the study by Bailey, Badway, and Gumport (2001). The second source is from results of Bailey and Morest's (2004) fieldwork carried out at six community colleges. At those colleges, presidents, other administrators, and faculty were asked to list their competitors. These results are displayed in Table 4.4. The table first lists all of the institutions identified by administrators at the college as creating the most significant competition for the community college. The second panel lists all other competitors mentioned.

In only one case did community college personnel identify a local for-profit institution as among the most important competitors. In all but two cases, community college staff cited the local four-year *public* college or university. One exception was a very academically oriented community college in New York City, and the staff there perceived a local, private, not-for-profit college as providing the most serious competition. Two colleges said that both local four-year public and local community colleges were the most important competitors, and one listed a four-year public and a local private not-for-profit.

In reviewing the perceptions of community college personnel, it is important to note that misperceptions about the for-profits are common at community colleges. Some personnel did not realize that some for-profits granted bachelor degrees and others thought that they did not teach any general or developmental education courses. Community college faculty members were convinced that their institutions offered a better, more comprehensive education. They saw the comprehensiveness of the community colleges as an advantage, at least for many students. Community colleges offer a much more extensive variety of liberal arts courses. Even for students

TABLE 4.4
Perceptions of Competition among Community College Administrators

	Suburban Illinois	Urban Florida	Urban New York (1)	Urban New York (2)	Rural New York	Urban California	Suburban California (CS Site)	Suburban California	Suburban Washington State
Most significant	One private not-for-profit four-year college and one for-profit four-year college	One public university	Three private not-for-profit colleges	Two public community colleges	Two public universities and two community colleges	Two public universities, two community colleges	Two public universities providing extension, one community college	One public university	One public university and one private not-for-profit college
Other listed competitors	Two private not-for-profit colleges	One public university, local community colleges, one for-profit four-year college	Local public four-year college—business and computer proprietary schools, one for-profit four-year college, one for-profit two-year college	Public universities and one for-profit four-year college	Two private not-for-profit colleges, two public universities, two for-profit four-year colleges, and three for-profit two-year colleges	A private university that also confers associate degrees, one private not-for-profit college conferring both four- and two-year degrees. One for-profit four-year college	Nearby community colleges, companies providing training for their own employees	One private four-year university. Two community colleges	One private not-for profit, two community colleges, one for-profit four-year and one for-profit two-year college.

who do want a technical degree, community college faculty emphasize that their colleges offer much more opportunities for cultural enrichment and for a diverse and comprehensive educational experience. The more focused for-profits were not seen as good places for students who do not know what field they want to study. As one community college administrator quoted by Bailey, Badway, and Gumport (2001) argued, "[Our college] is more suited to allow students to participate in the exploration process of education rather than getting locked into a program before they have a chance to really know what they want. [Our college] provides students with options, not simply a job" (pp. 43–44).

Thus, community college faculty did not perceive that for-profit institutions were a significant threat to their college's enrollment. They also tended to hold traditional views about the narrowness and general low-quality of for-profit education, though in most cases they had little knowledge of the specific programs or students at the for-profits.

Administrators at community colleges, on the other hand, usually saw the for-profits as complementary rather than competitive. For example, in each of the sampled colleges that was located near a University of Phoenix campus, a representative from the university had visited the community college soon after establishing the campus. The purpose of the visit was to set up articulation arrangements to encourage community college students to transfer to the University of Phoenix. Similarly, the DeVry colleges in Chicago publish on their web sites detailed lists of Chicago City College courses that correspond to lower-division DeVry courses. The community college administrators suggested that transfer to the for-profits (and the private not-for-profits) was easier than to the public four-year schools. Thus, community college administrators were much more aware of the four-year for-profits than those in the two-year sector. (They had little awareness of the prevalence of associate degrees within the four-year schools.) This is perhaps not surprising, because it is the four-year, regionally accredited institutions that have, in general, attracted the most attention. These are, after all, the colleges that have been tracked and described in the pages of the *Chronicle of Higher Education,* other publications likely to influence community college personnel, and the popular press in general.

During the first five years of the 2000s, political and demographic events further reduced the potential for anxiety about competition from the for-profits among community college administrators. Enrollments increased as a result of the sharp growth of college-age students, the influx of immigrants (in some areas), and rising tuition at four-year colleges. In many states, these increases in enrollment were not accompanied by increases in state funding, either because funding formulae in some states were not based on enrollments or because state legislatures had simply reduced per student funding. Some community colleges were in effect turning away students simply because the classes that students wanted or needed were filled. Even if revenues were sensitive to enrollments, capacity was a problem; capital expenditures are constrained in times of fiscal stress. One effect of these developments was that community colleges, at least in their credit programs, were increasingly serving younger, more traditional-aged students. In the end, this is their preferred market. The average age of community college students had been dropping for several years (Adelman, 2005). Thus, to the extent that the for-profits targeted older, nontraditional students, the direct competition between community colleges and for-profits was further reduced. Finally, most community college administrators believed that the large tuition differences continue to provide a significant buffer between their colleges and the for-profits.

Indeed, in light of the attempts by the for-profits to recruit community college transfer students, the predominant relationship between community colleges and for profits may be complementarity rather than competition. Moreover, a college education that consists of two years in a community college followed by two years in a for-profit college would certainly be a lower-cost, from the point of view of the state, alternative to expansion of the four-year public system—though the narrower occupational scope of the for-profits suggest that this would be a limited strategy, useful primarily for students in some well-defined occupational fields.

Because competition from the for-profits is not a major cause of anxiety among community college faculty and staff, it is not surprising that the colleges have not made significant structural changes in their credit programs in response to the growth of the for-profits. Since the apparently successful for-profit model is based on a focused strategy that limits institutional goals and missions, one potential community college response might be to try to move toward a similar focused approach, but, overall, this is not happening. If anything, colleges are taking on more missions (Bailey and Morest, 2004; Morest, in this volume). Nor are colleges reducing (at least in their credit programs) their emphasis on academic education. To the contrary, college personnel, especially faculty, see the array of choices and the important role of academic education as a significant advantage vis-à-vis the for-profit competitors. In terms of the relative number of faculty members and course offerings, community colleges have either maintained or strengthened their emphasis on academic and general education during the past two decades (Morest, in this volume). Other trends, such as the high-profile growth of honors programs and the growing movement for community colleges to offer baccalaureate degrees, suggest that community colleges, for better or for worse, are increasingly seeking to follow a traditional academic collegiate model, rather than a focused occupational or technical alternative.

Noncredit Instruction

The reaction of community colleges to potential competition in noncredit in-struction is more complicated than their reaction to competition on the credit side. Over the past several years, community colleges have enthusiastically developed pro-grams to serve the workforce development needs of local employers and workers through customized training and noncredit programs. According to the National Household Education Survey ([NHES] 2002a), noncredit "job-related" enrollments at community colleges and public two-year vocational schools grew by 16% between 1995 and 1999 to more than 3.3 million students.[4] In 1999, another 4.3 million students were enrolled in other types of noncredit courses at these institutions. Overall in 1999, as many noncredit as credit students were enrolled in public community colleges and vocational schools.

Community colleges have embraced these activities for several reasons (Dough-erty and Bakia, 2000; Bailey, 2002; Bailey and Morest, 2004). Certainly a search for resources has been a primary motivation, though the relationship between noncredit offerings and net resources is not straightforward. Noncredit/workforce develop-ment activities may generate some financial surpluses for the college, and, if they do, one advantage is that presidents often have more discretion over their use than they do over other sources of revenue. On the other hand, in calculating surpluses from these activities, colleges rarely take account of fixed or capital costs. In some cases, customized training is paid for by state economic development funds that are, in effect, public subsidies to colleges (the money goes from the state through the busi-ness to the college). Alternatively, colleges also derive political benefits from work-force development. Such activities develop partnerships with local businesses and sometimes labor elites, which can strengthen the position of the colleges with state and local legislatures.

Workforce development activities often have a high profile at community colleges, and presidents are often proud of them as expressions of the college's commitment to serving the diverse needs of the community. To what extent are these activities threat-ened by for-profit providers and how are community colleges reacting?

Whereas the for-profits are in some sense the new participants in the credit market who are perceived to be threatening the established providers, the community col-leges are the outsiders in the world of noncredit job-related training. The private sector is already deeply involved with noncredit instruction, perhaps most obviously through training that takes place in workplaces that is either carried out by company training departments or by private consultants. Indeed, community colleges are minor players among workforce training institutions. According to the NHES, more than 3 million people report receiving noncredit job-related training or education from community colleges and public two-year vocational schools, but six times that number (more than 19 million) report receiving job-related education from business or industry. Even professional associations and labor unions (as a group) provide more noncredit training than community colleges (U.S. Department of Education 2002a).

Thus, to the extent that community colleges are active in noncredit markets, they have already been competing with for-profit providers. (The four-year colleges are also extremely active in noncredit training.) This is certainly part of the explanation for why noncredit programs at community colleges are often operated separately from the credit programs and operate more on a business than an academic model— that is, they do not adhere to semester scheduling, courses are often taught by industry professionals, the classes take place in a variety of locations, they can be organized and eliminated on short notice, and they have little or no commitment to academic or general education. For the most part, they are run completely separately from the credit programs.

Unfortunately, the data on noncredit instruction will not allow us to come to any definitive conclusions about for-profit competition. First, we do not have a good sense of the overall size and importance of these activities at individual colleges. Do they generate surpluses, or do they lose money? How valuable are the political benefits that they engender? Indeed, we do not have a sense of the nature and strength of the growth of for-profit competition for noncredit activities. The noncredit training reported by NHES represents a great diversity of activities, and it is not clear what percentage of them competes directly with potential community college offerings. Most college presidents see potential for growth in noncredit activities, and it is not surprising that some colleges turned to this source of revenue as state funding dropped. A major push toward expansion might reveal more obvious competition with other providers.

Community College Response to the Growth of Vendor Certification

We can get some sense of the response of community colleges to potential competition from for-profit providers and new forms of educational delivery by examining the involvement of the colleges in preparing students for information technology (IT) vendor certification exams. IT certifications became a prominent and controversial issue in the late 1990s.[5] The certifications were based on passing specific assessments designed by corporations such as Microsoft and Cisco. Students could become certified as particular types of technicians and engineers by passing the certification exam independent of how they learned the knowledge and skills assessed in the exam. These potentially represented a profound threat to traditional accredited educational institutions, because they cut the link between those institutions and credentials. The 2000 publication of Clifford Adelman's report, *A Parallel Postsecondary Universe* increased interest and anxiety about this trend. Adelman emphasized the growing importance of certifications and the involvement in preparing students for those certifications of corporations and other organizations that were not traditional educational institutions.

Moreover, IT-related instruction, in both the credit and noncredit areas, has been an important source of enrollments for community colleges. Thus, the colleges potentially faced a double threat: first, to a high-profile occupational area that generated significant enrollments and, second, to the necessary link between the services that they provide (classes and other types of formal instruction) and the credential that certifies competence (the degree or certification). How did the colleges respond to this potential threat?

This section of the chapter draws on material from the National Field Study and material presented by Jim Jacobs and Norton Grubb elsewhere in this volume. As they argue, community colleges have responded to these developments. All fifteen colleges adopted some form of IT certification programs, but there were many patterns of course delivery. In most cases, courses to prepare students for certifications did not offer credit. In some cases, however, this type of instruction was subsequently also introduced into the credit courses. Offering the instruction in both credit and noncredit modes allowed the colleges to serve different constituencies. In general, the noncredit courses were directed at adults who were either in the industry or knew exactly what courses they needed to find a job. Many of these students already had bachelor degrees or, in some cases, postgraduate degrees. In contrast, younger students, who were beginning their careers, were found in the more traditional credit courses.

In some cases, responding to local demand, colleges offered certification preparation even if they lacked the necessary faculty and equipment. A minority of the institutions sought out relationships with private vendors to deliver the training because they lacked the technical expertise. In other instances, the colleges partnered with the technology vendor to deliver the class. For example, in four colleges an outside vendor supplied the instructors and equipment while the college provided the facilities and marketing. The vendor received 70%–75% of the revenues. College staff members were enthusiastic about these arrangements. As one faculty member stated, "It's a fabulous partnership."

Community college administrators tended to see certification preparation as opportunities. There was not a sense of anxiety that a market was being eroded. Indeed, community college staff stated that they believed that the reputation of the colleges as established nonprofit instructors with a broad portfolio of college courses was an important advantage, in relation to consultants or other for-profit providers. Price was another advantage. As one administrator stated, "I hate to say this, but they [for-profits] are not actually competing with us because, number one, we charge so much less." On the other hand, in the cases in which the colleges saw these programs as sources of revenue, they charged what appear to be market rates for certification preparation. This was usually much more than they charge for credit courses or some other noncredit offerings.

In the end, initial anxieties that certifications would, in effect, replace traditional credit-based instruction have not been borne out. The collapse of the dot-com bubble is one important factor. Colleges reported a significant drop-off in enrollments after 2000. Also, college staff perceive the noncredit certification preparation courses as appropriate for adults, many of whom already have degrees. That is, high school graduates are not bypassing college, prepping for assessments, and entering the labor market armed with certifications but without college degrees. From this perspective, certifications are most effective for those who already have degrees or as part of a degree program. Research by Carnevale and Desrochers (2001) also suggests that certifications are complementary to, rather than competitive with, traditional degrees.

Thus, during the late 1990s and early 2000s, community colleges responded to the growth of interest in IT certifications. They did so by using a variety of approaches. Which strategy they chose depended on their own staff and facilities and the nature of local demand. This response has been incorporated into the existing structures of the colleges, characterized by more entrepreneurial and flexible noncredit programs and traditional credit-bearing degree programs. The incorporation of material for IT certifications has influenced some of the content of degree programs, but there has been no significant change in the structure or pedagogy of those programs. Administrators do not perceive significant competition between the credit and noncredit markets in these fields, so credit enrollments are not threatened. They appear to believe that they can compete effectively in the noncredit market. Overall, the colleges see the growth of the importance of certifications as presenting opportunities, rather than an opening for for-profit providers to siphon off community college enrollments.

Conclusions

In the early years of the twenty-first century, competition from for-profits is not a major preoccupation of community colleges. The for-profit market share in the two-year sector has actually fallen, and the for-profits account for a mere 4% of all enrollments. For the credit programs, college administrators perceive other public sector institutions as representing more significant competition. Moreover, it is perhaps not surprising that the colleges are not preoccupied with competition in an era when demographic trends are swelling college enrollments while state funding is dwindling. In many states, increased enrollments are a decidedly mixed blessing.

Community college personnel are much more aware of the four-year for-profits than those in the two-year sector. This is not surprising, because the four-year for-profit sector is growing rapidly (albeit from a low base) whereas the two-year for-profit sector is stagnant. Community college personnel tend to see the four-year institutions such as DeVry and the University of Phoenix as complementary rather than competitive. The significant number of associate degrees granted by four-year, for-profit institutions does not seem to create anxiety among community college personnel, probably because the numbers are still so low (5% of all associate degrees) relative to the number of associate degrees conferred by community colleges.

Any lessons for community colleges from the for-profit experience are most likely to be found among the four-year, for-profit institutions. The large majority of the two-year for-profits are not regionally accredited. There is some evidence that the four-year for-profits provide a more structured environment with more comprehensive and coordinated student services. One reason that they can do this is that they have a much more focused and limited mission. There is less emphasis on academic or general education, students have fewer choices, and counselors and job placement personnel can be more specialized. Community colleges, however, are not moving to emulate this model. In addition, there is evidence that community colleges continue to strive to at least maintain their adherence to a traditional collegiate model. Many community college faculty members believe that this is an important factor that sets their institutions apart from the for-profits. One could see this as an inflexible and anachronistic unwillingness to respond to changing markets or a principled commitment to preserving the broader goals of a liberal education.

Competition in the noncredit market is different. In contrast to the situation in for-credit markets, community colleges are relatively minor players in the noncredit, work-related market. On-the-job training, vendor instruction, and other forms of private sector training dwarf these activities at community colleges. Thus, there is not a sense that the colleges' established interests are threatened by upstart for-profit institutions. From this perspective, almost any part of this market that colleges can acquire seems like a plus. And indeed, for a variety of political and financial reasons, for at least two decades, many community colleges have sought to increase their work with local employers and their noncredit, workforce-related offerings. Moreover, throughout this time, the noncredit offerings at community colleges have had more in common with a for-profit model than the credit programs.

Certainly the most significant competition faced by community colleges in the first decade of the twenty-first century is the competition for public funds with other public activities and taxpayers. In the short to medium term, this financial crisis poses a greater threat to community college enrollments and to their broader public purposes, including the equity mission, than competition from the for-profits.

Nevertheless, we can speculate about whether the current fiscal problems in many states will eventually expose community colleges to greater competition from the for-profits. One possibility is that the current budget restrictions may encourage colleges to seek out more traditional college students who often have fewer academic and financial problems. Because they require less remediation and auxiliary support services, these traditional students are probably less costly to educate successfully; they also fit most easily into the traditional "collegiate" structures. And, unless they expand their capacity, community colleges may also in effect become more selective. The bulge in the college-age population only facilitates these trends. If the community colleges diminish their service to older and nontraditional students, those students may increasingly turn toward for-profits. When the baby boom echo passes through the system, as their parents did a generation ago, community colleges will once again look to nontraditional students to fill their classrooms. This time, they may find that the for-profits are more firmly established in those markets and that it is therefore more difficult to follow that strategy.

Trends in tuition at public institutions create even more potential for competition. Community college tuition in many states has risen sharply. This continues a long-standing trend in which students and their families are paying for a larger share of the cost of their education at public institutions. Whether this will increase the *relative* price of community colleges depends on what happens to tuition at competitor institutions. It is possible that community college tuition may rise relative to the for-profits but drop relative to four-year public institutions. The intensity of competition between public and for-profit institutions will also be influenced by trends in public tuition-assistance programs. The most advantageous situation for for-profits and private not-for-profits would be one in which operating subsidies to public institutions were cut significantly and partly offset by increases in public tuition assistance. In the current political environment, public support for higher education is likely to be increasingly in the form of aid to individuals rather than institutions, and developments in the early years of the decade lend support to that prediction (Arnone, 2003). Moreover, aid to individuals is also shifting from grants to loans (Hearns and Holdsworth, 2004), and the for-profits are notorious for making sure that their students take advantage of both the grants and loans for which they are eligible. Therefore, although the for-profits still have only a small share of the two-year market and many community colleges have more students than they can handle, it is certainly time for community college leadership to start thinking about how they will fare in an educational market with much smaller public-private tuition differentials.

During the 1980s institutions of higher education faced declining enrollments with excess capacity. In many states, that is not the problem in the middle of the first decade of the twenty-first century. Many states have inadequate capacity for a growing student demand in the midst of severe fiscal strain. Moreover, in light of the economic importance of higher education for individuals and low enrollment levels for low-income students and students from some minority groups, equity concerns suggest that the demand ought to be even higher. As states contemplate options for increasing enrollments, increases in community colleges appear to be one alternative. As Zumeta (2004) has argued, incentives to encourage expanded enrollments in private institutions may be cheaper than building new four-year colleges. The argument presented here suggests states might consider a policy that encourages two years in a community college followed by two years at a private institution, with appropriate financial aid to offset the higher tuition. Such a policy might particularly benefit the for-profits, in light of their more aggressive efforts to encourage transfer students.

Finally, what implications do these developments and the growing importance of the for-profit sector of higher education have for the equity and access mission of the colleges? The traditional complaint about for-profit institutions has been that they take advantage of low-income students as a means to gain access to their loan and financial aid eligibility. Many of these abuses were ended or reduced at the time of the reauthorization of the Higher Education Act in 1992, which tightened up institutional financial aid eligibility. Some of the for-profits, therefore, seem to do at least as well with low-income and especially minority students as public institutions. Minority students tend to be overrepresented in the for-profits, and, as we have seen, there is some evidence that the for-profits have higher graduation rates. Nevertheless, these can only be considered tentative conclusions, and additional analysis using longitudinal data is necessary. Unfortunately, the sample sizes in the national data sets administered by the National Center for Education Statistics are not large enough for a definitive analysis of the performance of for-profits, and the state data sets that are increasingly available often, but not always, only include data on public institutions (Ewell, Schild, and Paulson, 2003).

Promoting a policy that encourages transfer from a community college to a private college, particularly a for-profit institution, for upper-division education is worth considering, but we still need more information about the quality of the education at the for-profits and the experience in those institutions of low-income and minority students. In any case, the equity implications of such a strategy would depend on the tuition levels at both types of institutions as well as developments in financial aid policy.

At this point, there is little evidence that the for-profits in particular are either threatening the enrollments of community colleges or pushing the colleges to actions that would weaken the equity agenda, but this may be because they have such a small share of the two-year market and because of the particular conjuncture of demographics and fiscal policy. Furthermore, this analysis has focused on community colleges; the conclusions could be different for four-year public institutions.

To the extent that there are lessons for community college in the experience of the for-profits, the message seems to be that focus and structure are important. The for-profits have more limited missions, many fewer options, and more structured programs. For many reasons, community colleges are not, and probably cannot, move in that direction (Bailey and Morest, 2004). The question, then, is whether structure and focus can be provided within the context of a comprehensive institution. The answer to this has to do with the internal design of programs and the links and connections between them. These are issues taken up in other chapters in this book. In light of the narrower ambit of the for-profit institutions, they offer few insights in how to overcome the tension between focus and comprehensiveness.

NOTES

1. According to the NCES web site (http://nces.ed.gov/), completion of an IPEDS survey is mandatory for "all institutions that participate or are applicants for participation in any Federal financial assistance program authorized by Title IV of the Higher Education Act of 1965, as amended." NCES reports a 90% response rate for the survey.

2. Notably, the small number of regionally accredited two-year, for-profit institutions award credentials in proportions more like their public sector counterparts.

3. In the past, proprietary schools were criticized for being "diploma mills" or for providing an inferior education simply to garner federal loans and grants. Changes in 1992 in the Higher

Education Act ended many of these abuses. See Bailey, Badway, and Gumport (2001) for a discussion of this point.

4. U.S. Department of Education (2002a [NHES]), author's calculations.

5. There are certifications in other fields, but the IT certifications attracted the greatest attention.

CHAPTER FIVE

Virtual Access

REBECCA D. COX

Distance education has become a central component of the discourse on higher education. With descriptions such as "open education" and "e-learning," references to the most recent forms of distance education hint at the educational promises of the new technologies: increased access to higher education, a more engaging learning experience for students, and preparation for success in the new information technology (IT)–driven economy. A core assumption underlying most predictions for the future is that on-line education will serve to improve the educational opportunities for students at every level of higher education. As one policy analyst described this "foreseeable future," the task for "most secondary-school graduates" will involve selecting a combination of on-site and distance-education courses that is "educationally sound, accessible, and affordable. In this sense the Internet . . . will enrich the educational choices generally available to all categories of learners" (Baer, 1998, p. 18). From this perspective, on-line education symbolizes an as-yet-unrealized future, variously envisioned as making good use of cutting-edge digital technologies, broadening postsecondary students' opportunities, and facilitating more efficient and effective approaches to higher education.

Surveys indicate that student enrollment in on-line courses has been steadily increasing, particularly among public colleges and universities. Indeed, the 2004 survey conducted by the Sloan Consortium indicated that, at public institutions, more than 60% of the respondents—academic officers—agreed that "online education is critical to their long-term strategy" (Allen and Seaman, 2004, p. 3). In the context of such growth, community colleges continue to play a major role in providing distance education through a range of media (Council for Higher Education Accreditation, 2000; National Center for Education Statistics, 2002c; Allen and Seaman, 2004), enrolling approximately half of the postsecondary students studying on-line (Allen and Seaman, 2004).[1] The research data, however, describe community colleges' on-line involvement with only the broadest strokes.[2] Much of the literature on on-line education—both empirical and theoretical—focuses on the concerns and contexts of four-year colleges and universities but remains relatively silent about community colleges (e.g., Trow, 2000; Palattella, 2001; Meyer, 2002; Twigg, 2002). In addition, empirical studies have documented the extent and growth of on-line involvement across different sectors of higher education but have made less progress in addressing issues of pedagogy, student learning, and curricular quality within those on-line offerings (Zemsky and Massy, 2004a). Under these circumstances, the enthusiastic rhetoric of possibility continues to outpace the empirical evidence.

Although research on on-line education is relevant to the entire field of higher education, it is critically important for the community college sector, which provides access to higher education for the least advantaged students. As community colleges respond to the changing demands of the educational market, their ability to provide authentic educational and economic opportunities requires sustained attention to issues of equity. This is particularly true for digital forms of distance education, which offer a means of extending geographical access to college without necessarily increasing students' educational opportunities.

Access to higher education entails making college courses available and allowing students to enroll. The mere existence or availability of college courses, however, represents an ersatz form of access. Authentic educational opportunity requires access to a learning environment that is not fraught with obstacles to success. For virtual access to increase the educational opportunities for less advantaged students, it must do more than offer the chance to enroll. As Frank Newman (2000) has observed, there is an immense difference between fulfilling market demand, catering to "easy-to-educate students who have the resources to pay," and fulfilling a need, providing high quality instruction for "students who are poor and harder to educate" (p. 21). Attending to the quality of on-line instruction is essential to preserving the democratizing aspects of public, postsecondary schooling.

This chapter describes the conditions for and nature of community colleges' involvement in distance education during the early 2000s—the formative period of their investment in digital and web-based course offerings. Drawing from the extensive set of data from the Community College Research Center's National Field Study, the chapter examines the fifteen colleges' approaches to on-line education at that critical historical juncture. The discussion consists of five parts. The first describes the institutional contexts of the colleges' participation in on-line education, whereas the second locates the colleges' involvement within that broader landscape of heightened competition and external demands for accountability. The third section outlines the disjunction between the optimistic administrator rhetoric and the practical realities of colleges' on-line involvement. The disjunction emerged in two forms: the modest extent of colleges' on-line offerings and the contested nature of on-line education from the perspective of faculty. The fourth part reviews the implications of these disjunctions in terms of educational equity. The fifth and final section highlights two crucial components of improved on-line practice.

Colleges' On-line Involvement

The impetus for community colleges to invest in distance education, and in on-line offerings in particular, has been integrally linked to their role within the field of postsecondary education. In particular, respondents from our sample of community colleges consistently reiterated the pressures of competition in explaining the college's involvement in on-line education. At a suburban college in a state where college service-area agreements had not been extended to distance education, one administrator commented, "I think we need to do more [distance learning] in order to stay competitive. We're going to get knocked out of the box if other community colleges or other state ops [operations] or other states start taking over our territory."[3] At another college, an administrator expressed concern that local proprietary schools would "eat our lunch."

As subordinate members of higher education, community colleges face competitive pressure, reflecting the increasingly market-oriented postsecondary environment. In the face of reduced federal and state funding, public colleges and universities have been forced to rely on private sources for an increasing share of their revenues. At every level of higher education, the result has been intensified competition for critical resources: funding, student enrollment, and status. Within the community college sector, the typical enrollment-based funding procedures at the state level spur colleges to continually seek higher enrollment numbers.

As the community colleges in the study developed their initial on-line offerings in the late 1990s, they were also aware of the rhetoric from the business world, which avowed that Internet-savvy education providers would capture a crucial share of the educational market. This notion was promoted in various forums, including the educational policy discourse, as in RAND analyst Walter Baer's contention that "some institutions undoubtedly will be squeezed out by more entrepreneurial competitors, both nonprofit and for-profit. For e-learning, as for other sectors of e-commerce, the Internet rewards those who enter early, adapt rapidly and are ready to seize opportunities as they arise" (Baer, 1999). Burbules and Callister (2000), similarly defining their position in the debates over on-line education as "the middle ground," contended, "There really is no choice for colleges and universities. Where these technologies are widely available, where the cost and convenience factors are of such potential importance, and where the demand is increasing, someone will step into the vacuum if colleges and universities do not. . . . In such a competitive context, there may be a few schools with sufficient prestige not to worry that they will lose students to other providers. But for the vast majority . . . the race is on" (pp. 278-79).

The euphoria of the late 1990s over the Internet may have been punctured by the dot-com bust, but the rhetoric touting distance education as a key to colleges' competitive edge has not disappeared. More recently, Dan Carnevale (2004) reported in the *Chronicle of Higher Education,* "The recent explosion in distance-education enrollments is likely to continue over the next 10 years, forcing many institutions to seek outside help to manage rising student populations and demands for the latest technology. . . . Colleges that don't choose to buy packaged courses and find they cannot keep up with other institutions' offerings could be the early victims of a distance education shake out that some observers say is sure to come" (p. B8).

Threat Assessment and Colleges' Responses

Within any organization, executive leaders play a critical role in interpreting and responding to the organization's external environment (Thompson, 1967; Scott, 1998; Weick, 2001). In community colleges, a primary task of such "boundary spanners" requires that they make sense of what often emerges as uncertain and inconsistent messages from beyond the walls of the college to inform the college's approach to that broader environment. In the context of the serious fiscal restraints that community colleges face, it is not surprising that the specter of competition from a variety of postsecondary actors had prompted college administrators to embrace the on-line involvement. Ultimately, administrators at all fifteen community colleges felt compelled to respond to the potential threat posed by on-line education. Among the senior administrators in this study, the dominant perspective on distance education emphasized the necessity of providing web-based offerings. One administrator described this imperative by asserting, "You'd have to be blind not to see it."

In making the case for their college's on-line involvement, administrators reiterated the optimistic claims and unsupported assumptions of public discourse and, in the process, articulated two key themes: the competition for student enrollment and the community college's mission of postsecondary access. For instance, interview respondents from WRCC uniformly explained that on-line education had developed at the college as part of the "business" of education. According to one faculty member there, "We were told when we first got started, that these private schools are all getting into this, and we have to do it. A certain aspect of it is that it's a business; you have to stay competitive."

By implicitly defining educational access as course enrollment, college personnel described their efforts to address the threat of competition while simultaneously invoking the college's mission to increase access to postsecondary education and occupational training—particularly for "nontraditional" students. At WRCC, one of the colleges facing the most difficulties in pulling together faculty support for distance education, an administrator told us, "We are putting a tremendous amount of emphasis on technology. . . . As an access tool definitely, to give students who are place-bound, job-bound, child-bound, an opportunity to get back in the classroom from their homes by using technology—whatever avenue it takes to get them educated to a higher level."

From this perspective, technology-mediated access increases students' opportunities to acquire postsecondary credentials and in turn contributes to increased economic opportunities in the labor market. Often embedded in this vision of on-line education is an assumption that on-line education would foster students' acquisition of the technology-related skills required in the workplace. In fact, administrators explicitly described the educational value of using web-based technology in enabling students to pursue careers in high-technology fields. One administrator in our study even described the presence of an extensive on-line program as a sign that a college is "student-centered." Such rationales suggested that *not* to offer on-line courses would do a great disservice to students.

At the same time, senior administrators also asserted that investing in distance education would increase enrollment. For example, a fundamental impetus for expanding WRCC's on-line program lay in the state-funding formula, which had set WRCC's growth rate for that year at more than 10%. Surpassing the set growth rate would ensure a larger funding base for the future, which meant that for WRCC, where 90% of its funding came from the state, increasing its enrollment would substantially expand the college's resource base. Officials at another college, SMCC, asserted that a focus on technology would propel the growth of the college. There, the growth of the on-line program was linked to an aggressive expansion plan to become one of the five largest colleges in the state. Through the strategic action of senior administrators, SMCC's program had expanded from twenty on-line classes in 1999 to seventy-eight in the fall of 2002.

It is significant that these colleges' decisions to invest in on-line education were not driven by a conviction that it would cut their per-student instructional costs. Although administrators tried to minimize the cost of on-line instruction, at every college they explicitly asserted that the immediate cost of offering on-line courses was higher than that for on-site classes. The rationale for establishing and expanding on-line programs was, instead, based on a desire to increase enrollments and to be more competitive. In the end, most administrators believed that an on-line program was an essential component of an up-to-date college.

Many colleges were joining with others to form state- or regional-level consortia. The threat of competition was one motivation for this development. One respondent described the governance of the Virtual College of Texas as the result of an alliance of smaller Texas colleges, borne from the fear that the larger colleges with established on-line programs would dominate the state's on-line market. The four states with unified community college on-line consortia had implemented policies to regulate cross-college registration and functioned as information distribution centers for potential on-line students. Furthermore, such state- or regional-level organizing re-sulted in agreements among colleges, serving to both regulate and complicate the dynamics of on-line competition among community colleges.

In the end, the dominant perspective among senior administrators toward on-line education was that of advocacy. Fourteen of the fifteen colleges in the sample were dedicated to on-line expansion. At these colleges, the issue arose in 70% of the interviews with senior administrators. Ninety-four percent of the administrators who voiced their perspectives commented favorably on on-line education and expressed an interest in continuing to expand their college's distance-education program.

Public Rhetoric and Internal Realities

Regardless of the status of the on-line program or the specific conditions compos-ing the college's local environment, a consistent pattern emerged across many of the colleges—a disconnect between the public rhetoric and the realities of actual practice. As a rule, this disconnect manifested itself in a contrast between the public portrayals of each college's involvement in on-line education and the depth of the program's structural components. In fact, the symbols of a college's on-line participation ap-peared in numerous forms, including prominent mention of the on-line program on the college's home web page, the set of web pages devoted to the procedures and guidelines for potential on-line students, reference to the course-management system that the college had adopted, the number of on-line offerings, on-line course descrip-tions, class schedules that highlighted web-based (and other distance) courses, and, at some colleges, additional texts, such as brochures, separate on-line course schedules, and lists of frequently asked questions. In many instances, colleges' distance offerings were also advertised by state- and regional-level consortia. A consortium's web site typically consolidated information about the region's distance education, announc-ing each college's participation in on-line education and making the enrollment information available to students in one spot. By using the Internet to document the availability of on-line courses across the state, the community colleges—both as individual colleges and as a collective group—signaled their pursuit of cutting-edge technological and educational developments. Consequently, it should not be surprising that every college, regardless of its on-line capacity, had made efforts to incorporate these visible signs of on-line education involvement.

The colleges' involvement, however, was generally quite modest. Despite the legible signs of on-line activity and senior administrators' enthusiasm about expanding student access through on-line offerings, at the time of our study, most colleges offered only a smattering of courses. In some cases, colleges were depending on one or two instructors to teach a short list of offerings.

The extent of on-line offerings in the colleges in our sample corresponded to the college's capacity to assemble and coordinate six basic components: the technological infrastructure, student services for students at a distance, administrative support, a full-time distance-education coordinator, professional development for on-line instructors, and an adequate level of faculty participation. Five of the fifteen colleges had successfully assembled these components and were able to offer a consistent selection of on-line courses and had achieved a measure of stability in their on-line programs.[4] This basic capacity allowed these colleges to offer on-line courses as an organization, distinguishing them from colleges where instructors pursued on-line teaching on an individual basis (typically in partnership with another college or a regional consortium).

Although these five "high" end colleges had established the basic structural components, they were only beginning to address more controversial issues (e.g., faculty compensation, intellectual property) and substantive instructional concerns (e.g., course and program evaluation). In particular, the coordinators of the five established on-line programs expressed concern with student completion rates. In each case, completion rates in on-line courses lagged behind those of on-site classes. One coordinator reported that completion rates in distance-education courses were 15% lower; at another college, the average completion rate across the distance-education program was 52%, compared to a 71% average across the college's campus-based courses. At the other three colleges, respondents did not provide exact numbers, but noted that students were less likely to succeed in on-line offerings. On-line coordinators at these sites spoke of their plans to examine and improve the quality of the on-line programs but had not yet implemented many of their ideas.

The majority of the colleges, however, had not developed this basic capacity. In light of administrators' passionate advocacy of on-line education, the absence of these key components was striking. Even more surprising was the minimal level of functioning of some of the program components. Student services, for instance, posed a huge challenge to nearly every college. One college conducted all course registration in person. Although the coordinators could make exceptions for distance students when absolutely necessary, standard policies did not allow phone registration, much less on-line registration. In addition, on-line coordinators at several sites noted the weaknesses of advisement—in terms of both the quality of academic advising available to distant students and the accuracy of advising about on-line courses. One on-line coordinator noted that, although on-line students could receive academic counseling by phone, the advisors were not well informed about the on-line program and therefore often dispensed misleading advice.

At the low end of on-line involvement were three colleges with minimal capacity to offer on-line courses. Located in three different states, these colleges (two urban and one rural) were unable to afford the cost of establishing a program. Each was able to offer a few on-line courses via its state-level consortium but not to allocate enough resources to developing components on its own campus. In the case of WUCC, as of the fall of 2002 the college offered a total of three courses, all of which were taught by the same instructor. WUCC represented an extreme case. Located at the lowest end of the on-line capacity continuum, the college's administrators offered the most passionate endorsements of on-line education. In other words, it was at WUCC where the division between rhetoric and reality was the widest.

Two colleges proved to be partial exceptions to this pattern.[5] At one college (WSCC), still in the process of assembling the components of an on-line program, the majority of administrators shared a vision of the college as one that did not "do" on-line education. This contention, however, did not prove to be accurate. Although the college was not actively working to build an on-line program, it did offer a range of on-line courses, some of which were part of a well-established program in allied health. Although the college lacked an on-line coordinator or professional development for on-line instructors, a number of instructors were engaged in on-line innovations. The existence of distance-education (including on-line) offerings was prominently displayed on its home web page, advertising the college's commitment to new educational technologies.

Administration-Faculty Polarization

Although the vast majority of senior administrators interviewed at each college expressed a consensus about the value and purposes of on-line education, faculty respondents offered a contrasting set of assertions about the impetus for and consequences of its development. The consensus among the majority of administrators reflected two assumptions: community colleges must offer on-line education to maintain their competitiveness, and the advantage of on-line education is that it increases the community college's accessibility. For faculty respondents, however, on-line education was a highly contested area of college activity, and the experiences of on-line faculty participants at each college presented a sharp contrast with the views expressed by the majority of college's senior administrators. The views expressed by faculty members, including both on-line instructors and those uninvolved with distance education, fundamentally challenged the administrator maxim that the mere availability of (access to) on-line courses benefited students.

Patterns of Faculty Participation

Initial on-line offerings at every college had emerged from the work of a small number of "pioneers." These instructors, intrigued by the prospect of exploring new technology, had invested immense amounts of time and energy developing, teaching, and refining their on-line courses. The on-line pioneers interviewed for this study came from a wide range of disciplinary backgrounds, began their on-line explorations with varying levels of technical expertise, and pursued a variety of instructional goals. One of the few constants across colleges was that the earliest participants included instructors of technology-based courses, such as IT and digital media. The large colleges had access to a broad pool of faculty, so in some cases the number of on-line pioneers was sufficient for significant expansion. Once a college's on-line education offerings had been developed around the efforts of the pioneers, however, the program eventually reached an impasse. As the NESCC distance-education coordinator noted, "We've had our first wave of innovators who have jumped off, and they are moving along; some are working on their second and third courses. And we have a much smaller but equally motivated group coming through now. So I don't see a lot of new people. We're attempting to go out and recruit more faculty."

Once the pool of early on-line innovators had been exhausted, different strategies and resources were needed to promote faculty participation. This is not a startling phenomenon. Research on the spread of innovative practices has repeatedly confirmed Rogers's (1962) theory of diffusion, thereby reiterating the distinct differences among individual approaches to new technologies (see Cuban, 2001, and Garofoli and Woodell, 2003). Those in the early-adopting groups share similar motivations and expectation for experimenting with new technologies. In contrast, the majority of people, though not resistant to change, do not understand or respond to technological innovation in the way that the early experimenters do.[6]

For every college, accommodating even a small number of on-line students required an immense investment in the technology, technological support, and student support services. Once those basic structures and services were established, encouraging greater faculty participation required administrators to appeal to a new set of faculty members. The resources that had proven adequate for the colleges' earliest on-line faculty were insufficient to encourage the majority of college faculty to participate. In fact, respondents at every college viewed the initial on-line instructors as a distinctive minority. In an interview with two early on-line participants, one explained, "Until many of us were involved in distance learning, it wasn't understood how much work it is to create a course; even a course that only has three students is still a lot of work. Of course, Sarah (a pseudonym) was a pioneer; I was a pioneer. We weren't driven by the bottom line, we were driven by the challenge that we had." This instructor perceived clear differences between SMCC's first on-line instructors, an elite group of "pioneers," and the rest of the faculty. Acknowledging the amount of time and effort required to teach on-line, she distinguished her colleague Sarah and herself from instructors who worried about financial compensation. Once the college tapped into a wider faculty pool, on-line instructors began voicing concerns that, though entirely legitimate, had not yet been addressed. These two instructors exhibited a sense of pride for belonging to the initial group of on-line innovators, eschewing the need for financial incentives, but most SMCC faculty members were not as sanguine about the issue of adequate compensation. Indeed, across every college, the typical instructor was more skeptical of on-line education than the early innovators, and they demanded greater levels of organizational support, both while preparing to teach and while teaching on-line.

The amount of work required of on-line instructors presented another, related obstacle to faculty participation: the problem of reform-related burnout. Indeed, research studies of school reform efforts indicate that the excitement of engaging in reform can be squashed if the work demands increase and continue indefinitely (Little, 1996; Miller, 1999; Bartlett, 2004). This appeared to be the case at multiple sites. As one instructional dean admitted, "I do have instructors that teach [on-line] for a couple of semesters and get burnt out. That's something new I am noticing."

Faculty Perspectives

Because the topic of distance education was incorporated into all of the faculty interviews, the data include comments from faculty across academic disciplines and occupational fields. Across all fifteen colleges, the faculty members we interviewed consistently questioned their colleges' approaches to on-line education.

Faculty respondents expressed their objections to on-line education in terms of the workload and by questioning the quality. Many described how the current policies—or the absence of established policies—created unfavorable conditions for undertaking on-line work. At MWUCC, where distance-education courses did not count as part of a normal teaching load, a faculty pioneer observed that, especially for full-time instructors, the amount of work for developing and teaching a course was not worth the money: "So I got the short end of this deal. No money to do revisions; and I have to teach it in 10 weeks, rather than the regular 16 week semester." Another MWUCC instructor agreed, contending, "It's just a black hole in terms of the amount of time and energy you put into it."

Expressing a common concern heard across the sample colleges, an interdisciplinary group of faculty at WRCC mentioned discomfort with the administrative pressure to put courses on-line. "There's a lot of talk about modularizing our courses and putting them on-line and teaching components. Many of us who take more of a holistic perspective of course curriculum are finding ourselves having a hard time with that piece." Underlying that concern, and other similar comments, was the fear that instructional integrity and course quality were being undermined in the on-line marketplace. The interview respondents who expressed the most criticism of on-line educational quality were often the most active in their colleges' on-line programs, functioning as program directors, on-line course developers, or on-line teachers. For instance, one of the original on-line instructors at one of the basic capacity colleges described his on-line teaching and course development experiences in the context of changing organizational priorities. Summarizing the changes he had witnessed at his college, he explained, "There's a real emphasis on cost savings, and there just seems to be no serious attention to academic issues. . . . There's been a shift, from regard for academics to a regard for fiscal control."

This kind of polarization between senior administrators and faculty emerged at thirteen of the fifteen colleges. At those thirteen colleges, administrators expressed frustration by what they perceived as faculty resistance to new technologies. Administrators at nine of the colleges cited their inability to increase faculty involvement as an unresolved problem. At six colleges, distance-education administrators lamented the constraints imposed by faculty contracts and, in some cases, by union regulations. One program director remarked that he found his job "very tough in terms of getting the faculty to accept the use of technology and then to effectively use technology." In the most aggressive strategy for increasing the number of on-line faculty, WRCC had recently begun requiring all new full-time hires to teach on-line and employing adjunct on-line instructors who lived outside the area—often outside the state.

Administrators who viewed faculty as unreasonably recalcitrant, however, may have been ignoring the conditions of faculty work and dismissing reasonable instructional concerns. For example, WRCC, where instructors expressed vehement objections to teaching on-line courses, also happened to be the college that had responded to the funding differential between on-site and on-line courses by enrolling fifty to sixty students in each on-line section—approximately twice the average enrollment of its on-site courses and twice that of the other colleges' on-line courses. In other words, WRCC administrators were trying to minimize the financial burden of their ambitious expansion of on-line education by doubling the enrollment in each class. Faculty members resisted participation in the on-line program, which, in turn, led to the recruitment of adjunct instructors, often from other states, and the establishment of new hiring criteria for full-time faculty. During interviews, WRCC instructors voiced their shared concern: that the administration's cost-saving measures were undermining an already questionable learning environment.

Statements from respondents at other colleges further suggested that instructors were willing to experiment with on-line courses when the college supported their efforts with the necessary resources and provided opportunities to learn in ways that coincided with their pedagogical philosophies. For instance, at SWUCC, instructor involvement increased dramatically around the start of 2001—a phenomenon that one of the college's on-line coordinators attributed to the increase in support resources available to faculty" "[The faculty members] see that we're interested in supporting them. And I think that makes a big difference. And so we've instigated different levels of training for Blackboard. I've got an instructional design person that works for Distance Learning. She's really good, and we talk the same language about curriculum development and pedagogy. Nobody talked that before. Not at all. They never looked at that." In this way, the coordinator, the person most intimately connected to the on-line program at SWUCC, asserted that the focus on curricular design and on-line pedagogy was responsible for instructors' willingness to participate in on-line instruction.

On-line Education and the Equity Agenda

The race to build viable on-line programs was at a formative stage during this study. As a result, the research data reveal how colleges' early on-line development was shaped by the perceptions of fierce competitive pressures exerted on community colleges. Unfortunately, the nature of colleges' involvement highlighted preexisting inequities within the community college sector. Furthermore, the evidence also suggested that those inequities would not be remedied by future on-line participation.

For example, the crucial difference between the colleges at the "high" end of on-line development and those with minimal on-line offerings revolved around the geographic locations of colleges and the socioeconomic status of their student popu-

TABLE 5.1
Colleges with Basic On-line Capacity

College	Geography	Enrollment	% Black and Latino	County/Service Area Income[2]
SUCC	Florida, mixed[1]	42,000	31	Equal to median statewide income
NESCC	New York, suburban	9,000	9	Equal to median statewide income
SWUCC	Texas, urban	26,000	28	17% greater than median statewide income
NWSCC	Washington, suburban	22,000	7	16% greater than median statewide income
MWUCC	Illinois, urban	>25,000	65	Equal to median statewide income

1. Mixed geography refers to a service district that encompasses both urban and rural regions.
2. 1999 U.S. Census figures: median household income for the county. For colleges in multi-college districts, the median household income of the service area was calculated.

lations. The colleges that had established basic on-line capacity included four of the five largest colleges in the sample and did not include any rural colleges.

These five colleges' early investment in on-line education was facilitated by pre-existing resources, which in turn enabled them to attract industry support and to take advantage of emergent community partnerships. In other words, generating additional revenue streams proved much easier for the most advantaged colleges. In addition, the size of the colleges had helped ensure an adequate number of on-line innovators among the faculty.

In contrast, the three colleges with minimal on-line capacity shared one basic attribute: their students resided in relatively low-income areas. At the same time, the crucial set of factors for each college complicates any additional generalizations across cases. In fact, the three colleges differed on many counts, including state and local funding formulas, statewide on-line policies, service-area competition, administrative capacity, and prior investment in distance education. At WUCC, despite district-level pressure to build an on-line program, a fundamental lack of administrative capacity had prevented much progress. Once WUCC lost the bid for an important (and anticipated) military contract to the other college in the district, several administrators focused their attention on on-line course development. Their efforts, however, did not alter the district-level dynamics, which resulted in further expansion of the other college's on-line program and, by virtue of that on-line growth, the accrual of additional resources.

NWRCC, a very small, rural college, had faced similar challenges in offering on-line courses. Very few faculty members were interested in exploring on-line instruction, and the college's financial resources were already stretched very thin. At the time of the site visit, the college was already facing repercussions. The combination of minimal on-line offerings and the calculus of state funding had previously forced the college to pay $16,000 to another community college in the state for the provision of on-line courses during a single semester.[7] In effect, NWRCC, like WUCC, struggled

TABLE 5.2
Colleges with Minimal On-line Capacity

College	Geography	Enrollment	Percent Black and Latino	County/Service Area Income[1]
WUCC	California, urban	15,000	53	22% below median statewide income
NEUCC	New York, urban	7,000	94	36% below median statewide income
NWRCC	Washington, rural	2,000	20	23% below median statewide income

1. 1999 U.S. Census figures: median household income for the county. For colleges in multi-college districts, the median household income of the service area was calculated.

to move beyond a low level of on-line capacity while facing financial sanctions for being a particularly low-resource organization.

Inconsistencies in Access

By the time our study was complete, virtual access had proved problematic in two ways. First, on-line courses at the sample colleges did not necessarily attract new populations of students. At each site, the majority of students in on-line courses also enrolled in on-site classes. This meant that, for the most part, the on-line courses were fulfilling the demand for convenience, rather than access. Significantly, administrators at several colleges noted that future on-line courses would most likely not draw new students from their service areas. In practice, virtual access was synonymous with higher enrollment numbers, but those increased enrollment numbers did not necessarily include students otherwise unable to attend the college.

The second and more serious complication involved the learning environment afforded to students on-line. At several sites, the bulk of student enrollment in on-line courses occurred after on-site sections had filled, which suggests that students would have preferred to take the face-to-face versions of those classes. Indeed, the on-line coordinator at one such site lamented this pattern, because the students who enrolled at the end of the registration period tended not to be the highly motivated and self-disciplined individuals who typically enjoyed the most success in on-line courses. This view—that only certain types of students would succeed in on-line courses—was reiterated by respondents at every college. Finally, the lower completion rates in on-line courses than in on-site ones undermined the claim that on-line courses promoted access to educational opportunity.

Virtual Quality

The consensus expressed by a group of occupational faculty was that community colleges were embracing on-line education as part of a national movement. They declared, "[W]e don't see that the quality is there yet . . . [but] we are in a situation where you feel like you've got to do it." This statement neatly summarizes the friction between colleges' responses to the pressures exerted by the broader postsecondary environment and their mission to educate students of wide-ranging goals and varying levels of preparation.

On-line Delivery versus On-line Instruction

Senior administrators implicitly contended that the existence of on-line courses (i.e., the use of digital technology) was an essential component of an up-to-date college. From their perspective, establishing the requisite technological components and "putting courses on-line" deserved priority status. In light of the organizational and technological complications of supporting initial on-line courses, the majority of resources targeted by on-line education went to the technological infrastructure and administrative support—the components most visible to potential students. This defined on-line education as a technological product rather than an interactive or relational process.

This conceptualization of on-line education, neatly separating the web-based components from the instructional practices, left the on-line faculty (and, in some cases, the on-line program directors) to work out the practical complications of developing and teaching courses with very little organizational assistance. Although the faculty and coordinators in the study worked very hard in their efforts to offer high-quality on-line instruction, the institutional imperative to provide on-line courses took precedence over most considerations of teaching and learning quality. Thus, the issue of quality, while of great concern, was subsumed by the logistics of getting those courses on line. The nearly exclusive focus on structure at the organizational level reified the conception of web-based technology as a "delivery" system. Within such a framework, on-line teaching consists of "delivering" instruction or transmitting course content. Indeed, the virtual classrooms observed in this study were highly text oriented, with the substance of the courses comprising text-based information. In some cases, students were able (or required) to buy print-based document packets that contained information identical to that on the web site. In these cases, web-based technology truly served as a delivery system.

The approaches to on-line education constrained rather than enhanced faculty members' understandings of how to wed instruction and technology. The most compelling example lay in the learning opportunities that faculty had been afforded. The dominant paradigm for course development at these community colleges structured professional development as opportunities for instructors to learn how to use the technologies that comprise the "delivery system." One instructor explained the inadequacy of such an approach: "I took a course on Web CT . . . and it was glaringly obvious from the moment I walked in that the course was taught by someone who knew the technology inside out and backwards, but had no sense of how to communicate that material. No sense of what classroom assessment is about or how to get input from the students." Individuals at every college offered challenges to that paradigm. Furthermore, increased concern with the quality of classroom-level learning and greater understanding of the immense challenges of on-line teaching had led on-line coordinators—particularly at SUCC, MWUCC, and NESCC—to provide more robust opportunities for faculty learning. In the end, however, the resources the colleges were able to draw upon did not offer faculty the kinds of expertise or learning opportunities that would allow them to rethink or redesign their curricula.

Citing a range of problems affecting course quality, such respondents also noted their concerns for the future. For instance, after describing her college's on-line program as a means of transmitting information, one instructor remarked, "I think there are some of us, myself included, who believe that there is a very, very different emphasis in education as opposed to information, and I don't want us to lose a sense of that distinction—that you can inform a person without really educating them. Giving a person information doesn't help them know what to do with it, and we are a very, very information-rich society as it is, with a lot of people who don't know how to apply information, who cannot "synthesize." For this instructor, on-line courses at her college emphasized "information," not "education." Access to higher education through technology-mediated instruction, she feared, would constitute only superficial learning experiences for her students.

On the quality of the resulting courses, the on-line coordinator at the same college commented, "Probably the same range of practices that we have in our face-to-face courses is being replicated on-line, when that might have been an opportunity not just to teach people technology, but to have them think about engaging students and what kinds of things you can do better online, rather than just post your lecture, or whatever it is that might be happening." Implicit in such comments is an important critique of "access." Indeed, the question of access to what remains crucial and unanswered.[8]

Access to What?

These interview data echo the work of other researchers who contend that, as yet, on-line courses throughout higher education do not reflect dramatically different approaches from on-site courses. Zemsky and Massy (2004b) for example, report a sense of disappointment with web-based education among participants at six colleges with reputations for their on-line investment. Similarly, a survey of college students conducted by ECAR (Educause Center for Applied Research) revealed a "surprising" number of "negative comments about how professors used technology" (Young, 2004, p. A31).

With regard to an extensive body of research on learning processes, Bransford, Vye, and Bateman (2002) noted that instructors who are asked to imagine an on-line version of one of their current courses consistently envision a course that results from transferring classroom-based course to the Internet. In fact, the authors assert that, when asked to redesign the lesson for any course (whether on site or on line), every individual can suggest improvements, but only rarely does an instructor redesign the course (e.g., rethink the use of a lecture-driven format). As a result, "most on-line courses have tended to look much like 'porting' existing classrooms onto the Internet." Furthermore, in light of their work in cognitive development and the resulting *How People Learn* framework, they contend that "neither traditional face-to-face courses, nor their online cousins, represent environments where opportunities for high-quality learning are consistently strong" (Bransford, Vye, and Bateman, 2002, p. 190).

In other words, there is an immense difference between putting a course on-line and redesigning a course by starting from the learning goals and integrating various forms of knowledge and expertise to build a course that realizes those goals. Redesigning courses is far from simple, however, and doing so requires expertise that may be distributed among different people (e.g., knowledge of the subject matter and learning, expertise in assessment practices and technology). The resource supports and organizational structures that would facilitate a truly different approach to faculty learning, course development, and on-line instruction were absent from every college. Thus, despite the determined (and, in some cases, heroic) efforts of individual faculty and on-line administrators, the kind of organizational communication and coordination needed to support such an approach—both within the college and with the external environment—was missing. In sum, web-based communication could potentially support a rich educational experience in virtual classrooms, but to do so would require the fundamental redesign that Bransford, Vye, and Bateman discuss, starting at the core interactive processes of teaching and learning, then building structures that support those priorities and needs. This would ultimately involve institutionalizing a more sophisticated approach to both on-site and on-line education. In the context of the divisions found inside these community colleges, such coordination faces formidable obstacles.

Teaching involves more than simply making information available to students.

Similarly, the fundamental challenge for faculty in making effective use of digital technology is not located at a superficial level of application—in how to use a web browser or a search engine or how to import content into WebCT, a course management system commonly used in the early 2000s for on-line programs. These invisible processes of teaching and learning, however, were marginalized as colleges tried to build on-line capacity.

This, in turn, meant that the assessment of the on-line program or of the individual on-line courses focused on the technological components rather than the processes of teaching and learning that constituted the on-line courses and the on-line program. Indeed, a consistent feature across every college was the scarcity (or, more frequently, the complete absence) of assessment data for on-line courses. Although colleges maintained records of on-line enrollments and retention rates, the work of evaluating and improving the quality of courses was, at best, in a preliminary stage. Furthermore, at nearly every college, although administrators expressed deep concern with the consistently low retention rates in on-line courses, none of the colleges had attempted to document the types of students who tended to fail to complete or conducted research or follow-up investigations to determine the causes.

SUCC represented a notable exception. It was unique among the colleges in the study, in that a group of administrators had sought out and read recent research findings on on-line education. Furthermore, the on-line program had undergone a formal evaluation, an activity that had been undertaken at only one other college in the sample. Ironically, these assessment activities led several top administrators to advocate the development of hybrid offerings, rather than purely distance courses.

Possible Paths of On-line Practice

Increased concern with the quality of classroom-level learning and growing understanding of the immense challenges of web-based teaching had led on-line coordinators at some of the colleges to provide greater organizational support for faculty learning and move beyond their reliance on the efforts of individual innovators. In fact, we observed promising activities at several colleges, where on-line coordinators were pursuing ways of developing individual faculty members' expertise and building college-wide communities to support instructors' engagement with on-line practices.

An administrator at NESCC described the college's philosophy of on-line course development as one in which "the major concern is the pedagogy, the instruction and the student, not the technology." To support the focus on learning, the on-line program supported several platforms and enabled both asynchronous and synchronous interaction; in this way, the program provided "a technology pool, and instructors are picking and choosing the technologies that will let them accomplish their academic objectives."

During our visit, MWUCC was in the midst of implementing a three-stage process for new on-line instructors, incorporating on-line instruction for the instructors themselves. Drawing from external resources, one stage required completion of University of Illinois's faculty development offering. Another stage would target pedagogical issues. In addition, the coordinator envisioned disciplinary-based faculty groups, which would enable ongoing discussion and reflection about teaching specific subjects. Similarly, SMCC had recently instituted a weekly workshop for on-line course developers, bringing faculty together to discuss pedagogical issues and receive peer feedback on the design of their courses. Finally, on-line faculty at SUCC were investigating recent research findings, forging a collaborative relationship with the nearby research university to increase their knowledge base. These efforts had initiated a substantive change in the on-line program, as the college decided to move toward hybrid courses.

Such accomplishments attest to the possibilities of faculty development, particularly those fostering generative learning and ongoing inquiry into the challenges of teaching and learning—with old and new technologies. Ultimately, however, they were only glimmerings of promising practice. In fact, the landscape of these colleges' on-line programs reflected the phenomenon eloquently summarized by Randy Bass: "Too commonly the approach in higher education to technology and teaching separates discussions of technology from pedagogy, isolates pedagogy from disciplinary practices and methods, and overall, fails to approach innovation as a matter of ongoing intellectual and practical inquiry. In such conditions, technology integration likely will proceed along the path of least resistance, stressing productivity and efficiency over quality and learning, with only isolated pockets of innovation" (quoted in Hatch, Bass, Iiyoshi, and Mace, 2004, p. 44).

Conclusions

Fulfilling the promise of increased educational opportunity depends, at least in part, on providing educational environments that center on students' learning. Careful consideration of the quality of instruction that community college students are afforded is therefore a crucial component of fostering a more equitable approach to postsecondary education. In other words, a sincere offer of postsecondary access to the less-well-prepared students requires more than course availability or the chance to enroll. Students' opportunities to learn and to succeed are shaped by many factors beyond the mere availability of postsecondary courses. As Cohen, Raudenbush, and Ball (2003) assert while outlining the multiple resources involved in teaching practice, "Access creates opportunities for resource use, . . . but resources are not self-acting" (pp. 120–122). The resources themselves are not as important as how they are used.

On the whole, the conditions at the colleges during the time of this study functioned as constraints, severely limiting the potential for on-line education to benefit community college students. Indeed, the promise to deliver more on-line courses to community college students under such conditions (Allen and Seaman, 2003) is a rather gloomy prospect.

Improvement is, nevertheless, possible. The quality of on-line education ultimately rests with the faculty members who are developing and teaching on-line courses. The insights from this study, in conjunction with current research on learning, suggest two key areas to target organizational resources: professional development and course assessment. In both cases, supporting faculty work in the virtual classroom involves more than creating a program of professional development or constructing a systematic approach to assessment. Such an approach comprises (1) locating the processes of student learning at the center of attention; (2) envisioning learning as the ongoing interaction among students, instructors, and course material; (3) facilitating meaningful opportunities for faculty learning; and (4) collecting and analyzing evidence in a way that can (and will) inform improved performance at all of these levels.

From an organizational standpoint, this necessitates a strong commitment in desire, practice, and policy at the senior-most levels of administration. In the absence of such commitment to reshape the colleges' approaches to on-line education, the existence of high-quality on-line courses will most likely be the exception, rather than the rule. In fact, constructing high-quality virtual environments demands a variety of resources and knowledge largely unavailable within individual community colleges.[9] As a result, although the colleges have spent efforts making incremental (albeit necessary) improvements to their on-line programs, the trajectory of on-line involvement may exacerbate existing postsecondary educational inequities. Perhaps the commonly held assumptions about the potentials of "e-learning" hold true for high-status colleges and more advantaged postsecondary students, but much more needs to be learned about how to teach community college students effectively with on-line delivery. Community college student have often encountered educational difficulties in the past and face some of the most serious barriers to college completion. Without empirical evidence about exactly how and under what specific conditions on-line processes facilitate robust learning, a great deal of work remains before the promises of on-line education can be realized at the community college.

NOTES

1. Courses may take the form of live or prerecorded telecourses or use digital technologies such as interactive video-conferencing, multimedia CD-ROMs, and web-based instruction. Web-based technology can support "real-time" (synchronous) computer conferencing or, more commonly, asynchronous interaction through e-mail, listservs, and/or threaded discussion groups.

2. Some reports of web-based education conflate different levels of web use, grouping courses with minimal web use—such as course web sites and peripheral e-mail use—together with courses in which the majority of instruction occurs in the virtual classroom. For a logical rubric for categorizing different levels of web use, see Allen and Seaman (2003). For this study, we defined an on-line course as one in which 95% of instruction occurred at a distance. Thus, courses with an initial on-site meeting are considered "on-line." We also made note of other distance courses, especially those using newer technologies. Several colleges had invested in interactive ITV (instructional television) courses, but the focus of efforts in new forms of distance education—even at those sites—was on on-line education.

3. New York was the one state in the sample that had not established service districts for on-line providers. In other states, community colleges had formed consortia and as a collective group negotiated the terms by which one college's student enrolls in an on-line course offered by a different college in the state.

4. At these colleges, infrastructure consisted of relatively up-to-date computers for on-line faculty and access to an on-line course management system (e.g., Blackboard). The existence of the basic infrastructure did not necessarily mean that a college had put student services on-line. The availability of student services, therefore, constituted a distinct component of basic on-line capacity. This involved making services such as course registration, advising, and access to library materials available to distance students—though again, not necessarily through web-based media. Administrative commitment required the support of at least one senior administrator who maintains the authority to allocate (or redistribute) resources. A full-time on-line coordinator spent a majority of time on curricular and programmatic issues, as opposed to technology support issues. A basic level of professional development involved targeting resources at the college level to assist instructors with course development and on-line teaching issues. Underlying these faculty resources was a planned approach to developing instructors' on-line knowledge. Finally, basic on-line capacity required an adequate level of faculty participation. The nature of *inadequate* faculty participation was quite clear: few on-line innovators (fewer than four) among a faculty whose representatives voiced strong criticism of the college's approach to on-line education.

5. The only exception in this instance was WSCC. SUCC proved not to be an exception; although the president had expressed a strong desire to reduce on-line offerings; the majority of senior administrators did not express that view.

6. Rogers's (1962) theory of diffusion involves discussion of individuals who are likely to be early adopters of innovative practices, revealing distinct differences among individual approaches to new technologies. Applying Rogers's heuristic, Garofoli and Woodell (2003) estimate the following distribution of faculty among Rogers's categories: innovator (2.5%), early

adopter (13.5%), early majority (34%), late majority (34%), and laggard (16%). In their discussion of the dividing line between "early adopter" and "early majority" faculty, they note the typical characteristics of early adopters as "visionary," "risk-takers" who "favor revolutionary change," "willing to experiment," and "generally self-sufficient." In contrast, "early majority" instructors are typically "pragmatic," "risk averse," in favor of "evolutionary change," "want proven applications," and "may need significant support." This is not to suggest that other faculty members at these colleges did not exhibit these characteristics in other areas of practice. We saw evidence of innovation—both technology related and not—on the part of many instructors who were not involved in on-line education.

7. NWRCC's solution to this financial burden involved collaborating with another rural college in the state. This was the only example in the study of intercollege collaboration in process.

8. When paired with research that questions the instructional practices of on-site courses (Hull, Rose, Fraser, and Castelano, 1991; Grubb, Worthen, Byrd, Webb, Badway, Case, Goto, and Villeneuve, 1999; Hillocks, 1999), continued reference to the "no significant difference" phenomenon reveals a disturbing disregard for the quality of learning opportunities afforded by what is currently available. For a different critique of the "no significant difference" discourse, see Sener (2004).

9. For a brief discussion of the "substantial basis" for community college complaints of being under-funded, see Grubb, Worthen, Byrd, Webb, Badway, Case, Goto, and Villeneuve (1999, p. 322).

CHAPTER SIX

The Limits of "Training for Now"

Lessons from Information Technology Certification

JIM JACOBS AND W. NORTON GRUBB

Students need to have other things that feed into that learning experience so that they're not left with just a training that's only good
for now, but an education that will carry on. And that's why certifications are folded into courses; they're not standing out there as a
course. We're not going to train you in just this Cisco, it's folded into a
wider thing.

—*A community college dean, National Field Study*

Workforce development in the United States is largely carried out in community
colleges, particularly for middle-level jobs, as well as in four-year colleges and universities for middle-level and professional positions. Typically, students complete a series
of courses designed by educators to meet the skill demands of relevant occupations,
and then they receive credentials based on courses passed—often disparaged as "seat-
time" credentials, because they depend on sitting still long enough to accumulate the
required course credits.[1] Unlike some other developed countries—particularly the
German-speaking countries—the United States does not maintain a work-based system to prepare those entering the workforce, and the criteria for credentials are
largely decided by education providers rather than employers.

In the past two decades, however, this approach has been challenged in several
ways, particularly by those who believe that relatively low skill levels among the technical workforce can be attributed to school-based education rather than job preparation more closely aligned to the workplace (Secretary's Commission for Achieving
Necessary Skills, 1991). The failure to prepare an adequate workforce has been widely
cited as a potential threat to U.S. competitiveness, particularly during the 1980s and
1990s, when the presumably superior Japanese and German workforce-development

systems were seen as major threats (Commission on the Skills of the American Workforce [CSAW], 1990). One response has been to strengthen the academic preparation of all students, but other responses have included the efforts to develop more work-based learning—through the ill-fated efforts of the 1994 School-to-Work Opportunities Act, now abandoned and viewed as ineffective (Hershey et al., 1998; Stull, 2003) —and efforts to create new kinds of credentials to replace seat-time credentials. In particular, as part of the boom in information technology (IT) during the 1990s, specific high-profile firms, including Microsoft, Novell, and Cisco, created firm-specific certificates to certify the abilities of individuals to work with the hardware and software of that firm only. Their promoters vowed that such certificates would reshape the workforce preparation system and establish new modes of learning (Flynn, 2002), and others suggested that firms were creating a parallel educational universe outside of the traditional institutions, threatening to displace community colleges (Adelman, 2000).

As one of the apparent challenges to the future of colleges, we included the issue of IT certification in the National Field Study. In each of the National Field Study colleges, therefore, we surveyed all the firm-based certificate programs offered by the college, interviewed instructors and administrators, and tried to collect information on the magnitude of such efforts and their effects on students. We wanted to address three specific questions:

- What is the involvement of community colleges with certification programs?
- What is the impact of these activities on the future delivery of workforce development at these colleges?
- What implications do these developments have for the equity role of community colleges?

Four years later, the demand for IT certificates has waned, and the supposed threat of these practices to community colleges has disappeared. The responses of colleges to IT certificates, however, have been instructive about a more general set of issues, including the role of formal schooling in workforce preparation, the linkages between colleges and employers, the balance of specific versus general approaches to workforce preparation, the equity of alternative approaches, and the nature of community colleges themselves. In this chapter, we first examine the roles of credentials in workforce development. We then describe the rise of IT certificates (and several other alternative credentialing efforts) and the multiple ways community colleges incorporated them into broader programs. We clarify the potential negative consequences of firm-based certification, to counter the sometimes exaggerated claims of some supporters. The final section presents our conclusions about this instructive episode, the characteristics of successful credentials, the benefits for students, and, particularly, the implications for the ability of colleges to respond to economic changes.

The Roles of Credentials in College-Based Workforce Preparation

Over time, the emphasis on formal schooling as the dominant way to prepare the labor force has been justified by the superiority of school-based forms of learning over work-based and apprenticeship forms, especially for the competencies required by knowledge-intensive jobs and professional positions (Grubb and Lazerson, 2004). School-based preparation, however, creates an immediate problem: how to keep the competencies taught in schools, colleges, and universities reasonably aligned with the needs of employers. Educators use a variety of strategies to do this, including guidance and counseling to inform students about the demands of employment; institutional linkages (such as advisory councils) to provide direct information from employers to providers; and credentials. When an educational credential works as intended, it provides uniform expectations among all participants. Employers specify the competencies they need; education and training programs use credential requirements to shape their curricula and motivate students with the promise of employment; and students know what competencies they must master to become marketable. This is the positive sense of credentials: they coordinate the activities of employers, education providers, and students, by providing consistent incentives.

If, however, one of the three groups of participants does not have its interests fully represented, problems are likely to arise. If, for example, employers hire on the basis of experience or other qualities and ignore credentials in hiring, credentials may seem superfluous. If for any reason (including the pace of change or the distance between educators and the workplace) the competencies taught are not those required on the job, students and employers alike are disappointed with the results. The value of a credential thus becomes uncertain, and "credentialism" takes on the negative connotation of educational requirements not rationally related to employment requirements (Collins, 1979; Grubb and Lazerson, 2004, chap. 7). As a result, credentials in the United States—usually developed by providers rather than employers, relatively informal rather than highly structured (as in England or Germany, for example), and usually assessed in classrooms rather than under joblike conditions—have come under attack.

In addition, credentials require considerable institutional effort to create and enforce, including three potentially controversial requirements: (1) competencies or standards must be established, (2) a method of assessing competencies must be created, and (3) a mechanism for policing the process must be developed. Again, any one of these three may go awry—for example, when education providers rather than firms specify standards, methods of assessment are invalid ways of measuring performance on the job, or individuals are hired regardless of the credentials they have or the quality of the credentials. The United States has not, with the important exception of licensing mechanisms for professions, created the highly elaborated systems of credentials that exist in some other countries, and so again the negative aspects of credentialism may emerge.

During the 1990s at least three alternatives to traditional credentials developed, as workforce experts concluded that this informal system both failed to align the supply and demand for skills and presented a chaotic picture to young people (CSAW, 1990). Policy makers responded with growing interest in skill standards (e.g., U.S. Department of Education, 1993); this led in turn to the establishment of the National Skill Standards Board (NSSB) in 1994 to establish standards for occupations throughout the country and to provide assessments for them. Eight years later, the NSSB had generated a great deal of useful discussion about skills and had created a few standards for broadly-defined occupations, adopted by a few states. The efforts, however, failed to become self-sustaining; educators found it difficult to use national standards because of inconsistencies among state and national frameworks, a lack of technical assistance, and low levels of academic competence (MPR Associates, 1996; Haimson and Hulsey, 1999). The NSSB was phased out in 2003 by the Bush administration.

A second and potentially more effective approach to creating skill standards has been generated by industry associations, which in some cases—notably the National Automotive Technicians Education Foundation (NATEF) for automotive technicians —created standards for occupations, certified education providers, and developed credentials based on assessments (including performance-based assessments) of student competencies. (For a compendium of some industry-based standards, see Wills [1993].) They promised to replace provider-developed credentials with employer-created credentials and align the demands of employers with the offerings of providers. Such approaches also appear to be spreading to newer occupations. For example, one college of the National Field Study reported that the national hospitality associations were developing skill standards and credentials for different types of hospitality workers. Industry-based credentials, however, still appear to be relatively restricted—for example, after twenty years of development, the NATEF program is still considered "voluntary," many automotive dealers do not participate, and most programs have fewer than 100 students completing the program. They have never been extensively studied, and we did not find enough examples in the National Field Study colleges to examine them.

A third development has encompassed the efforts of IT firms to develop firm-specific credentials. During the 1990s, more than 2.4 million jobs were created in IT—in new occupations whose names and skills were unfamiliar to educators. At first, firms created in-house programs to train staff with their own equipment, but larger firms then saw the potential for training efforts to become profit centers and began providing the certification programs to individuals outside their firms (Information Technology Association of American, 2001). The IT sector then developed a system of assessments to certify whether individual workers had acquired the skills for specific IT jobs by using the hardware and software of the particular firms. According to industry sources, the goal was to provide an adequate supply of individuals with the skills necessary to operate specific software programs and networking equipment (Carew, 2004); the appropriate connection between employer skill needs and educational outcomes would be established as firms created the assessments.[2] Unlike school-based credentials, the final assessment of learning is designed by the firm and is administered by a third party, not the provider. In addition, skills could be learned in a variety of places—community colleges as well as trade schools, on-the-job learning, and self-study—so firm-specific certification offered an alternative to the monopoly of conventional schooling over entry into occupations. Such a system presented the possibility of significant competition for community colleges in educating technical workers.

Certification programs grew rapidly during the 1990s. In 1991, there was one certification program, the Certified Novell Engineer (or CNE); by 1999, there were 300 different IT certifications and more than 2.4 million certificates conferred through these programs (Adelman, 2000). More recent data indicated that Microsoft alone issued a total of 1.4 million certifications by January 2003, which suggests a total number higher than Adelman's estimates (Haimson and Van Noy, 2004). Within the IT industry the "certs," as they were called, became a means by which individuals were able to demonstrate their competencies. Only a minority of individuals, however, prepared for these exams through some formal postsecondary courses. A survey completed by Prometric, a firm that administered tests for some IT firms, indicated that the majority of individuals prepared through self-study, using books or on-line material, or attending short courses in proprietary trade schools. Only 6% reported attending a program at a two- or four-year postsecondary institution (Haimson and Van Noy, 2004).

Certifications were significant departures from traditional vocational education programs, which have emphasized educational processes rather than outcome measures. The new approach was developed around clusters of occupations and work, which more closely reflected the realities of the occupational structure and organized the curriculum around functional activities of the workplace, rather than conventional occupational education departments (such as business, technology, and allied health) that failed to provide students and employers with knowledge about specific jobs. Instead of requiring all IT students to master many program languages, courses could be designed around specific functions of IT occupations such as networking, system maintenance, and software security in addition to programming. Thus, in many ways, the development of firm-based certification created a threat to the ways community colleges carried out occupational education.

Industry Certification and the Reactions of the Community Colleges

This new educational market did not go unnoticed by community colleges, which initiated subassociate degree certifications, especially in IT, by use of the certification systems marketed by various firms. Most colleges organized these within their non-credit and continuing education programs. By the end of the decade, a survey of colleges estimated that 25% of all community colleges maintained one or more certification programs (U.S. Department of Education, 2002; Haimson and Van Noy, 2004). The rapid growth of the programs and the large student enrollments suggested that these efforts were altering the nature of workforce development.

Because firm-based certificates concentrated on the needs of companies, they permitted colleges to draw on their strengths in customized training and incumbent worker training, often operated separately from the traditional occupational programs (Rothwell, Gerity, and Gaertner, 2004). These entrepreneurial units were the first to react to the growth of IT certifications. In addition, community colleges were interested in developing subdegree credentials to increase statistics for completion rates. IT certifications also gave workforce-development educators a new way to argue that real outcomes should be based on workplace demands. Thus, in several ways, IT certificates were consistent with preexisting trends in community colleges.

In other ways, the new certification systems pushed colleges out of traditional approaches. Most customized training at community colleges is performed on a contractual basis for specific "clients"—companies or even governmental agencies such as the Department of Labor—but relatively few conclude with a demonstration of specific competencies. Indeed, in many instances, the client requests the college not to test students, to create a more positive atmosphere in the class. As a result, "seat time" still dictates the completion of the course, but the new certifications systems required mastering a test at the end, more consistent with other efforts—these efforts include, for example, the Workforce Investment Act (WIA) and its precursors, the federal government's funding for occupational education, and some state accountability systems, which rely on outcome measures rather than seat time.

For these reasons, many practitioners in community colleges seized on the certification movement as an indication that credentials in community colleges needed to be reformed. Organizations such as the American Association of Community Colleges (AACC) viewed these developments as signs of change in the traditional system. In a publication written for its 2000 Convention, the AACC summarized this view: "As governments and employers demand evidence of learning, the inadequacy of traditional college transcripts has become more obvious. . . . Traditional benchmarks like degrees and certificates do not capture or reflect the value of these varied experiences" (AACC, 1999a).

In the same year, two councils affiliated with the AACC—the National Council for Occupational Education (NCOE; now the National Council for Workforce Education) and the National Council for Continuing Education and Training (NCCET) — produced a position paper on credentialing that argued, "Community colleges need to redesign credit and non-credit curricula, training programs and learner support systems to be able to respond quickly to stakeholders' certification and credentials requirements. One bright spot for many community colleges has been their rapid adoption of certification programs in many of the information technologies. Colleges need to learn from these experiences and apply the learning in other areas of their curriculum, as it is highly likely that other areas of the private sector will follow the lead of the informational technology sector" (NCOE-NCEET, 2001).

By now there are some signs that reformed approaches to certification are being implemented. Maryland has begun a process by which firm-based certificates are used within the community colleges. Many colleges hope to develop transcripts for students that include e-credit and noncredit courses, as well as industry certifications and other forms of learning recognized by employers (Stanley, 2000). Several community colleges are using new transcript formats that take into account noncredit education, and ongoing discussions between noncredit administrators and college registrars have examined how to account for noncredit instruction (Warford, 2002).

Although the development of firm-based IT certification has prompted some colleges to develop new courses and new approaches to certification, there has been very little empirical work on how colleges incorporated these new certificates—and particularly whether they provided the substantial challenge that their supporters assumed. Therefore, the National Field Study examined all examples of firm-based IT certificates in the fifteen colleges we studied, to shed some light on these issues.

Certifications at the National Field Study Sites

As all the chapters of this study reveal, community colleges are diverse institutions, and their use of certificates is no exception. Table 6.1 reveals the wide variety of community college responses to IT certification. Although all fifteen colleges incorporated some IT certification programs, the range of responses was quite broad and included

- Altering existing curriculum within IT degree programs to include specific subjects covered in certification exams, such as networking or streaming.
- Developing noncredit courses and related certificates providing training in specific equipment or products of IT firms, which did not certify learning within a traditional college framework but did prepare students for the examination.
- Providing new continuing education classes, either through private training vendors contracted by the college or through college personnel skilled in specific equipment programs.
- Targeting firm-specific programs to specific groups such as unemployed workers, usually under contract from the local workforce-development board or some other state-sponsored job-training program.
- Creating specific programs to prepare students for certification examinations and marketing them through noncredit or continuing education divisions.
- Developing partnerships with vendors to become regional training centers or testing centers, as a service to the community and other educational institutions. In some instances, these regional centers served a technology dissemination function and trained other instructors, either from high schools or other colleges.

No one of these six strategies dominated, and many of the larger colleges in the National Field Study used more than one of the approaches. The distinctions among the six modes of delivery appeared tactical, rather than based on any particular education philosophy or desire to change the institution. Rather than viewing IT certification programs as a separate format, they were implemented within current institutional structures, usually as noncredit or continuing education classes rather than traditional credit courses. Only one of these colleges offered IT certification courses only for credit. Seven institutions, however, maintained both credit and noncredit instruction for certifications; the credit programs were longer and permitted students to earn credits toward associate degrees, whereas the noncredit

TABLE 6.1
Colleges and Certification Programs

College	Number of Certifications	Credit	Noncredit	Private Vendor Provides Certification	Involve High School[1]	WIA[2] Programs in Information Technology	Regional/Test Center for Certifications
MWRCC	4	Yes	Yes	No	No	Yes	No
MWSCC	5	Yes	Yes	Yes	No	Yes	Yes
MWUCC	3	No	Yes	Yes	No	Yes	No
NERCC	4	Yes	Yes	Yes	Yes	No	Yes
NESCC	4	No	Yes	Yes	No	Yes	No
NEUCC	3	Yes	Yes	No	No	?	Yes
NWRCC	1	Yes	Yes	No	No	No/Yes[3]	No
NWSCC	6	Yes	Yes	No	Yes	No	Yes
SMCC	6	Yes	Yes	Yes	Yes	Yes	Yes
SUCC	8	Yes	Yes	Yes	Yes	?	Yes
SWSCC	3	Yes	Yes	No	Yes	?	Yes
SWUCC	9	Yes	Yes	No	No	Yes	Yes
WRCC	2	Yes	No	No	No	Yes	No
WSCC	4	Yes	Yes	No	No	No	No
WUCC	8	Yes	Yes	No	Yes	No/Yes[3]	Yes

1. A "no" response for high school involvement means there was no information that could be found about it.

2. WIA stands for the Workforce Investment Act. This column indicates whether the colleges maintained informational technology programs that were being financially supported through the WIA system, normally the local Workforce Development Board.

3. NWRCC and WUCC did not maintain WIA-funded programs, but they have some joint program with outside WIA providers.

courses were shorter and were usually provided in an open-entrance, open-exit format. Administrators generally believe that noncredit programs are chosen by students who already have degrees and are looking for specific skill training—including training to upgrade the skills they need in existing jobs—while credit programs are more likely to be taken by younger students entering the workforce for the first time.

In explaining the creation of new courses, colleges referred to some well-established principles of community colleges. One was responsiveness to the labor market. An administrator from California described the variety of programs as such a response: "We are probably the largest single trainer of people in Java and C++; we're one of the largest in the country. You need to do what's in demand."

In addition, administrators responsible for these programs believed that diversity of responses reflected different niches in the market for IT certification, in turn reflecting the heterogeneity of students. Unlike secondary schools, which can focus on young adults before they enter the "adult" workforce, workforce-development programs in community college enroll many groups, including people just out of high school, immigrants who have never attended any formal education in the United States, experienced workers looking for retraining, and individuals like the long-term unemployed and welfare recipients looking for second chances to enter the labor market. By offering different types of programs, colleges can cater to the diverse needs of these students, and potential students can choose which programs best meet their needs. One dean from a Florida community college justified the multiple responses of his institution: "We try not to duplicate them [courses offered by other vendors], but at the same time, we're serving a different population. The person who is taking the credit computer course . . . this is a person who is associate degree and eventually bachelor degree oriented. The majority of the people that we have taking our classes are those people who want short-term skills training. They maybe already [have a degree]. So what we do is offer certification programs that people want because they know exactly what their goal is." The major goal of these administrators was to be responsive to training and education needs within their own community, a central way of being a community-serving institution. Taking this approach meant colleges were also eager to serve students who already had degrees, and indeed the presence of such students was a point of pride, validating the usefulness of the college in serving a new constituency. As one dean put it, "They may already have bachelor's degrees. So they don't care, they don't even look at the credit route if it looks like the [noncredit] courses are what they want there and the times they want."

In addition to noncredit courses, the colleges in the National Field Study participated in the new forms of certification in different ways, described in Table 6.2. Eleven colleges offered Cisco and Microsoft certification, and nine were providing programs leading to A+ certification. Four institutions were authorized Microsoft testing centers; one institution was attempting to become an authorized Microsoft academic trainer, and one had applied to be a testing center for a computer testing service organization. At least one college developed a regional academy, serving students from many community college districts. In many cases these services were provided by noncredit or stand-alone "institutes" established within their colleges, somewhat separate from the rest of the college.

In one sense, however, IT certification programs at community colleges did represent a significant change in the way that the colleges organized workforce development. Instructors and administrators traditionally determined the needs of employers and the skills they taught through advisory committees and other forms of gathering labor market information. In the case of firm-based certification, however, colleges focused on student demand—the willingness of individuals to pay for courses, rather than the employer demand for individuals with these certificates. Most colleges saw student demand as sufficient proof of employer interest in certificates. This assumption, however, may not be valid, in light of the limited information about the economic benefits of certificates as well as the limited access of many students to career counseling.

TABLE 6.2
Noncredit Certification Programs of Information Technology in Community Colleges, Summer 2001

College	IT Program	IT Cost	General Tuition	Location	Potential for Credit
MWRCC	A+	—	$49: District Resident $147.3: State Resident $223.6: Out-of-State	Center for Business and Industry	—
MWSCC	Cisco	$43: District $124: State Resident	$43: District Resident $124: State Resident $171: Out-of-State	Occupational/Vocational Program	Credit Side (Digital Micro-processor Tech program)
MWUCC	—	—	$52: District Resident $122.5: State Resident $202.3: Out-of-State $30: Continuing $45: Vocational	—	—
NERCC	A+, Cisco, Microsoft	—	Full-Time: $1,300: State Resident $1,475: Nonresident Part-Time: $99: State Resident $108: Nonresident	IT Career programs (Continuing Education)	Credit and Noncredit
NESCC	A+, N+, Microsoft	—	Full-Time: $1,175: State Resident $3,067: Nonresident Part-Time: $98: State Resident $255: Nonresident	Workforce Development Institute (Continuing Education)	Credit—free

Institution	Certifications	Cost	Tuition	Division/Program	Notes
NEUCC	A+, Microsoft, Cisco	$975 (72 hours) $1,200 (96 hours) $3,480 (280 hours)	Full-Time: $1,250: State Resident $1,538: Nonresident Part-Time: $105: State Resident $130: Nonresident Non-Degree $120: State Resident $175: Nonresident	Business and Technology Division (Continuing Education)	—
NWRCC	N+, Microsoft, Cisco	$599 (30 hours) $695 (40 hours) $799 (semester)	$63.05: State Resident $234.75: Nonresident	Center for Business and Industry Services	Credit for Cisco (3 hours/day, 2 days/week)
NWSCC	A+, N+, Cisco, Microsoft, Oracle, Linux	$895: (112 hours) $695 (72 hours) $149 (6 weeks by on-line) $2,195 (4 subjects) $695 (72 hours) $695 (72 hours)	$64.26: State Resident $235.96: Nonresident	Academic Program Continuing Education On-Line Education	Noncredit in Continuing Education; Otherwise Credit
SMCC	A+, N+, Microsoft, Cisco, Novell	—	$51.5: State Resident $193: Nonresident	Advanced Technology Division	—
SUCC	A+, N+, Microsoft, Cisco, Linux, Oracle	$599 (56 hours) $1,199 (35 hours) $1,199 (35 hours) — $1,199 (35 hours) $845 (36 hours)	$53.67: State Resident $201.6: Nonresident	—Institute IT Certification Program —Computer IT Department	Credit for A+ and N+ Certification Programs in Computer IT Department

TABLE 6.2 *continued*

TABLE 6.2
Continued

College	IT Program	IT Cost	General Tuition	Location	Potential for Credit
SWSCC	Cisco, Microsoft, Linux, Oracle	$529 (70 hours) $2,000 (112 hours) $259 (30 hours) $599 (40 hours)	$37: District Resident $41: State Resident $212: Out-of-State and International	Workforce Development Division (Continuing Education)	—
SWUCC	Cisco, Linux, Microsoft, Oracle, Sun	$3,790 (280 hours) $645 (36 hours) $1,690 (104 hours) $3,925 (155 hours) $3,360 (112 hours)	$47: District Resident $96: State Resident $215: Out-of-State and International	High-Technology Institute	—
WRCC	A+, Microsoft, Novell	—	$11: State Resident $130: Nonstate Resident	Business and Computer Information	—
WSCC	Cisco	—	$11: State Resident $130: Nonstate Resident	Computer Science/Technology Department	—
WUCC	A+, . N+, Microsoft, Cisco, Linux, Oracle	Free for Cisco and A+	$11: State Resident $130: Nonstate Resident	Centers for Education and Technology	—

In general, as for other credit and noncredit offerings, program success—and success in competing with other vendors of certification courses—was defined by enrollments, again a reflection of *student* demand. One administrator expressed a typical view: "I know we enjoy more success then any of the other proprietary or educational providers. But we have far more contact hours and far more one-on-one work, and our graduates are far more successful in getting jobs and thriving. . . . We know that for a fact, we get people coming in here taking A+ courses after taking an entire A+ course from one of our competitors."

Colleges generally cited their reputations in the local community as providing them a competitive advantage over other vendors—particularly because, as we clarify in "The Dark Side of Industry-Based Certificates," they did not seek to attract students on the basis of lower tuition. In two institutions, administrators cited the local reputation of the college and the quality of the existing program as the reason for its competitive edge. As one dean stated,

> What gives us an advantage over the other companies is that people like the name of the college, rather than the [vendor]. When we give a Continuing Education certificate it's a Southern Accreditation Association certificate with official Continuing Education Units. It means that when they take that to their company they know that this is a course that was taught as a regular official college course, and not just by some little place down on the corner here that opened up a room in an office building, put some computers in there and started doing computer training. They know that our instructors are going to have qualifications that are going to be on file. The curriculum is going to be on file. We're going to be maintaining quality control over the instruction that is taking place and that gives us an advantage. So I think that a lot of companies prefer to use us.

Even administrators in noncredit or entrepreneurial units of their institutions emphasized college reputation as giving them a competitive edge. A director of continuing education articulated this common theme: "I think our competitive advantage is the fact that [this college] itself has a good reputation in the district. Nationally, as well as in the district, the other competitive edge is the quality we deliver." Another emphasized that this reputation would apply even when the college subcontracted with vendors: "I think the content that we give is, we don't cut any corners. Again, we contract with a third party to provide this. We provide the space, we assist with the recruitment and we monitor for quality control. But, it's a national curriculum . . . so it's not like it's any mystery or secret."

At some colleges, the student demand for IT certification was so strong that they turned to private vendors to provide courses. These relationships were initiated by colleges because of their difficulty in hiring instructors and their inability to stay current in the field. At four colleges, the outside vendor supplied instructors and equipment while the college provided the facilities and marketed the classes. In all these instances, courses were noncredit; the vendor kept 70%–75% of revenues and the college kept 25%–30%. As one administrator outlined the process of using a private subcontractor,

> The teachers are provided by [company X]. It's a fabulous partnership; it's a revenue share. They take care of the entire curriculum; they order all the books. And they provide us with industry instructors. We did not want it to be a typical academic, computer information systems class. These certificate programs are practical in nature, and so they, by providing us with people from industry, are a perfect match. We have never been able to get these certification programs off the ground before, and we needed the expertise of a company who had a system in place for us to be able to do it.

Another administrator who had just initiated a new relationship with a vendor described it this way:

> We're in our third A+ class. We've got two brand-new computer labs, they're small labs, and they only hold sixteen people. That's all we wanted in the classroom. And then Net+ will start in the spring. Our responsibility is to provide a classroom, tables, chairs, chalkboards, to register students, to collect their money, to keep a permanent record of a student's attendance, and they [the contractor] invoice us, it's a 25/75 share. We keep 25%, but as you know for training programs, the bulk of the responsibility is in curriculum and finding an instructor. So, we think that's very, very fair.

The alternative, in the colleges that chose not to hire outside vendors, was to retrain existing staff or hire new instructors.

For the most part, colleges were readily able to incorporate firm-based IT certificates into their existing practices and structures, relying on the traditional justifications for serving the local community and different groups of students. Indeed, the practice of offering certification courses in both credit and noncredit formats gave students maximal choices and allowed some students to opt for specific training while other students could complete such certificates as part of a broader associate degree. The tendency to use outside vendors, however, presents a potentially new departure for colleges.

The Dark Side of Industry-Based Certificates

Although colleges were readily able to respond to the new demand for IT certificates, some aspects of their response are potentially worrisome. The first and most-obvious of these is the tuition charged for IT certificates and its effects on the colleges' traditional equity role. Access to community colleges by low-income students is facilitated by low tuition, often offset by federal and state tuition assistance (both grants and loans); however, neither of these subsidies operated in IT programs. Most colleges established specific fees for the IT certification, not the traditional credit-hour tuition. The costs varied from program to program and from institution to institution, as the results in Table 6.2 indicate. Although one college did offer free Cisco and A+ training (though they charged fees for the test), certification classes were generally much more expensive than traditional credit programs, costing as much as $3,500 a program. This indicates that most colleges focused on working adults who could afford to pay. None of the colleges offered any scholarships or student aid—outside of the normal federal aid programs, which are available only for students taking credit courses at least half time, automatically excluding most students enrolling in IT certification. Although no college kept records on the characteristics of students in IT courses, the high tuition suggests that there were few lower-income students. In light of the high tuition and the unconventional scheduling of classes, it also seems unlikely that many recent high school graduates would be attracted to these classes.

The equity problems with these credentials illustrate the potential dangers of colleges charging what the market will bear, as trade schools sometimes do. Individuals enrolling in short certificate programs are ineligible for federal and most state grants, both because these are likely to be noncredit courses and because they are less than half-time students. (They are, however, eligible for the Hope Tax Credit and Lifelong Learning Tax Credit, though many moderate-income students may not earn enough to qualify, and others may be unaware of these tax breaks.) If they take out loans and go into debt to pay for tuition and then find that these certificates do not in fact pay off, they may default on their loans—just as students from proprietary schools often do. Although there are no data on the numbers of students who have defaulted as a result of industry certificate programs, this possibility illustrates another problem with high tuition in the absence of greater assurance that such programs will pay off.

Furthermore, IT certification courses were not linked to other courses and support services of colleges, including developmental education. The expansion during the 1990s of IT jobs provided new employment opportunities. However, the preparation in mathematics, basic literacy, and communication skills of individuals wanting to enter such jobs can be formidable and time-consuming—particularly for adults without high school diplomas, but also for the substantial numbers of high school graduates who still need developmental education once they enroll in community colleges. Without access to developmental education and other "academic" courses, students intending to complete IT certification might find it difficult to learn the material and pass the test. For example, three of the fifteen colleges in the National Field Study had certification programs funded by the WIA: one accepted WIA voucher recipients into its IT certification courses, another ran specific programs for WIA recipients in A+ and Microsoft Certified Systems Engineer (or MCSE) programs, and a third was waiting for state approval to run such classes. These programs appeared to be general computer awareness and computer literacy classes rather than certification classes. Although this emphasis is understandable because of the academic preparation necessary to pass any test, none of the colleges offered developmental programs for students in WIA programs. None of these colleges had data on how well students performed in these classes; but, in light of the common need of WIA recipients for basic skills instruction, we suspect that such students would fare poorly.

Beyond the National Field Study sites, there are some strong examples of certification programs for low-income workers. These are small, carefully controlled programs, designed by coalitions of firms, workforce-development boards, and local colleges (Alssid et al., 2002). Although such "boutique" programs may work well, they require services and forms of collaboration not present in most colleges providing IT certification.

A second serious problem with certificates involves the age-old debate about specific versus general programs. The IT certificates created by individual firms are obviously firm-specific: they provide certification of the ability to use the particular software and hardware of Novell, Microsoft, Oracle, and other IT firms, but they do not certify broader abilities, and they do not therefore encourage training providers to give students a broader understanding of IT—for example, the difference between networking in general and the specific approach to networking software of Cisco. In the language of pedagogy, they encourage "systematic" or skills-oriented instruction, in which instructors teach students to master a series of commands rather than understanding what a computer application is supposed to accomplish. They generally discourage a "minimalist" or constructivist or systems approach in which students learn the underlying purpose of particular applications and then learn specific computer applications as ways of carrying out more general tasks (Carroll, 1990; Jonassen, Mayes, and McAleese, 1993). As a result, firm-specific certificates violate a widely understood maxim in occupational education: that narrow and specific forms of education should be avoided because they may become obsolete over the long run, whereas broader conceptual approaches are more likely to benefit the student over a career.[3] Indeed, part of the broader problem of not knowing the employment benefits of these certificates is the ignorance of what happened to individuals with certificates when the IT crash took place in 2000, when their specific skills are likely to have become less valuable.

Some community colleges in the National Field Study got around this problem by embedding IT certificates in broader Associate programs. This approach provides both the broader education for the long run and the specific training in individual applications for the short run. The problem of overly specific training is precisely what a dean of occupational education referred to in his comments: "Students need to have other things that feed into that learning experience so that they're not left with just a training that's only good for now, but an education that will carry on. And that's why certifications are folded into courses; they're not standing out there as a course. We're not going to train you in just this Cisco; it's folded into a wider thing."

Many college providers were clear that IT certificates were not primarily useful for younger students just entering employment; instead they tended to be used by older workers with experience in the IT field but who needed upgrade training on particular software or hardware to stay current. This corroborates Bartlett's findings (2002) that employers relied more on information about degrees and previous work experience for hiring new workers, whereas certificates were more important as a means of upgrading within the firm. Similarly, a comparative study of IT career pathways in the United States and Denmark indicated that certifications were less important than degrees in hiring individuals, but certification was more important for mobility within the company or sector. One senior administrator at an engineering firm stated, "[C]ertifications without experience are totally useless" (Regional Technology Strategies, and Technology Institute, Copenhagen, 2004). An IT worker in the National Field Study corroborated this: "Technical schools that are pandering certs to IT neophytes ought to be ashamed of themselves! Regardless of the outlook for IT workers, certs are practically worthless to people trying to break into IT. IT is like anything else: experience counts. . . . Saying you have an MCSE or CCNA (Cisco Certified Network Associate) in lieu of experience is like saying you're Catholic, but you've never stepped inside a church!" Although IT certificates may be used as part of broader programs, their creation by firms interested only in firm-specific preparation is part of a larger problem where employers—either through advisory committees or hiring standards or certification mechanisms—push colleges and other providers toward overly specific training.

Unfortunately, colleges had very little idea about what happened to students enrolled in IT certification courses. No college collected data on whether credit or noncredit students performed better on the assessments or even maintained any form of records on passage rates in certification tests. (The only exceptions are the few programs under contract with local workforce boards.) Indeed, it would have been difficult to do so, because students can take certification exams in many different test centers and the centers are under no obligation to provide information back to providers. Even in the three colleges that acted as test centers, this information was unavailable. In contrast, when students are in programs subject to state licensing, like nursing programs, the pass rates are regularly reported to the institution, and colleges often use this information in their marketing and assessment efforts. Therefore, one crucial difference between private certification procedures, as for IT certificates, and public licensing procedures is the extent of information available on what happens to students. Without this information, it is impossible to verify the claims of IT firms that such certificates provide ready access to employment or to ascertain employment experiences over the booms and busts of the IT sector itself or—of crucial importance to community colleges—whether broader approaches to education are more effective over the long run than narrowly firm-specific training. Although firm-specific certification opens up new possibilities, it also brings new dangers.

Assessing the Challenges of Firm-Based Certification

Certification programs at community colleges are still new and emerging. The boom of the 1990s created an environment of great excitement, in which it was easy to predict revolutionary change, but the bust of the IT sector after 2000 has moderated interest in these approaches. In retrospect, these certificates were ways for firms to increase the supply of potential workers, given a sharp spike in demand. When the demand for workers declined, however, employers returned to their normal screening and hiring procedures, which emphasize degrees and general competencies; certificates are important primarily for mobility within the industry. As the boom ended, enrollments in certification courses fell. As one dean running a Cisco certification program noted, "We actually see it in our enrollment. Right now we have 450 students enrolled but probably two years ago we probably had 700 students in any given semester. Some of them are actually employed. But a lot of them are not. They are carrying on with other aspects of networking. They are not making near the money that they did in the past."

At the same time, it is probably unwise to dismiss the influence of certifications simply because they did not live up to the exaggerated expectations of the bubble economy. Although they have not profoundly changed the delivery of workforce education and the alarmism of the late 1990s proved to have been unwarranted, they have contributed to modest shifts of emphasis and they have clarified many of the underlying issues.

One clear implication of the past four years is that community colleges are usually flexible enough to accommodate changes in workforce delivery. Most colleges in the National Field Study incorporated IT certificates without much difficulty—most in noncredit formats, but some in both credit and noncredit programs. Consistent with their local missions, local developments were quite varied, but there is no indication that colleges somehow resisted the new certificates or found them difficult to incorporate. Indeed, the inclusion of certificates within existing programs has developed a kind of hybrid program, with both specific and general components, that is probably more powerful that either alone. This has potentially positive implications for the equity agenda because it means that the more expensive proprietary schools do not hold a monopoly over granting these certifications.

On the other hand, colleges did not incorporate some innovative features of IT certification such as smaller modules instead of semester-long courses, industry-driven tests, or pass/fail grading systems into conventional occupational programs. None of the colleges planned to hire private vendors to teach credit classes, even those that used such vendors for IT certification. The effects of new certificates on colleges' dominant practice were therefore limited. In addition, the changes that did take place were consistent with other developments, particularly the steady expansion of noncredit courses and the increases in older students taking courses for upgrade training. Administrators often referred to the certification students as adults interested in taking only these classes, because they already have degrees and are looking only for upgrade training.[4] This suggests that focusing too intently on certifications could lead community college IT departments to shift their focus away from first-time college students who may be more difficult to educate and require greater support than their older, more-experienced peers.

The recent experiences also clarified some of the inherent problems of firm-based credentials. One, of course, is the problem of being overly specific, or focused too much on "training for now" rather than "an education that will carry on." Especially in the absence of information about employment effects, in a sector with wide swings in employment, there are good reasons to worry that the promised employment benefits associated with firm-specific training will not materialize. Therefore, even if they benefit *employers*, firm-specific certificates may be a particularly bad deal for *students*—though in the absence of information about employment benefits it is difficult to know. A second inherent danger is related to the effort to develop *national* certification. In the National Field Study colleges, there were few attempts to fashion courses that would fit the needs of local employers of IT specialists; colleges implicitly assumed that the national certificate was in the interests of local employers. In contrast, conventional occupational programs generally use advisory committees and other local contacts to modify curricula for the needs of local employers—another practice that is unlikely to be seriously changed in response to firm-based credentials. To better establish the role of industry credentials in upholding the equity agenda, much more needs to be known about what students receive in return for their investment in IT programs, and this needs to be assessed at a *local* level.

Another issue is whether firm-based certificates help remedy the possible problem of supply- or provider-driven education and shift toward demand-driven education more responsive to demands of the labor market. In theory, the development of certificates by particular employers ought to shift toward demand-derived education. Colleges and other vendors, however, have paid attention to *student* demand, without worrying about whether student demand is well informed about employment options. In general, we are concerned that students are not well informed, because career-oriented guidance and counseling in many colleges is weak. (See "'Like, What Do I Do Now?': The Dilemmas of Guidance Counseling," by Norton Grubb, in this volume.)

This is particularly the case for new credentials whose market value has not yet been established, and for IT certificates in particular whose market value is completely unknown. This result clarifies that the development of certificates by firms is not sufficient to create demand-driven outcomes, as long as colleges and other vendors benefit from enrollments rather than outcomes over the long run.

In one way, however, community college responses to firm-based credentials provide a vision of a different institution. By creating programs with high tuition levels (Table 6.2), often for courses in institutes set apart from the rest of the campus, some colleges behaved more like trade schools, charging students what the market would bear for firm-specific training and ignoring the equity implications of high tuition. Because of the absence of any information about the employment consequences of IT certificates, students bore the entire risk associated with finding related employment. For experienced individuals using these certificates to upgrade their skills for the places they work, these risks were certainly minimal. For students new to the workforce, without the experience that would allow them to judge the role of certificates among the other potential criteria for hiring, however, the risks must have been substantial—particularly when the demand for IT professionals crashed after 2000. The tendency to develop independent entrepreneurial units, following different tuition and marketing policies, has happened elsewhere in some community colleges, particularly in units responsible for customized training and other services to specific firms (Bailey and Morest, 2004). But, as Jacobs and Teahen (1997) have noted, any substantial expansion of these independent units would seriously undermine the community college as an open-access institution, serving the public interest by providing general forms of education and by making access for all students possible.

Similarly, the tactic of providing IT courses through vendors also suggests a very different institutional model. Colleges justified this practice by high levels of demand that they would otherwise be unable to accommodate, and they insisted that their quality control was strong and the college's reputation would extend to their vendors. However, they provided little evidence of how they monitored quality; such subcontracts were money-making devices—through the "revenue share" and the 75/25 split of revenues—that may have benefited the colleges and the vendors alike, but not necessarily employers or students. And if colleges decided to become large subcontracting institutions, charging high tuition for specific courses taught by freelance instructors in the region, they would be little different from private trade schools. There may be sound educational reasons for subcontracting, but none of the National Field Study colleges described them as anything more than opportunistic efforts to meet high demand.

Overall, however, the adventure with IT certificates reveals how stable conventional college- and university-based preparation of the workforce is. Although many different ways of preparing for these exams developed, the exams themselves proved overly narrow; they precluded modifications to local employment conditions, and in the end a great deal of preparation was embedded in conventional educational programs anyway. When the enormous surge in demand for IT workers of the late 1990s receded, employers themselves reverted to their customary reliance on conventional degrees and experience. Similarly, the failure of the National Skills Standards Board clarifies how difficult it is to create an alternative system of credentials, at least without a powerful demand from industry itself. We suspect that licensing mechanisms and industry-based standards represented by NATEF might be more fruitful to examine, because they reflect employer demand while avoiding the problems of overly specific credentials, but this would require a different study.

At the end of the day, the expected increase in alternative forms of learning driven by external competency-based exams did not take place. Community colleges have now augmented their IT programs with some certificate-oriented courses, and some trade schools offer them as well, but the educational system as a whole remains much the same as it was. And thankfully so, we should add, because the trade school model for community colleges violates some of their most important values, particularly their commitment to serving public interests, their participation with local employers and varied groups of students, and their belief in access and educational equity.

NOTES

1. We use the term "credentials" as an all-inclusive term encompassing certificates, diplomas, licenses, and other less-formal awards, including those cranked out on photocopy machines.

2. Any effort to develop credentials should have a theory underlying how they should work. For example, the conception of credentials as aligning the interests of employers, providers, and students is such a theory, taken from Grubb and Lazerson (2004, chap. 7). The theory of credentials implicit in IT certificates assumes that providers and students will follow the lead of employer demand. This did in fact happen, in the sense that providers developed courses and students applied for certificates in large numbers. In the absence of a policing mechanism guaranteeing that certificates will provide some advantage in employment, however, their success cannot last. Indeed, the reversion of firms to conventional hiring practices after the IT bust of 2000 meant that ultimate source of demand weakened substantially.

3. One could argue that these credentials lead to firm-specific training that workers pay for themselves (see Table 6.2), and expect to benefit from, whereas public support ought to go only to relatively firm-general education (Becker, 1993). Becker's analysis, however, is usually interpreted as saying that firms ought to provide firm-specific training and that students and governments should pay for general education that generates a flow of both private and public benefits over time. Firm-specific certificates requiring students to pay shift the entire burden of firm-specific training onto students rather than having firms bear the costs.

4. Both national data on noncredit students and a survey of IT students indicate that, in comparison to credit students, they are better educated and have higher wages (Haimson and Van Noy, 2004).

CHAPTER SEVEN

"Lights Just Click on Every Day"

DOLORES PERIN AND KERRY CHARRON

More than twenty years ago, academically underprepared students were described as "the thorniest single problem for community colleges" (Cohen and Brawer, 1982, p. 236, cited in Smittle, 2003), and the same seems to be true today. Within higher education, community colleges "often have the neediest students, the most academically underprepared, and the economically disenfranchised" (Hebel, 2003, p. A21). Students entering without adequate literacy and math skills form a diverse group that includes recent high school graduates, immigrants, refugees, "Generation 1.5" (Blumenthal, 2002), and older, returning students. The already challenging task of educating nontraditional students is becoming even more difficult with demographic shifts currently under way in the United States that exist alongside increasing expectations that employees hold college degrees.

National difficulties in teaching academic skills extend from preschool emergent literacy programs through college. Despite the considerable amount of attention that has been directed to improving basic skills instruction for young children (Foorman, 2003) and adolescents (Jetton and Dole, 2004), large numbers of young adults graduate from high school with poor reading, writing, and math competency (Kirst, 2004). From a kindergarten-to-grade 16 (K–16) perspective, community colleges are attempting to solve educational problems begun much earlier. Today's community college remedial student is often yesterday's second-grade "struggling reader."

Because academically underprepared students also tend to come from low-income households (Cohen and Brawer, 2003), the existence and outcomes of community college remedial programs affect the ability of the United States to achieve educational access and equity goals. The community college is the one site within public postsecondary education that ensures admission to academically underprepared degree aspirants. Access through an open-admissions policy is, however, only one step toward educational equity, which is achieved when low-income students have the same chance of graduation as more privileged students (Hauptman, 2004). Community colleges can increase low-income, academically underprepared students' chances of graduation through effective remedial programs. The role of such programs is clear if postsecondary completion is to be a measure by which institutions are to be held accountable (Ewell, 2004). In this chapter, we examine current practices in remedial education in order to contribute to an understanding of how community colleges are trying to increase access and equity for underprepared students, many of whom are casualties of inadequate K–12 education.

Community colleges' open-admissions policy for which community colleges are well known has a strong impact on everyday life in the classroom: estimates of the proportion of students who enter these institutions with difficulty in reading, writing or math range from one-third to 90% (Richardson and Elliot, 1994; U.S. Department of Education, 1996, 2003g; Spann, 2000). Remediation, called "developmental education" in postsecondary settings (Casazza, 1999)—and "intervention" in the K–12 system (Coalition for Evidence-Based Policy, 2003) —is a feature of almost all publicly funded community colleges (McGrath and Spear, 1991; Dougherty, 1994; Zeitlin and Markus, 1996; McCabe and Day, 1998; Shults, 2000). In fact, remediation has become a central mission of these colleges (Howard and Obetz, 1996; Raftery and VanWagoner, 2002).

Remediation has been defined as "a class or activity intended to meet the needs of students who initially do not have the skills, experience or orientation necessary to perform at a level that the institutions or instructors recognize as 'regular' for those students" (Grubb, Worthen, Byrd, Webb, Badaway, and Case, 1999, p. 174). Underprepared students enter community colleges needing academic, social, and emotional support (Reynolds and Bruch, 2002; Liff, 2003), and developmental education services include placement testing; reading, writing, and math courses; tutoring; academic advisement; and personal counseling (Boylan, Bonham, and Bliss, 1994a; Simpson et al., 1997; Phipps, 1998; Casazza, 1999; Roueche, Ely, and Roueche, 2001; McCabe, 2003). According to advocates, developmental education should be comprehensive (Roueche, Ely, and Roueche, 2001; Boylan 2002), and the achievement of underprepared students may depend on use of a large number of services. For example, a program aiming to increase the math and science performance of students from a Latino agricultural migrant community in California included educational planning, academic advisement, career counseling, remedial course work, early alert of academic difficulty, workshops and tutoring in math and science, study groups, and field trips (Kane et al., 2004).

Within the array of developmental education services, the most frequently offered are courses in basic reading, writing and math skills, and tutoring at academic learning centers (Perin, 2004), none of which counts toward degree completion. Tuition is usually charged for the courses, whereas the tutoring is free. Remedial course work, which has been described as "the most controversial part of the developmental education equation" (Oudenhoven, 2002), and the most prominent (Grubb et al., 1999; Boylan, 2002; Lundell and Higbee, 2002; American Association of Community Colleges, 2000), is the focus of this chapter.

A particularly challenging issue that community colleges face is the setting of standards for entry to college-level degree-credit courses. Most community colleges assess incoming students to determine readiness for the college curriculum (Jenkins and Boswell, 2002), but there is no general agreement as to the specific reading, writing, and math skills needed to learn from the postsecondary curriculum. The lack of a common benchmark creates problems for deciding what should be taught in developmental education courses (Phipps, 1998; Merisotis and Phipps, 2000; Oudenhoven, 2002). Other challenging issues concern the appropriate organization of remedial courses within the college structure and teaching methods within remedial classrooms—administrators and faculty have many options from which to choose (Boylan, 1999; Grubb et al., 1999; Perin, 2002). Strong views have been expressed on these topics, but there is a serious shortage of controlled evaluation research to support them, which is troubling in view of claims that postsecondary remedial course work is ineffective (Johnson, 1996; Crowe, 1998; Grubb et al., 1999; Lundell and Higbee, 2000).

The grades and retention, graduation, and transfer rates of students who enroll in developmental education courses have been used to assess the effectiveness of remedial programs (e.g., Roueche, Ely, and Rouche, 2001). As we shall see, however, much of the research on developmental education is based on data from single institutions, making generalization difficult, or is plagued with serious methodological problems. Moreover, for the most part, it examines developmental education classes, which are extremely varied and in any case are only one, albeit the best known, strategy for strengthening the academic skills of underprepared community college students.

This case study reported in this chapter, using the multisite qualitative data gathered by the National Field Study, is designed to understand developmental education at the study sites, and to set the stage for additional rigorous analysis. In the current study, we asked: Have there been changes in the level of remedial need? How are developmental education courses organized within the colleges? What approaches to curriculum and instruction are used? The chapter ends with several questions emerging from this qualitative case study that can inform quantitative investigation in the future.

Academic Preparedness of Community College Students

By using conventional measure of academic preparedness—developmental educa-tion course enrollments—it is evident that many community college students are entering without the reading, writing, and math skills needed to learn at the college level. Developmental education course enrollment rates have been high and flat in recent years. Forty-two percent of freshmen entering public community colleges across the country in 2003 enrolled in at least one remedial course, approximately the same as in 1995 (U.S. Department of Education, 2003g, table 3). A national sur-vey conducted by the American Association of Community Colleges (Shults, 2000) found that approximately 36% of entering freshmen, and a median of 20% of all community college students, were enrolled in developmental education courses. The survey showed remedial course enrollments to be higher in institutions in large cities, with half reporting that at least 27% of students were enrolled in developmental education courses. State data indicate that up to half of the first-time freshmen across the country take remedial courses (Crowe, 1998). Rates of 87%, 50%, and 27% are reported for the community colleges in two states and one municipality in the Na-tional Field Study sample: New York (Mayor's Advisory Task Force on the City University of New York, 1999), Texas (Texas Higher Education Coordinating Board, 1999, Table A-2), and Washington (Washington State Board for Community and Technical Colleges, 1994), respectively.

At first glance, it appears that the large number of remedial course enrollments may be mitigated by the fact that 90% of students spend less than one year in remediation (NCES, 1996), taking only two or three remedial courses (Shults, 2000). Many of the students, however, never enroll in credit courses. Developmental educa-tion course enrollments, moreover, underestimate academic skills difficulty. In fact, many students who enter community colleges with inadequate reading, writing, and math ability do not enroll in these courses.

The National Field Study found much variation across states and institutions regarding the existence of mandatory placement for academically underprepared students and, where it exists, whether the mandate is enforced (Perin, 2006). Where mandates existed, they were often softened within the colleges—for example, depend-ing on the institution, not all skills were assessed; not all students were assessed; subjective rather than objective placement measures were used; instructors could override the assessment or placement requirements; remedial prerequisites could be overridden, not enforced, or removed altogether; placement was not required in all weak areas; career students were exempted from assessment; cutoff scores (the scores below which students are considered to be in need of developmental educa-

tion) were lowered; assessment tests were readministered; students could pass remedial courses with less-demanding instructors; college-level courses were substituted
for remedial courses; limits were placed on remedial course repetitions; and low-
skilled students were steered away from demanding college courses (Perin, 2006).
Because participation in developmental education courses may often reflect student
choice rather than need, it is necessary to augment remedial course enrollment data
with other kinds of information to obtain a realistic estimate of the level of academic
preparedness.

Trends in Levels of Academic Preparedness

Table 7.1 summarizes calculations of students' readiness for college work in the
participating states and colleges on the basis of three indicators of academic preparedness used in a national study by Jenkins and Boswell (2002): the proportion of
test takers who scored below institutionally or state-defined cutoff points on placement tests, the number of developmental education enrollments, and instructors'
observations of classroom performance in both remedial and degree-credit classrooms. Even though the standards across these different indicators and across institutions vary considerably, using all of them provides a truer picture of remedial need
than developmental education course enrollments alone. At the state level, academic
preparedness, according to this measure, varied from a low of 14% in Illinois to highs
of 65% and 68% in Florida and the New York municipal system. These measures, like
simple enrollments, also may reflect state policy that determines who is required to
take developmental education as much as academic preparedness. It cannot be a
coincidence that the National Field Study states that either do not mandate remedial
placement—Washington and California—or do not enforce a placement mandate—
as in Illinois—show lower rates of remedial "need" than the states with a strong
placement mandate—Florida and New York. At the time of the study, Texas mandated
remedial placement for those in need but subsequently changed its approach, leaving
placement policy to the individual colleges. This state reported a high level of remedial need at the time, but whether the removal of the state mandate will be
associated with a fall in the reported rate of academically underprepared students in
the future remains to be seen.

The relation between testing standards and classroom demands complicates the
understanding of academic preparedness. For example, discipline-area instructors
described reading, writing, and math difficulties in their degree-credit classrooms,
even among students considered academically prepared according to college measures. A member of the academic faculty of MWSCC, for example, stated,

TABLE 7.1
Students' Academic Preparedness

State	Site
Proportion of Students Academically Underprepared[1]	
Washington: 38% of community college entrants need remediation; 50% of recent high school graduates enroll in remedial math courses, 20% in writing, 10% in reading.	NWSCC: 60% enter with low skills; 43% take developmental education course in first year; developmental education enrollments account for 11% of FTEs annually.
	NWRCC: 91% of incoming students need developmental math, 52% need developmental English; recent growth in non-English-speaking immigrant population
California: 22% of community college students enroll in at least one remedial course	WUCC: 60% enter with poor skills, much demand for higher level developmental math, very wide range of skills, socioeconomic status, and ethnic background
	WSCC: Specific proportion not known but poor skills among many entering students described
	WRCC: Specific proportion not reported but decline in skills described
Texas: 41% of first-time freshmen enroll in at least one remedial course	SWUCC: Developmental enrollments have dropped to 5% reading, 3% writing, 20% math but a larger proportion have low skills
	SWSCC: Need for remediation based on placement scores: 25% reading, 15% writing, 44% math; enrollments lower than placement, especially in writing area; increase in students with limited English proficiency who need remediation
Illinois: 14% of community college students enroll in at least one remedial course	MWUCC: 20% enter with baccalaureate degrees but among the others, 85% need developmental math, 74% need reading and/or writing; 51% of students enrolled in developmental math, 51% reading, 81% writing.
	MWSCC: Proportion not reported but low skills among many entering students described; 30–50% estimated to need remediation
	MWRCC: 64% of incoming students need developmental math, 33% need developmental reading or writing
Florida: 65% of new students need at least one course	SUCC: 85% of incoming students need at least one developmental education course; of recent high school graduates, 46% need remedial reading, 34% need writing, 54% need math
	SMCC: 51% of incoming students need developmental math, 36% need reading, 26% need writing; 80% take at least one remedial course; 40% of the local population did not complete high school
New York (municipal system): 68% of first-time freshmen enroll in at least one course.	NEUCC: 75% test into at least one developmental education course, was 90% two years ago

TABLE 7.1
Continued

Proportion of Students, Academically Underprepared[1]	
State	Site
New York (state system): information not available	NESCC: 70% of students enter with poor skills; 10% enroll in developmental education NERCC: 34% of students take at least one remedial course, 17% take courses in all three remedial areas; 90% of entering students come from lowest third of high school class

1. Types of information vary across states and sites. Estimates of level of academic underpreparedness based on placement scores, developmental enrollments, interviewees' observations, and previous research (e.g., Jenkins and Boswell, 2002).

I'll have students in my class who have passed the reading test, who can actually read the words of things that I've assigned, but they have no way to interpret them. For example, I assigned Voltaire's *Candide,* which . . . the bulk of the class found funny and there were some students in the class that simply didn't understand that it was all irony . . . they kind of understood what the story was but they didn't understand the meaning at all. Because their reading level was too low. And they actually passed the reading test which I think requires reading at the sophomore in high school level. I think is the standard.

Math performance was an area of strong concern, as shown in Table 7.2, and examples of "hidden remediation" (Grubb et al., 1999, p. 104) were described, for example, by an accounting instructor who found it necessary to teach skills such as conversion of fractions to decimals and the formula for simple interest. Pessimism about student abilities led an administrator at WSCC to propose the right to fail:

[Academic preparedness is] a real problem for our social sciences especially because we do require writing across the curriculum and many of these classes have required . . . up to eight thousand words. And if you get a philosophy class like a critical thinking class that maybe has five papers, and they can't write, they're dead. And we find a lot of drop outs and things like that. So . . . we're not doing a good job of that I don't think. But I don't know how you'd do a good job. I mean, the students they don't know what they don't know. So maybe it's a good experience for them to fail to find out that they're not ready to succeed yet. I mean that's just a personal feeling. I mean I'd rather have people try and fail than not try at all.

As with the national data cited above, no major change in the levels of college readiness was reported at the National Field Study sites. The situation appeared to be chronic but stable overall, with some slight improvements at NEUCC resulting from recently implemented high school graduation exams. Despite the stable numbers,

TABLE 7.2
Issues in Academic Preparedness

| | College | | | | |
Issue	WRCC	WSCC	WUCC	NWSCC	NWRCC
Academically underprepared students in degree credit class-rooms:					
Reading, writing and math difficulties observed in college-level courses		×		×	
Applied clinical skills may not be compromised by low academic skills				×	
Students poorly prepared for writing across the curriculum		×			
Low academic preparedness attributed to state policy to remove remediation from four-year colleges		×			
Developmental education students may be attracted or steered to education major		×	×		
Math skills:					
Math especially problematic			×		
Slight decrease in need for math remediation in recent years attributed to new high school graduation exam				×	×
Overlap between academic skills and language proficiency:					
Demand for both developmental education and ESL exceeds supply, developmental reading courses serve native and nonnative English speakers together; recent reduction in developmental reading sections, increase in ESL			×		
Foreign-born students have better skills					
Native and nonnative English speakers have similar pattern of academic need				×	
ESL students have particular difficulties learning writing skills					
Students who opt for remediation tend to be older, non-English speaking			×		
Most students who test into all three remedial areas have limited English language proficiency					
Native Spanish-speakers' academic performance hindered by lack of everyday use of the English language					
Differing reactions to college academic demands—native-English speakers' shock at difference between high school and college, nonnative speakers' lack of confidence					
High school role:					
High schools preparing students adequately for community college	×				
Decrease in need for remediation attributed to increased high school standards					
Students taught applied rather than theoretical math in high school better prepared for community college allied health program				×	
High schools have low standards and poor teaching methods			×	×	
High school senior year insufficiently demanding					
Difficulties in communication between college and high school				×	
Special projects with high schools to increase academic preparedness			×		×

SWSCC	SWUCC	MWRCC	MWUCC	MWSCC	SUCC	SMCC	NERCC	NESCC	NEUCC
			×	×		×		×	
				×					
×			×			×		×	
			×						
×									
×									
									×
									×
									×
	×				×			×	
				×				×	
×				×	×				

TABLE 7.2 *continued*

TABLE 7.2
Continued

Issue	College				
	WRCC	WSCC	WUCC	NWSCC	NWRCC
Student learning patterns, behaviors, and motivation:					
Learning disabilities observed in developmental education students			×	×	
Many students prefer not to disclose learning disabilities diagnosis					
Growing number of nontraditional, at-risk students:					
Variation in motivation and behavior	×		×	×	
Many math students unmotivated					
Classroom rules needed					
Older students more motivated than younger					
Older students are better skilled than younger students but have learning disabilities, younger students immature and unmotivated					
Older students anxious, have low self-esteem, main outcome of remediation for this group is increased self-confidence					
Low academic scores may reflect motivation rather than ability					
Academic difficulties result for social problems					

remedial need at community colleges is likely to grow, due to major increases in recent years of the number of school-aged children with limited English language proficiency (Hawkins, 2004) as well as an anticipated expansion of Hispanic and Asian-American immigration in the near future (Harrell and Forney, 2003; Kim, 2003; McCabe, 2003; Reuters, 2004). An academic preparedness problem may be brewing in the K–12 system, because, as reported by Hawkins (2004), there is a severe shortage of teachers who have experience with English language learners. These children may be part of a growing achievement gap and may take their first post-secondary steps in open-admissions community colleges.

Reasons given by National Field Study interviewees for the current high levels of academic difficulty included the colleges' open-admissions policy, inappropriately low cutoff scores on placement tests, and state policy confining remediation to the community colleges. Low high school standards were also mentioned, though previous literature has described calls to abolish college remediation on the basis that its mere availability lowers high school students' academic motivation (see Oudenhoven, 2002). Further, it is troubling to note that passing high school college-preparation courses in English and math does not guarantee passing scores on college placement tests (Hoyt and Sorensen, 2001). However, further research is needed to ascertain the relation between students' secondary and postsecondary experiences. For example, a developmental math student at NWSCC interviewed for the study (who unknowingly

	College								
SWSCC	SWUCC	MWRCC	MWUCC	MWSCC	SUCC	SMCC	NERCC	NESCC	NEUCC
	×	×		×				×	
				×					
						×			
	×			×					
								×	
								×	
				×		×		×	
			×						
								×	
				×					
		×			×		×	×	

contributed to the title of this chapter) perceived the teaching in the community college to be easier to understand than in high school, saying, "I get everything explained to me so much better. It's kind of like lights just click on every day."

Some interviewees in the study attributed the high level of remedial need to the presence in the colleges of immigrants and refugees with low English proficiency and limited schooling. Apart from these foreign-born students, there was also a growing number of "Generation 1.5" nonnative speakers of English, who were educated in the United States and speak fluently but display many "fossilized language errors" and are academically underprepared (Blumenthal, 2002, p. 49). As in the previous literature (Kimmel and Davis, 1996), National Field Study interviewees described the needs of English-language learners and native-English-speaking, academically underprepared students as generally similar.

Interviewees at a number of sites reported that a substantial proportion of students in developmental education had learning disabilities, head injuries, and other impediments that limited their achievement (Table 7.2). Among the older students, previously undiagnosed learning disabilities became evident in the postsecondary setting. At the same time, some students who had in fact been identified as learning disabled in the K–12 system preferred not to reveal this information.

There are many descriptions in previous literature about the economic, social and emotional difficulties of community college students (Roueche and Roueche, 1993,

1999; O'Banion, 1994; Richardson and Elliot, 1994; Grubb, 1996; Hammons and Barnsley, 1996; Cohen and Brawer, 2003). Certainly, an underlying assumption of developmental education is that academically underprepared students have difficulties beyond reading, writing, and math skills (Casazza, 1999; McCabe, 2003). Returning students were described by National Field Study interviewees as better skilled but lacking self-confidence and younger students as unskilled, unmotivated, and immature. Whatever the perceived source of the academic difficulties, developmental education and degree-level course instructors alike expressed frustration with students' approach to task, and some seemed at a loss to know how best to teach these students. One factor in planning instruction is the location of developmental education courses within the college structure.

Organization of Developmental Education within Community Colleges

Because developmental education courses rarely count toward degrees, it is not necessary that they be administratively connected to degree-granting programs. In fact, developmental education courses are organized in three ways in community colleges: mainstreaming, in which the courses are housed in academic departments along with the degree-credit courses; centralization, where the courses are taught in a stand-alone developmental education department; and mixed, where one remedial area, such as reading, may be centralized and the others mainstreamed (Shults, 2000; Perin, 2002). There have been strong calls for centralization (Boylan, Bliss, and Bonham, 1997; Roueche and Roueche, 1999; McCabe, 2003) on the grounds that this model makes it more likely that instructors will have a primary interest in teaching basic precollege academic skills rather than seeing it as an unpleasant chore. Also, it is argued that centralization makes counseling and ancillary tutoring more readily available. On the other hand, centralization may result in instructors' isolation from the regular college program and declines in student motivation (Oudenhoven, 2002). Despite the recommendations for centralization, McCabe (2003) reported that most institutions mainstreamed their developmental education courses.

As shown in Table 7.3, twelve of the fifteen National Field Study sites mainstreamed the remedial courses in the academic departments, one site centralized them, and two used a mixed model. Although not reported in previous literature, two forms of mainstreaming were seen at the National Field Study sites. In one, which we call "full mainstreaming," the developmental education courses were administered alongside the degree-credit courses. This organization was found in seven of the twelve sites that used a mainstream model. Five other sites used "partial mainstreaming," in which the remedial courses were taught in the academic departments but coordinated by separate personnel. The main reason for mainstreaming, whether full or partial, seemed to be organizational and budgetary efficiency.

Mainstreamed and Mixed Organization

There was variation in the way each type of model was implemented. SWUCC provides an example of a mainstreamed organization without the benefits of a disciplinary connection. The college had reorganized developmental education several times in recent years. Centralized in the mid-1990s, the reading and writing courses were subsequently moved to a liberal arts department and developmental math to the math department. Although an advantage of mainstreaming is the connection to the regular academic disciplines (Perin, 2002), at SWUCC college-level English was not taught in the department in which the developmental reading and writing classes were now housed. Thus, developmental education was fully mainstreamed in form (in the regular academic departments) but not in content (developmental reading and writing separated from college English). Several reading and writing instructors at the college were unhappy with the mainstreaming in itself because regular academic instructors were not able to meet the needs of remedial students. One instructor explained, "We don't believe English teachers can teach reading. Reading is a very specialized skill, and to help a disabled reader, you have to know a lot of things about what goes on in the brain to bring them forward. So we don't think reading is just low level English. . . . [The English instructors] feel the same way. The faculty wanted the other structure. They don't really want the students. [The] English people don't want them" (Developmental education faculty, SWUCC).

This sentiment was echoed at SWSCC, where remediation was partially mainstreamed under the leadership of a single dean for developmental education. The dean's attempts to centralize remediation had not received college support: "[I]t sounds like an oxymoron but I wanted to create a center of excellence in developmental education and they wouldn't do it here. . . .. They want us to stand for transferring students to great universities; they don't want to stand for a center of excellence for remedial education. In fact, they want to hide from it."

NWSCC and MWSCC used fairly complex partial-mainstreaming approaches. In a "diffusion model," the developmental education courses at NWSCC were operated by one department and the labs by another, which caused management difficulties. At MWSCC, self-paced computer-assisted developmental education courses were taught at five different learning centers. A reading instructor oversaw the delivery of reading instruction in the centers and reported to one administrator regarding curriculum

TABLE 7.3
Organization of Developmental Education by College

Issue	College				
	WRCC	WSCC	WUCC	NWSCC	NWRCC
Mainstreamed	×	×	×		
Mainstreamed, coordinated separately				×	×
Centralized					
Mixed (writing, math in academic departments, reading in separate department)					
ESL and/or adult basic and developmental education in same department				×	×

and another regarding program operation. NESCC, which used a mixed model, experienced frequent change in organization. A developmental education instructor commented, "Some years I think that we're centralizing, and then all of a sudden there are little study centers all over campus."

Although there is overlap in the academic needs of native-speaking and academically underprepared students who are learning English, developmental education and English as a second language (ESL) courses were not always organized together. For example, SWUCC had a large ESL program administered separately from developmental education. Instructors argued that this organization was detrimental to both developmental education and ESL students. At NEUCC, ESL courses were administered in the English department along with the developmental writing courses but separate from the developmental reading and math courses. At SWSCC, the ESL and developmental education courses were in different departments, both of which reported to the same dean.

A mixed model, where one part of developmental education, such as reading, is in a separate department and the other areas are housed in the academic departments, may be more effective at smaller institutions than at larger ones. At NERCC, a relatively small institution, for example, the location of developmental education courses in different departments was not thought to impede communication among the remedial reading and writing instructors, but at NEUCC, a larger institution where developmental reading, writing, and math were taught in different departments, there was little interaction among instructors across the remedial areas, though they often taught the same students.

Centralization of Developmental Education Courses

The only National Field Study site that centralized developmental education, SMCC, had done so since the early 1990s. Although some interviewees argued that

College									
SWSCC	SWUCC	MWRCC	MWUCC	MWSCC	SUCC	SMCC	NERCC	NESCC	NEUCC
	×		×		×		×		
×		×		×					
						×			
								×	×
						×			×

this approach was optimal, several cited the disadvantage that developmental education instructors did not teach college-credit courses and thus were not fully aware of
college standards. Correspondingly, many thought that, if degree-credit instructors
taught remedial courses, it would help them "remember where these kids are coming
from." A member of the SMCC developmental education faculty summarized a
sentiment that instructors should teach both remedial and college-level courses: "The
thing that I see that can be . . . a disadvantage to [centralizing remediation], is if you
do not have people from faculty that will sometimes teach in the [developmental
education] courses or vice versa, there could be a tendency for people to sort of split
themselves and not really pay attention to what needs to go on or what the upper
courses are going to be expecting." In contrast, in the mainstreamed and mixed
models at MWUCC, NESCC, and SWSCC, remedial instructors also taught degree-
credit courses, which, according to an interviewee at NESCC, made them familiar
with the standards that the developmental education students would have to meet at
the college level. This arrangement would promote "seamless vertical connections" to
the college curriculum (McCabe, 2003, p. 68).

A remedial reading instructor at NESCC, which offered developmental reading in
a separate department, however, liked this arrangement because it allowed specialization and more freedom than would be possible if reading courses were taught in a
regular academic department. An administrator echoed the point that centralizing
remediation made it more likely that instructors would have relevant experience.

Besides being the only site to centralize developmental education courses fully,
SMCC was one of only three colleges in the sample (NWSCC and NWRCC were
the others) that offered developmental education and adult basic education (ABE)
courses in the same administrative unit. At SMCC, both areas reported to a separate
dean. ABE students, youth and adults who have not earned a high school diploma,
include both high school dropouts and recent immigrants with limited schooling.
Most community colleges offer ABE in continuing education departments (Morest,

2004), but, because many ABE students hope to enter college, the creation of formal administrative connections between ABE and developmental education would be useful (Reder, 2000). In the current sample, NWSCC and NWRCC, as well as SMCC, combined ABE and developmental education. This type of organization, which provides a bridge for students from continuing education to the degree program, may be a new trend. These types of bridge programs are easier to organize in states such as Washington (where NWSCC and NWRCC are located), in which the ABE programs are administered by and located at community colleges.

Approaches to Instruction

Remedial courses are the most visible form of developmental education in postsecondary education. An administrator at MWSCC noted that the demand for remedial courses was high and represented a significant portion of the departmental budget, and, "depending on how you look at it, either fortunately or unfortunately . . . that is almost the bread and butter of a lot of those particular fields in terms of the number of students involved." The colleges varied widely in terms of criteria for placement in and movement through these courses. At MWSCC, tuition was waived for developmental education if the student was simultaneously enrolled in at least one three-credit, college-level course.

As in the K–12 system, the developmental education field is actively searching for appropriate ways to teach literacy and mathematics to academically underprepared students. Periodicals relevant to developmental education in community colleges are replete with instructional recommendations, a sampling of which is found in Table 7.4. Many of the items are typical of approaches recommended in literature for individuals with learning disabilities in the K–12 system. Also, as with K–12 interventions, the great majority of recommended approaches have not been evaluated in controlled studies.

One issue identified in Table 7.4 pertains to class size, a problem throughout education (Winerip, 2004). At the National Field Study sites, remedial courses were usually capped at a lower number (between eighteen and twenty-eight) than the college-level courses (often thirty-five). Increases in enrollment hindered intentions to keep classes small, as was the case at SWSCC, where, according to an administrator, the ideal class size for developmental reading was twelve but had grown to eighteen.

Following conventional practice, the remedial courses did not bear degree-credit, except at NERCC, where all developmental education credit counted toward the associate degree. This practice was justified by an administrator on the basis of what was perceived as a broad state definition of remediation. In any case, the college

TABLE 7.4
*Examples of Recommendations for Improved Developmental Education Instruction in
the Previous Literature*

General principles

Provide explicit, structured, sequential instruction and prompt feedback (McCusker, 1999; Simpson
and Nist, 2000; Carifio et al., 2001; Smittle, 2003)
Present information in small chunks, related to already-known information (Smittle, 2003)
Use mastery learning (Boylan and Saxon, undated)
Use learner-centered, meaning-based instruction (Grubb et al., 1999; Mohr, 2002)
Link basic skills instruction to applications and content-areas (McGrath and Spear, 1991; Biermann
and Sarinsky, 1994; Commander and Smith, 1995; Boylan and Saxon, 1998; Boylan, 1999;
McCusker, 1999; Minkler, 2002; Snyder, 2002; Smittle, 2003; Illich et al., 2004)
Teach for transfer of skill (Simpson et al., 1997)
Teach metacognition and self-regulation, such as goal setting, critical thinking, transfer across
domains, self-directed learning (Boylan and Saxon, 1998; McCabe and Day, 1998; Nist and
Holshuh, 2000; Nist and Simpson, 2000; Ausburn, 2002; Elder and Paul, 2002; Oudenhoven,
2002; Liff, 2003; Smitle, 2003; Bruch et al., 2004)
Vary teaching methods, select methods based on cognitive theory (Boylan and Saxon, 1998)
Use computers for word processing, electronic communication, web access (McCusker, 1999)
Keep class size to 20 or below (McCusker, 1999)
Align developmental education and college standards, state standards and requirements explicitly;
express high expectations (Boylan and Saxon, 1998; Smittle, 2003)
Allow sufficient time for task completion (Smittle, 2003)
Teach for independent learning (Smittle, 2003)
Incorporate student identity issues in teaching (Reynolds and Bruch 2002)
Promote student-faculty contact and cooperation among students (Smittle, 2003)
Accommodate different learning styles and abilities (Rochford, 2003; Smittle, 2003)
Provide supplementary computer practice, tutoring, mentoring, vocational counseling, LD
advisement (Boylan and Bonham, 1998; Boylan, 1999; Roueche et al., 2001)
Award degree-credit for developmental education courses (McCusker, 1999)
Hire instructors who are credentialed, experienced in special education, and sympathetic to needs
of at-risk students (McCusker, 1999; Roueche and Roueche, 1999; Smittle, 2003)
Evaluate programs and provide professional development (Roueche and Roueche, 1993; Boylan and
Bonham, 1998; Smittle, 2003)

Examples of instructional strategies that demonstrate principles

Explicit instruction, student collaboration, independent learning: reciprocal teaching (Hart and
Speece, 1998)
Teach summarization and composing from sources (Johns, 1985; Selinger, 1995; Maloney, 2003;
Perin et al., 2003)
Provide feedback: specific comments for revision of writing (Carifo et al., 2001)
Incorporate student identity: interpret text in terms of ideology, race, class, gender; use critical
inquiry strategies based on personally-relevant themes (Weiner, 2002; Maloney, 2003)

generated a substantial number of full-time equivalent credits from these courses. In
addition, NESCC offered a transferable, college-credit, remedial math course for
students who had passed the placement test but had weak math skills, and NEUCC
offered a nontransferable degree-credit reading course.

Two major categories emerged in the analysis of the parts of the National Field
Study interviews that pertained to developmental education: course formats (form),
and instruction (content). Remedial course formats include conventional, stand-

alone skills courses and special programs (Simpson et al., 1997). At the National Field Study sites, three formats were found, which we call standard remedial courses, modified remedial courses, and special programs.

Standard Remediation

Standard remedial courses teach word-identification skills, spelling, vocabulary, grammar, reading comprehension and writing strategies, math computation and problem solving, and other basic skills that will sound familiar to elementary school literacy and math teachers. There is an emphasis on drilling (Grubb et al., 1999) by use of generic materials that are unrelated to students' educational and career aspirations, except by accident. Although these courses appear to employ methods that were not effective for underprepared students in their earlier academic history, they are a standard offering. Asked why little attempt was made to integrate remedial instruction to the students' substantive areas of interest, National Field Study interviewees tended to respond either that generic basic skills were needed to learn all subject matter or that the goal of the courses was to prepare students for the first level of college-credit English composition and math rather than specific content courses. Simpson et al. (1997), however, suggested that separating instruction of skills from the content areas to which they will be applied limits the transfer of skill.

The National Field Study sites offered two to four levels each of developmental education course work in reading, writing, and math. There was a large volume of offerings, with multiple sections of each of these six, nine, or twelve classes. The number of levels tended to be stable from year to year, though WUCC reduced the number of levels of writing remediation from five to four on the basis of changes in cutoff scores. SWSCC added a lower-level math course, which conflicted with the administration's agenda of more quickly freeing students to take college-level courses.

Standard courses ran for one semester or quarter, with the contact hours divided between classroom instruction and a required lab component (Boylan, 2002) consisting of computer-based practice or tutoring. The lab component was required in at least one skill area at all sites except MWSCC, which recommended supplementary tutoring in the college learning center. Class periods ranged from fifty minutes to more than two hours. At both SUCC and WUCC, instructors indicated that the time allotted was insufficient to teach all the skills needed, and interviews in many of the sites suggested that teaching students of lower skill levels was a significant challenge. A developmental education instructor at SUCC conveyed some typical concerns: "[D]uring those five hours we have to teach them everything they need to know. And it's really not enough time to truly get them as ready for [freshman composition] or taking a psychology class, or writing a paper for [the government course], or being in a humanities class as I would really like to have them. I would want them to be able to write essays from day one, but I know they can't. I have one or two in each class that could. . . . But I also have the ones [with extremely poor skills]."

The students at the lowest remedial levels appeared to be indistinguishable from those attending ABE, except for the possession of a high school diploma:

> English [level 1] is a catch-all class and the student level there could be 6th grade reading to 9th grade reading and you have students in that class who can't write a single sentence. So it's a very difficult class to teach because the curriculum that you give them, the vocabulary is something they always struggle with. They have very little knowledge and vocabulary, little knowledge in world events and so it's hard to sort of tap out where they are. At English [level 2], your students are more sophisticated, they have a little bit more worldly knowledge, more of them are computer literate, and they are able to formulate sentences and paragraphs a little better. But still there are students in there who are on the bottom level and have been sort of pushed up from [level 1] (Developmental Education Faculty, WUCC)

At MWUCC, students with extremely low test scores were assigned to a preremedial introductory program.

Modified Remediation

Table 7.5 identifies thirteen different modifications of the standard developmental education course format at the National Field Study sites: self-paced remediation, personalized remediation, tutor-based remediation, on-line remediation, accelerated remediation, intensive summer remediation, contextualized remediation, combined reading-writing remediation, combined remedial and college English, study-skills courses, off-site remediation, alternation of instruction and application, and instruction in a quarterly rather than semester schedule. In some cases, both the standard and modified forms of instruction were offered, whereas in others all of the courses were in modified form.

Remedial math students at WUCC were offered a choice between a standard developmental math course and a self-paced open-entry, open-exit course provided in a specialized math lab. Two-thirds of the students opted for the self-paced instruction. Although WUCC had not evaluated the effectiveness of the course, previous research in a college for underprepared students in Minnesota showed that math

TABLE 7.5
Modified Instructional Services and Special Programs, by College

	College				
Type of Service	WRCC	WSCC	WUCC	NWSCC	NWRCC
Modified developmental education courses:					
Self-paced remediation			×		
Tutor-based remediation					
On-line remediation					
Accelerated remediation					
Intensive summer remediation					
Contextualized remediation					
Personalized remediation					
Combined reading-writing remediation					
Combined remedial and college English					
Study-skills courses					
Off-site remedial courses					
Semester rather than quarterly schedule					
Special programs:					
"Developmental Learning Community" clusters reading, writing, and math courses for students who test into all three areas					
"ESL Learning Community" clusters reading, writing, and ESL courses for students with limited English proficiency and remedial needs				×	
"Special Program" clusters developmental reading and writing courses for students at grade levels 5.6–10				×	
"Achievement Program" for students who have not declared a major and/or test low in all three remedial areas, largest program in the college					
"Freshman Program:" 5-week modules for low-scoring entrants					
"Success Program" for students whose scores are close to level needed to enter 4-year college, conditionally accepted to 4-year college					
"Summer Program:" Free summer remedial program initially intended for students who have failed course during academic year but open to all					
"Introductory Program:" reading, writing, math and ESL for students who score too low for remediation, connected to remedial program, includes vocational education and counseling					

skills did not improve in computer-based math instruction compared to traditional math lectures, but satisfaction and persistence were higher for the computer instruction (Kinney, 2001).

At SUCC the developmental math courses followed a format of self-paced and small-group work in class, supplemented by tutoring during the lab hours. Students could take the state test for exit from remediation when they were ready. An administrator expressed that self-paced instruction was appropriate for math but low motivation would limit its feasibility in the reading and writing areas. In light of students'

College									
SWSCC	SWUCC	MWRCC	MWUCC	MWSCC	SUCC	SMCC	NERCC	NESCC	NEUCC
					×				
×									
×									×
×	×			×			×		×
							×	×	×
		×			×				
		× ×							
		×	×						
									×
×		×						×	
							×	×	
				×					
		×							
								×	
									×
									×
									×
			×						

difficulties with time management and self-discipline, it seems likely that students would need preparation in monitoring, evaluating, and regulating their learning processes (Garrison, 1997) to benefit fully from self-directed learning. Research in an urban occupational education technology center in Oklahoma indicated that self-paced, computer-assisted learning was more effective for adults than for high school students (Ausburn, 2002). Adding tutoring to self-paced instruction may help overcome the younger students' difficulty. Another modification that was found in the National Field Study was a few personalized remedial courses at MWSCC that combined tutoring and self-paced computer-assisted learning in the college learning center.

Tutor-based remediation was available at SWSCC for students who scored within ten points of passing the state placement exam and was offered in response to students' requests for test preparation. Individualized and group tutoring was provided by three full-time professional tutors. Although this option was not widely advertised, demand was so great that the tutors were overwhelmed. Another modification of standard remediation was found in on-line math and study-skills courses at SWSCC and NEUCC. At NEUCC the study-skills course was selected as the first on-line option when venturing into the area of distance learning. The concerns expressed above regarding self-paced instruction apply equally to the on-line options.

Five of the colleges (SWUCC, MWSCC, NEUCC, NESCC, and NERCC) provided accelerated remedial courses. At SWUCC, students had a choice between half- and full-semester-long remedial reading courses. A student interviewee relayed that he had been told by a counselor that he was "smart enough" to take the shorter course. MWSCC offered a few accelerated remedial courses for which there was good demand, though an interviewee suggested that they were ineffective because the students lacked self-discipline. NEUCC provided a separately coordinated, special program of five-week developmental math and writing modules to hasten the preparation of students for the college curriculum.

Accelerated remedial instruction was also found in the form of intensive summer remedial courses at the three New York sites. The summer courses at NESCC lasted for two weeks and were designed for new students. An older student appreciated these classes because they had helped with skills and provided an orientation to the college. NEUCC provided five-week-long summer remedial courses mainly intended for students who had failed a remedial course, but open to all. The summer courses at NERCC also lasted five weeks, but some of the developmental math instructors at NERCC, voicing the same concerns about insufficient time noted above, argued that the courses were too demanding and advised their students not to take them. WUCC was asked by the district to provide a fast-track remedial option, but administrators resisted and an instructor who had tried to reduce the length of his course from eighteen to fifteen weeks was unable to find classroom space. Corroborating the concern expressed at MWSCC noted above, a member of the developmental education faculty at SWUCC doubted the feasibility of accelerating remediation because of the seriousness of students' academic difficulties:

> [A] lot of [SWUCC administrators and instructors] really don't understand what we are doing, and I think that also applies to our legislatures. They really don't have an idea of

the challenges we face when we get students who are reading and writing on a sixth, seventh grade level . . . they are not educators. So they don't have that background, and they are concerned primarily, from what I can tell, with the university systems in Texas, who get far less of these kinds of students than we do . . . what they fail to understand is that the students are going to need a lot of time to overcome their bad educational experiences, the older you get, the harder it is to learn how to read and write. And they don't understand that you want to push these students through, but these are probably the wrong students to fast track.

Another modification of the standard remedial offering was contextualized instruction, in which reading, writing or math skills were directly linked to the subject matter in the disciplines, compatible with Simpson et al.'s (1997) recommendation that remediation be connected to subject matter. Two kinds of contextualized courses were found at the National Field Study sites, akin to models of academic-occupational integration in community college career programs (Perin, 2001): developmental education courses that were infused with content from the disciplines, called "applied academics" in career programs, and remedial courses that are paired with credit-level content-area courses, a type of learning community. For the current purpose of identifying examples of modification of standard remediation, learning communities can be seen as instances of contextualized learning. A barrier to pairing developmental with credit-bearing courses and thus to providing contextualized learning in this format is that many of the discipline-area courses apply remedial or college-English prerequisites. Thus, the content-area courses with which developmental education courses are paired tend to be introductory general education courses.

Two examples of applied academics were identified. One was a developmental writing course for SUCC nursing aspirants that included technical writing and preparation of documentation for the health care profession. The other was a course at MWRCC that was based on a Midwestern university college athlete program comprising five weeks of skills instruction followed by five weeks of application of the skills to subjects such as criminal justice.

Four of the fifteen sites offered learning communities that involved developmental education (Table 7.5). The largest number was found at WSCC, where there were six learning communities that paired a developmental education course with a college-credit course in media or the health sciences. An instructor stated that, in the linked developmental education courses, "the readings are flavored with issues related to that field." This instructor went on to explain that, although in theory linked to a discipline area course, there was no faculty collaboration or curriculum alignment, so the developmental courses resembled the applied academics courses described above.

Similar to WSCC, SWSCC's learning communities paired developmental writing with history, reading with psychology, and ESL reading with humanities. The ESL reading instructor attended the humanities course to identify reading skills that needed attention. An interviewee indicated that linkage had been effective but the effort was not expanded because not enough instructors were interested in participating, possibly because of increased workload (Boylan, 2002).

SWUCC used learning communities that pair remedial with college-level courses as a retention strategy for upper-level developmental education students: "[W]hen . . . they're getting a little antsy, they're really tired of the developmental stuff, we have paired courses. We have certain courses that we will let them take their developmental along with the paired course in order to keep them in college and have them start earning college credit toward their degree" (Administrator, SWUCC). SWUCC's learning communities included three-course clusters of developmental writing, study skills, and college composition; developmental reading, history, and psychology; and also a reading course for students who had passed the writing portion of the state skills test, paired with history. In the latter, similar to the ESL example from WSCC, the reading teacher sat in on the history class and taught reading skills in her class based on the history textbook. In a learning community for education majors only, a developmental writing course was paired with a childhood education course.

Finally, MWSCC offered one learning community involving developmental education, which paired remedial reading with a human anatomy course. There was interest in expanding this effort, and the college was studying the effectiveness of the paired courses. Two other National Field Study sites had tried unsuccessfully to incorporate developmental education into their learning communities. WUCC was unable to recruit students to the designated courses and at the time of the site visit was offering learning communities consisting only of pairings of college English with courses in humanities and anthropology for students in an honors program. Similarly, WRCC had tried to create learning communities to address writing problems but was unable to recruit enough students. WUCC had also attempted to pair courses such as automotive technology and vocational math with college English but abandoned the attempt because they were a "nightmare to schedule."

As mentioned above, remediation is conventionally provided separately for reading, writing, and math. Although academic assignments at the college level integrate reading and writing skills (Perin, Keselman, and Monopoli, 2003), they are often taught separately in developmental education, as was the case in most of the colleges visited. Exceptions were found at MWRCC, which offered a combined reading-writing developmental education course for the lowest-scoring students, and MWUCC, which offered several seven-hour combined options. Instructors at

WUCC who were interested in offering a four-credit reading-writing remedial course, however, met bureaucratic obstacles in the college district.

Similarly, an administrator at NEUCC had been interested in combining reading and writing instruction but decided that it was not feasible:

> [I] never understood [why reading and writing are taught separately] . . . except for political reasons of course . . . part of what I think has happened is that writing is easily legitimized, you might say, by the English people. . . . But reading isn't. Reading is seen as really a remedial skill . . . remedial at least at the college level . . . and so they really haven't legitimized it. The truth of the matter is that as we move toward this [rising junior] test, it has become a little bit clearer that the two ought to be joined. But I'm not sure I want to take on that political battle right now . . . [but] teaching in a way that combined [reading and writing] would maximize the opportunity to pass.

The same institution, however, offered a modified remedial course that combined college-credit and developmental English, a seven-hour offering for students with borderline scores on the writing portion of the placement test. Students could retake the test twice during the semester and, if they passed, continue with and receive credit for college-level English. Institutional data showed that this modification yielded high pass rates.

Among the developmental reading courses, MWRCC, NESCC, and SWSCC offered study-skills courses to teach students general learning strategies and textbook-reading skills. SWSCC's version was a free study-skills course open both to students and the community, including parents. Some of the classes were specifically for nonnative English speakers.

Further modifications of standard remediation were some off-site remedial courses that NERCC taught in the local prison and that NESCC provided for local industry. A final remedial modification involved scheduling: at MWSCC, although the college-credit courses were scheduled quarterly, the remedial courses were taught in semesters because instructors had found that the students were unable to master all required skills with a college quarter. Plans to increase the use of computer-assisted remediation and to subcontract remediation were rejected at MWSCC. As an administrator explained, "[W]hen a third of your incoming, traditional-age students or more require some form of remediation, farming that out for a community college to me seems to be problematic."

The majority of the thirteen modifications of standard remediation functioned either as solutions to learning difficulties or to accelerate exit from remediation. It was beyond the scope of the study to ascertain the effectiveness of these options, but an evaluation would be useful in the future.

Special Programs

As shown in Table 7.5, eight special developmental education programs were identified at six sites: the Developmental Learning Community at MWRCC; the ESL Learning Community and Special Program at NWSCC; the Special Program at NWSCC; the Achievement Program at NESCC; the Freshman, Success, and Summer Programs at NEUCC; and the Introductory Program at MWUCC (all fictitious names). These programs reflect community colleges' capacity to attend to students' specific needs. Nowhere else in higher education does one see so many customized programs within a single concentration. Several of the programs were designed for the lowest-functioning remedial students.

The special programs at MWRCC, NWSCC, and NESCC were learning communities that were, however, different from the contextualized course pairings already described; in the special programs, the learning communities comprised clusters of remedial courses but no discipline-area courses. Learning communities are considered extremely beneficial in postsecondary education in providing opportunities for student bonding and mutual support (Gabelnick, MacGregor, Matthews, and Smith, 1990; Tinto, 1997; Boylan, 2002), as well as faculty collaboration and curriculum alignment (Grubb et al., 1999). Positive outcomes reported for community college developmental education students include increased satisfaction, retention, performance, and completion rates (Boylan, 2002; Raftery and VanWagoner, 2002; Bloom and Sommo, 1995).

The Developmental Learning Community at MWRCC was a cluster of remedial reading, writing, and math courses for students who tested into all three remedial areas. Similarly, the ESL Learning Community at NWSCC was a set of reading, writing, and ESL courses for students who entered the college with limited English-language proficiency as well as remedial needs. In these two learning communities, the students formed cohorts and were block-scheduled in the set of courses.

At NWSCC, many students began their developmental education work in the Special Program in the English department, designed for a maximum of sixty-six students who read on grade levels 5.6 to 10. (Students who scored in this range but passed a writing sample were placed in a standard, higher-level remedial class. Those scoring below 5.6 were placed in ABE.) The Special Program was a two-hour block of reading and writing courses and a lab component for a total of eleven to twelve institutional (nondegree) credits. After taking a standardized reading test and a locally developed writing test on the first day of class, the sixty-six students were divided into three classes of twenty-two students each, corresponding to low, medium, and high test scores. On the last day of class, students retook both tests and had to pass both to place out of the Special Program. At this point they could proceed to a standard developmental writing course in which subsequently they had to earn a B or better to place into college-level English. The English composition instructors expected the remedial completers to write full sentences and apply correct grammar and paragraphing. Corroborating the experiences of the allied health instructors cited above, however, a remedial instructor described "a mismatch" between the English composition course and the type of writing required in the health sciences courses. According to an NWSCC administrator, assigning the lower-scoring individuals to the special program protected the stronger students in other classes from a slow pace of instruction: "[T]here's a certain group who is never going to get to that level [i.e. college]. They end up in a lot of community college classes that go too fast for them, but we're totally open enrollment so they're in the classes that do not meet their needs. Often because they're there, it slows down the class . . . the teachers are not trained to teach people who have special needs like that. It's just not a good situation for everybody. So you take that and you create a situation that works for this special group and everyone is happy."

The Achievement Program at NESCC was designed for students who needed work in all three skills areas and were, according to a developmental education instructor, in degree programs "by the skin of their teeth." The special program was also for students who had not decided on a major or had performed poorly in a career degree program such as health. The Achievement Program was the largest program at NESCC, enrolling 1,800 of the college's 9,304 students. Academic advisors worked with the students to formulate a program of study and monitored their progress.

NEUCC offered three different special programs for developmental education students, the Success Program, Summer Program, and Freshman Program, each administered by different personnel. The Success Program was designed to facilitate the entry to a four-year college of students who had low placement scores. These students were counted as NEUCC students but were conditionally accepted by a senior college in the same system. The Summer Program provided developmental education courses to approximately 1,200 students of the college's 6,928 students who were required to attend because they had failed a remedial course during the academic year. The Freshman Program provided the fast-track modules to prepare students for college-level courses.

The seventh special program identified in the National Field Study was the Introductory Program at MWUCC, which provided twenty hours of skills classes, tutoring, vocational education, counseling, and ESL instruction to 350 of the college's total 8,147 students each semester. Participants tested at the seventh-grade level or below in reading, writing, or math, levels considered too low for the developmental education.

The instructors worked closely with the regular English faculty (remediation was mainstreamed at MWUCC). The program director stated that remediation at low skill levels was a critical first step toward workforce preparation but noted that individuals who tested into the program sometimes had a rude awakening when they realized how long it would be before they could start taking college-level courses.

Three of the National Field Study institutions—SWSCC, MWRCC, and NEUCC—stood out for the sheer number of remedial options. SWSCC and MWRCC each offered five different forms of remediation, including the standard courses. NEUCC also offered five types of remediation in addition to its three different special programs. Although not a current objective, the efficiency and clarity of multiple offerings would be worth exploring in future research.

Effectiveness of Developmental Education Courses
Previous Research

A survey conducted early in the days of open admissions (Roueche, 1968, cited in Simpson et al., 1997) found that 90% of students failed or dropped out of remedial courses; now, more than thirty years later, retention and graduation rates of developmental education students are still low (Lundell and Higbee, 2000), which suggests a long-lasting problem in the effectiveness of developmental education. At the same time, some authors (Boylan, 2002; Roueche, Ely, and Roueche, 2001) have concluded that remediation is effective under some circumstances. The differing conclusions may stem from differences in the methodology used to evaluate developmental education. There are four kinds of reports about effectiveness. First is literature pointing to a lack of systematic data or suggesting that remediation is ineffective, on the basis of anecdotal or survey evidence (Johnson, 1996; Crowe, 1998; Grubb et al., 1999); second is a national study conducted in the early 1990s; third are descriptions of outcomes within single institutions; and fourth are a small number of rigorous quantitative evaluations that use random assignment and sophisticated control group methodologies.

The national study was carried out by Boylan and colleagues (Boylan and Bonham, 1992; Boylan, Bonham, and Bliss, 1994b; Boylan, Bliss, and Bonham, 1997). Developmental education data were gathered from 150 four-year research universities and community and technical colleges. First-semester grade point averages (GPAs), cumulative GPAs, developmental course-pass rates, and retention (expressed as graduation or still attending at the five and a half-year point) were compared as a function of the presence of absence of developmental education centralization, mandatory assessment, mandatory placement, tutoring, tutor training, advisement or counseling, and program evaluation. These studies yielded several observations about remedial education in community colleges. Within the community colleges, retention and remedial English pass rates were higher for students in centralized programs. Remedial placement also showed measurable benefits: retention rates and remedial math and English pass rates were higher for students when remedial placement was mandatory. In a similar vein, first-term GPA and remedial English pass rates were higher in programs where tutoring was available, remedial math pass rates were higher in programs where counseling and advisement was available, and retention and remedial English and math pass rates were higher in programs that engaged in evaluation. Cumulative GPA was not systematically related to any of the input variables within the community colleges.

It is difficult to draw definitive conclusions from this national study because details of the methodology are sketchy. For example, Boylan et al. stated that the institutions were selected by use of a "systematic circular sampling procedure" (1994b, p.1), but details of the procedure and response rate per institutional type were not provided. Although the authors state that the "subsamples were stratified by institutional type and geographic region to insure representativeness," details were not provided. At each institution, a "project liaison" completed a survey and collected information requested by the investigator. The role of this individual in the college, what steps were taken to ensure objectivity of reporting, and how the information provided was categorized by the research team were not reported. A random sample of 6,000 developmental education students was identified for the purpose of transcript analysis, but, again, details are not provided on how this was accomplished and whether the sample was representative in proportion to institutional type.

Boylan and Bonham (1992) reported that 83% of students who completed remedial reading went on to pass a social science class, 92% who passed remedial writing went on to pass college-level English, and 77% who passed remedial math went on to pass college-level math (in each case with a grade of C or better). The number of remedial students who failed or dropped out of the remedial courses, however, was not reported. Further, the study's lack of random assignment or other controls for differences in student characteristics across programs limits conclusions about effectiveness (Grubb et al., 2000; Dougherty, 2002).

The third source of information about program effectiveness, descriptions of outcomes within single institutions, result from expert review, where cases considered exemplary are described by highly respected individuals in the field. In this tradition, a series of program descriptions provided by Roueche and McCabe and colleagues (Roueche, 1968; Roueche and Roueche, 1993, 1999; McCabe and Day, 1998; McCabe, 2000; Roueche, Ely and Roueche, 2001) suggest that effective developmental education programs have many of the characteristics listed in Table 7.5: for example, they not only target academic skills, but also foster social and emotional development, provide support services such as study-skills courses, tutoring, counseling, and advisement, provide ongoing student assessment, and receive a high level of institutional support. Roueche and Roueche (1993) emphasized the need for structured courses and also argued that credit should be given for remedial course work. They further suggested that programs are more effective when they tailor length and format of courses to student needs.

Several authors have presented the developmental education program at the Community College of Denver (CCD) as a success. The program incorporated many of the best practices described above (Crespin, 2004). Longitudinal data indicated that students who started college in remedial courses had first-semester performance, retention, graduation, and transfer rates similar to those of students who started in credit courses (McCabe and Day, 1998; McClenney and Flores, 1998; Hebel, 1999; Rouech, Ely, and Rouech, 2001; Roueche and Roueche, 2001). Although these are encouraging findings, the reports on this very influential case do not provide enough details to evaluate the validity of the results. Which students were included in the two samples? How large were the samples? How long were they tracked, and what were the rates of retention, graduation, and transfer? How did the characteristics of the two groups of students compare? How was the need for remediation assessed? Were all students who were advised to enroll in remediation required to do so, or were some students with low academic skills still allowed to bypass remediation? Was there attrition between assessment and initial enrollment? Without this type of information, the reader does not know whether the two groups were comparable, so it is difficult to differentiate between the possible effects of differences in initial characteristics from the effects of the program.

The type of degree that academically underprepared students pursue may also be related to developmental education outcomes. Nationally, many occupational programs do not require initial assessment or remediation, and may not require developmental education course work even for students who fail the assessments. Further, occupational courses tend to have lower completion rates than academic courses (Alfonso, Bailey, and Scott, 2005). Without knowing whether developmental education enrollees and students who did not take remedial courses aspired to the same college degrees, it is difficult to draw conclusions about the effectiveness of CCD's developmental education program. Moreover, evidence gathered from the National Field Study sites indicates that many colleges circumvent placement rules and guidelines, thereby allowing many low-skilled students into college-level courses (Perin, 2006). The CCD research does not report whether all students scoring below the college's cutoff score on the initial placement test were mandated to attend developmental education courses. Although the results from the CCD case are encouraging, for the reasons just stated, more analysis is needed to determine whether the conclusions would hold up under a more comprehensive and rigorous methodology.

Another methodological problem in the expert panel studies is the lack of information on criteria for site selection or indicators of effectiveness. For example, McCabe and Day (1998) stated that their programs had "80% success levels" in English, reading, and math, and 90% of the students in the programs had GPAs of 2.0 or better. Information concerning the nature of the courses—for example whether they were precollege or college-credit classes—was not provided. Also, in McCabe and Day's description, course performance for remedial students was described as equal to or better than that for nonremedial students, and retention rates were "as high as 82 percent" (p. 25), but neither course performance nor retention was defined.

The fourth type of research on remediation includes a small number of rigorous quantitative studies. A study by Bettinger and Long (2004) is of interest because it uses a statistical technique designed to differentiate between the effects of initial characteristics and the impact of the program itself, though, unfortunately for the purpose of understanding community colleges, the study was restricted to four-year institutions. The study used a longitudinal student record data set from Ohio and focused on a large sample of first-time, full-time students of traditional age enrolled in the states' nonselective public four-year colleges in the fall of 1998. The results suggest that students placed in remediation are more likely to withdraw from college, but they also indicate that participation in remedial courses does not seem to decrease the likelihood of transferring to more selective institutions or attaining a bachelor degree. The growing availability of state longitudinal unit record data sets will make it possible to carry out this type of analysis on samples of community college students.

Finally, in 2003, MDRC, a nonprofit research organization, conducted the first random assignment evaluation of the community college remediation model. The research evaluated learning communities for full-time students with low placement scores. The communities were comprised of cohorts of about twenty-five students who took three first-semester courses together: English (usually at the remedial level), a course on another academic subject, and a one-credit freshman-orientation course. The students received extra counseling, tutoring, and vouchers to purchase books. Students who applied for the learning communities were randomly assigned to a community or to a control group. Members of the control group received the remediation services available to all students. One year after enrollment, the students in the learning communities were twice as likely to have completed their remedial English requirements as students in the control group (Bloom and Sommo, 2005).

The random assignment process guaranteed that there were no systematic differences between the experimental and control groups. These findings support the findings of Kane et al. (2004), mentioned earlier in this chapter, and suggest that academically underprepared students require a full range of instructional and support services. Although there are some promising beginnings, little systematic research is available regarding the effectiveness of community college remediation as it is conventionally offered. With respect to the two more rigorous studies cited above, one was focused on students in four-year colleges and the other tested a very specific type of remediation program on one campus. Pending further information, the conclusions of the available research on remediation are best treated as hypotheses that can provide a useful basis for future evaluation research. A rigorous, well-reported, replicable, peer-reviewed national study of the effectiveness of community college remedial programs remains to be conducted. Such research would need to seek interactions between program components, student characteristics, and instructional quality.

Indicators of Effectiveness of Developmental Education Courses at National Field Study Sites

The most common measures of developmental education outcomes are retention and graduation rates, though, following from the lack of agreement on college entry standards mentioned earlier, there is little consensus on what levels of retention or graduation are needed to demonstrate remedial effectiveness (Lundell and Higbee, 2000). Despite the lack of common metrics, a look at performance data on commonly used institutional measures provides the beginning of an understanding of remedial effectiveness.

The National Field Study sites used six indicators that relate to the effectiveness of developmental education: (1) remedial completion; (2) return following semester; (3) remedial dropout; (4) movement to higher-level courses, which includes advancement to both higher remedial levels and college-level courses; (5) test scores and grades; and (6) college performance and graduation. Because institutional data were not readily available and definitions of the variables were sometimes unclear, and an evaluation of remediation was beyond the scope of the study, the findings on remedial effectiveness must be considered preliminary.

Remedial completion rates, defined as exit from remediation according to institutional criteria, were available for nine of the fifteen sites. As shown in Table 7.6, the completion rates ranged from 47% to 92%. The completion data are based on students who persisted in the courses. Because they persist through the remedial courses in which they are placed, completion rates indicate the extent to which they are able to meet criteria for exit from remediation, such as passing an exam. Evidently, dropouts were excluded from these data.

The two institutions that reported on the second indicator—proportions of remedial students who returned to the college the subsequent semester—showed similar outcomes. At SWSCC, 65% of remedial freshmen, compared to 73% of nonremedial freshmen, returned. At MWRCC, 65% of remedial math students returned, compared to 74% of the remedial writing students. Fewer writing students returned than in the past (81%).

The third indicator—remedial dropout—is defined as the number of students who are no longer attending the class at the end of the semester, as a proportion of the initial enrollments. Dropout rates were 25%–50% for three of the four institutions that reported this information. The fourth institution, SWUCC, showed better outcomes, for example, a dropout rate of 24% for full-time remedial students. At the time of the study, the state of Texas, in which SWUCC is located, required students to drop all courses if they dropped a remedial course (Perin, 2006). One must keep in mind that dropout does not always signify negative outcomes. For example, at both NEUCC and WUCC some of the dropouts had left in good academic standing. At the same time, lower-performing students at SUCC showed higher attrition, which corroborates previous research showing poorer outcomes for lower-skilled students (Adelman, 1996). Interventions at NESCC and WUCC including class rescheduling and curriculum revision were reported to be effective in stemming dropout.

Information concerning remedial students' move to a higher-level course, the fourth indicator, was reported by all of the California sites, where placement is voluntary. The rates were low. The best figure was at WUCC, where 32% of the remedial English students proceeded to a higher-level course. At this institution, however, an interviewee suggested that some of the writing students were permitted to advance to a higher level despite poor skills.

Two of the Illinois institutions provided information on the fifth indicator, test scores and grades. At MWRCC, the ability to pass remedial writing on the first attempt was a strong predictor of persistence in the college. A curious finding was reported at MWSCC, where an institutional study found that reading scores were higher when students entered the college than when they had completed -sixty to ninety credits.

Six sites reported varying types of information and outcomes on the final indicator, performance and graduation. Little numerical information was available, and interview testimony was mixed. At SUCC, the academic performance of remedial completers was said to be as good as that for students who entered the college with

TABLE 7.6
Outcomes by Measure and College

Outcome Measure	College						
	WRCC	WSCC	WUCC	NWSCC	NWRCC	SWSCC	SWUCC
Percent remedial completion (different years, some state and some institutional data)	64	54	54	74–81	60	76–92[1] (78 CR; 76 HM; 92 LR)	47–79[1] (67 CR; 47 HW; 79 LW)
Percent returning subsequent semester	—	—	—	—	—	65 RF; 73 NF	—
Percent remedial dropout	—	50 M	—	—	—	—	76 FS; 62 MS; 48 PS
Percent moving to higher level courses	15 E 28 M	21 E 26 M	32 E 17 M	—	—	—	—
Test scores and grades	—	—	—	—	—	—	—
College performance and graduation	—	—	Recent revision of higher-level math course resulted in better performance in college math	—	—	—	—

| College | | | | | | | |
MWRCC	MWUCC	MWSCC	SUCC	SMCC	NERCC	NESCC	NEUCC
—[2]	—	49–72[1] (72 CR; 49 BM; 72 HW)	28–68 (68 R; 60 W; 28 M)	—	—	—	—
65 M; 74 W[3]	—	—	—	—	—	—	—
—	25–35	50	—	—	—	—	—
—	—	—	—	Reduction in dropout resulting from improved registration and attendance-monitoring	—	—	—
71% who pass developmental writing course on first attempt are still in the college one year later, compared to 34% of those who did not pass on first attempt	—	Entering students have higher reading scores than those at 60–90 credit mark	—	—	—	—	—
67% of students who test into remedial writing but opt not to take it fail college composition	Students who test into developmental writing but do not need developmental reading more likely to graduate	—	Remedial completers do as well in college program as non-remedial students	Students who start in remediation or ESL have lower chance of graduating	Students who take developmental education better prepared for college-level work	—	Remedial completers better prepared than high school graduates who place in the college program; remediation seems effective based on time spent in remediation and ability of completers to meet college-level academic demands

TABLE 7.6 *continued*

TABLE 7.6
Continued

| | College | | | | | | |
Outcome Measure	WRCC	WSCC	WUCC	NWSCC	NWRCC	SWSCC	SWUCC
Emerging Issues	—	—	Some lower level writing students advance to next level despite poor skills	a. Some low-skilled students pass college-level courses without remediation b. English courses do not prepare students for writing at college level	—	Need for appropriate outcome measures	a. Reasons for remedial dropout: immaturity, demanding schedules, social problems b. Need for appropriate outcome measures

NOTES: E=English; M=Math; R=Reading; W=Writing; CR=College credit course completion; HM=Higher level math; BM=Higher/lower levels of math; LR=Lower level reading; HW=Higher level writing; LW=lower level writing; RF=Remedial freshman; NF=Non-remedial fareshman; FS=Full-time remedial students; MS=Remedial student taking 6–11 credits; PS=Remedial student taking <6 credits
1. Depending on skills area
2. Dashes indicate information not provided by Site
3. Down from 81%

higher skills, echoing claims made by Roueche, Ely, and Roueche (2001) and Boylan et al. (1997). At NEUCC the performance of remedial completers was characterized as better than that of initially higher-skilled students; however, it was reported at SMCC that students who began their studies in remediation or ESL had less chance of graduating. At both MWRCC and NERCC, performance was better for initially low-skilled students who opted for remedial classes, compared to similar students who decided to skip developmental education.

In summary, the colleges had different ways of measuring outcomes for developmental education students. The data provided by the sites do not necessarily represent the whole compendium of measures they used; rather, it appeared that the institutions submitted to us only the information that was readily available. The lack of available data suggests that the measurement of developmental education outcomes was not a high-priority objective in most of the institutions. On the basis of the spotty data available, there were a sufficient number of negative results to raise alarm about the effectiveness of remedial courses. Many low-skilled students did not complete a remedial sequence, dropped out of remedial courses, or did not move to higher level courses. In addition, remedial math performance was particularly poor, and reports were mixed concerning the ability of remedial students to earn degrees.

College							
MWRCC	MWUCC	MWSCC	SUCC	SMCC	NERCC	NESCC	NEUCC
High persistence rate may mask sporadic attendance	Graduation outcomes hard to determine because students in the college transfer to four-year as soon as they can without earning associates degree	a. English courses do not prepare students for writing at college level b. Reasons for remedial dropout: immaturity, demanding schedules, social problems c. Effectiveness defined as readiness for transfer program, data not available	a. Highest attrition rates in lower level remedial courses b. Students who take optional 3-credit freshman orientation show better persistence rates but state reluctant to add credits to program	State indicator of effectiveness: number of students who pass course, move to higher level and pass that course, tracking begun, data not available	—	a. Completion of math more difficult than completion of reading or writing remediation b. College changed schedule and slowed instruction to reduce dropout rate from math	20% dropouts left in good standing, personal reasons

Discussion and Emerging Questions

As with national estimates, there were large numbers of academically under-prepared students at the National Field Study sites but no major increases in recent years. Although the small size of the current sample prevents definitive conclusions, it is notable that the proportion of underprepared students was not systematically related to geographic region or institutional placement policy. Further, the levels of preparedness were fairly similar in colleges in rural, suburban, and urban locations, a pattern different from that reported by Shults (2000). A question for future research is whether the populations served in the various locations are becoming more similar.

Developmental education course enrollments underestimated the need for reading, writing, and math skills. Academic skills difficulties interfered with teaching and learning in college-credit courses regardless of placement policy. The presence of academically underprepared students in degree-credit classrooms meant that the problem extended beyond developmental education and spilled out to the whole college.

With regard to the organization of developmental education courses, the model used by most of the National Field Study colleges did not resemble the recommendation made in the literature that developmental education be centralized in separate departments. Among the large majority of sites that integrated the courses in the regular academic programs (mainstreaming model), however, the varied approaches and recent changes reported suggested that an optimal method of organizing developmental education had not been found. Further, one change that was not reported but nevertheless may be expected in the future concerns the teaching of academically underprepared students who are also not fluent in English. Despite the overlapping needs of English language learners and language-proficient underprepared students reported by National Field Study interviewees, ESL and developmental education were rarely organized in same department. On the basis of projected immigration patterns, the colleges may need to overcome existing internal political barriers and organize developmental education and ESL together rather than treating them as two different services. As the two populations come to resemble each other even more than they already do, developmental education instructors will need professional development in methods for teaching linguistically diverse students and ESL instructors will need to increase their ability to teach basic academic skills.

Developmental education curriculum and instruction took many forms. Although many of the classes used traditional teacher-centered generic drills in reading, writing, and math, modifications were numerous. Further, some of the colleges were "remediation-heavy" in offering multiple remedial services. None of the fifteen institutions in the sample had evaluated the effectiveness of any of the new approaches. The interest in speeding up remediation indicates that the colleges were trying to balance the improvement of skill with retention of at-risk students. The attempt to accelerate remedial exit appears to be part of a larger trend to soften placement policy (Perin, 2006). A contradiction is noted between the desire to speed up remediation and reports in both the National Field Study interviews and previous research that remedial students needed more time on task. If remediation is more than preparation for placement tests, it is likely that acceleration of remediation will not result in a student body that is better prepared for the reading comprehension, writing, and math demands of college-credit courses.

The organizational and instructional heterogeneity across the National Field Study sites may be interpreted as a struggle to find ways of teaching a challenging population. This pattern, also seen in the developmental education literature (summarized in Table 7.4), suggests that community colleges have not reached consensus on the characteristics of satisfactory methods to teach basic reading, writing, and math skills.

The measures used to determine developmental education outcomes also varied widely. Overall, completion rates were low, regardless of skill area and placement policy. Among the sites reporting, dropout rates were high and movement to higher level courses was low. Several sites implemented interventions that had positive ef-

fects on attrition. Although reasons for attrition included personal and social difficulties, some of the dropout may also have resulted from student perceptions that
their academic needs were not being met. As in previous research, National Field
Study remedial completers seemed capable of achievement in the college program,
but this population included only a fraction of students who began remediation. This
finding raises a central methodological question: should effectiveness be measured by
studying outcomes of what seems to be a small number of completers or that of all
enrollees?

Despite the centrality of the remedial mission, systematic evaluation studies are
rare. The indications of low effectiveness found in this study make rigorous evaluation particularly urgent. Numerous questions emerging from this qualitative case
study could usefully be incorporated into such an evaluation. Controlled research is
needed to determine outcomes among three groups: remedial completers, remedial
dropouts, and adequately prepared college entrants. Differential use of support services (e.g., counseling and tutoring) should be folded into the research to determine
their effects on academic outcomes. It is also important to confirm the accuracy of
the placement tests currently used to determine readiness for the college curriculum
(Perin, 2006).

The different course modifications and programs in progress at the sites should be
studied to learn which of the initiatives is effective for which populations and to what
extent some of the options may be inefficient duplications. In particular, the effectiveness of accelerated remedial instruction needs attention, because several interviewees
doubted its appropriateness. Also of special interest would be outcomes of summer
immersion programs for recent high school graduates, such as at NEUCC, the use of
which appears to be growing (Arenson, 2004). Similarly, the ability of students of
different skills, ages, and backgrounds to benefit from self-paced versus traditional
math remediation should be studied.

The value of incorporating the content and skills from the discipline areas should
be studied. A primary issue to investigate is the relation between performance in
freshman English and, math on one hand, and content area courses, on the other. If
closely related, it makes sense to prepare developmental education students for English and math courses rather than content-area study. A weak relation would signal
the value of contextualization of developmental education curricula in the content
areas that students plan to pursue. Because the students in any one remedial course
aspire to different degrees, it is difficult to customize remediation in terms of subject
matter. Two ways to contextualize the instruction of reading, writing, and math in
discipline content are learning communities in which remedial courses are paired
with subject-matter courses and the use of tutoring in learning centers to provide

literacy and math instruction as support is provided for degree-credit course assignments (Perin, 2004). Information about the relative effectiveness of these two approaches is important. In any research on developmental education outcomes, factors on student background should be entered as covariates to determine whether initial skill level, age, language proficiency, and other variables affect students' ability to benefit from one approach over another.

Remediation is fundamental to the community colleges' ability to pursue the equity agenda. It is well known that students arrive at community colleges with a vast range of backgrounds and levels of academic preparedness. A sadly common scenario is that of the student who graduates from high school with As and Bs and is placed into developmental classes in college. It becomes the task of community colleges to offer all of these students—those who have succeeded academically in the past and those who have not—the same chances of completing college. The National Field Study findings suggest that we remain far from this ideal. The questions raised in this chapter are examples of issues on which answers are needed to inform efforts to create a productive learning environment that simultaneously serves the needs of academically underprepared students and enables the community colleges' equity goals.

CHAPTER EIGHT

"Like, What Do I Do Now?"

The Dilemmas of Guidance Counseling

W. NORTON GRUBB

My whole [high] school went to this community college. . . . There is not a lot of career counseling there. So everybody is like, well, what do I do now? So they come here to figure it out.

—*Community college student, National Field Study*

In a simpler world without occupational choices, where sons succeed their fathers and daughters become mothers and homemakers, there are few decisions for young people to make about their occupations. As occupational possibilities expand, some mechanisms must facilitate the choice among them. This process has increasingly taken place in schools and colleges, as occupational preparation has moved into formal educational institutions (Grubb and Lazerson, 2004). So most education programs from the high school through postsecondary education have developed forms of guidance and counseling, initially *career counseling* helping students choose occupational directions, then *academic counseling* assisting students enroll in the right courses and make progress toward academic goals, and sometimes including *personal counseling* focusing on personal and psychological issues. Finally, *financial counseling* may be necessary, especially in postsecondary education, where students have to juggle schooling and work and tuition and grants and loans—though financial counseling usually takes place in financial aid offices, separate from other forms of guidance and counseling.

The issues of guidance and counseling are especially difficult in community colleges. The variety of students is challenge enough, because different kinds of students usually need different help (Healy and Reilly, 1989). First-generation college students with little information from their families about progress through college, immigrants unfamiliar with the education and employment options in this country, and "experimenters" or "undecided" students unsure of their educational and occupational goals (Manski, 1989; Grubb 1996, chap. 2) all present special problems. Furthermore, the "equity agenda" of the "people's college," serving nontraditional students, requires programs that target at-risk or low-income or minority students. So there is widespread acceptance in community colleges of the enormous need for guidance and counseling, "essential to the success of students," as one counselor said.

Counseling, however, has long been criticized. It has sometimes been attacked for directing women to traditionally female occupations, working-class and minority students to working-class jobs and occupational education, and immigrants to menial positions. Within their own institutions, counselors often have checkered reputations. Many instructors in the National Field Study complained about misinformation from counselors, and many griped that "they're not aware of our programs," a particularly common criticism from occupational instructors. Many charged that counseling is not especially innovative, or is "fifteen years behind," and that counseling is isolated and insular: "it's this little vested-interest place," asserted one dean. There is not much consensus about what guidance and counseling should do (as documented later in this chapter, in "What Guidance and Counseling Mean: What Do Counselors Do All Day?"), and very few efforts in most colleges to develop a coherent plan or vision. Noninstructional programs such as student services remain peripheral in most colleges, and the resources are almost always inadequate.

The great dilemma of counseling and guidance is that it seems particularly important, especially for nontraditional students, even though it is underfunded, underused, and sometimes embattled. Furthermore, despite its presumptive importance, there has been relatively little investigation into the nature of counseling in community colleges (Grubb, 2001b). In light of limited information, the National Field Study included guidance and counseling among the issues to examine in fifteen colleges. We interviewed the directors of guidance and counseling, as well as the directors of student services in general; we spoke with several counselors in each college, either individually or in focus groups; and we visited counseling centers. Instructors also provided valuable insights, both positive and negative. We could not observe counseling sessions because of privacy issues, and—although we talked to a number of students in focus groups—we did not systematically interview them about their use of guidance and counseling.

In the first section, we examine the special needs of community colleges students. The second section describes the basic structure of guidance and counseling, and the third analyzes what counselors do in their interactions with students. The fourth section describes some innovative practices that are potentially more effective because they correct some dilemmas of standard practice—though there is very little evaluation evidence to judge whether practices that seem promising are in fact effective. In the conclusion, we present an agenda for colleges as they design their programs, for researchers, and for state policy makers as they contemplate reforms.

The Varying Needs of Students in Community Colleges

The most persistent challenge in community colleges is the vast variety of students, generating needs for very different forms of guidance and counseling. Many older students are there to upgrade their skills, and they need only to be steered to the appropriate courses. Other older students, including dislocated workers preparing for new careers, may need to know much more about employment options. Many younger students entering community colleges from high schools are "experimenters," unsure about the relationship between schooling and their aspirations. Such students come to community colleges because they are low-cost and convenient places for generating more information about their career and educational options. These students, however, usually develop information by taking courses almost at random, and this is not necessarily an effective route. As one dean acknowledged, "It troubles me, and drives me to be finding a better way and more focused way [to help experimenters], 'cause I don't believe that it serves people well to just come here and shop and shop. And I think it's almost—well, it does keep them off the streets, but on the other hand, it's somewhat wasteful."

The deans and counselors in our fifteen sites were all well aware of "experimenters." One counselor declared that "the undecided population is huge," citing figures that of 15,000 credit students only 3,000–4,000 students had chosen majors. In another college that prides itself on being a transfer institution, the dean of student services noted that 67% of students entered undeclared,[1] so "the bulk of our work is to help guide students to career decisions"—even though her college had almost no career counseling. Many noted that even students who have declared an intention often change their majors—"after they've had the experience of being here for a semester [they] realize they want to change their goals"—so that initial decisions are often unstable. Many colleges have majors like General Studies or Liberal Studies, usually a grab bag of courses required for transfer and general education but requiring no special plan from students. One counselor noted, "General Studies is, you know, the next step up from undecided, since such majors don't require any special commitment." And several individuals noted that students without clear goals cannot complete any program; as one president declared, "People who don't have a plan to graduate don't graduate," So resolving the dilemmas of "experimenters" is crucial to completion.

A second complexity is that many students enter without adequate academic skills and need to be placed in appropriate developmental courses. Where placement in such courses is voluntary, students may want to avoid developmental education even if this may not be best for them. As one counselor said, "When students are self-advising and when students are navigating through a curriculum that allows them to step over some prerequisites, they will do some things that don't support the likelihood of their succeeding." The problem of false-positives in assigning students to developmental education—assigning students who do not need it—is obvious, and "it fries people if you put them in the wrong course," but the problem of false-negatives—students who avoid taking developmental courses but are unprepared for classes—is much less recognized. Counselors therefore face tricky issues in guiding students to the right combination of developmental and "regular" classes. Here a potential conflict arises between instructors, who want students to complete prerequisites, and counselors, who often want to help students complete *programs* in the shortest amount of time. As one academic instructor described the tension, "Student services are concerned with students' scholarships running out. . . . It's very important to stay in real close contact with them, like counselors . . . because if you don't, they start thinking your program is a waste of time, and they start figuring out ways to counsel students out of it."

In the National Field Study colleges, there was a widespread consensus about the need for guidance and counseling. The dominant perception is that students are needier now than they were twenty or thirty years ago—less prepared academically, from lower-income backgrounds, less likely to get information and moral support from their parents, less attuned to what "college" involves and less socialized to academic routines. Many faculty and counselors report more students with anxiety, stress, depression, and other mental health issues than they remember from the past. To explain the large number of "experimenters," many note that career information and guidance in high school has virtually disappeared: "a lot of our students who graduate from our feeder [high] schools are not ready for anything. They simply come here because it's the next convenient step." Another ventured a similar opinion: "I think they have trouble seeing the future, but I don't think they've been asked questions to this point in their life that make them think about how they're going to get to their future. . . .We have conversations about things they really haven't conversed about—their values, their principles." And, two successful transfer students noted that the goal of becoming an independent decision maker does not occur in

high school because much of the high school curriculum is programmed for students.[2] As one counselor summarized the case for guidance and counseling, "They
are essential to the success of students. The area in which we really need to be strong is
the counseling and guidance area—given that the students that we work with are
academically at-risk, and that they require a lot of intervention. We have a lot of issues
related to mental health, to disabilities, to economic disadvantage, to unawareness of
higher education and the value in terms of money. So for all of those reasons, we get a
population that can really benefit from counseling and guidance."

Discussions about students occasionally veer into language suggesting that some
students are not ready for college and real commitment. A dean of counseling noted
about undecided students, "It wasn't the natural tendency of these students to be
aggressive, to be astute, self-directed, and all those kinds of strategies that the successful student is able to do." Another dean of counseling described them: "I'm continually reminded of the fact that the students we see here are students who, for a
variety of reasons, come here without . . . the guidance or initiative that many
students have that go on to research institutions or to quality, private colleges. The
parents . . . have in many cases missed the opportunity to invest in the kind of
guidance or direction that kids need to early on make that commitment to pursuing. . . . Most of the students we see, for lots of reasons . . . there's something missing
there. I see students who are lacking direction, who are not inspired, who have
tremendous informational gaps. . . . You know, we have to work on them from
ground zero." These perspectives tend to view initiative, planning, and commitment
as capacities that develop in families. But the second of these comments, contrasting
community college students with those who go to research institutions, clarifies a
little-recognized point about selection mechanisms in higher education. Students
who are unsure of what they want to do are more likely to go to two-year colleges. As
one student said of his decision in an earlier study, "I don't want to spend all of my
parents' money going to a four-year school when I don't really know want I to do yet"
(Grubb, 1996, p. 69). In addition, students who have not been taught to plan carefully
are less likely to complete the necessary requirements to enroll in four-year colleges—
taking the SAT or ACT and the right combination of high school courses, completing
applications the previous year. In this manner, the higher education system is a
filtering mechanism ensuring that a higher proportion of community college students are "experimenters," or lack initiative, or fail to connect current actions with
future consequences.

Another dimension of students is a nontraditional attachment to schooling. For
most community college students (and many in four-year colleges, too), postsecondary education is neither full time nor residential. Even though they recognize that

some postsecondary credential is necessary to get ahead, schooling is not the central focus of their lives. As one dean noted, contrasting her traditional view with those of many students, "They look at the schedule, and they don't know what to do. So then they start just fitting it in with the rest of their life. And I want to say school is not something you fit in with the rest of your life—that school is something that helps you to do what it is you want to do, and you have to make that commitment to doing it, so it becomes at the forefront." Similarly, a counselor in a focus group noted that "they will temper their [college] schedules based on their work schedules because work is primary"—rather than developing a college schedule first and then finding work to fit around it: "they don't see themselves that this [college] is their job."

The most obvious consequence of marginal attachment to college is that such students make little progress. They do not show up for guidance sessions or counseling courses. The "guesstimates" of how many students do not receive any counseling are usually "about a half," a substantial proportion but not an overwhelming majority. The dominant view acknowledges that many of the neediest students never receive any student services. One counselor articulated a kind of triage model, where students who learn about college only from family members do not show up, the neediest students who "fall through the cracks" do not show up, and students in the middle are most likely to come in.[3] Similarly, the head of counseling in another college asserted that academically stronger students and those more focused on career goals tended to show up "more than the students who really need the service." She also noted that many students who attend college for reasons aside from their own decisions—for example, students who attend because friends do, or whose parents pressure them, or who do not know what else to do—fail to use services even though they need them. One counselor summarized the problem of these students:

> They didn't think about what they wanted to do. Sometimes they're in school here for two or three years before they finally figure out what they want to do. Some of them just didn't plan. And some of them get misinformation from their friends. . . . But they don't come to see a counselor and then their friends say, well, you need to do your general education to transfer. And no, you need your general education *and* the courses in your major, and if you're a science major, you want to start the courses in your major the first semester.

On the contrary, another dean of student development noted that motivated students, those in courses where instructors encouraged them to make use of counseling, nursing students (who are generally highly selected), honors students, and international students show up at counselors' offices. In general, the most-motivated students show up, as do some students who are required to participate in counseling

—welfare recipients, those enrolled in special programs for low-income or minority students—but large numbers of unmotivated and indecisive students fail to use the services that might help them formulate goals.

Unfortunately, although counselors are sure that many needy students never receive help, there is rarely any systematic effort to find out why students do not show up. Part of the lack of planning around guidance and counseling has been an unwillingness of most colleges to profile their students carefully, to ascertain which ones have stable goals and which are experimenters, to determine why some of them do not make use of services. And so, although counselors acknowledge the special needs of their nontraditional students, their colleges have done little to meet these needs systematically.

The Basic Structure of Guidance and Counseling

While it is helpful conceptually to distinguish among *academic counseling, career counseling,* and *personal counseling,* in practice it is almost impossible to make clear distinctions. Career counseling may be necessary before academic counseling can take place, and academic counseling often leads to personal issues. As one counselor noted, "Initially, people come because of the pressure of the [academic] requirements and then it ends up being a personal issue; that's always a problem. Too much work, not enough childcare, just went through a divorce, just got laid off, it could be a lot of different reasons. . . . Not that many students will come and say I need to see a counselor because I'm having a lot of personal problems."

In the colleges of the National Field Study, there is very little sustained personal counseling. Although counselors are often trained in psychological counseling (because of state requirements), and provide limited help to students with personal problems, they refer students with serious issues (those needing more than two or three sessions) to personal counseling available in the community.[4]

Relatively little career counseling exists in most (but not all) colleges. Counselors do help "undecided" students find a major to declare, usually using the conventional trait-and-factor approach described below; but the real crush of students needing academic advising—particularly at the beginning of every semester—precludes much career counseling.[5] Most counselors are not trained in career counseling, and many colleges have only rudimentary career counseling offices. One college with 35,000 enrolled students had a staff of twenty-two counselors, but only a half-time career counselor funded by welfare-to-work, in a tiny office in an out-of-the-way location; many other colleges have no specific facilities devoted to career counseling.

In addition, financial counseling may be important because most community college students—from lower-income backgrounds than their peers in four-year colleges—usually have to support themselves and either have to navigate the complex maze of federal and state financial aid or combine education with employment. Financial counseling, however, usually takes place in financial aid offices, disconnected from other sources of guidance and counseling. In the National Field Study colleges, there was not a single mention of financial counseling among student services staff.[6] There are some indications that financial aid offices are understaffed (summarized in Grubb and Tuma, 1991) and in any event their help would be limited to information about grant and loan eligibility and application procedures, rather than a broader array of aid and employment alternatives. In addition, students who need to figure out how to support themselves while they attend college, and also need more precise career goals rather than "shopping and shopping," may also have family problems to complicate the situation. This means they may have to seek help from several different offices at the college. Unfortunately, these are the elements of the "family-work-schooling dilemma" described by several interview studies of students (Gittell and Steffy, 2000; Matus-Grossman and Gooden, 2002; Woodlief, Thomas, and Orozco, 2003) and are often responsible for students dropping out. It is no wonder that some colleges are moving toward one-stop services, to provide individuals with the full array of counseling and guidance they may need.

As a result of the lack of personal counseling, career counseling, and comprehensive financial counseling, most counseling is academic in nature, helping students navigate the courses necessary to complete credentials or to transfer but leaving undecided students without much help in formulating goals. Most colleges also make a distinction between *counseling* and *advising,* often with separate offices and different individuals. *Counseling* includes discussion and advice about academic issues, almost always one-on-one, and is usually carried out by professionals trained to be counselors (usually with counseling or social work degrees). *Advising* involves the provision of information only, about course requirements and sequences, transfer requirements, "the 'go do your schedule' thing," and is usually carried out by non-professional staff (or, in some colleges, by faculty in specific departments). Intentionally, then, many resources devoted generically to guidance and counseling are limited to academic *advising.* If an "undecided" student or someone with personal issues shows up in the offices of an *advisor,* he or she is sent to a *counselor*—the two kinds of personnel are not interchangeable. In theory, this provides a customized service, where students who need only simple information get it from advisors whereas others with greater needs are able to see counselors.

In practice, however, it may be difficult for the neediest students to see counselors. In many colleges, particularly with serious fiscal limitations, there has been a slow process of hiring advisers in place of counselors, to substitute less costly staff. As a counselor in one of these states noted, "It's a money issue: faculty/counselors are more expensive than advisors." (A new community college in this state opened without any counselors, replacing them with nonprofessional "student success facilitators.") In another college in the National Field Study, the number of counselors went from eleven to three while enrollments were increasing, and advisors took up the slack. A counselor explained that "what they're trying to do here is to get the biggest bang for the buck—bring in the most people and pay the least amount of money to deliver it." Another college essentially abandoned counseling in favor of advising, so "we don't really have bone fide counselors like we used to." Similarly, the City Colleges of Chicago eliminated counselors and replaced them with nonfaculty "registration specialists" (Evelyn 2002a, 2002b). This is a familiar process of "deskilling"—of substituting advisors who have lower skills and cost less in place of more-skilled and more-expensive counselors (Braverman, 1974). Thus, fiscal pressures also contribute to the dominance of advising over counseling.

Most colleges have an extensive array of information and advising (if not counseling) available to their students—indeed, sometimes a bewildering array. In the modal college, there is generally a counseling department; a separate staff of advisors, including some faculty; a separate career counseling office (even if it is small); a special program for low-income or minority or immigrant students, with its own counselors or advisors; yet another program for disabled students; a transfer office; sometimes a separate division for international students; informal procedures where faculty (especially occupational faculty) provide career and academic advice, and sometimes a formal program of faculty advising; a new student orientation session at the beginning of each semester; jobs fairs offered during the school year; and workshops on finding jobs, writing resumes, and interviewing. Any financial counseling is provided by financial aid offices, though the advice is usually limited to eligibility and application issues, and such offices may be understaffed. Three colleges have early-alert systems, warning students if their progress falls behind norms. In addition, every college catalogue is a gold mine of information about course requirements, course sequences, requirements in every major, and requirements for transfer—though faculty and counselors often complain that students do not read the catalogue.

In addition, most colleges offer short courses to help students wrestle with career and educational decisions. These go by many different names—Career Exploration, College Success, College Strategies, Personal Development—and offer a mix of career exploration, introduction to the services available on campus, and study skills. They allow students to explore career options at greater length, and in some colleges they are explicitly used to help "undecided" students find a major. In one college, they guide students through the assessments necessary for career counseling: "It doesn't do a lot of good to put the student through the battery of assessment, of career and interest assessments, and give 'em the results and they never pick up the information and do anything more with it. . . . The class guides them through that entire process." Most of these courses require students to write about their life circumstances and goals, a potentially helpful feature, because writing can play a critical role in helping students examine issues of identity (Hull and Zacher, 2002). These career-related courses have also become part of learning communities for new students (further described in "Promising Practices: Integrating Guidance and Counseling into the Core"). Unfortunately, enrollments in such courses appear relatively low, so that, although they may be widely available, they are not widely used. For example, in the college where the dean of student services estimated that two-thirds of students entered undeclared, career development courses were taken by only 5.5% of entering students. We suspect that students with highly instrumental and credentialist views of college avoid such courses, just as they avoid other nonrequired and "irrelevant" courses including developmental and general education (Cox, 2004).

In most colleges, students have access to *distributed* information and counseling services, in different places and programs, rather than *centralized* services. The underlying logic is partly that different groups of students need different services, so students who need only advising, those who need some counseling, and those who need more intensive services can find what they need—a continuum of services to meet every need. Another justification is that students who do not find advice in one format may happen across it in another. Distributed services, however, seem to have evolved without much planning, and no college articulated a deliberate strategy of providing services in various places and programs. Moreover, distributed services have obvious drawbacks. Students may not be informed about the variety of services available; they may find the variety of services bewildering; and the information available may be inconsistent. A counselor worried about "students meandering around the institution," not knowing what services are available and unable to find the counseling office. Several colleges claimed that they try to coordinate counseling services, but acknowledged that coordination is "not as formal as we'd like it to be." The problems caused by uncoordinated and fragmented services in education have often led to efforts at coordination or creating comprehensive service centers. Indeed, two colleges in the National Field Study are developing one-stop approaches, where every counselor can carry out every aspect of student services. Although the idea of one-stop services is relatively well-known, it has not been widely developed in community colleges.

The distributed approach makes it difficult to ascertain the resources in counseling. One conventional approach has been to calculate the student-counselor ratio. In the National Field Study colleges, ratios of full-time counselors and advisors to full-time-equivalent students were generally in excess of 1000:1, ranging from 914:1 to 1400:1. More than fifteen years ago, Keim (1988) found that the national average for the student-counselor ratio was 951:1. Our numbers therefore suggest that this problem has not improved since then. Moreover, if part-time students (including many "experimenters" and "undecided" students) need as much counseling as full-time students, the ratio per enrolled student rather than per full-time-equivalent student is the appropriate measure. Then the college with 914 full-time-equivalent students per counselor had 1,625 *enrolled* students per counselor and advisor—in a state where a committee on the enrollment process recommended a 500:1 ratio.

Calculating student-counselor ratios, however, understates the resources available if faculty members are used as advisors, if career development courses are available, or if learning communities and work-based learning are used as counseling mechanisms. In addition, the resources in guidance and counseling are unevenly distributed: some counselors are available only to disabled students, some only to low-income or minority students, and some colleges have several campuses with different resources at each. Furthermore, a peak-load problem exists at the beginning of each semester, when a flood of students try to see counselors and advisors. As one counselor noted, "They don't really premeditate the need and see a counselor on a regular basis." The periods of peak demand are therefore frantic, with students limited to ten to fifteen minutes each; the remainder of the semester, counselors find their office hours relatively empty. In addition, one college noted that students do not show up to about 40% of appointments, even when there is a long waiting time to see counselors. Counselors are busy in the sense that their appointment schedule is filled, though their offices often remain empty.

Despite the complexity of this issue, almost everyone agreed that resources are inadequate. Some mentioned that "student overload means cutting courses" or reducing the length of appointments. Another noted, "If you look at the number of full-time counselors for this many people, they obviously don't begin to reach the number of students who are here. The resources are there [only] for a student who asks a few questions and gets going on the right track." The lack of resources means, once again, that only students with initiative and direction can get access to counseling. Furthermore, no one believes that resources are likely to increase substantially, because of the precarious fiscal situation of all student services: "As we move to cutting costs, and perhaps student services being a non-revenue-generating program, they often then look to student services for budget cuts." And so the lack of resources is a chronic problem.

Another persistent and unresolved dilemma involves whether to make services voluntary or mandatory. In most colleges, services are entirely voluntary. The only requirements fall on students in academic trouble—those on probation or those who have fallen behind in their coursework. In addition, students who sign up for special programs—disadvantaged students, for example, or welfare recipients—are often required to go to counseling. The usual presumption, however, is that students are no longer children who need to be directed. On the other hand, some counselors voiced serious misgivings about leaving all decisions to students. The dean of counseling at one college, where too many students avoided counseling until it was too late, suggested that students need something more "coerced," something he called "intrusive advising": "Someone has to do some outreach and it has to be deliberate, no longer leaving students to their own devices to find their way to us." This echoes the language reported by Muraskin (1997), describing "intrusive advising" and "active counseling" as requiring multiple meetings during each semester, midterm evaluations by faculty, and ongoing tracking of student performance—all of these mandatory. Another counselor, in a college with many resources including learning communities incorporating counselors, argued for more mandatory elements: "One of the frustrations is a student will come in after they've been here two or three years and never seen a counselor, and pretty much have not been following their plan. . . . I just went on an accreditation visit to another school. Because it was a private school they have been able to make orientation mandatory, even though they don't use that word. They are able to state it in a stronger way that all the students go through it. And I wish that we could do that."

One college has an early-alert system, described as "an intrusive system that really goes to the student rather than wait for the student to come in," and as a "Velcro system, that's what it is: whenever they [students] need the test, they [counselors] stick to you." Requiring students falling behind their planned programs to see counselors is another way of making counseling mandatory. There may not be an elegant solution to the dilemma of making counseling mandatory, because it is difficult to distinguish a priori the students who might benefit from mandatory counseling from those who would not. But where there are strong presumptions that all students benefit from a range of services—as in the LifeCourse program profiled below—the need to differentiate students in this way vanishes.

Although the dominant approach to guidance and counseling is to provide counselors and advisors, along with various other distributed activities, there are two major variants—specialist counselors and faculty advising.

Specialist Counselors

In two colleges, counselors were assigned to particular academic and occupational departments, or to groups of related departments such as the sciences. Counselors become more familiar with the courses and programs within these departments and more knowledgeable about transfer requirements to related four-year college programs. They could also work on a continuous basis with students in those majors. Specialist counselors also served as a source of information from each of the departments back to other counselors and advisors. There are many advantages to such specialization. As one counselor specializing in science, biotechnology, and medical occupations said, "The truth is that you can't be an expert on everything. . . . There's areas they [students] are specializing in, so as a student has greater needs, we can provide those greater needs. . . . You get to know some of the faculty in the program. So whenever they've come to me for information about oh, you know, what does a student need to do to get into a biotech program at Cal Poly Pomona, they have come and asked me to help them find information."

On the other hand, there is a potential tension between having specialist counselors and the kinds of generalist personnel envisioned in one-stop service centers. In addition, specialist counselors cannot readily help "experimenters" who have not yet found their way to specific departments.

Faculty Advising

Another variant found in four National Field Study colleges was to place greater emphasis on faculty. For example, one college provided undecided students with initial counseling but then sent them to departments for subsequent advising. Students with specific questions also went to department advisors, and counselors saw only those students who were in danger of flunking out. Students received better-informed advice from faculty who were intimately involved in departments; occupational faculty in particular were often actively involved in advising students and finding them jobs.

It is unclear, though, how well the process of faculty advising works. Instructors vary in their interest, and many academic instructors are unable to provide much beyond information about the content and sequence of courses. One faculty member noted that distributing advising among instructors meant that "advising is everybody and nobody's job—nobody knows exactly what the college's advising system is and [instructors] often feel inadequate about it." The faculty had asked for institutional support (like in-service education) without success; lacking training or accountability, the administration was "just sort of symbolically carrying it out." Another academic instructor noted that "they've kind of separated it [staff counseling from instructor counseling], so now you have that territory, that invested-interest fighting against full-time faculty. The lack of respect that goes on between the two cannot be quantified." Finally, placing greater responsibility for advising with faculty members may come at the cost of attention to teaching, which is never a good thing (Grubb and Associates, 1999, chap. 8). To work well, then, faculty advising requires strong institutional support and professional development. It might, for example, be part of an overall counseling plan providing detailed information to students in their majors, but not appropriate as a comprehensive approach.

Overall, the most distressing aspect of guidance and counseling is that most colleges did not have any coherent plan for what they provide. One counselor described his department as full of "Lone Rangers," working individually but without any plan for what they all did. Many counselors confessed that they had never determined which students were experimenters and why. They recognized that some students suddenly figure out what they want to do—"Whammo, the light went on, and he got his skills together and he actually got into the university"—but they can't say why this happens or what they can do to increase its likelihood. Many noted that large numbers of students needing counseling never find their way to these services, without systematically investigating why some students do not show up. There is widespread awareness that many students fail to complete coherent programs, and some acknowledgement that, "if you don't know where you're going, you don't know how to get there," but little effort to determine why students fail to complete. The conventional practices, including widely distributed services, have grown up without any plan or rationale, and many promising ideas—various career development courses, the learning communities we describe in the fourth section, the extended use of work-based learning—are provided in only small amounts.

Finally, there appears to be no national consensus about what guidance and counseling should be. The National Council on Student Development, a community college group, promotes student services but says almost nothing about what they might look like. The National Academic Advising Association, a group based in four-year colleges, has developed five widely held beliefs, some of which are obvious—for example, advising should support student learning and personal development. The Association also holds that counselors should work collaboratively with students rather than lecturing them, that career advising and the development of life plans are crucial components, and that the counseling relationship should be developmental as the student changes (Gordon, Habley, and Associates, 2000), but these relatively obvious beliefs say little about what practices should be adopted. Finally, we detected little discussion in the National Field Study colleges about current practices, or directions for the future. Particularly with limited resources, a more systematic approach to guidance and counseling might be an important way to address the substantial needs of students—the subject of the concluding section.

What Guidance and Counseling Mean: What Do Counselors Do All Day?

Before we conclude whether counseling should be redirected rather than simply expanded, an important question is what counselors (and advisors) do in their interactions with students. Because these interactions are necessarily hidden, we have to rely on counselors' own statements, small hints and indirect statements, as well as some comments from students.

Although counselors tend to rely on indirect methods—such as interest inventories or informational approaches to allow students to guide themselves—it would be foolish to argue that directive approaches are completely absent. One dean of student services noted that "most of them [counselors] are quite direct" in counseling students, and anecdotes persist of women steered toward traditionally female occupations and working-class students tracked into traditional vocational areas. There is, however, little career counseling in most colleges, and most of it provides information only. The way most counselors speak of the needs of "undecided" students is that *students* need to establish goals for themselves—"if *you* don't know where you're going, *you* don't know how to get there." The dominant trait-and-factor approach—in which counselors help students uncover their preferences, personality traits, and strengths, by using interest and personality inventories and providing them information about occupations most suited to their interests and abilities—is explicitly nondirective and aims to provide students with the information necessary for *them* to make decisions. Within the counseling profession, the directive approach has very much fallen out of favor (Krei and Rosenbaum, 2001; Rosenbaum, 2001). In addition, most colleges have an array of services aimed specifically at low-income, minority, immigrant, and (less often) female students, and those student services personnel act as advocates for particular groups. In light of these programs, the notion that guidance and counseling are responsible for overt tracking in community colleges seems far-fetched. It ascribes entirely too much power to a service that is, in most colleges, determinedly student centered and relatively peripheral in any event.

More subtle problems may in fact be sources of bias. One is an error of omission rather than commission: If the variety of courses and programs in a college is large and the complexity of degree and transfer requirements substantial, the lack of access to counseling may discourage some students—particularly nontraditional students, or those with marginal or nontraditional attachment to college. In this case, the kind of triage noted in the first section—where the students most in need of counseling never find their way to services—constitutes a serious barrier or mechanism of "cooling out" (Clark, 1960b), even if counselors try to eliminate overt bias from their advice.

Furthermore, the dominant approaches to counseling may serve as another subtle source of bias. Most guidance involves the provision of information—or the "information dump"—about prerequisites, graduation requirements and sequences, general education requirements, and transfer requirements. The head of student services in one college—who observes counseling sessions as part of evaluating counselors—noted, "Some just try to inundate students [with information]. There's a time for what they need to know but we have some people, I think, who probably overwhelm them." Another noted that "some people [counselors] can't tell how much information they [students] can process in that short period of time."

Here a disagreement becomes apparent, particularly well articulated in a college with an internal schism between "broad" versus "narrow" (or "low-end") counseling. One counselor, a proponent of a "student-first" approach stressing student needs over institutional requirements (like enrollments in low-enrollment courses), defined "narrow" counseling as providing information about course and degree requirements and responding to questions that students raise without inquiring about the conditions of their lives. Another described "low-end" counseling as providing information without help in interpreting the information, as counselors do who "just try to inundate students" with information. "Narrow" counselors might, if asked by students for an education plan, simply provide one, especially a general-purpose plan such as completing the generic requirements for transfer—a plan not tailored to the interests and conditions of students. Indeed, there is a tendency for counselors to advise students, especially undecided students, to "get their gen ed requirements out of the way." As the student quoted at the beginning of this chapter described her college, "It gives you more time to mature as yourself and to figure out what you want to do, but I haven't really talked to anyone about a career here. But this is a good spot for you to knock out your electives and see what's going on and save your money." This talk of getting gen ed "out of the way" and "knocking out electives" is distressing partly because it suggests how peripheral general education is. As a method of counseling it may provide some kind of plan, but it is not tailored to the interests or capacities of students and it is simply a delaying tactic hoping that students will happen on some genuine interest in the process.

In contrast, advocates of "broad" counseling tend to probe the conditions of a student's life. They claim that they will not simply provide an education plan, but instead try to engage students in discussions of life goals. (This stance also clarifies the difficulty of separating academic planning from career advising and suggests an inherent weakness in hiring *advisors* who provide information without knowing anything about a student's plans.) Counselors operating within this approach are "trying to answer the questions students would ask if students knew what to ask"— which indicates that some come in with so little understanding of occupations and postsecondary options that they do not know where to begin. "High-end" counseling means "doing as broad a job as possible," helping students figure out their goals considering the state of their lives, their interests, and capacities, and providing a wide range of alternatives. The insistence from the "broad" perspective that counselors must learn more about students' lives recognizes that some programs are simply impossible, especially for students with employment and family responsibilities. As a math instructor noted, "The advice they [students] get in a cookbook from a counselor might be, 'Well, if you want to get your degree in two years, then you have to follow this schedule,' and it's not realistic." There are also racial and class dimensions to this kind of counseling, because counselors who do not know about the conditions of students' lives cannot engage in "high-end" counseling. This is an argument for having more counselors of color, as well as counselors with working-class or occupational backgrounds.

The differences between "broad" versus "narrow" (or "cookbook" or "low-end") approaches appear in other ways, too. Several counselors reported that some instructors teach career development courses in a "narrow" fashion—providing a great deal of information, often through lecture—and sometimes in a "broad" approach, pushing students to interpret information and getting them out of the classroom in various projects.[7] The use of internships and work placements is also more consistent with a "broad" approach, because it assumes that experience and not simply information is necessary.

When counselors do engage in career counseling, the dominant approach is the trait-and-factor approach. One counseling head noted that career planning is oriented toward "instruments and tools," and many others referred to the battery of assessments—the Meyer-Briggs personality assessment, various interest inventories, the Discover system developed by ACT—that they use with "undecided" students. Sometimes counselors mentioned finding internships as ways of exploring particular jobs, but these references were relatively rare; most community colleges have relatively little work-based learning, except perhaps in health occupations, where internships are standard (Villeneuve and Grubb, 1996; Stern,1999).

Although the trait-and-factor approach has deep roots in this country (Parsons,

1909), it often amounts to little more than providing information about selected occupations—a process sometimes belittled as "test 'em and tell 'em," Together with the volume of information provided by advisors, various centers, including transfer centers concerned with course requirements, and web-based sources available in career offices, the tactic of providing information is the dominant approach to counseling in most colleges—the "information dump."[8] If students are not sophisticated in their use of information, however, an "information dump" cannot be an effective way to help students make decisions in their own interests (Grubb, 2002b). Students also need to be able to judge the information they receive and distinguish well-intentioned but inaccurate information (from friends, for example) from deliberately misleading information (from proprietary schools, for example) from accurate but unhelpful information (from statewide surveys of labor markets, for example). To make rational decisions, individuals must have well-formed preferences, which "experimenters" and "undecided" students lack by definition. They need to be able to weigh present and future possibilities and the trade-offs among them; without the capacity of "planfulness," it is hard to know what career and course planning might mean. They must understand probabilistic events and be able to weigh educational and occupational alternatives with different probabilities of success. They must consider a wide range of alternatives including some, like formal schooling itself, where they have been treated badly in the past and that they may not be able to consider dispassionately and rationally (Reay and Ball, 1997). For some students, the "choice" of an occupational area involves the complex process of developing a very different identity (Hull and Zacher, 2002)—a particularly difficult process for women contemplating nontraditional employment, working-class youth and first-generation students trying to move into middle-class occupations, or immigrants trying to assimilate into a new country.

Decision making therefore proves to be a multifaceted competence in its own right—but one that conventional guidance and counseling do not address. More substantial experiences—semester-long courses such as Career Development or College Success, internships or co-op placements, service and experiential learning—may be necessary. Counselors in the "broad" tradition often stress the need for a more "holistic" approach, using a variety of services to lead students to understand themselves, their capacities, and their alternatives in much deeper ways, but they never pretend that information alone is enough; even if information is available, "it just stays there," inert and unused by students in decision making.

To be sure, in colleges with varied students, many need little more than information, and they may be well served by simple information sources. As one counselor noted, "If a student knows how to use the information in the catalogue, and actually works through it, that person will understand and build their own ed plan that makes sense." But many other students fail to show up in counseling, and the range of services available in most colleges does not include the activities beyond the conventional "information dump." In practice, nontraditional students require a continuum of services that are not present at most community colleges. These institutions may need to invest more substantially in nontraditional approaches to guidance and counseling.

Promising Practices: Integrating Guidance and Counseling into the Core

In the fifteen colleges of the National Field Study, a number of practices have been developed to self-consciously strengthen guidance and counseling. The ones we profile in this section provide more systematic approaches, better integrated into the core functions of their colleges; they move away from peripheral student services provided by nonfaculty in offices apart from classrooms and workshops. They are more likely to go beyond the "information dump," and they usually incorporate "broad" rather than "cookbook" approaches.

The LifeCourse Program

The "Start Right" initiative in one college is one of seven strategic learning goals that the college has articulated. Start Right assumes that focusing support as students enter will result in better adjustment to the college and reduced attrition. The advising component of Start Right is called "LifeCourse": "Life's a trip—you'll need directions." "LifeCourse is a student's guide to figuring out 'what to do when' in order to complete your career and educational goals. LifeCourse links all of the components of the college (faculty, staff, courses, technology, programs, services) into a personal itinerary to help you succeed in your college experience." The explicit goal of LifeCourse is to prepare students to become independent, symbolized in the following diagram:

$$A \rightarrow As \rightarrow AS \rightarrow aS \rightarrow S$$

The small and capital letters represent advisors playing a smaller role as students become more independent. The LifeCourse program is explicitly developmental in the sense that it moves students through five stages:[9] the Postsecondary Transition, where high school students can learn more about postsecondary options; Introduction to College, for students in their first fifteen credit hours of college work, giving them "connections and directions to plan a successful college experience"; Progression to Degree, for students between fourteen and forty-four credit hours, implementing their career and education goals; Graduation Transition, for students with more than forty-five credit hours, completing their degrees and planning either to transfer or to enter the workforce; and Lifelong Learning, in which students recognize "the need for continued learning, the retooling of skills/knowledge and the need to create new skills."

LifeCourse therefore presents a plan for a series of decisions and actions culminating in completion of a program. LifeCourse makes the process of becoming independent particularly concrete, with more sources of support at earlier stages and then less support as students become more independent. It also integrates career planning with academic planning, rather than separating academic *advising* and career *counseling*. Counselors are assigned to different stages in the LifeCourse process and, presumably, become experienced with the special issues of each stage. In addition, LifeCourse is not simply a way to create an education plan, though it does do that; it also provides information about services at every step in the plan, clarifying the value of many different services. For example, outreach to high school students is part of the Transition to College stage, and services to help students complete programs are part of the Progression to Degree and Graduate Transition stages. The information about LifeCourse is available both on the Internet and in a student handbook. In addition, this college is trying to develop a one-stop approach to student services, so all the services that facilitate the LifeCourse process are available in one place.

LifeCourse is a framework that organizes a student planning process, a set of clear expectations for completing programs that all students, counselors, and faculty share, and a series of student services. Rather than being a peripheral service, LifeCourse organizes all activities in the college, *including coursework,* so students become independent. It creates a set of expectations from the outset. As one counselor noted, "The key is just [students] knowing they need a plan." It specifically rejects the notion of "coming here and shopping and shopping," and it rejects the notion that nontraditional students are "a different kind of student, looking for something different"—"as quick as he can get it and as cheap as he can get it"—or, more precisely, it encourages any such students to slow down, consider their options more carefully, and plan accordingly. So, partly by developing very different assumptions about students and their needs, LifeCourse creates a much richer conception of what guidance and counseling might be.

Learning Communities Incorporating Counseling

A second novel approach has been to incorporate counseling into learning communities. Learning communities (or linked courses) typically include two or three (or even more) courses that students take simultaneously, with instructors jointly planning the content, developing common projects, teaching the prerequisites for one course in the other, and occasionally team-teaching (Smith, 1991; Matthews, 1994; Tinto, Russo, and Kadel, 1994; Grubb and Associates, 1999, chap. 7). They encourage both students and faculty to develop communities of support and create linkages among what is otherwise disconnected and fragmented coursework. Modest evidence indicates that they increase grades and progression in coursework (Tokina, 1993; Tinto, Goodsell-Love, and Russo, 1994; Tinto and Goodsell-Love, 1995; Bloom and Sommo, 2005).

Counseling shows up in learning communities in several different ways. In one example, a college integrated a college success course taught by a counselor with a learning community including history and English instructors. In other cases, colleges have developed learning communities incorporating career exploration with introductory courses in a particular occupational area. This practice allows students who have selected a broad occupational area—business or health occupations, for example—to begin learning the basic material of the occupational area at the same time that they become more knowledgeable about specific occupations. In a third example, several colleges have created learning communities combining career development or college success with developmental courses in reading, writing, and math. Such learning communities address simultaneously the needs of many new students for both basic skills and education plans. They also overcome a dispiriting aspect of developmental education—that students seeking occupational advancement are shunted into coursework unrelated to their progress. Such learning communities also connect counselors and instructors, something that can help reduce the gulf that can exist between these two groups.

Sometimes learning communities incorporating counselors are developed for specific students. One prominent example is the Puente program in California, which exists in both high schools and community colleges and focuses on Latino students (Gandara and Moreno, 2002; Grubb, Lara, and Valdez, 2002). The organizers of each Puente program are counselors who serve in many different capacities: they cooperate with instructors to identify academic barriers; they work with students to develop education plans moving them toward completion and transfer; they arrange for mentors from the Latino community; and they set up field trips (including trips to four-year colleges), parent meetings, and other enrichment activities. Puente thereby creates roles for counselors that go far beyond the conventional role. Similarly, the PACE (Program for Adult College Education) program is a learning community for older adults, often women returning to college after child-rearing, that uses an unconventional schedule in which students meet on Saturdays and in the evenings.[10] Within a PACE program, counselors are assigned specifically to provide guidance and information to a group.

Other Planned Innovations

Other innovations are being planned in the fifteen colleges of the National Field Study, though it is too early to tell how some of them will fare.

Two colleges (including the college with LifeCourse) are developing comprehensive one-stop student service centers. This approach hopes to correct the fragmentation typical of distributed services. These programs, however, require staff members who are knowledgeable about many different aspects of counseling and cannot be undertaken without considerable commitment to staff development.

One college's dual-enrollment program with local high schools drew the attention of high school counselors to the need to prepare students better for college. As the coordinator described it, "The counselors and the principals are very involved in making sure that the students are actually ready for college-level work." In light of the tendency to blame high schools for the large number of "experimenters," such involvement with high school counselors provides one way of reducing the magnitude of this problem.

Several colleges are developing computer-based student record systems to follow the progress of students, share information among instructors, and trigger visits to counselors if students lag behind their academic and occupational goals. These too have the advantage of being relatively systematic efforts affecting all students.

Some colleges have taken special steps for students in occupational programs. One college used federal funds to hire three career transition counselors to help occupational students complete certificates or degrees rather than random courses. As the vice president for workforce development commented, "Many students will come in, take this, take this, that's what they need, that's what they want. They leave and go get a job"—even though small amounts of coursework do not provide substantial employment benefits (Grubb, 2002a). Similarly, one dean of math, engineering, and technologies hired a counselor specifically for occupational programs: "Ever since I was able to take a counselor under my wings and direct her to the programs, it's made a tremendous, tremendous change in the way students' needs are met in the vocational program." These are methods of correcting the particularly large distance between counseling and occupational programs.

The Systematic Use of Work-Based Learning

A number of counselors in the National Field Study colleges said that they would find "undecided" students work placements or internships as ways to learn more about employment. In addition to teaching occupational competencies, this approach recognizes that work-based learning can also serve the purposes of career counseling by allowing students to experience occupations directly. In the vast majority of the National Field Study colleges, however, work-based opportunities are comparatively rare. They are common only in medical occupations and therefore aimed at students who have already determined their occupational area.

At some colleges not in the National Field Study—colleges in the Cincinnati area (Villeneuve and Grubb, 1996) and LaGuardia Community College in New York (Grubb and Badway, 1998)—work-based learning and cooperative education are used more uniformly for career guidance. Although co-op placements are intended primarily as forms of work preparation, they also have real benefits as career exploration. As a co-op coordinator at that college explained, "It's like practice. You get a chance to do a job. . . . That's the neat thing about co-op, because you're not sure and you get to go out and you try it out and you get to see what those people do, day in and day out, and you get to say, 'Yes, this is what I want to do the rest of my life' or 'No, it's not really what I want to do the rest of my life,' so you get an opportunity to make a change without a lot of investment into it." At LaGuardia, evening seminars during co-op placements teach some of the skills necessary for finding jobs, but they also require students to think about career options, to understand the nature of work, to analyze the value of classroom learning on the job, and to explore the larger social issues surrounding employment.

What is unusual about the Cincinnati and LaGuardia co-op programs is that they are systematic and provide large numbers of students with work experiences. Furthermore, these programs prepare students for their work experiences, provide coordinators to keep track of what students are learning on the job, integrate work-based and school-based learning, and create time for students to distill the implications of their work experiences for future activities. These are rich and multifaceted educational experiences, with career guidance serving as one of several benefits.

These promising practices have several elements in common. First, they have clear visions for improving guidance and counseling rather than continuing practice as usual. Second, these innovations are built into the core of these institutions, and particularly into teaching and learning, preventing counseling from being isolated and peripheral. Third, they try to make guidance and counseling less dependent on the initiative of students or on the resourcefulness of individual counselors and instructors and create expectations that all students can benefit from advising and counseling as part of a larger developmental process.

Although there is very little evidence about the effectiveness of student services, a study of student support services under the TRIO program—including both a quantitative study of outcomes and case studies of five exemplary programs—corroborates the value of these promising practices and helps us understand when guidance and counseling are unlikely to be effective.[11] Student services—dominated by counseling and peer tutoring—did increase GPAs, credits earned, and retention, but improvements depended on the extent to which students participated. Most improvements were limited simply because the extent of services was small. This suggests that restricted access to guidance and counseling constrains its effectiveness, hardly a surprising finding. A structured and directive freshman year experience seems to have been particularly valuable, as was "active counseling," also described as "intrusive academic counseling"—which indicates that what National Field Study counselors described as mandatory and "intrusive" counseling might be more effective, particularly for disadvantaged students, than leaving contact to the discretion of students. More holistic services, and services provided in a "home base" on the campus serving the "whole student," were more effective, which indicates that centralized services and one-stop centers might be beneficial. Integrated services, where staff provided more than one service, were more effective, again supporting the notion of one-stop centers where individual counselors work with students in a variety of ways. And programs that blended student services with other programs showed increased retention, which suggests that learning communities combining counseling with academic or occupational content are valuable. There is no evidence in these results, however, to suggest that unplanned services, provided in small amounts, relying on the initiative of students themselves, and unintegrated in any way with the rest of the college can make any difference to outcomes.

Overcoming the Dilemmas of Guidance and Counseling

The results of the National Field Study indicate a number of dilemmas that many—perhaps most—colleges face. Perhaps the greatest dilemma is that many students—particularly nontraditional students and "experimenters"—need a variety of counseling services. Whereas focused and aggressive students can find what they need, many students who need it the most do not show up in counseling, or not until they are on probation. Second, the substantial consensus about the escalating needs of community college students is not matched by any consensus about what guidance and counseling should be. Career and personal counseling are weak compared to academic counseling, and academic *advising* dominates; financial counseling is limited and divorced from other kinds of counseling. Most guidance and counseling takes the form of information alone, but many students need much more than information. There is no consensus on "broad" versus "narrow" counseling, or on "coercive" versus voluntary approaches. Similarly, there no consensus on whether distributed counseling services versus centralized services are more effective, though some colleges are moving to one-stop centers partly to provide students the array of information — career, academic, personal, and financial as the case may be. Despite the great variety of services, everyone agrees that resources are inadequate. Finally, very few institutions have created coherent visions or plans for their guidance and counseling services. Although there are some exceptions—LifeCourse, the use of learning communities, the systematic use of work-based learning—most programs of guidance and counseling seem to have developed piecemeal, without careful thought about what different students need.

Remedying this situation requires that colleges recognize guidance and counseling as central rather than peripheral to several missions, especially to the equity agenda and to helping students complete coherent programs rather than "come here and shop and shop." Simply acknowledging the problem is inadequate, because calls to revitalize counseling have been repeated in other institutions—particularly high school —without anything being done. A second step is to engage in systematic planning, to determine why students do not complete programs and how much noncompletion is due to factors that could be remedied through guidance and counseling. This institutional research would correct the current situation where faculty and administrators are aware of problems students face but are unclear about the magnitude, the causes, or the solutions.

A third step would then be to develop activities appropriate for different groups of students, a continuum of services for those with different needs. Some would look like services now offered—transfer counseling, for example. Colleges might find particular solutions to specific problems—perhaps systematic work experience for students with little knowledge of the labor market, special courses and mentors for immigrant students, or learning communities for students considering broad occupational areas, to help them narrow their goals. In addition, different approaches to counseling—for example, the "broad" or "high-end" or "intrusive" counseling that some college officials mentioned—might be a better substitute for conventional trait-and-factor approaches, at least for some students. A coherent program of guidance and counseling would also have to resolve tricky issues about voluntary versus compulsory counseling, and some colleges might be able to formulate larger frameworks, like the LifeCourse program, to integrate a variety of activities.

Next, implementation might require a new division or office responsible for all activities, to avoid the fragmentation of services. It might also require personnel with different qualifications than counselors and advisors now have. Ongoing professional development, keeping all personnel up to date on patterns of student success and failure and on new program developments, would be critical, because, as one counselor observed, "you learn on the job—it's a high-info job." Furthermore, a student monitoring system would not only urge students to establish goals and meet them but would also provide information to counselors about student progress and patterns in using student services.

The final step of a systematic approach would be the evaluation of student services to determine where these services are working and where they are failing to reach students. This approach envisions a kind of virtuous circle, of initial efforts based on better knowledge about the needs of students, leading to better-designed activities, leading in turn to better information to improve counseling in a subsequent round.

In such efforts, guidance and counseling need the support of senior administrators. There is also little question that, with a well-developed plan to spend resources wisely, the expansion of funding would be necessary—for additional staff development, for hiring internship coordinators, for creating new learning communities or courses such as career exploration, for creating additional "broad" and necessarily time-consuming counseling. Without such a plan, however, even substantial increases in funding might simply be wasted.

Unfortunately, states have played almost no role in guidance and counseling. In the colleges we examined, several states require that counselors have degrees in counseling or psychology—not a particularly helpful requirement, in light of the lack of personal counseling. At the time of our field research, Washington had been trying to get colleges to substitute advisors for counselors, a shift that is unhelpful to some students. Both Illinois and Florida have developed transfer information systems. Otherwise, no state had any policy about guidance and counseling, but states could be helpful, in addition to providing additional resources, in several ways. They could help in the collection and validation of information about promising practices; fund demonstration projects to provide information for new directions; and develop and test student tracking systems to provide information to counselors about students falling behind in their programs. States can always serve a convening function, bringing colleges together to discuss issues of common concern related to guidance and counseling. Finally, the personal problems of community college students, particularly their employment and family responsibilities, suggest that states could coordinate mental health and social services, child care policies, and perhaps family support centers or referrals to agencies in the community. These are not issues that colleges can resolve on their own.

Finally, researchers should also pay more attention to guidance and counseling. Institutional researchers have important roles to play, particularly in ascertaining student needs and examining the effectiveness of different counseling activities. Other studies, particularly studies of effectiveness, probably need to be conducted by outside researchers. Until more is known about the special needs of community college students and the programs that are effective for their great variety, though, efforts to develop more effective approaches will continue to be ad hoc.

So we see many ways to escape the century-old dilemmas of guidance and counseling. Otherwise the current situation—in which many colleges make do with conventional services and inadequate resources, without much planning—cannot improve practice. Fiscal pressures are unlikely to abate, the needs of students will probably become increasingly serious, and there is no end in sight to the numbers of unprepared high school graduates, immigrant students, dislocated workers, and others needing second chances to find stable careers.

All the forces that have contributed to the current dilemmas of guidance and counseling are likely to continue—and without coherent planning and careful resource use, guidance and counseling are all too likely to remain peripheral. The peripheral position of guidance and advising in college priorities works to undermine the community college equity agenda. Although efforts in the classrooms can help to level the playing field for students academically, without support and quality advising students may never be able to reach many of these classrooms. In this way, developing high-quality guidance and advising is critical to increasing retention, graduation, transfer, and job placement rates.

A great deal more can be learned by community colleges about their students' enrollment patterns. Which courses act as gatekeepers, with large numbers of students withdrawing or failing? Do all students have similar success in developmental education courses, or are there identifiable patterns in which students that are low-income, first-time college-goers, racial or ethnic minorities, or full-time employees fail at higher rates? What happens to new cohorts of students once they enter the colleges—how many change their majors? How many persist to graduation? These questions can be answered with institutional data, and by conducting these types of studies colleges will be able to learn about their students and about how their institutions are supporting those students.

NOTES

1. In the goals students declared when they applied for the fall 2000 semester, 29.4% said they wanted to transfer; 3.3% said they were there to "formulate plans"; 21.9% were undecided; and 30.9% did not respond to the question, which I interpret to mean that they were undecided. This means that 56% of entering students were unsure, compared to 29% who said they wanted to transfer.

2. For evidence that high schools fail to provide their students much help in finding direction, aside from preaching "College for All," see Krei and Rosenbam (2001), Rosenbaum (2001), and Grubb and Watson (2002).

3. This triage model is consistent with the findings in Grubb (1996, chap. 2), based on interviews with about fifty community college students in California. The students with the clearest career plans and those with the least initiative and sense of purpose admitted to not using counseling services.

4. The one exception is a college that hired an additional counselor specifically for mental health issues, because the local deinstitutionalization of mental health had increased the numbers of students needing specialized services.

5. This finding confirms results in the literature, particularly from Keim's (1988) survey and from research by Coll and House (1991).

6. The split between financial counseling and other types of counseling is also reflected in the sparse literature, none of which mentions the potential need for financial counseling.

7. Similarly, the seminars included in cooperative education programs at LaGuardia, intended to serve as career exploration for liberal studies students, are sometimes taught as simple information transfer through lecture and sometimes taught in more conceptual and constructivist ways (Grubb and Badway, 1998).

8. The provision of information is the dominant approach to counseling in this country, in virtually all institutions. See, for example, Table 10.a in Herr and Cramer (1992), in which three of the top five services are occupational information, educational information, and individual assessment information.

9. Many developmental conceptions of career planning are described in Herr and Cramer (1992), especially chapter 4. These concepts, however, were rarely mentioned by counselors in the fifteen colleges. The typical system of advising, where students see counselors on a drop-in basis, cannot possibly be developmental, because there is no continuity.

10. None of the National Field Study colleges had PACE programs; on this approach see Grubb and Associates (1999), chapter 7.

11. The results should be interpreted cautiously: they are based on 5,800 students in forty-seven institutions, both two- and four-year colleges, half of whom were enrolled in the TRIO Student Support Services program for disadvantaged students with the other half a matched sample. Their application to *all* students, in community colleges *only*, is therefore a leap of faith. On the other hand, these are some of the only evaluation results of student support services at the college level. See Muraskin (1997) and the third-year longitudinal study results at www.ed .gov/offices/OUS/PES/higher/sssyr3html and sss3.html (accessed January 31, 2006).

CHAPTER NINE

Twice the Credit, Half the Time?

The Growth of Dual Credit at Community Colleges and High Schools

VANESSA SMITH MOREST AND MELINDA MECHUR KARP

It is Wednesday afternoon and students are taking their seats for Nancy Johnson's English 101 class at NWSCC, in Washington. These are not typical community college students. Although about 30% of the enrollments at this college are nonwhite, there are no African American or Hispanic students in the class. Of twenty-four students here today, four are of Asian descent, roughly reflecting the distribution of Asian students schoolwide. The students are strikingly different from those in other classes we have observed because they all know one another. Before the beginning of class, they turn in their chairs and chat in small gender-differentiated groups. They appear to be very young, and the three visibly older students sit on the periphery of the noisy mass of younger students, quietly looking through the materials they brought to class. We notice that several of the students flash smiles full of braces.

Nancy begins class by collecting papers. As she does so, she explains that the purpose of the homework was to develop analytical writing skills. As an example, she asks students how they would structure an essay around convincing readers about the characteristics that make a successful Running Start student: determination, good study skills, and reliable transportation are the suggestions made by students. Elaborating on her example, Nancy asks the class what the study-time rule is for college. A number of the students respond "two hours at home for one hour in class." No doubt, Nancy's example was contrived for our benefit, because later, as we walk out of the classroom together, she tells us that within the last few years she has had to reformulate her curriculum and pedagogy since well over half of the students in her English classes are now local high school students who are able to attend NWSCC tuition-free through the state's Running Start program. Nancy is nearing retirement and has been teaching English 101 at NWSCC for around thirty years.

Community colleges are increasingly engaging in partnerships with high schools that seek to provide high school students with the opportunity to enroll in college courses. These arrangements, usually called "dual enrollment" or "dual credit" programs,[1] are not new, because colleges have long allowed academically gifted students to enroll in advanced coursework. But dual enrollment has seen rapid growth over the past few years, both in terms of the numbers of students involved and the types of students targeted.

As programs expand, dual enrollment is drawing from a wider student population, providing the opportunity for college-level study to middle- and even low-achieving students in addition to the most advanced. These developments reflect a belief on the part of policy makers and educators that participation in rigorous academic experiences such as dual enrollment can promote student access to and success in college (Adelman, 1999; Martinez and Bray, 2002). Engaging in college-level work prior to high school graduation may encourage students to enter into postsecondary education when they might otherwise have chosen to forgo college.

In today's policy environment, dual enrollment programs are frequently seen as mechanisms for making access to postsecondary education more equitable and increasing the likelihood that disadvantaged and academically disengaged students will be successful in college (Bailey and Karp, 2003). Because students often participate in dual enrollment free of charge, these programs are also assumed to save families money and shorten students' time to degree. Though we will describe in this chapter other reasons for secondary and postsecondary institutions to encourage the expansion of dual enrollment, such as financial incentives and the opportunity to enhance institutional prestige, the potential for positive outcomes for students is perceived to be a primary motivation.

There is an inherent tension between opening access and ensuring that only students ready for college-level work participate in college courses. Colleges may be interested in ensuring the integrity of their academic programs, even more so than high schools. In addition, educators do not want to put their students in jeopardy of failure by enrolling them in college-level courses too soon. Thus, they may want to maintain high admissions standards for dual enrollment programs. Doing so, however, may exclude the middle- and low-achieving students most in need of an extra "push" toward college.

It is not surprising that institutions have both incentives and disincentives for expanding the range of students in dual enrollment programs. Although there is a growing literature on dual enrollment and other credit-based transition programs (cf. Hoffman, 2005; Karp et al., 2005; Kleiner and Lewis, 2005; Waits, Setzer, and

Lewis, 2005; Hughes et al., 2005), this study takes a unique approach by analyzing the incentives that both community colleges and high schools have to participate in dual enrollment. What are the pressures shaping dual enrollment at community colleges and their partner high schools? What are the motivations and drawbacks for developing the programs? This institutional analysis allows us to develop a stronger understanding of the equity implication of the dual enrollment movement.

In this chapter we begin by discussing the history and background of dual enrollment. We then describe the dual enrollment programs at our study sites, including a discussion of the characteristics of dual enrollment students, looking at whether they are typical college-bound students or a more academically diverse group of students. The subsequent section analyzes the incentives that colleges and high schools have to participate, and we end with conclusions, focusing on the implications of dual enrollment for the community college equity agenda.

Background

Dual enrollment allows high school students to enroll in and earn credit for college courses while they are still in high school. Unlike the College Board's Advanced Placement (AP) program, dual enrollment courses are offered directly by the colleges, and students receive college transcripts indicating their successful completion of courses. Course requirements and standards are set by the colleges themselves, as opposed to an external coordinating board. Both four-year and two-year institutions may sponsor dual enrollment programs, though community colleges are more likely than other postsecondary institutions to offer dual enrollment (Johnstone and Del Genio, 2001; Kleiner and Lewis, 2005). During the 2002–2003 school year, 98% of public two-year institutions enrolled high school students in college-credit courses, compared with 77% of public four-year and 40% of private four-year institutions.

There is a long history of collaboration between high schools and community colleges. In fact, a substantial number of public community colleges began as junior colleges in the early 1900s. Early community colleges were extensions of local K–12 school districts, and students continued from high school to junior college without leaving a common school building (Cohen and Brawer, 2003). These continuing students received instruction from the same teachers they had in high school, and the school administrators who provided leadership for their prior education often championed the creation of junior colleges. In these early days, the local public education systems at the secondary and postsecondary levels were virtually indistinguishable from one another. As the community college sector grew following World War II, however, a division between high schools and community colleges developed. Community colleges increasingly became part of state community college and higher education systems, and their involvement in local school districts became less direct.

Still, the linking of colleges and high schools existed in various forms throughout the twentieth century. High school students have long been able to earn college credit through programs like the AP program, the International Baccalaureate Organization's diploma program, and the College Board's College-Level Examination Program (CLEP) tests. In general, however, these programs have been targeted at academically advanced students and require financial and time commitments from students that make widespread participation unlikely.

The establishment of LaGuardia Middle College High School on the campus of LaGuardia Community College in New York City in 1974 represented a major organizational development linking high schools and colleges. Located on community college campuses, middle college high schools began providing students with access to high school and college-level courses simultaneously, as well as with counseling and other support to help them succeed academically. This organizational approach is interesting from the standpoint of community colleges because the schools tend to focus explicitly on students at risk of dropping out of high school as opposed to high achievers.

In the early years of the new century, this model has been expanded on by the Bill and Melinda Gates Foundation. According to the foundation's web site (www.gates foundation.org), by 2005 it had invested more than $114 million to create early college high schools around the country. Like middle colleges, early college high schools are located on college campuses; however, rather than taking a few college courses during high school, early college students accrue enough college credits to earn an associate degree or the equivalent of the first two years of a bachelor's degree. The Gates Early College Initiative has funded the start-up of these schools in more than twenty-five states; by 2008, 170 early college high schools are expected to be operating throughout the United States (Jobs for the Future, 2004).

During the early to mid-1990s, Tech Prep and the School-to-Work Opportunities Act began offering federal funding for the creation of institutional partnerships between community colleges and secondary schools for occupational education. Tech Prep encourages the development of a variety of programs linking high schools and community colleges. In some instances, high school students in Tech Prep programs take occupational courses at their high schools that can later be assigned college credit if the student decides to attend a community college with articulation agreements in place. Alternatively, some Tech Prep programs allow high school students to enroll in college technical courses. Finally, some Tech Prep programs emphasize career aware-ness through short-term activities such as mentoring and job shadowing.

In many communities, high school students have regularly been able to enroll in community college courses. Under this arrangement, students in need of academic enrichment or challenge could register at a college for a course or two, as a supple-ment to their regular high school curriculum. Dual enrollment began to receive widespread attention at the state level in the late 1980s and early 1990s, when a number of states passed legislation ensuring that all students had access to college courses while still in high school. In 2005, the National Governors Association rec-ommended expanded access to dual enrollment and other college- level courses as a key action strategy for states engaging in secondary education reform (National Governors Association, 2005).

Minnesota is credited with being the first state to adopt a policy supporting dual enrollment (Boswell, 2001; Clark, 2001). In 1985, the state created Postsecondary Enrollment Options (PSEO) to "promote rigorous academic pursuits and provide a variety of options" to high school juniors and seniors (Minnesota Statute Sec. 123.3514). Five years later, the state of Washington followed, implementing the Run-ning Start program. Like PSEO, Running Start provides public high school students with the opportunity to take college courses.

State policies addressing dual enrollment have become more common during the past fifteen years. Forty states have some sort of dual enrollment policy, though the comprehensiveness of these policies varies widely (Karp et al., 2005). Some states require schools to provide dual enrollment opportunities to students, whereas other states permit these options but let individual institutions decide whether to offer them. Likewise, some states place many regulations on course content or student admissions, while others do not.

With respect to the states in the National Field Study, Washington established its Running Start program in 1990. Texas and Florida both developed state dual enroll-ment policies during the early 1990s. California passed dual enrollment legislation in the late 1990s, formalizing what had until then been an informal process of al-lowing high school students to take college courses. Illinois began implementing a scholarship-based dual enrollment program in the late 1990s. Of the states in our study, only New York did not have a statewide policy for dual enrollment at the time of our research. Despite this, dual enrollment programs were common at the institu-tional level, and the City University of New York developed a system-wide policy for dual enrollment in 1999.

Reflecting the situation nationally, the content of the dual enrollment policies in the National Field Study states varied widely. California, Florida, and Washington mandated that postsecondary institutions offer dual enrollment opportunities to students, but in Texas and Illinois offering dual enrollment was voluntary. In California, students paid tuition for their dual enrollment courses, whereas in Illinois the state paid students' tuition. In Florida, the participating institutions paid tuition so that the program was free to students. At the time of our research, California and Illinois double-funded dual enrollment, meaning that both high schools and colleges received their average daily attendance (ADA) or full-time equivalent funding for high school students enrolled in college classes. In Texas and Washington, high schools lost ADA funding for students enrolled in college dual enrollment courses.

Nationally, participation in dual enrollment has increased as state systems have matured. The National Center for Education Statistics (NCES) estimates that 813,000 high school students nationwide took a course through a postsecondary institution during the 2002–2003 twelve-month academic year (Kleiner and Lewis, 2005); 619,000 of these students enrolled at public two-year institutions. In the 1990s, dual enrollment grew rapidly in some states. For example, in Virginia the number of students in dual enrollment more than tripled between 1991 and 1997 (Andrews, 2001). The number of students enrolled in dual credit courses in Illinois has grown from 2,220 in 1990 to 25,554 in 2001 (Barnett, 2003). Enrollments in the state of Washington have experienced rapid growth as well, more than tripling from 3,350 in 1992 to 13,699 in 2000 (Washington State Board for Community and Technical Colleges, 2001b). In New York City, the number of colleges offering dual enrollment increased from six to seventeen between 2000 and 2001 (Kleiman, 2001). Nearly 13,000 New York City high school students enrolled in a credit-based college course during the 2002–2003 school year (S. Cochran, personal communication).

This rapid program growth results in part from widespread beliefs about the potential benefits of dual enrollment programs for a wide range of students. Policy makers find many reasons to support dual enrollment. First, research has shown that many students do not challenge themselves during the senior year of high school (National Commission on the High School Senior Year, 2001). Dual enrollment provides value-added for students who have finished their high school curriculum early by allowing them to learn college-level material and prepare for the academic rigors of college. Second, aside from curricular benefits, dual enrollment offers the practical advantage of lowering the cost of postsecondary education. Because students are living at home and the cost of dual enrollment is frequently state-subsidized, they are able to accrue transferable credits that may shorten their time in college. In some states and localities the high schools also pick up a share of the cost, and high school students pay only for books and transportation when they enroll in college courses. As the cost of attending college continues to rise, the potential savings of dual enrollment are a significant benefit for students and their families.

Finally, some policy makers have taken the view that attending college classes can be beneficial to middle- and even low-achieving high school students (Lords, 2000). The central assumption is that dual enrollment will increase access to and improve retention in postsecondary education because students will enter college with a more realistic understanding of the skills they need to succeed in college. Moreover, many dual enrollment programs require students to pass college assessment tests before entering the program. Even if students fail these tests and cannot enroll, they have received an early warning about their lack of preparation (Kleiman, 2001).

The rest of this chapter looks at the development of dual enrollment at the National Field Study colleges. Data on dual enrollment programs were collected through interviews with personnel at the colleges who have direct involvement with high school partnerships, and interviews with admissions counselors and senior administrators. High school partnership personnel included Tech Prep directors, dual enrollment program directors, and a charter high school principal. Often these individuals had responsibility for more than one high school partnership program. At some sites, high school students who had participated in dual enrollment were interviewed in focus groups and faculty were interviewed whose classes enrolled large proportions of high school students.

In addition to conducting interviews at the fifteen National Field Study colleges, we interviewed guidance counselors of high schools partnering with eight of the colleges. Fourteen high schools were contacted, representing a geographically diverse subset of National Field Study college partnerships. Our questions of high school counselors fell into several categories. First, we asked about the features of the schools' dual enrollment programs, including course location and teachers, funding streams, and student recruitment and selection processes. We also asked about the history of the programs and the primary motivations for offering them. Next, we asked about student and parent views of dual enrollment, as well as the impact of dual enrollment on the school as a whole. Finally, we asked informants to tell us about other curricular options within their schools and districts.

The results of college and high school interviews were analyzed using N5 software for qualitative research (QSR International, 2000). Data were coded deductively, as a way to identify key themes related to institutional incentives and disincentives to participation. Because this analysis was exploratory in its framework and goals, we also sought and documented themes emerging from the data. Relatively little is

TABLE 9.1
High Schools in the Study

School	State	Location	Enrollment	Percent Free Lunch	Percent Non-white	Percent Attending College after Graduation[1]	Percent Participating in Dual Enrollment[2]	Dual Enrollment Selection Criteria
SWSHS#1	Texas	Rural	1,428	7.8	24.9	75	20	College placement test
SWSHS#2	Texas	Suburban	358	22.5	21.8	50	31	Counselor recommendation
SWSHS#3	Texas	Rural	480	24.8	26.7	85	3	College placement test
WRHS	California	Small Town	1,924	13.1	52.0	85	13	College placement test
NESHS	New York	Urban	1,299	40.1	25.9	87	55	Counselor recommendation
NEUHS	New York	Urban	437	83.7	99.8	90	18	College placement test
SUHS#1	Florida	Suburban	3,400	44.7	60.0		11	3.0 GPA
SUHS#2	Florida	Suburban	2,137	17.3	13.5	65	30	3.0 GPA
NWRHS#1	Washington	Small Town	1,742	30.6	26.0	50		College placement test
NWRHS#2	Washington	Rural	1,254	3.8	6.4	71	14	College placement test
NWSHS#1	Washington	Suburban	1,274	13.4	8.5	60[3]	13	College placement test
NWSHS#2	Washington	Suburban	1,392	0.0	20.3	75		
NWSHS#3	Washington	Suburban	1,497	1.7	13.8	92	8	College placement test
MWSHS	Illinois	Suburban	2,875	0.0	20.7	97		College placement test

SOURCES: U.S. Department of Education (2000a) Common Core of Data 2000–2001 and interviews with high school counselors.

1. This is an estimate given to us in interviews by the school counselors.

2. In schools where juniors may take dual enrollment courses, percent of juniors and seniors participating. In schools where only seniors may participate, percent of seniors only.

3. Sixty percent to four-year colleges; "a lot" go to two-year colleges.

known about the practices and scope of dual enrollment, and therefore our primary aim is that the findings presented here will pave the way for further research.

The Sites

All of the National Field Study sites partnered with high schools in some way. Specifically, all but one (SWRCC) offered Tech Prep. Three colleges partnered with middle college high schools (WSCC, SMCC, and WUCC). The most significant differences among the colleges included where courses were taught (at the high school or the community college), who taught the courses (high school teachers or community college faculty), and how students were taught (classroom or distance learning such as NERCC's offering of dual credit courses through a fiber optic network funded by Cablevision). Of the fifteen community colleges studied, one allowed only high school faculty to teach the classes and six allowed only college faculty, with the remaining eight allowing either high school or college faculty to teach courses. Similarly, one college allowed dual enrollment courses to be taught only at the high school, three allowed them to be taught only at the college, and the rest allowed them to be taught at both.

The characteristics of the high schools in our sample are described in Table 9.1. The high schools ranged in size from fewer than 400 students to nearly 3,500. Somewhat contrary to the popular perception of large urban schools and small rural ones, some of the largest schools in the sample were in rural areas, whereas the smallest was in a central city. The schools also varied in their racial and ethnic diversity. Although a few schools enrolled students who were predominantly or nearly all nonwhite, others enrolled only small numbers of minority students. Some of these partnering high schools enrolled high proportions of students from low socioeconomic backgrounds, but most had fewer than 25% of their students receiving free or reduced-price lunch.

Dual enrollment participation rates in the high schools varied widely. At one school, only 3% of students in the junior or senior classes participated in the dual enrollment program, whereas at another school 55% did so. In general, between 10% and 20% of juniors and/or seniors at the high schools were participating, with seven schools falling within this range. These proportions are quite high, given that in many cases we learned that students spend between half and all of their time on the college campuses.

In light of the eagerness of policy makers and college administrators to expand access to dual enrollment, we expected to find a wide range of students participating at our fourteen high schools. Program entrance requirements and counselor interviews, however, indicated that was not the case. In general, the dual enrollment programs targeted high-achieving or academically proficient students. All but two schools required students to pass a college placement test or have a certain grade point average (GPA) to enroll in a dual enrollment course. The two schools without such standards relied heavily on individual counseling to ensure that only students with potential for success could enroll. One of these schools explicitly counseled only the most advanced students into the program. The other school worked with students to place them in dual enrollment courses that were most appropriate to their abilities—the most advanced students enrolled in math and science courses, while lower-achieving students took a personal computing course.

These findings reflect the practices of dual enrollment programs nationally. Sixty-two percent of respondents to a survey of high schools conducted by NCES indicated that their school had admissions requirements for students wanting to enroll in a dual credit course (Waits, Setzer, and Lewis, 2005). These requirements commonly included meeting a set GPA, being recommended by a teacher for the course, or meeting a minimum score on a standardized test. Many schools required students to meet multiple admissions requirements.

Almost all informants in our study described dual enrollment students as focused, intellectually curious, and academically able. Many also commented that successful dual enrollment students were more than just academically proficient. Rather, they were emotionally mature and more responsible than the average high school student. One counselor said that "it is much easier to qualify for the program than it is to succeed in it" (NWRHS#2). Many students may be academically, but not socially or developmentally, ready for college work.

Most respondents said that the "typical" dual enrollment student was in the top 10%–20% of his or her class, but informants at three of the schools noted that the most advanced students tended not to enroll in dual enrollment, preferring to earn college credit through the AP program. Instead, dual enrollment students were those who are college-bound but shy away from the high-stakes nature of AP or are reluctant to commit the time necessary for success in AP courses.

Interviews with college staff indicate that participation in at least some dual enrollment programs is limited to those students coming from families with significant resources. Washington provides the clearest example of this. Although the Running Start program is popular with multiple interest groups such as legislators, parents, and students because of its cost-saving and choice-providing options, the director of these programs at NWSCC described the program as primarily a middle-class phenomenon, in part because students must have a car to drive to the community college to take dual enrollment courses.

Pressures Shaping Participation

From the standpoints of institutions and individuals, the incentives to participate in dual enrollment outweigh the disincentives. First, for community colleges, dual enrollment is well aligned with the mission "to meet the total post–high school needs of its community" (President's Commission on Higher Education, 1947). Community colleges can keep policy makers and taxpayers content by framing dual enrollment programs as community services that support the local high schools. Second, there appears to be a great deal of enthusiasm on the part of students and parents for dual enrollment programs. This means that dual enrollment can aid in recruitment for both college and high schools and help them maintain positive relationships with stakeholders. Finally, dual enrollment was perceived by some of the colleges in this study as being an important new revenue source.

Dual enrollment was frequently seen by college administrators and staff as a way to meet the needs of the local community and, as such, was perceived as fitting into the larger mission of the community college. Dual enrollment programs fit into this community service–oriented view of the college in a variety of ways. Dual enrollment programs frequently enabled the colleges to share institutional resources with local high schools. For example, when enrollments at high schools surge, dual enrollment allows for the absorption of increases without expanding buildings, particularly if high school students leave their building to attend dual enrollment classes at the college. On the other hand, community colleges make use of empty high school classrooms in the evening by running classes that enroll both college and high school students. This allows for a synergy in which each institution can maximize the use of its classrooms. From the standpoint of the colleges and high schools, dual enrollment allows for enrollment increases without capital investment.

Another type of resource sharing occurs around technical education, which is expensive for both community colleges and high schools to provide. For example, a Midwest urban college administrator mentioned that the original intent behind creation of dual enrollment programs was to share resources supporting career-technical education (CTE) courses so CTE would continue to be available to high school students. This administrator alluded to the possibility that secondary schools would eliminate CTE courses viewed as expensive or duplicative of those available at the postsecondary level. Current developments in federal support for dual enrollment hint at a shift of technical education from the secondary to postsecondary levels (U.S. Department of Education, 2003h).

In lower socioeconomic-status communities in particular, community colleges may offer dual enrollment as one of several college-preparation programs that may help high school students improve their odds of successfully transitioning to college. For example, at NEUCC, dual enrollment is one option among many, including Gear Up, Upward Bound, Liberty Partnerships, Tech Prep, and Project STEP. At a college in Texas, three high school-to-college transition programs provided a package of options through which high school students could earn college credit, rather than as individual programs. In this way, the colleges can contribute to local efforts to improve high school students' educational outcomes.

Some colleges also saw dual enrollment programs as helping local economic development efforts. For example, a technical education dean at SWUCC told us that, "because our region is in the high tech area, they are screaming for entry-level technicians, and the pipeline is not large enough. There aren't enough adults ready to go to work in these jobs. . . . [The] pipeline needs to expand to the high school level and start bringing more kids through." In teacher education, another high-demand field, WSCC had initiated planning for an articulated program to recruit prospective students in high school and provide dual enrollment opportunities at the community college along with a capstone option allowing students to matriculate to the local four-year institution to complete a bachelor's degree.

Although the motivation to provide services to the community was strong in the National Field Study colleges, the most compelling reasons to offer dual enrollment seemed to stem from other sources, including educators, policy makers, parents, and students. The enthusiasm for dual enrollment found among various stakeholders, encouraged colleges and high schools to offer dual enrollment options. Second, educational institutions, particularly colleges, saw dual enrollment as financially beneficial.

Much of the enthusiasm for dual enrollment programs stemmed from educators' beliefs that dual enrollment is beneficial to students. High school counselors, for example, reported that the primary motivation for high school involvement in dual enrollment was a conviction that students benefit from a variety of curricular options. Although most respondents described multiple benefits to dual enrollment, the positive nature of customizing students' educations was the most frequently stated. From this perspective, dual enrollment was a way to offer students more options, such as the ability to take interesting or challenging courses not available at the high school level. Explained one guidance counselor, "[O]ptions can't do anything but help kids succeed" (SUHS#1). Another asked, "Why should [the students] sit in English IV when they could do more?" (SWSHS#2). Likewise, one high school principal saw this as an extension of the individualization that occurred in the junior high school, in which students could begin to take high school courses earlier than their freshman year. He believed that students were "exhausting" the high school curriculum. Dual enrollment allowed these students to supplement their coursework and, in his opinion, increased their motivation through more individualized learning.

Two counselors reported that, for those with very specialized interests or clear career goals, dual enrollment allows students to build their own areas of interest. For example, students who desire intensive study in the sciences often cannot obtain it in high school because of the expense of lab equipment. Instead, students can take science-related courses at local colleges, or they can begin to take the prerequisites for their college majors (such as nursing) rather than taking high school courses that might not be interesting and would not benefit them as much in the future.

Some high schools offered dual enrollment in an attempt to reduce "senioritis." They believed that offering seniors the opportunity to take college classes increased students' motivation and made the senior year more meaningful and worthwhile. The staff of one school believed that dual enrollment courses exposed their students (who were primarily from low-income homes and whose parents had not, by-and-large, attended college) to the social and academic demands of postsecondary education.

Students also benefited from dual enrollment, according to high school staff, because it enabled them to receive free or low-cost college credit. This benefit seemed particularly salient for schools with a significant portion of students from low-socioeconomic-status families: "Even private local [colleges] as well as state schools accept credit from [the partner college]. So, dual enrollment kids really do end up with a full semester of college credit, which has a huge financial benefit" (SWSHS#3). In fact, college personnel take advantage of these programs for their own children.

At the colleges, individual instructors felt that they benefited from dual enrollment. Many college instructors perceived dual enrollment students as highly motivated and intelligent. Explained a math instructor at NWSCC, "[The Running Start] students were very pleased to say who they were because they were so proud of it because they wanted to learn because they were going to take calculus earlier. I mean they had a whole different perspective and the mix was marvelous. So I find them to be quite a treat."

Some regularly matriculated students concurred with their instructors, noting that the Running Start students in their courses were difficult to tell apart from other students. In addition, they perceived the dual enrollment students as interested in academic success and highly motivated, in contrast to recent high school graduates who were in college only because "it's their next step that they are supposed to do" (NWSCC student).

Sensing parental enthusiasm for dual enrollment—the counselor at school SUHS#1 said that parents' "eyes light up" when they learn about the program—some high schools and colleges found that there were institutional benefits to participation. In one urban high school (NESHS) that had been losing its students as their families moved to the suburbs, dual enrollment was an explicit mechanism for stemming white flight and salvaging the reputation of the school. This school was actively expanding dual enrollment offerings, in part to increase student motivation and help the students save money on college tuition, but also because dual enrollment was an important factor in maintaining enrollment levels. A counselor explained that the school needed to be seen by parents as "flexible and offering good courses so that families will stay in the area and not move to the suburbs" (NESHS). Dual enrollment was a good public relations tool in this way, and it helped maintain a reputation as "a good school."

Similarly, some colleges hoped to parlay student participation in a single dual enrollment course into increased prestige for their institutions. Community colleges have long been stigmatized as the bottom rung in the postsecondary hierarchy. Dual enrollment gave the colleges an opportunity to provide convincing evidence to parents that their curricula overlap with those of four-year institutions. For instance, at MWSCC, a suburban college in Illinois where dual enrollment was just beginning to take root, an admissions officer noted that this was a long-awaited opportunity for the college to prove its value to reluctant parents and students: "This particular demographic here is a pretty affluent area, and what we battle, particularly in the high schools, is parental pressure, social pressure of the families, for the students to go to a four-year institution and not the local community college."

Community colleges viewed dual enrollment as a valuable mechanism for allowing high school students to sample community college programs. For example, a K–12 partnership director at NESCC told us that "a lot of our high school students are opting to go someplace else. So by beginning to broaden the appeal of the collaborative programs, we're beginning to help high school students see the college as slightly different. Collaborative programs, in my opinion, are the first line of contact for many school administrators, teachers, and students too, to the college. So, we're your first impression."

Finally, colleges in our sample agreed that financial incentives were an important element in their decision to offer dual enrollment opportunities. An administrator at SWSCC referred to the dual credit program at his college as a "cash cow." Another SWSCC official commented that financial benefits have made dual credit attractive to community colleges in the state and also to universities that are seeking new revenue streams. This official pointed out, "[Dual credit has] grown to the point now that four-year colleges and universities are wanting to get in on the game, and [the state] has legislation pending now saying we should be able to go into the high schools and offer college credit courses as well. They [referring again to the universities] were never interested in it until it became big business."

An NESCC administrator confirmed the importance of dual credit as a new funding source, admitting that the program helped to make up for lost revenue associated with the college's regular curriculum, saying, "[I]n the last two years, the college has made its budget because of this [dual credit] program and the growth in it, because our [regular] enrollment has decreased." He went on, speaking glowingly about the funding incentives associated with dual credit courses: "It's sort of a gold mine. It doesn't cost them [the community college] anything. Very little. They don't have to have a classroom. It's all done in the high school. [M]any times high school teachers have master degrees so that they actually certify the high school teacher as a community college professor, taught in the high school classroom by the high school teachers. They get state and local reimbursement, and of course the high school continues to get whatever funding they've raised." At this particular college, both the state and the county reimburse community colleges on the basis of full-time equivalent enrollments.

It is important to point out that, although funding for dual enrollment may benefit colleges and individuals, it is not clear that it benefits states. This has come to be known as a problem of double-dipping, in which both the colleges and high schools receive state funding for the same students. An example of this comes from Illinois' Accelerated College Enrollment (ACE) initiative. In 1997, a new funding formula permitted both high schools and community colleges to collect state funding for students enrolled in dual credit courses. In 2001, the state of Illinois implemented the ACE program, which provided state funding at the rate of $55 per credit hour to public community colleges to underwrite all or a portion of students' dual enrollment expenses (Barnett, 2003). Since the initiation of the ACE grant, dual credit enrollments have risen dramatically, to 25,554 during the 2001–2002 school year, with 17,006 of them supported by the state's ACE grants.

Although community service, individual and institutional benefits, and financing are all compelling reasons for colleges and high schools to engage in dual enrollment, the data also revealed some disincentives. In particular, community college faculty were not unilaterally supportive of the programs, logistical and scheduling problems were common, and high school counselors reported several disadvantages for their institutions.

Faculty resistance focused on quality, job security, and territorial issues. According to a vice president at NESCC, dual credit courses were perceived as threatening student enrollments and therefore teaching jobs, saying, "The union has been trying to bury the high school program ever since we started it. You are taking students out of seats. You are taking work away from faculty by shifting it to another area." A K–12 director at another college (NESCC) noted that "there is a suspicion on the part of the faculty that the high school teachers aren't doing as good of a job." Other faculty felt that teaching high school students threatened their status, because they were "the lowest one[s] on the totem pole if you go out to the high schools and teach. They're [college faculty] not used to discipline; they're not used to interruptions and announcements" (SUCC, Director of Dual Enrollment Programs).

Some faculty also found that including high school students in their classes created additional pressures to which they were unaccustomed. For example, according to the K–12 director at SWSCC, parents of seniors in danger of failing a dual enrollment course sometimes tried to pressure their instructors to give passing grades for failing work.[2] The performance of dual enrollment students had to be carefully followed, so high school graduation was not threatened by failure of college courses (NWRCC, Tech Prep Coordinator). Other faculty members reported feeling constrained by the young age of dual enrolled students. Explained the director of dual enrollment at SUCC, "I've had calls from parents, like in the psychology class, a parent had complained that they touched on sexuality and things. And I have to tell them, that's the content of a college course." This respondent also indicated that such concerns should not—but might—change the tenor of a college classroom: "But there's a maturity thing, particularly when they [high school students] come to campus. There's a poor maturity thing. People in the class shouldn't have to feel uncomfortable because there's a child in the class, a fourteen-year-old and they don't want to say something that should be part of the discussion in a college classroom."

Colleges sought ways to minimize faculty resistance. In response to parental concerns regarding sexuality and other course content, SUCC limited dual enrollment participation to high school juniors and seniors. Administrators at MWRCC were successful at putting conciliatory language into the union contract about dual credit courses: "Dual credit courses shall not be used for the purpose of reducing the number of, consolidating, or eliminating bargaining unit positions at the college" and that "specific policies and procedures for dual credit at [the college] shall be reviewed annually by representatives of the faculty and the administration." Further, SWSCC began to offer financial incentives to encourage college faculty to teach courses at high schools.

High school teachers and counselors also saw disincentives to participation, because, from their point of view, some of the best students may be abandoning high school to attend college classes. In some high schools, dual enrollment was seen as competing with other curricular offerings or school goals. Some of these schools were losing funding when their students enrolled in dual enrollment courses and therefore felt budgetary constraints when a critical mass of students participated. One school, for example, was facing staff cuts because they had lost too many full-time-equivalent students in the past year. Although this loss was not directly attributed to dual enrollment, the counselor we spoke to noted that if the sixty-two dual enrollment students were on the high school campus instead of at the college, the school might not be confronting this situation (NWSHS#3).

As a result of the loss of funding for dual enrollment students, some schools were reluctant to advertise the program: "We'd rather keep [the students] here . . . but we live with it, we cooperate with it, we realize we're going to have to send kids to [the college]" (NWRHS#1). Counselors' reluctance was often magnified because, at least in some states, high schools are expected to counsel dual enrollment students and keep track of their progress toward high school graduation, even when the students no longer attend the high school and the high school receives no funding. This added burden was understandably troublesome for schools and counselors already strapped for both time and money. A few interviewees, however, did note that the loss of funding, while unfortunate, was something that the schools could adjust to and learn to budget for, and so it could become less of a concern over time.

Other schools felt negative consequences from dual enrollment in terms of the loss of students, particularly those at the top of their class. Three schools described the difficulties of maintaining large AP or honors programs while encouraging dual enrollment participation. One school (SUHS#2) had dropped its honors English course for seniors in favor of dual enrollment. Administrators at the other two schools (SWSHS#3 and NWSHS#3) had considered doing this as well, although at the time of our interview they had not yet dropped any courses. In essence, there was competition for the best students between the high school-based courses, such as AP, and the college courses. In light of the prestige of AP and honors courses and the desire on the part of many high school teachers to teach these classes, the loss (or threat of the loss) of advanced high school courses is an undesirable side effect of offering dual enrollment. At some schools, teachers resented the pressure put on AP courses by dual enrollment and, in the words of one informant, "talk[ed] it down to their students" (SWSHS#3) in an attempt to maintain AP and honors enrollments. The difficulty of balancing the schools' desire to offer AP courses and please their teachers while offering students dual enrollment was not lost on a number of our interviewees.

Three schools also noted that, even if course offerings themselves were not affected by dual enrollment, the loss of the most advanced students to dual enrollment had a negative impact on the school. Because dual enrollment students tend to be some of the best in their classes, their loss was felt in terms of a changed academic atmosphere in the classrooms. Course discussions, for example, were perceived to be suffering without the input of the brightest students. One counselor called this aspect of dual enrollment a "brain drain" for the school. As he explained, "[I]t takes some of the best students away from the school . . . and that's fine but we won't actively recruit [students to dual enrollment]. We are trying to maintain the academic integrity of our programs" (NWRHS#2).[3]

Navigating the different organizational structures and institutional cultures at the K–12 and higher education levels poses additional challenges to dual enrollment programs. A dean at WUCC related the ways that different schedules and requirements complicated dual credit offerings: "The college had its normal seventeen-week structure, and we discovered that many times, that [the local high] school was successful at football, so the students were not allowed to come to school because they had to go to a pep rally. Or teachers had some in-service, so the students had the day off. . . . It was gumming up the system. We'd have to make up classes because the students were being taken out of class, and we [would still] have to meet a minimum number of Carnegie hours."

Offering related complaints, a K–12 administrator at SWSCC reported a similar observation on institutional differences, saying that faculty of dual credit courses "had to get grades out every six weeks, unlike the college. It was a hassle. They are grading on a high school basis, maintaining the high school hours and holidays, which aren't consistent with ours and so there's extra effort." Such challenges were not insurmountable. In both cases creative scheduling and shifting school calendars helped bridge the two educational sectors. Nonetheless, it is evident that these programs create many logistical challenges to participating individuals and institutions.

Discussion and Conclusions

In general, the incentives to offer dual enrollment outweighed the disincentives at the institutions in our study. Faculty at both colleges and high schools appeared to be some of the programs' most significant detractors. Their voices, however, are not likely to be heard amid the din of enthusiasm generated by policy makers, college financial officers and other college officials, and parents. Furthermore, we found no shortage of faculty at both levels who were supportive of the programs.

Many educational institutions have a financial interest in dual enrollment. Community colleges, and in some cases high schools, are able to obtain additional funds for dual enrolled students. There are also hidden savings for the colleges, depending on how the dual enrollment classes are structured. In some cases, dual enrollment classes are being run off-site at high schools, using high school faculty with master's degrees. These classes do not require the time of full-time college faculty, and they do not displace college-age students by using college classroom space. From the standpoint of high schools, the savings may be even greater, because enrolling in college courses potentially costs less than K–12 per-student expenditures. Finally, high schools whose dual enrollment students attend class on a college campus may be able to alleviate some overcrowding. This, however, does not take into account economies of scale, because high schools cannot easily eliminate teachers even when class sizes drop below normal.

Many at community colleges see dual enrollment as a recruitment strategy. From the perspective of community colleges, high school students are a relatively untapped resource. Although it is true that, in some communities, many students may attend the local community college after high school, the colleges can now enroll them prior to graduation. Furthermore, our interviews indicated that the students who are taking advantage of dual enrollment are not the ones who typically would attend community college. In this sense, community colleges are tapping into the resources of four-year colleges. At one of our sites (NESCC), this had been recognized by four-year colleges, which were either starting their own programs or developing strict criteria about coursework that would be awarded transfer credit.

High schools, as we learned through our interviews, are also using these programs as recruiting tools. The concept of the "shopping mall high school" evolved at the beginning of the last century with the expansion of compulsory secondary schooling (Powell, Farrar, and Cohen, 1985). As long as we have laws mandating that students stay in high school until they reach a certain age, high schools are likely to diversify curricula to keep as many of their constituents as happy as possible. In today's climate of expanded "consumer" choice in public education, a program of dual enrollment that promises to save parents on college tuition can become a significant factor in a school's ability to retain the best students.

Prestige also accrues to community colleges with dual enrollment programs. Certainly from the standpoint of community colleges, the opportunity to enroll students who would otherwise attend four-year institutions can distinguish the colleges. College personnel spoke about these connections as offering opportunities to inform high school counselors about their programs. Community colleges are also expanding honors programs that aim to prepare students to transfer to top universities, both public and private. These programs can recruit high school students early, helping to recast the colleges as part of a pipeline to higher status postsecondary education options. From the standpoint of the high schools, the availability of dual credit expands the college preparation possibilities for students who do not qualify for honors or AP programs.

There are many questions about dual enrollment programs that remain unanswered. To begin with, there is little evidence of their effectiveness for high school students or their efficiency from the standpoint of state governments, because colleges and high schools do not track the progress of students in these programs. For example, what proportion of participants successfully earns college credits? Do they apply the credits toward further postsecondary education? If so, which colleges and universities accept the credits, and what do they count toward? If the situation is anything like the articulation between community colleges and four-year colleges in traditional transfer programs, it is likely that dual enrollment credits only count as electives. While elective credits are helpful, they may end up displacing other credits that can encourage students to develop cultural awareness or expand their experiences into new fields. Research may later show that dual enrollment credits may not count toward graduation.

In addition, our data indicate that dual enrollment may not actually increase middle- or lower-achieving students' access to college-level coursework. All but two of our high schools had admissions requirements for their dual enrollment programs; the majority of these schools required students to pass a college entrance exam or have a high GPA to participate in dual enrollment. Guidance counselors were mixed in their assessment of a "typical" dual enrollment student, and, although some indicated that dual enrollment reaches a broader range of students than do AP or honors programs, most indicated that dual enrollment students are academically strong and oriented toward college attendance prior to their participation. It is not clear, then, that dual enrollment enables a broader range of students to take college-credit courses in high school. Instead, dual enrollment may be an additional curricular option for those students already being well served by honors or AP courses. In fact, in one high school in our sample, dual enrollment supplanted honors courses, and others felt that dual enrollment and AP courses competed for the same students.

The admissions requirements put in place at the schools in our sample may have excluded many middle-range and academically disadvantaged students. A 2004 set of case studies of college and high school dual enrollment programs that purposefully sought a sample of programs serving a wide range of student came to similar conclusions (Hughes et al., 2005).

One way to minimize the negative impact of admissions requirements on access is to implement comprehensive and enhanced comprehensive dual enrollment.[4] These programs build students' skills over time by aligning developmental coursework (often offered by the partner college) with the program's admissions standards so that, ultimately, students are able to meet the necessary requirements. By including a pathway of developmental coursework culminating in a college credit dual enrollment course, such programs ensure that students are ready for college-level work while at the same time maintaining access for those students in need of additional assistance (Hughes et al., 2005). None of the sites in the current study used this strategy. Therefore, students who could not meet the college course entry standards were prevented from participating in the dual enrollment program altogether.

In light of the academic proficiency of dual enrollment students, and the selection bias that may occur, it is not at all clear that dual enrollment is helping disadvantaged or even middle-achieving students enter and succeed in postsecondary education. If dual enrollment students are more successful in college (which, it should be noted, has not been indicated by any current research), this may be an artifact of their already strong academic performances, not their dual enrollment participation. Even more disconcerting for those concerned with expanding educational equity, it seems unlikely that dual enrollment is expanding curricular options for students in need of such opportunity. It is possible that dual enrollment programs actually increase, rather than reduce, curricular stratification within high schools.

From the standpoint of equity and access, the implications are therefore mixed. These programs increase access for some students to postsecondary education. Students need not leave home and may save significant amounts of money by enrolling early. The equity implications, however, are not as clear. First, it is too early to tell whether the quality of these courses is equivalent to other college options. We have yet to find out how acceptable these credits are to four-year colleges and universities, and, in all likelihood, these outcomes may be influenced by market pressures. Colleges and universities most in need of enrollments may be most likely to accept the credits. Furthermore, it may take a substantial amount of self-advocacy for the average student to maximize the value of credits earned in high school. Both of these results will favor students who have access to the best information and financial support.

Finally, from a public standpoint, the structure of financing for dual enrollment suggests that state governments pay a large part of the bill. In some cases, state governments are paying the bill twice by compensating both high schools and community colleges. In instances where only one institution is compensated, arrangements have to be made between the school districts and the college. Because community colleges subsidize the cost of tuition with state funds, there is no question that some of the local cost of public education is being shifted to the state. Although high school–age students win in this game, it remains unknown whether there is a population of college-age students who ultimately lose if colleges shift their focus toward enrolling a younger population.

Although there is considerable variation in the structure of dual enrollment by state and institution, the findings of our study suggest that its underlying motivations do not necessarily favor increasing equity. As with other programs at community colleges, the financial stakes of dual enrollment are linked to enrollment of students rather than retention. In fact, as we have said, community college faculty and administrators reported the perception that most dual enrolled students do not attend community colleges after high school, making retention a moot point.

Furthermore, motivations make it unlikely that dual enrollment will move in the direction of serving low-income or disadvantaged students for several reasons. Because increased institutional status is one byproduct of dual enrollment programs, along with strengthened connections to taxpayers, community colleges are unlikely to abandon the opportunity to serve higher-income, better-prepared students. Dual enrollment is also seen as financially beneficial by colleges in part because participating students require limited support services. For colleges to focus on lower-income or disadvantaged students, they would have to increase their student support services (Bailey and Karp, 2003; Hughes et al., 2005). Along with the problem of support services, we know that most dual enrollment programs are avoiding the issue of remediation by having entry requirements in place. In most cases, it would be very difficult for a community college to provide college preparatory or explicitly high school–level education to high school students, as would be the case with developmental coursework.

Developing the equity agenda in dual enrollment is thwarted by the shortage of data. Some of the colleges in the study had a coordinator for dual enrollment who kept track of the names of dual enrolled students. Unless the colleges do something in their data system to flag high school students or have a coordinator who tracks them, there is no way to distinguish between high school and college students. On the other side of the equation, high schools are generally ill equipped to collect and analyze data on their students, though this is sometimes done at the district level (particularly since the development of No Child Left Behind). Systematic data at the high school level on postsecondary activities of students is particularly scarce. Research conducted by Hughes et al. (2005) finds that, even if data on students are collected at one level, they are rarely shared with the other.

The result of this shortage of data is that knowledge of dual enrollment is formed mostly through anecdote and individual perception. Although colleges and high schools claim that the students they enroll in dual enrollment come from the middle range of students, they may be serving lower-income and disadvantaged students without realizing it. They might also significantly improve the ability of students to apply their college credits if more were known about where students go to college and whether retention should be a concern.

Addressing these problems would probably best be done at the system or state levels, because the incentives and time are not available at the institutional level. Furthermore, if education is conceptualized as a PK–16 pathway, centralizing information about where students are earning and applying their credits would be essential to understanding how well students move through the system. This is particularly true of dual enrollment, where students may earn credits at a community college and apply them to a four-year college. In light of the current uses and motivations underlying the development of dual enrollment, it is therefore fair to say that much work is needed if these programs are to increase equity by providing not only access but also outcomes to a broad range of students.

NOTES

1. All high school students taking college courses are participating in dual enrollment, as they are simultaneously enrolled in high school and college. Sometimes, these students earn high school as well as college credit under an arrangement referred to as "dual credit." Both arrangements existed at National Field Study colleges, though most colleges sponsored dual enrollment, rather than dual credit, programs. In this chapter, we tend to use the more general term.

2. In some cases, students took dual credit courses to fulfill high school graduation requirements. If they failed these courses, the students not only missed out on earning college credit, but also did not earn credit needed for their high school diploma. Occasionally, this could prevent students from graduating with their class. Students, however, were often not aware of this potential consequence when enrolling.

3. The colleges were not blind to high schools' reluctance to encourage dual enrollment participation. A director of dual credit programs at a northwest suburban college described the behavior of secondary administrators as "passive-aggressive," pointing to problems with their failing to inform students of dual credit course options, saying, "They just don't circulate the info as much as they should. They don't promote it to parents as much as we [community college administrators] think they should."

4. Bailey and Karp (2003) define comprehensive dual enrollment programs as those programs containing a sequence of dual enrollment courses such that they encompass much of a students' educational experience. Enhanced comprehensive dual enrollment programs also include support services for students, such as counseling and assistance with college applications.

CHAPTER TEN

The Community College Equity Agenda in the Twenty-First Century

Moving from Access to Achievement

THOMAS BAILEY AND VANESSA SMITH MOREST

In 2001, community college faculty, staff, and students celebrated the hundredth anniversary of the founding of the first junior college, originally designed to provide lower-division college education to allow elite universities to concentrate on research and advanced professional training (Brint and Karabel, 1989; Dougherty, 1994). At that time, access to higher education in general was still restricted to a small elite. Since then, community colleges have taken on a plethora of functions and post-secondary education has become a mass activity, experienced by about three-quarters of each age group, and now considered a prerequisite for access to "good" jobs, however "good" is defined.

Conceived as institutions to relieve colleges of the burden of educating eighteen and nineteen year olds, community colleges now play a crucial role in opening the opportunity of higher education to all of the population. As the economic impor-tance of college has grown, providing all of the population the opportunity to acquire a college education has become a more important element in a search for equity and justice in society.

How well have community colleges realized this equity agenda? Have recent de-velopments in the past decade threatened that agenda? What are colleges and policy makers doing to advance that agenda, and what can they do to strengthen it? These are the questions that have preoccupied the authors of this book.

The past decade has seen a shift in thinking about community colleges, from an emphasis on access to one on overall educational attainment, especially degree attainment—that is, a shift from getting students into college to what happens to them once they are there. The presence of community colleges has opened access to higher education for a broad range of students. This access is based on lower costs, proximity, and efforts to accommodate the needs of even those students who are not prepared academically for college. Enrollment data show that community colleges attract a disproportionate number of low-income students and students who face other barriers to college, and, if community colleges were not available, fewer students would attend college at all (Rouse, 1995; Alfonso, 2004; Dougherty, 1994).

Community colleges have played a crucial role in opening access to college, but more work remains to be done. Almost one-quarter of high school students never enroll in any college. Although it could be that it is not necessary that every student attend college (Rosenbaum, 2001), what is disturbing about the students who never do so is that the group is dominated by students from the poorest families. This is not to say that solving this problem is the sole responsibility of community colleges, though they can play a role. Our point is that, despite the progress in providing postsecondary opportunities, access to college remains limited for low-income students and those from some minority groups.

It is fair to say that community colleges have made a crucial contribution to opening college access, but their role in providing overall equity in higher education outcomes is less clear. The majority of students who start community college do not earn a degree or certificate. Certainly some of those students did not intend to complete a degree, but completion rates are still low even after taking student goals into account (Bailey, Jenkins, and Leinbach, 2005). Research continues to show that students who want to complete a bachelor degree are less likely to do so if they start in a community college, even for similar students (Pascarella and Terenzini, 2005). In a *New York Times* article about the large number of students who do not complete college, Glenn Dubois, the chancellor of the Virginia Community College System summarized the problem in his state in a statement that could apply to most states: "We here in Virginia do a good job of getting them [students] in. We have to get better at getting them out" (Leonhardt, 2005). The need to do a better job of "getting them out" will grow if states and individuals increasingly turn to these colleges because of their relatively low cost.

Thus, over the past decade, policy makers, researchers, and staff at the colleges themselves have increasingly turned their attention to community college outcomes as well as access.[1] Researchers have been concerned with retention and especially transfer for many years, and community college staff and faculty have always worked to improve outcomes for their students. Nevertheless, the concrete incentives that influence college behavior are based on enrollments rather than student progress. Moreover, in most cases, the data systems and records that colleges could use to understand the experience of their students were designed to count enrollments at a given time, rather than to follow individual students through their college careers. Thus, the good intentions and hard work of community college faculty in promoting the success of their students are generally not reinforced by the institutional incentives and information systems. As a result, completion rates for community college students have not been widely known, and their significance has often been disputed. At the institutional and state levels, the emphasis has been, and remains, on cross-sectional rather than longitudinal tracking and analysis.

This book seeks to strengthen the community college equity agenda, by assessing a series of developments that could threaten that agenda, analyzing the measures that a sample of fifteen colleges have taken to address those challenges, and developing recommendations for how that agenda could be strengthened.

Challenges to the Community College Equity Agenda

At the turn of the century, when this project was conceived, there was widespread anxiety among educators in community colleges concerning various developments in the higher education system that might threaten the health of community colleges and their equity agenda. The turn of the millennium was a time at which higher education institutional boundaries and control seemed to be challenged.

The rapid and well-publicized growth of the for-profits led to warnings that these dynamic institutions were going to threaten the enrollments and missions of public institutions, that "their students should be our students" (Zeiss, 1998; Newman, Couturier, and Scurry, 2004). The growth of industry certifications appeared to usher in a new era of competency-based education that would sever the ties between credentials and the institutions providing the instruction (Adelman, 2000). In the extreme case, any organization might prepare students while colleges would simply provide the credential by administering the test. What role would traditional community colleges play in this "parallel universe?" On-line education foreshadowed the end of the bricks-and-mortar-classroom, leaving behind any colleges that did not get in early enough to the on-line game—geographic service areas would be a thing of the past, and every college would potentially compete with every other college in the world (Levine, 1997). Controversies around the restriction of developmental education to community colleges worried some that community colleges would be seen more and more as colleges for the ill-prepared. The growing accountability movement loomed as a threat, too. Regulators seemed to be focusing on what community college personnel considered inappropriate outcomes, such as simple graduation rates, to measure and pay colleges. These initiatives neglected the community college-level perspective that multiple missions meant that graduation rates provided at best a distorted picture of community college performance.

The chapters in this book have shown that these anxieties were exaggerated. The for-profits did continue to grow, but they retained only a small share of the market. For community colleges in particular, complementarity seems a more appropriate description of the public community college/for-profit interaction than competition. From the point of view of the state, both community colleges and the for-profits (and private colleges in general) were lower-cost alternatives to public four-year institutions. The certificate frenzy, closely associated with education for information technology skills, faded with the dot-com bust. On-line education has continued to grow, but at least so far it has had its main influence in hybrid courses rather than stand-alone on-line education with no bricks and mortar. Many community colleges have steadily absorbed the on-line modality into their standard operating procedures. Colleges in states that have concentrated developmental education in community colleges seem to have adjusted with no major discontinuities in the four-year or the two-year sector, though profound problems with the developmental function remain.

Accountability, especially performance-based funding, so far has been a paper tiger. It has not threatened college funding or enrollments, though it does appear to be contributing to the broad shift of focus from enrollments to outcomes and may create incentives for community colleges to become more selective. Although its direct impact has been limited, it has had indirect influence by promoting more discussion of student outcomes. Thus, it is part of a broader set of influences, including pressure from accreditors, pushing colleges to shift their attention from access to student success.

Looking back from the second half of the decade, the anxieties of the late 1990s seem difficult to understand. Perhaps the turn of the millennium promoted an apocalyptic perspective. More likely, the economic frenzy associated with the dot-com bubble probably accounts for much of the aura. The information technology industry was directly associated with on-line education and the certification movement. In the days when analysts predicted that the Dow Jones Industrial Average would rise to 36,000 and that the rules of the "old economy" no longer applied, and before the scandals at Enron and other companies came to light, the private sector seemed to be a risk-free source of wealth and productive solutions. This environment surely made it seem as though anything was possible with on-line education and that the for-profits could develop into particularly formidable institutions.

Emerging Challenges

Although some of these anxieties were exaggerated, different challenges have emerged. The flush state coffers of the 1990s gave way in the new century to deficits and powerful resistance to tax increases. Indeed, the growing tax revenues at the end of the century hid a trend in many states in which the postsecondary education share of state budgets was actually declining as the budget share of medical costs, corrections, and, in many states, K–12 education grew (Kane, Orszag, and Gunter, 2003). The economic recovery that took place during the middle years of the first decade of the century did begin to restore revenue to state governments (Fischer, 2006), but there were many claims on those resources and pressures to increase expenditures on medical care and K–12 education continued to be strong. These fiscal trends took place just as the baby boom echo and continued high levels of immigration swelled college enrollments. Thus, whereas at the turn of the century colleges worried that the for-profits, distance education, and certification might empty their classrooms, by the middle of the decade they were more concerned about is how to keep their classrooms from overflowing while their budgets shrank (Boggs, 2004).

As state institutional funding has dropped, colleges have raised tuition, leading to an increase in the "privatization" of higher education. Public sector financial assistance, especially needs-based aid, has not kept up. This raises the financial bar for higher education in general, but it also casts new light on community colleges as lower-cost alternatives to baccalaureate-granting institutions.

The accountability movement has continued to grow, although the Bush administration's focus on elementary and, later, high school education has shifted accountability attention away from higher education. Various trends suggest that colleges may face greater pressures for accountability in the future. In 2005, Bush administration officials began to emphasize a desire to apply the accountability principles on which the No Child Left Behind (NCLB) Act is based to higher education. As the consensus has grown that some college or a baccalaureate degree has become almost essential for access to good jobs, as we have emphasized, there has been increased discussion of strengthening the K–16 pipeline. In addition to any incentives or sanctions imposed by regulation or accountability, the federal government, states, private funders, and the colleges themselves have become more aware of the leakage in the educational pipeline and that this leakage is much too closely related to income and race than it ought to be.

It remains to be seen how seriously state and federal legislators and education officials will take the inequalities inherent in these numbers. Nevertheless, as of now, state and federal officials are focused on these efforts. At the federal level, NCLB does emphasize closing the gap among groups, so, to the extent that these concepts are transferred, this approach will become part of higher education. High-profile foundation initiatives, including those of the Gates Foundation, the Ford Foundation, and the Lumina Foundation, are working to create an environment in which gaps are closed. Several states have joined these initiatives.

Therefore, in the middle of the first decade of the twenty-first century, the community college environment is characterized by fiscal constraint and the growing importance of tuition, accompanied by increasing discussion about outcomes with a focus on achieving overall educational equity among income and racial groups. This shift has profound implications for community colleges.

Enrollment simply involves getting a student through the college door. Community colleges have made important contributions to college access by providing educational opportunity to a wide range of students. As open-door institutions they enroll, in one way or another, almost any student who applies. Even those students who are not prepared for college level work can enroll in developmental education. Ironically, such a focus reduces the incentives for colleges to be concerned with the preparation of their entering students. To be sure, they need to provide remedial education, but a greater emphasis on what happens to students once they are enrolled immediately highlights the problems of their initial preparation. An enrollment focus also requires less attention to connections both within the colleges and among them.

Colleges emphasizing getting students in the door can operate in "silos." There need not be any connection between credit and noncredit programs. Certificate programs need not lead to associate degrees. Divisions and barriers between "terminal" occupational associate degrees and academic transfer programs can be maintained. Transfer itself does not necessarily receive much attention. Indeed, most community college faculty and administrators have only vague ideas about what happens to their students after they leave.

A shift from enrollment to outcomes, especially as educational demands grow, however, calls for much greater integration and connection among these different segments of the community college. It is not enough to get someone in the door; a student needs to be prepared to have success in college. This gives colleges a stronger stake in the quality of high schools. We have argued that data on certificates and noncredit suggest that these programs may not have strong economic benefits. Students may want to enroll in occupational programs to be able to work in the short term but also want eventually to move on to a bachelor degree, and of course those students who explicitly want to transfer and complete a baccalaureate degree must get help in that endeavor.

Despite the personal commitment of community college faculty and administrators to the success of their students, funding incentives and data systems are funda-mentally driven by enrollment. For the most part, with respect to funding, a brand-new student, a retained student, or one about to graduate is equivalent for almost all colleges. Moreover, as we will show below, most colleges cannot or do not track students in such a way that they have much sense of the progress of students among institutions or even within their own institutions. Most colleges do not know how many noncredit students are enrolled in credit programs, whether their graduates or nongraduates transferred or earned bachelor degrees, or what the records of their students were when they were in high school. So, although college personnel are concerned about their students' progress and get great satisfaction seeing students cross the stage on graduation day, in most colleges, officials simply do not have the information to understand the outlines of the process or to analyze where, how, and especially why leakages occurred.

Our investigations of community college practices have revealed both deep chal-lenges, as well as potential bright spots, in the effort to promote student success, connect institutions and units within institutions, and, in general, strengthen the community college equity agenda. In the first chapter, we argued that equity in higher education involves issues of preparation for college, access to college, and success once in college. We will review our overall findings within that framework.

Dual Enrollment

Community colleges are most involved with preparation for college through their participation in dual-enrollment programs. This creates an explicit high school to community college link. There is now a great deal of discussion about the reform of high schools. National-level reform efforts have shifted attention to high schools, and other initiatives are attempting to align high school graduation requirements with college entrance requirements (Achieve, Inc., 2004). As is clear from the chapter by Vanessa Smith Morest and Melinda Mechur Karp, dual enrollment is potentially a much deeper reform than alignment, because it is based on the notion that students will actually experience college. This not only gives them a good sense of what they will need to know to be successful in college but also attempts to acclimate them to the culture and broader demands of college.

The significant new development in dual enrollment is the extent to which re-formers now see it as an innovation that can reach beyond the traditional higher-achieving, college-bound students. Educators hope that dual enrollment can help prepare middle- and lower-achieving students for college, by helping them understand what will be expected of them, but also by setting high expectations, to which a broad range of students will respond.

Although the model is good in principle, it is still unproven empirically. Moreover, Morest and Karp argue that, although colleges and high schools have incentives to participate in dual enrollment, those factors do not necessarily push them to serve a broad range of students. Many of the institutional benefits would accrue to colleges if they limited participation to higher-achieving students.

In practice, there is a tension between using the program to reach a broad range of students, among them students who might not traditionally be expected to go to college or to have success once there, and keeping the program at a college level. Colleges often react to this tension, either through "prerequisite creep," in which high school enrollment in dual-credit programs becomes increasingly selective, thereby making it more difficult to serve the target students, or the watering down of "college-level" courses so that high school students can manage. The first tendency is no longer a solution to the problem, and the second might be even worse than the present situation, in that students will get the wrong idea about their preparedness for college.

Thus, any fully developed dual-enrollment program must include a noncollege-level preparation component, in which the high schools develop special programs for future dual-enrollment students that will allow them to accelerate their preparation for college, at least in some areas or fields. Viewed more broadly, this means dual enrollment is a lever for pushing high schools toward a model of accelerated preparation for college. If this is possible for nontraditionally college-bound students, why should it not be a model for all high school students? Perhaps it should be, but in the current context, one could argue that the presence of a special college program within the high schools creates additional incentives for some high school students to enroll and work toward that proximate goal. With proper guidance, this could very well reach down into a broad cross-section of students. Perhaps it should be seen as a transitional experiment to see whether high school can actually be shortened or whether, as a general rule, college material could be incorporated into the final two years of high school. This could increase the overall efficiency of the education system by telescoping the learning and eventually shortening either high school or college. Despair about the actual value of the senior year in high school suggests that this might be possible.

As it stands now, this is all conjecture. Little evidence exists to demonstrate that this can actually work. A few studies have suggestive evidence, but it is surprising how far this effort has gone without much empirical support (Bailey and Karp, 2003). The inability to track students from high schools to various colleges prevents even rudimentary descriptive analysis of the educational trajectories of dual-enrollment students. State and local data bases usually do not allow analysts to track students as they make the transition from high school to college. The data base maintained by the Florida Department of Education (2004b) does track students between high school and college and has allowed officials to begin to conduct useful descriptive research on the state's programs.

Developmental Education

The proponents of dual enrollment would like to see college-level work begin to permeate the last two years of high school. Unfortunately, high schools have a long way to go to achieve that objective. Indeed, at least for community colleges students, a more common situation is that high school–level work dominates the first two years of college. A shift in focus from enrollment to outcomes puts the emphasis on getting students out of developmental education rather than getting them into it. The connection between developmental education and regular credit courses is another link that must be strengthened.

Dolores Perin and Kerry Charron suggest that colleges are trying many different strategies to improve remediation, with limited success. The plethora of formal and informal methods found just in our fifteen case sites speaks to the lack of consensus about the most effective approach. Ironically, although there is consensus among remediation experts that developmental education ought to be centralized in its own department, centralization was not the dominant approach among the study colleges. This lack of correspondence between research and practice may simply reflect the lack of strong empirical evidence to support the expert consensus. Indeed, as Perin and Charron show, researchers have few definitive answers about the best design and characteristics of developmental education services.

Overall, most colleges do not have a systematic understanding about which students are placed in developmental education, what sorts of academic assistance they receive, and what subsequently happens to those students in the developmental and regular credit classes, if indeed they remain students. Thus, whereas college officials know that many students require and enroll in remediation and that many of those students have trouble, in most cases they do not have the descriptive base of information on which they could begin to fashion a comprehensive strategy to strengthen the academic skills of their students.

The problem is not that the data do not exist, but rather that the colleges do not compile it and analyze it in ways that allow them to track and understand the progress of their students. More comprehensive analysis is possible. For example, using transcript data supplied by the Los Angeles Community College District, Linda Hagedorn (2005) has carried out detailed analysis of what she refers to as the "developmental climb." It is significant that Hagedorn relied on special funding from the U.S. Department of Education and private foundations. Miami Dade College does carry out useful longitudinal analysis of their developmental students to identify specific barriers to successful completion of the developmental education sequence (Grubb, 2001a). Nevertheless, this type of focused longitudinal analysis of the experience of developmental education students is not carried out at the large majority of community colleges.

Developmental education is in many ways the foundation of the community college equity agenda. In many colleges, for a majority of students, it is the key to transforming enrollment into student success. In light of the immense human and financial resources spent on developmental education, and because most of the necessary data are available within the colleges, all colleges should track and analyze the experience of students in these courses.

Noncredit Courses

Developmental education courses generally do not carry credit toward degree completion. As we have seen in both the chapters by Vanessa Morest Smith and by Jim Jacobs and Norton Grubb, community colleges maintain many other types of noncredit programs and traditionally these have not been well connected to the regular credit-bearing courses. Once again, within the context of a focus on enrollment or access, such connections are not necessarily emphasized. They become more central in a framework of concern about the long-term experiences of students.

Generalization about noncredit is difficult, because there are many different types of noncredit courses and programs. Many community colleges teach adult basic education (ABE) or English as a second language (ESL) courses. For these noncredit students, simplified transitions from noncredit credit to credit are particularly important. Recent research suggests that ABE students must go on to regular credit programs and accumulate at least a year's worth of credit before they accrue any economic benefit from their studies (Prince and Jenkins, 2005). Some students have very specific goals that can be met by one or two courses, and, for them, connections to the credit program may not be important. Indeed, we know that many students in noncredit occupational programs at community colleges already have degrees (Phillippe and Valiga, 2000). Colleges and foundations are increasingly working to build so-called career pathways that consist of sequences of noncredit courses, employment, and credit courses that could eventually lead to transfer and higher-level employment (Alssid et al., 2002).

Jacobs and Grubb's chapter can be read optimistically in that they suggest that, in many cases, the material taught in the industry certification programs has been incorporated into regular credit-bearing courses in information technology departments. They judged this to be a positive development, not only because it joined this instruction to an educational progression toward a degree but also because it made the instruction available at lower costs to students. The fees for noncredit certificate instruction were generally much higher than tuition for regular courses and were also less likely to be eligible for financial aid, thereby reducing access to these programs for low-income students. Morest argued that, although in many cases noncredit occupational programs were connected to credit-bearing programs, courses in those programs often were not transferable to four-year colleges. Thus, the noncredit programs at community colleges could come into conflict with the equity mission, either because their cost discouraged low-income students or because they were not well connected to the credit programs and therefore to subsequent educational opportunities.

Both Morest's and Jacobs and Grubb's chapters discussed the inadequacy of existing data and research for understanding the growth of noncredit programs at colleges. Jacobs and Grubb argue that colleges have no idea how successful they are in preparing students for certification exams. Exam results are not provided to the colleges, and the colleges have no way of evaluating the effect of these certifications on subsequent student earnings. Most colleges do not track students across the noncredit/credit divide. This is something that will have to be changed as noncredit enrollments grow and if colleges want to better understand the influences of these programs on students. Students and employers might also like to know the value of their noncredit education.

The value of having data on the credit to noncredit transition is clearly revealed in Washington state, which also links these data to earnings information provided by the state unemployment insurance system. In Washington, research has shown the conditions under which the ABE program at community colleges has an economic payoff (Prince and Jenkins, 2005). These data have also been used to show that even small numbers of courses (both credit and noncredit) in technical areas have an economic payoff for displaced workers (Jacobson, Lalonde, and Sullivan, 2005). Colleges can already do much to link data on credit and noncredit, relying only on data that they have in-house, but, clearly, links to high school and employment information and to information from other institutions would also be useful.

Counseling and Student Services

Student progress through college often depends on the quality of counseling and advisement. Grubb's chapter reveals the immense scope of this task. Community college students often have few social resources on which they can draw for information and guidance about their college trajectories. As predominantly part-time, commuter students, they often have little opportunity to learn informally on campus through interactions with other students or faculty members. Formal counseling and advisement must fill those gaps, but the resources devoted to those functions are so limited that counselors at the best community colleges must work with hundreds of students. Many students never interact with counselors, relying instead on information they pick up from catalogs or web sites.

Grubb finds that, for the majority of community college students at the National Field Study colleges, student services take a form designed to cope with large numbers of students efficiently, by providing them with quantities of written information about their options. Grubb refers to this as the "information dump" approach. In general, student service functions were too short of resources and information to provide high-quality, frequent interaction with the extremely large number of students in need of services who attend community colleges.

Whether they have adequate information to make educational decisions and whether those decisions are consistent with their goals and needs remain unknown. As we found with developmental education, the plethora of approaches to student services suggests that there is no firm consensus about the best models. Grubb recommends student services develop more systematic approaches that are better integrated into the core functions of their colleges and that are based on the conviction that deluging students with information is not analogous to providing guidance and advice. The LifeCourse model used at one case study college provides evidence that models exist. It offers a method for integrating useful information about progression through the college into a process through which students can develop independent decision making in stages.

The experience with the for-profit institutions, as revealed in Thomas Bailey's chapter, may also offer some insights about student services for community colleges. Although these institutions, at least for now, do not seem to threaten community college enrollments, some tentative data suggest they have somewhat higher graduation rates. In general, the for-profits have a much narrower focus and tend to have more integrated student services. Colleges that specialize in a few occupational areas can build up expertise in the substance of those areas and contacts with local employers. The registration, advisement, and financial aid application processes also tend to be streamlined, making it easier for students to navigate these steps.

Unfortunately, most community colleges do not have the option of focusing on a few substantive areas or degrees, so counselors at community colleges must have knowledge and contacts in many more occupational fields than counselors at for-profits. Specialization of this type, however, may be possible in large occupational areas, such as nursing, or health in general. Indeed, many nursing programs in community colleges have good contacts with employers and clear counseling practices. Community colleges are also working toward streamlining their registration and initial academic advisement processes.

Overall, as we found with developmental education, colleges have very little sense of the effects of the student services that they provide. There have been a small number of formal evaluations of counseling models at community colleges, and they do show some suggestively positive results (Bailey and Alfonso, 2005), but they are usually conducted by outside evaluators. Thus, although they may offer colleges insights in choosing how to design student services, the type of analysis and tracking that could reveal the effectiveness of activities on a particular campus was not done on the campuses in our sample. Even for a well-known and admired program such as Life Course, college staff could not point to evidence that it influenced retention or graduation. Furthermore, the argument that the focused and centralized student services found in for-profit institutions leads to higher graduation rates is at best suggestive. A better understanding of the relationship between student services and student success would require both focused evaluation studies as well as the development of methods for incorporating information on student services into college and state data systems.

For the most part, colleges provide services based on widely used models, and those services are provided by dedicated professionals, but these professionals go home at the end of the day with little specific knowledge about the impact that they are having.

Distance Education

In addition to student services, the pedagogic activities also influence the probability that students will persist and eventually have a successful experience in college. A focus on enrollment, rather than student success, downplays the importance of pedagogy. If the college's emphasis is to get students in the door, the foundational educational activities—teaching and learning—are not set as the highest priority. This tension between enrollment and pedagogy was clearly revealed in Rebecca Cox's chapter on distance education. The wave of enthusiasm for distance education, especially during the late 1990s, was driven partly by anxiety among colleges that innovators and fast movers in on-line education would threaten community college enrollments. From a more positive perspective, distance education was seen as an approach that would open access by allowing working students, those with families, or those who did not live close to a college (and could not move), to attend college without scheduling or geographic constraints.

Colleges in the sample had made progress in implementing on-line education, though some faculty resistance and inadequate professional development slowed that progress. Most progress had been made in developing hybrid rather than entirely distance-based courses. Enrollments in on-line classes often picked up only after face-to-face classes had been filled, which suggests that students still preferred the regular courses.

What was most striking about Cox's findings was her conclusion that colleges underemphasized the difficult pedagogic issues associated with on-line instruction. Developing on-line education was seen in technical terms focused on getting students connected and getting the class material, often the same material used in regular classes, onto the server. Despite the widely shared perception that on-line students completed courses at lower rates than regular students, less attention was paid to how to teach and engage students in the on-line world. Potentially, the spread of on-line instruction could be used as a tool to strengthen teaching throughout the college, but the typical implementation strategy diverts this impulse to an emphasis on technology. Cox argues that, without sustained consideration of the quality of on-line education and the capacity of community colleges to offer high-quality on-line courses designed for students who already face academic problems, it is likely that developments in on-line education will continue to favor the most organized and purposeful students and may weaken the community college access and equity missions.

This technical emphasis on getting students enrolled in on-line courses and the underemphasis of what happens to them once they are there is a legacy of a cross-sectional, enrollment-driven model that clearly needs to change as colleges move toward a focus on student experience and success. A first step would be to conduct focused analyses of the characteristics and experience of students in distance education courses. This would require the simple step that administrative data bases establish coding to differentiate on-line from face-to-face courses. As with many of the topics we have covered, however, the problem is not so much the availability of data as whether the college establishes a priority of using the data thoughtfully to improve student success.

Transfer

Transfer to baccalaureate granting institutions remains a central mission of the community college. Indeed, it was the mission of the first community (or junior) college. Still, a relative minority of community college students make such a transfer. According to the 1988 National Educational Longitudinal Survey, only about one-third of students who start in a community college transfer within eight years of their initial enrollment—about two-thirds of those actually complete a bachelor degree. Although these numbers seem low, it is important to emphasize that many students do not intend to transfer. Nevertheless, more than three-fourths of students who start in community colleges state that their long-term goal is to complete at least a baccalaureate degree (Bailey, Jenkins, and Leinbach, 2005), so policy makers, educators, parents, and students would like to see higher levels of transfer.

In the past few years, analysts and college advocates have argued that opening transfer for community college students is increasingly important as the relative economic value of the bachelor degree has risen (Wellman, 2002; AACC and American Association of State Colleges and Universities, 2004; Long, 2005). Moreover, this will become that much more urgent if states expand their dependence on community colleges for lower-division education as a strategy to reduce the cost of higher education. As we pointed out in the introduction, research suggests that students who start at a community college are less likely to complete a bachelor degree than otherwise similar students who start college at a four-year institution (Dougherty, 1994; Kienzl, 2004; Rouse, 1995; Pascarella and Terenzini, 2005, chap. 8).[2] Most of the issues and suggestions that we have raised so far are relevant to transfer and bachelor degree attainment, because students must have a solid educational foundation at the community college if they are to transfer successfully and complete a baccalaureate degree. Any comprehensive policy to promote opportunity for community college students and strengthen the colleges' role in promoting educational equity, however, must deal with the transfer process itself. This means analyzing who transfers, what credits they are able to transfer, and whether they succeed in earning bachelor degrees.

Our fieldwork has shed light on several issues associated with transfer. First, in her chapter, Morest shows that the academic component of the community college organizational structure has remained remarkably constant over the past two decades. Thus, although some critics have suggested that community colleges are becoming more "vocationalized," therefore placing less emphasis on transfer, Morest demonstrates that the segment of the college organization on which transfer preparation is based has held its own, at least within the community college credit programs. She also shows that there continues to be a strong component of community college occupational education in both the credit and noncredit segments of the colleges that is not transferable. Indeed, in light of the growth of noncredit during the past decade, by some measures the nontransferable segment has actually grown. This reinforces our emphasis on the need to address issues associated with the relationship between credit and noncredit programs.

Although colleges can work to prepare their students for transfer, transfer policies must be developed at the state level. Even the best-prepared, transfer-ready students will not be able to transfer if local four-year colleges do not accept their transfer credits. Many of the colleges in our sample had extensive bilateral agreements with specific programs at individual four-year colleges, but this is a much narrower definition of articulation than state systems of two- and four-year colleges would suggest. Our investigations of the for-profits revealed that, in many cases, community college staff felt that the for-profits and the private not-for-profits were more hospitable than the public four-year institutions to the community college transfer students. It makes much more sense to develop transfer and articulation agreements at the state level.

A central theme of this book has been the need for better and more analytic student tracking, and, certainly when it comes to transfer, states are in a much better position than individual institutions to track students across colleges. Revealing patterns of student movement between institutions and the credits they transfer will be the first step to informing better articulation policies.

Wellman's (2002) study of transfer policies in six states revealed that these states have developed transfer policies and indeed have tracked at least some segments of the transfer populations.[3] She cites two states that are in our sample, Texas and Florida, as examples of states with good student-tracking capabilities, though, according to her, Florida had a more successful transfer system. Wellman's overall conclusion is that states with strong centralized higher education systems do a better job with transfers. For example, she argues that transfer in New York is facilitated because the two- and four-year systems report to the same governing board.

Although Wellman (2002) identified stronger and weaker states, she concluded that "2/4 transfer seems somewhat of a back-burner issue in postsecondary education in all six states" (p. 37). Furthermore, of particular significance to our argument, although low-income and minority groups transfer at lower rates than middle-income and white students, Wellman found no evidence that states were "systematically trying to reach at-risk students or institutions as priorities for 2/4 transfer" (p. 43).

Community colleges, four-year institutions, and states have an imperative to strengthen the transfer option. To accomplish this, the conflicts of interest inherent in one institution—in a sense, giving away credits to other institutions—needs to be acknowledged. A major role played by community colleges in state higher education systems is to make education affordable and accessible to larger numbers of students than can be served by the more costly four-years alone. This system, however, is inequitable if the credits earned at community colleges do not transfer or if other barriers prevent students from moving smoothly between sectors.

Researchers have used national data to study transfer, but more progress will be made on understanding and improving transfer when individual colleges and states can analyze in more detail the transfer experience of their own students. For this to happen, institutions must have data that track students across educational sectors and over relatively long periods of time. They will need access to state data systems to begin to be able to do this. Such data will facilitate understanding of the transfer system and make sure that it strengthens rather than thwarts the community college equity agenda.

Accountability

Accountability is often seen by college-level staff and faculty as a potentially punitive system that could do more harm than good. Colleges have also complained that accountability measures based on graduation rates are misleading because community college students have so many other goals. In principal, though, accountability measures could provide incentives for colleges to improve their performance in ways that policy makers would like to see. As Kevin Dougherty and Esther Hong's chapter indicates, there has been a great deal of activity associated with accountability at community colleges during the past decade. The question we are addressing here is how that movement influenced the community college equity agenda, particularly in the context of a shift from a focus on access to one on student outcomes and success.

Despite the increased activity, Dougherty and Hong's conclusion is that, so far, accountability measures in community colleges have not had strong direct effects on student outcomes. Indeed, they argue that there is suggestive evidence that accountability may have created incentives for creaming—shifting enrollments to better-prepared students in an attempt to improve outcome measures. On the other hand, the state fiscal problems of the first half of the decade tended to overwhelm funding accountability regimes, in that states simply did not have the resources to pay for their outcome-incentive systems. This therefore weakened whatever effect, positive or negative, accountability might have had on enrollments and student outcomes.

Funding and budgeting accountability therefore have not had strong direct effects so far. Nor have states successfully incorporated features in their systems that would particularly encourage successful service to low-income and minority students, such as setting graduation targets for minorities or requiring reductions in achievement gaps as the No Child Left Behind Act does for elementary schools. Although there is growing discussion of the need to develop an integrated, or at least coordinated, K–16 structure and an accountability system that encourages and measures system performance, so far data are not available that would allow that to be put into effect.

Accountability and accreditation systems could contribute to the equity agenda, though we are a long way from a comprehensive system that strengthens the community college equity mission and promotes success for minority, low-income, and other traditionally underserved groups. One problem is that data are not available— or, when available, they are not used to reinforce that goal. First, states need to reach a consensus on the appropriate accountability measures. Time-limited graduation rates such as the three-year community college graduation rate for first-time, full-time students collected by the National Center for Education Statistics (NCES) give a limited and highly distorted image of college performance (Bailey, Jenkins, and Leinbach, 2005). Second, that would almost certainly require multi-institutional measures especially as states take a broader look at accountability and improved performance for the whole elementary, secondary, and postsecondary systems.

Information Systems and Institutional Research

As we have emphasized in our discussion of the issues addressed in this book, a shift from a focus on enrollment to one on outcomes creates daunting demands on information and data systems.[4] Community college data and funding systems have been based on cross-sectional counts of students by various categories—age, sex, race, and other demographic characteristics. Most colleges are funded on the basis of this type of cross-sectional information. The large majority of student information reported to the NCES through its Integrated Postsecondary Data System (or IPEDS) is also cross-sectional, including enrollments, demographic characteristics, financial aid, and degrees awarded.

Throughout the work on this book, our efforts to understand what happens to community college students and how to make their experiences more productive have been thwarted by a lack of data and analysis. At what point do students leave college, and why? What is the most effective way to organize and administer developmental education and student services? Why do students in on-line course complete those courses at lower levels? How do students combine credit and noncredit classes, and how successful are noncredit students at moving into credit work? Do dual enrollment programs improve college outcomes for middle- or even lower-achieving high school students? Research using national-level data sets has addressed some, but certainly not all, of these questions, but, for the most part, these questions are not answered, and often not asked, at the college or district level, where faculty and administrators are in a better position to address the particular problems that they and their students face. A shift to answering these questions and in general to focusing on student success requires a unit record system that tracks students longitudinally. In the late 1990s, Congress began requiring colleges to track cohorts of first-time, full-time students for three years (for community colleges) and six years (for four-year colleges), but a comprehensive emphasis on student success requires more than simply the ability to tell whether a particular student graduated. If officials want to improve the performance of their colleges, they must also analyze the determinants of outcomes and get a better understanding of what they do or can do that will promote greater student success.

Ideally, college officials would need to be able to maintain records on the characteristics of their students, including information on their previous educational records, a detailed description of their courses and the services that they received, and their destination and activities after their departure. This would allow colleges to know what happened to their students, search for the causes of the problems that their students encountered, and assess the effectiveness of measures that the colleges have taken to address those problems. This is, of course, an ambitious plan, and there are several barriers that stand in the way of achieving this goal.

First, colleges and states already have extensive data records on their students, yet this information is not exploited. Even a cursory exploration of college web sites or searches for college reports can yield large quantities of data and tables, mostly reporting detailed information on enrollments. But somewhere in their files, colleges have information that would allow much more sophisticated and comprehensive analysis. Most colleges do have a complete record of students' experiences at the college, including their grades and course attempts. In most cases, however, colleges do not maintain these records so that they can be easily analyzed or do not devote the time and resources necessary to analyze them in useful ways. For example, with existing data, colleges could track every credit student, identify points where students drop out or get lost, calculate course completion ratios, determine various measures of retention, and analyze the relationship between these factors and a variety of demographic characteristics. Nevertheless, surveys and work with samples of colleges in 2005 indicate that very few colleges carry out this type of analysis (Morest, in press). Colleges devote most of their institutional research resources to reporting cross-sectional information. In the more advanced institutional research departments, colleges are able to report longitudinal rates such as semester-to-semester or year-to-year retention and, occasionally, cohort graduation rates. Transcript analysis allows a much more specific understanding of barriers to student progress, but it is extremely rare.

We see three broad barriers to implementation of a more comprehensive and effective data and information system. These include institutional and human resource capacities and priorities, the absence of crucial information in data systems, and the inability in most cases for colleges to track students across institutions. To some extent, there are technical problems with storage and software. Nevertheless, the most important barriers include human-resource capacity and, even more, institutional priorities. Although a few colleges have sophisticated research departments, many community college institutional research offices consist of a sole individual. Some colleges have only a part-time faculty or staff member who may not have research or quantitative research training. Even among colleges with larger institutional research departments, those offices are often preoccupied with accountability and enrollment reports—once again, mostly based on cross-sectional data. Without greater capacity and a commitment to longitudinal tracking, colleges will never have a comprehensive sense of how they are doing or even of whether their efforts to improve student outcomes are effective.

A second problem has to do with important information that is not currently in college data bases. For example, colleges do not know much about the specifics of the socioeconomic background of their students. Recovering income data for students is difficult, except for those who apply for financial aid. Nor do colleges know what sorts of services students received or the types of activities in which they participated. Recording the services received by students is conceptually possible, though it would require the development of a consistent system for categorizing services. For example, some colleges are now experimenting with using electronic identification cards to determine whether and how students use tutoring centers.

Keeping track of the experiences of noncredit students is also not possible in many college databases. In some cases, the colleges have the information, but it is not linked in any way to data on credit students. Thus, colleges do not know whether students who entered the college in noncredit programs ever end up in credit courses and what happens to them if they do.

The third problem concerns tracking students across institutions. For the most part, this is not something that an institution can do on its own, though it could be possible for colleges to collect information on the educational experiences that students have before they arrive at a college. But efforts in 2004 and 2005 to collect data

from twenty-seven community colleges in Texas, New Mexico, Florida, North Carolina, and Virginia revealed that none of the colleges could provide information on
their students' educational records before entering the college.[5] A survey conducted
by Ewell, Schild, and Paulson (2003) found that thirty-nine states maintained unit-
record databases that contained almost three-quarters of the national postsecondary
enrollments. Most of these databases included only enrollments in public institutions, though about a quarter of them included at least some information on private
institutions.

These data systems vary in their usefulness. Sometimes different sectors of higher
education within one state are recorded in different data sets and, in most cases, high
school and college data are not linked. State data bases generally lose students who
leave the state, but some neighboring states are developing sharing agreements. Some
colleges and states have made use of data from the National Student Clearinghouse,
which allows them to know whether (and where) their students registered at another
college, even if it is out of state. In any case, despite the limitations of the state
databases, they represent a rich opportunity for colleges and researchers to analyze
student experiences. More analysis of these data is essential if colleges are to shift their
emphasis from enrollment and access to student success and overall equity.

Strengthening Research

So far, we have emphasized data requirements, but when data are available, they
must be used thoughtfully. Indeed, even though there are many inadequacies in the
existing data, many questions could be addressed using those data if colleges and state
systems were willing to devote the necessary time and resources. Nevertheless, the
fundamental strategy for improving the use of data to advance the community college equity agenda involves improving the capacity of colleges to analyze and evaluate
their own practice—that is, increasing and strengthening their institutional research
capacity. The suggestions that we have outlined certainly require resources, but many
colleges are operating with only the most superficial knowledge of what happens to
their students, what problems they face, what specifically might help them, and then
whether the strategies that they choose to address those problems are effective. If
colleges are serious about focusing on student success rather than student enrollments, this must change. College administrators understand that they have to track
college finances, and it is safe to say that all colleges devote more resources to tracking
finances than they do to understanding their main "product"—student learning and
success. We have found that, not surprisingly, small colleges tend to have extremely
limited research capacity, devoting what they do have to responding to state and

federal reporting requirements. It is possible that districts, or groups of colleges, might work together to fund an effective research office.

Increasing institutional research capacity is not merely a matter of expanding the number of researchers at the colleges. In a sense, this type of change may not be realistic for community colleges, in light of their declining share of state resources and relatively small budgets. Instead, this means revising the role of institutional research and elevating its priority in contributing to institutional decision making. Specifically, the role that institutional research can play in community college institutional policy is to generate directions for change and then evaluate the productivity of change as it happens.

Developments in information technology create an environment in which more data can be collected with increasing efficiency. Access to data can be vastly improved so that all levels of college administration and faculty can analyze the students and programs that are most important to their roles. This kind of access to data will eventually break down some of the resistance to the use of data that is so prevalent at community colleges. Although in the past, much of this resistance stemmed from the way in which data can be used to support unpopular decisions that have already been made for other reasons, we are suggesting a bottom-up approach to data analysis, in which problems are identified and reforms studied as a part of daily practice.

In view of a stronger research capability, there are some areas among those that we have studied in this book, in which the colleges can increase their knowledge right away, using the data that are already available. These include developmental education, the relationship between credit and noncredit (at many colleges in any case), and on-line education. Progress on student services and the credit/noncredit relationship (at some colleges), would require some additional data collection, but much could still be done within each institution. A better understanding of dual enrollment and transfer clearly requires at least state-level data, as does the development of a productive accountability system. In some cases, state data sets are already available and in extensive use. In many other cases, the data are there but need to be organized (and, in some cases, separate data sets must be combined or linked) and ultimately used both for description and analysis.

Finally, we have emphasized the importance of quantitative data, but in many cases better quantitative data simply allows us to ask more useful questions. Data could show that a particular type of student tends to fail to complete college-level math courses. Knowing this, the college staff can start to find out why that is and work to correct it. Thus, quantitative data are a first step but need to be followed with interviews with students and faculty and other types of more qualitative investigations.

Conclusion

Community colleges clearly face a challenging new era. State fiscal constraints will reduce funding and put upward pressure on tuition, but they may also bring more students to the community college as individuals and states look for less-expensive alternatives to the higher-cost four-year colleges. Combined with the effects of the baby boom echo and increased immigration, community colleges may have the opportunity to, in effect, become more selective. This would, of course, run counter to the access function that, for many faculty and staff, is the heart of the community college mission. As we have seen in the first chapter, the access mission in any case is not complete, because about a quarter of high school students do not enter post-secondary institutions within eight years of their high school graduation dates. What is more, these are disproportionately low-income students.

Will a greater reliance on community college lead to a more or a less equitable education system? Research is equivocal on this conclusion. Community colleges expand access to the first two years of college, but for otherwise-similar students seeking bachelor degrees, those who start college in a community college are less likely to complete that degree. This suggests that, if the privatization of higher education funding increased the concentration of low-income students in community colleges, if nothing else changed, greater reliance on community colleges would probably lead to a more inequitable system.

The overall equity of the higher education system depends fundamentally on many factors outside of the control of community colleges, or indeed any colleges. Financial aid, transportation, and employment, day care, welfare, and other social policies are all crucial (Grubb and Lazerson, 2004).

In light of the importance of community colleges in absorbing the expansion of higher education, there is a great imperative for community colleges to do what they can to improve student outcomes. In this book, we have reviewed many approaches to accomplishing this: better connections between high schools and colleges; the use of dual-enrollment programs to leverage better college preparation in high school; improved developmental education based on a stronger understanding of the student experience in remediation; stronger connections between credit and noncredit programs; better-focused and planned student services integrated into the overall planning and strategy of the college; expansion of on-line education based on much greater attention to pedagogy for this modality; and a more sophisticated accountability system designed to promote equity and based on the development of a consensus with respect to multiinstitutional outcome measures. All of this needs to be tied together with data systems designed to understand student trajectories (including multi-institutional trajectories), the barriers they face, and the effectiveness of strategies used to improve outcomes.

Although we have focused on specific activities at colleges, such as developmental education and student services, colleges need to take a broader and more systemic view of strategic reform. Most colleges we visited already had many individual initiatives to help selected (often small) groups of students. These "boutique" programs were usually funded through state and federal grants. Boutique programs are set up when they are funded, often with an administrative role which only exists during the life of the grant. The activities frequently cease when the funding stream ends, even if they have had positive effects for students.

Community colleges confront very difficult problems. Reform should not be seen as an accumulation of individual programs, but rather as a thoroughgoing process having to do with how the institutions diagnose, improve, and evaluate their own practices. Each chapter has emphasized how progress requires better information and better incorporation into the overall operation of the colleges. The uses of data we have described are a fundamental part of that process. We are calling for community colleges to hold themselves accountable institutionwide by understanding the organization of their services not as they are funded, but as they are used by students.

Community college faculty and administrators have justifiably been proud of the role that their institutions have played in opening up higher education to many lower-income, minority, and first-generation college students who would have had more trouble entering a four-year institution—even if the states could have afforded to open up the necessary capacity in those institutions. College personnel now agree that access is not enough. We must pay more attention and work harder to improve the student experience once they are enrolled. Although this does not seem controversial, the incentives and management systems that guide and channel community colleges remain grounded in an enrollment-driven model. We hope that this book will help encourage colleges and the state and federal systems that govern and regulate them to move into a world that focuses on the experiences, progress, and problems of each individual student as he or she enters the college and moves through to the next stage of their educational, personal, and employment lives.

NOTES

1. Our thinking on these issues has been influenced by our participation in two foundation-funded national initiatives explicitly focused on increasing student success for groups of students who have been underserved by the higher education system in the country. One is the

Achieving the Dream: Community College Counts initiative. According to the initiative's web site, "Achieving the Dream is a multiyear national initiative to help more community college students succeed. The initiative is particularly concerned about student groups that traditionally have faced significant barriers to success, including students of color and low-income students." The work emphasizes using longitudinal data to identify problems and design effective solutions. For more information on Achieving the Dream, see www.achievingthedream .org. The second program is the Bridges to Opportunity initiative funded by the Ford Foundation. Bridges focuses on working with states to improve the ability of community colleges to serve low-income (especially adult) students. Both initiatives are emblematic of the growing emphasis on using data to improve college outcomes. At the same time, experience with these efforts also shows the seriousness of the problems colleges must confront to achieve their equity goals and improve student success in general.

2. There are methodological problems with this type of analysis. Nevertheless, researchers have used a variety of approaches to address those problems and consistently come up with this result.

3. Wellman studied three "high-performing" states (with respect to overall college completion in the state) and three "lower-performing" states to try to understand how their transfer policies and systems differed.

4. This section draws on research on community college institutional research capacity and practice conducted in 2005 and 2006 as part of the Achieving the Dream: Community Colleges Count initiative funded by the Lumina Foundation and others. As part of the project, we conducted a web-based survey of 189 randomly selected colleges. We also conducted intensive telephone interviews with 125 individuals at twenty-eight colleges. At each college, the research design called for interviews with the president, the head of institutional research, the dean or vice president of academic affairs, the person in charge of student services, and a faculty member (Morest, in press). For more information on Achieving the Dream, see www.achieving thedream.org.

5. These efforts were part of the Achieving the Dream initiative. The initiative is building an extensive longitudinal data base with data from all of the colleges participating in the initiative. The conclusion stated in this sentence was developed in the course of working with the colleges to create that database. For more information, see www.achievingthedream.org.

Achieve, Inc. 2004. *Ready or Not: Creating a High School Diploma That Counts.* Washington, D.C.: Achieve, Inc.

Adelman, C. 1996. The Truth about Remedial Work: It's More Complex than Windy Rhetoric and Simple Solutions Suggest. *Chronicle of Higher Education,* 43(6), A56.

Adelman, C. 1999. *Answers in the Tool Box: Academic Intensity, Attendance Patterns, and Bachelor's Degree Attainment.* Washington, D.C.: U.S. Department of Education.

Adelman, C. 2000. *A Parallel Postsecondary Universe: The Certification System in Information Technology.* Information Analyses General (070) no. PLLI-2000–8011. Washington, D.C.: Office of Educational Research and Improvement (ED445246), U.S. Department of Education.

Adelman, C. 2005. *Moving into Town—and Moving On: The Community College in the Lives of Traditional-Age Students.* Washington, D.C.: U.S. Department of Education, Office of Vocational and Adult Education.

Advisory Committee on Student Financial Assistance. 2001. *Access Denied: Restoring The Nation's Commitment to Equal Educational Opportunity.* Washington, D.C.: Advisory Committee on Student Financial Assistance.

Albright, B. N. 1998. *The Transition from Business as Usual to Funding for Results: State Efforts to Integrate Performance Measures in the Higher Education Budgetary Process.* Denver, Col.: State Higher Education Executive Officers (ERIC Document Reproduction Service No. ED418652).

Aldrich, H. E., and J. Pfeffer. 1976. Environments of Organizations. *Annual Review of Sociology,* 2, 79–105.

Alexander, F. K. 2000. The Changing Face of Accountability: Monitoring and Assessing Institutional Performance in Higher Education. *Journal of Higher Education,* 71(4), 411–431.

Alfonso, M. 2004. The Role of Educational Expectations and College Choice in Transfer and Baccalaureate Attainment of Community College Students. Doctoral dissertation, Columbia University, Teachers College.

Alfonso, M., T. R. Bailey, and M. Scott. 2005. The Educational Outcomes of Occupational Subbaccalaureate Students: Evidence from the 1990s. *Economics of Education Review,* 24(2), 197–212.

Allen, I. E., and J. Seaman. 2003. *Sizing the Opportunity: The Quality and Extent of Online Education in the United States, 2002 and 2003.* Needham, Mass.: Sloan Consortium.

Allen, I. E., and J. Seaman. 2004. *Entering the Mainstream: The Quality and Extent of Online Education in the United States, 2003 and 2004.* Needham, Mass.: Sloan Consortium.

Alssid, J. L., D. Gruber, D. Jenkins, C. Mazzeo, B. Roberts, and R. Stanback-Stroud. 2002. *Building a Career Pathways System: Promising Practices in Community College–Centered Workforce Development.* New York: Workforce Strategy Center.

AACC (American Association of Community Colleges). 1999a. *The Knowledge Net: Connecting Communities, Learners, and Colleges.* Washington, D.C.: Community College Press.

AACC. 1999b. *Performance-Based Funding: A Review of Five States.* Washington, D.C.: AACC.

AACC. 2000. *AACC Position Statement on Remedial Education: Policy Statement.* Washington, D.C.: AACC. Retrieved February 20, 2003, from http://www.aacc.nche.edu

AACC. 2002a. *Community College Growth by Decade.* Washington, D.C.: AACC.

AACC. 2002b. *The Workforce Investment Act: Implications for Community Colleges.* Washington, D.C.: AACC.

AACC and American Association of State Colleges and Universities. 2004. *Improving Access to the Baccalaureate.* Washington, D.C.: AACC and the American Association of State Colleges and Universities.

Andrews, H.A. 2001. The Dual-Credit Explosion at Illinois' Community Colleges. *Community College Journal,* 71(3), 12–16.

Arenson, K. W. 2004. Low Scores Bar Many Admitted to CUNY. *New York Times,* May 28, p. B3.

Arnone, M. 2003. States Increased Spending on Student Aid in 2001–2, Survey Finds. *Chronicle of Higher Education,* 49(34), A32.

Astin, A.W., and L. Oseguera. 2004. The Declining "Equity" of American Higher Education. *Review of Higher Education,* 27(3), 321.

Ausburn, L. J. 2002. The Freedom versus Focus Dilemma in a Customized Self-Directed Learning Environment: A Comparison of the Perceptions of Adult and Younger Students. *Community College Journal of Research and Practice,* 26(3), 225–235.

Baer, W. S. 1998. *Will the Internet Transform Higher Education?* (Rand Report RP-685). Reprinted from The Emerging Internet, Annual Review of the Institute for Information Studies. Retrieved October 2002, from http://www.rand.org/cgibin/Abstracts/abdb.pl?type=au&limit=0&query=baer,+walter.

Baer, W. S. 1999. E-Learning: A Catalyst for Competition in Higher Education. *iMP Information Impacts Magazine,* June. Retrieved October 2002, from http://www.cisp.org/imp/.

Bailey, T. R. 1988. Market Forces and Private Sector Processes in Government Policy: The Job Training Partnership Act. *Journal of Policy Analysis and Management,* 7(2), 300–315.

Bailey, T. R. 2002. Community Colleges in the 21st Century: Challenges and Opportunities. In P. A. Graham and N. G. Stacey, eds., *The Knowledge Economy and Postsecondary Education: Report of a Workshop,* pp. 59–76. Washington, D.C.: National Academy Press.

Bailey, T. R., and M. Alfonso. 2005. *Paths to Persistence: An Analysis of Research on Program Effectiveness at Community Colleges.* New Agenda Series, 6(1). Indianapolis: Lumina Foundation for Education.

Bailey, T. R., M. Alfonso, J. C. Calcagno, D. Jenkins, G. Kienzl, and T. Leinbach. 2004. *Improving*

Student Attainment in Community Colleges: Institutional Characteristics and Policies. New York: Community College Research Center, Teachers College, Columbia University.

Bailey, T. R., and I. Averianova. 2001. Multiple Missions of Community Colleges: Conflicting or Complementary. *Catalyst*, 20(2), 5–12.

Bailey, T. R., N. Badway, and P. J. Gumport. 2001. *For-Profit Higher Education and Community Colleges.* Stanford, Calif.: Stanford University, National Center for Postsecondary Improvement.

Bailey, T. R., J. C. Calcagno, D. Jenkins, G. S. Kienzl, and D. T. Leinbach. 2005. *The Effects of Institutional Factors on the Success of Community College Students.* New York: Community College Research Center, Teachers College, Columbia University.

Bailey, T. R., J. C. Calcagno, P. D. Jenkins, D. T. Leinbach, and G. S. Kienzl. (forthcoming). Is the Student-Right-To-Know All You Should Know? An Analysis of Community College Graduation Rates. *Research in Higher Education, 47 (5).*

Bailey, T. R., D. Jenkins, and D. T. Leinbach. 2005. *Community College Low-Income and Minority Student Completion Study: Descriptive Statistics from the 1992 High School Cohort.* New York: Community College Research Center, Teachers College, Columbia University.

Bailey, T. R., and M. M. Karp. 2003. *Promoting College Access and Success: A Review of Credit-Based Transition Programs.* Washington, D.C.: U.S. Department of Education, Office of Vocational and Adult Education.

Bailey, T. R., G. S. Kienzl, and D. Marcotte. 2004. *The Return to a Sub-baccalaureate Education: The Effects of Schooling, Credentials, and Program of Study on Economic Outcomes.* Washington, D.C.: U.S. Department of Education, National Assessment of Vocational Education.

Bailey, T. R., and V. S. Morest. 2004. *The Organizational Efficiency of Multiple Missions for Community Colleges.* New York: Community College Research Center, Teachers College, Columbia University.

Banta, T. W., and Associates. 1993. *Making a Difference: Outcomes of a Decade of Assessment in Higher Education.* San Francisco: Jossey-Bass.

Banta, T. W., and Associates, eds. 2002. *Building a Scholarship of Assessment.* San Francisco: Jossey-Bass.

Barnett, E. 2003. *Summary of the FY02 ACE Grant Final Reports: A Report to the Illinois Community College Board.* Urbana: Office of Community College Research and Leadership, University of Illinois at Urbana/Champaign.

Bartlett, K. R. 2002. *The Perceived Influence of Industry-Sponsored Credentials in the Information Technology Industry.* National Dissemination Center for Career and Technical Education Research Report no. RR2002. St. Paul, Minn.: National Research Center for Career and Technical Education, University of Minnesota.

Bartlett, L. 2004. Expanding Teacher Work Roles: A Resource for Retention or a Recipe for Overwork?. *Journal of Education Policy*, 19 (5), 565–582.

Becker, G. S. 1993. Human Capital: A Theoretical and Empirical Analysis with Special Reference to Education, 3rd ed. Chicago: University of Chicago Press.

Berkner, L., S. He, and E. F. Cataldi. 2002. *Descriptive Summary of 1995–96 Beginning Postsecondary Students: Six Years Later.* NCES 2003151. Washington, D.C.: U.S. Department of Education, National Center for Education Statistics.

Biermann, C.A., and G. B. Sarinsky. 1994. Hands-On Remediation: Alternative Strategies for a Community College Biology Course. *Community College Review,* 21(3), 53–61.

Bloom, D., and C. Sommo. 2005. *Building Learning Communities: Early Results from the Opening Doors Demonstration at Kingsborough Community College.* New York: MDRC.

Blumenstyk, G. 2000. How For-Profit Institutions Chase Community-College Students. *Chronicle of Higher Education,* 47(15), A30–31.

Blumenthal, A. J. 2002. English as a Second Language at the Community College: An Exploration of Context and Concerns. *New Directions for Community Colleges,* 117, 45–53.

Bogart, Q. J. 1994. The Community College Mission. In George A. Baker III, ed., *A Handbook on the Community College in America: Its History, Mission, and Management,* pp. 60–73. Westport, Conn.: Greenwood Press.

Boggs, G. R. 2004. Community Colleges in a Perfect Storm. *Change Magazine,* 36(6), 6–11.

Bogue, E. G. 2002. Twenty Years of Performance Funding in Tennessee: A Case Study of Policy Intent and Effectiveness. In Joseph C. Burke and Associates, *Funding Public Colleges and Universities for Performance: Popularity, Problems, and Prospects,* pp. 85–105. Albany, N.Y.: Rockefeller Institute.

Boswell, K. 2001. Dual Enrollment Programs: Accessing the American Dream. Education Commission of the States Office of Community College Research and Leadership. *Update on Research and Leadership Newsletter,* 13(1): 1–3.

Bowles, S., and H. Gintis. 1976. *Schooling in Capitalist America: Educational Reform and the Contradictions of Economic Life.* New York: Basic Books.

Boylan, H. R. 1999. Exploring Alternatives to Remediation. *Journal of Developmental Education,* 22(3), 2–8.

Boylan, H. R. 2002. *What Works: A Guide to Research-Based Best Practices in Developmental Education.* Boone, N.C.: National Center for Developmental Education, Appalachian State University, and the Continuous Quality Improvement Network.

Boylan, H. R., L. B. Bliss, and B. S. Bonham. 1997. Program Components and Their Relationship to Student Performance. *Journal of Developmental Education,* 20(3), 2–8.

Boylan, H. R., and B. S. Bonham. 1992. The Impact of Developmental Education Programs. *Review of Research in Developmental Education,* 9(5), 1–3.

Boylan, H.R., Bonham, B.S. & Bliss, L.B. 1994a. Characteristic Components of Developmental Programs. *Research in Developmental Education,* 11 (1), 1–4.

Boylan, H. R., B. S. Bonham, and L. B. Bliss. 1994b. Who are the developmental students? *Research in Developmental Education,* 11(2), 1–4.

Boylan, H. R., B. S. Bohnam, J. Jackson, and D. P. Saxon. 1994. Staffing Patterns in Developmental Education Programs: Full/Part Time, Credentials, and Program Placement. *Research in Developmental Education,* 11(5), 1–4.

Boylan, H. R., and D. P. Saxon. 1999. *What Works in Remediation: Lessons from 30 Years of Research.* Paper prepared for the League for Innovation in the Community College. Boone, N.C.: National Center for Developmental Education.

Boylan, H. R., and D. P. Saxon. 2001. *An Evaluation of Developmental Education in Texas Public Colleges and Universities.* Technical report prepared for the Texas Higher Education Coordinating Board, Austin, Texas. Boone, N.C.: National Center for Developmental Education.

Bransford, J., N. Vye, and H. Bateman. 2002. Creating High-Quality Learning Environments:

Guidelines from Research on How People Learn. In P. A. Graham and N. G. Stacey, eds., *The Knowledge Economy and Postsecondary Education: Report of a Workshop*, pp. 159–198. Washington, D.C.: National Academy Press.

Braverman, H. 1974. *Labor and Monopoly Capital: The Degradation of Work in the Twentieth Century.* New York: Monthly Review Press.

Brint, S., and J. Karabel. 1989. *The Diverted Dream: Community Colleges and the Promise of Educational Opportunity in America, 1900–1985.* New York: Oxford University Press.

Bruch, P. L., R. R. Jehangir, W. R. Jacobs, and D. L. Ghere. 2004. Enabling Access: Toward Multicultural Developmental Curricula. *Journal of Developmental Education, 27* (3), 12–14, 16, 18–19, 41.

Burbules, N. C., and T. A. Callister, Jr. 2000. Universities in Transition: The Promise and the Challenge of New Technologies. *Teachers College Record,* 102(2), 271–293.

Burd, S. 1998. For-Profit Trade Schools Win New Respect in Congress. *Chronicle of Higher Education,* 45(2), A47–48.

Burke, J. C. 1997. *Performance-Funding Indicators: Concerns, Values, and Models for Two- and Four-Year Colleges and Universities* (ERIC no. ED407910). Albany, N.Y.: Rockefeller Institute.

Burke, J. C. 2002. Performance Funding in South Carolina: From Fringe to Mainstream. In J. C. Burke, ed., *Funding Public Colleges and Universities for Performance: Popularity, Problems, and Prospects,* pp. 195–218. Albany, N.Y.: Rockefeller Institute.

Burke, J. C., and Associates. 2000. *Performance Funding Opinion Survey of Campus Groups, 1999–2000.* Albany, N.Y.: Rockefeller Institute.

Burke, J. C., and Associates, eds. 2002. *Funding Public Colleges and Universities for Performance: Popularity, Problems, and Prospects.* Albany, N.Y.: Rockefeller Institute.

Burke, J. C., and Associates. 2004. *Achieving Accountability in Higher Education: Balancing Public, Academic, and Market Demands.* San Francisco: Jossey-Bass.

Burke, J. C., and T. A. Lessard. 2002. Performance Funding: Campus Reactions. In J. C. Burke and Associates, eds., *Funding Public Colleges and Universities for Performance: Popularity, Problems, and Prospects,* pp. 60–83. Albany, N.Y.: Rockefeller Institute.

Burke, J. C., and H. P. Minassians. 2001. *Linking State Resources to Campus Results: From Fad to Trend: The Fifth Annual Survey.* Albany, N.Y.: Rockefeller Institute.

Burke, J. C., and H. P. Minassians. 2002. The New Accountability: From Regulation to Results. *New Directions for Institutional Research,* 116, 5–19.

Burke, J. C., and H. P. Minassians. 2003. *Performance Reporting: "Real" Accountability or Accountability "Lite"? Seventh Annual Survey, 2003.* Albany, N.Y.: Rockefeller Institute.

Burke, J. C., and S. Modarresi. 1999. *Performance Funding and Budgeting: Popularity and Volatility: The Third Annual Survey.* Albany, N.Y.: Rockefeller Institute.

Burke, J. C., J. Rosen, H. Minassians, and T. A. Lessard. 2000. *Performance Funding and Budgeting: An Emerging Merger? The Fourth Annual Survey 2000.* Albany, N.Y.: Rockefeller Institute.

Burke, J. C., and A. M. Serban, eds. 1998. *Performance Funding for Public Higher Education: Fad or Trend? New Directions for Institutional Research, No. 97.* San Francisco: Jossey-Bass.

California Community Colleges. 1999a. *Partnership for Excellence: District and College Baseline Data for 1995–96, 1996–97, and 1997–98.* Sacramento: California Community Colleges.

California Community Colleges. 1999b. *Partnership for Excellence: Frequently Asked Questions.* Sacramento: California Community Colleges.

California Community Colleges. 1999c. *Partnership for Excellence: Funding Allocations.* Sacramento: California Community Colleges.

California Community Colleges. 1999d. *Partnership for Excellence Report Specifications.* Sacramento: California Community Colleges.

California Community Colleges. 2000–2004. *System Performance on Partnership for Excellence Goals.* Sacramento: California Community Colleges.

California Community Colleges. 2005. *Performance Framework for the California Community Colleges: A Report to the Legislature, pursuant to AB1417.* Sacramento: California Community Colleges.

California State Job Training Coordinating Council. 2001. *Overview of the Performance-Based Accountability System (PBA).* Sacramento: California State Job Training Coordinating Council.

California Workforce Development Board. 2002. *Three Year Report of Performance-Based Accountability System.* Sacramento: California Workforce Development Board.

Cameron, S. V., and J. J. Heckman. 1998. Life Cycle Schooling and Dynamic Selection Bias: Models and Evidence for Five Cohorts of American Males. *Journal of Political Economy,* 106(2), 262–333.

Carew, D. 2004. *How Workforce Preparation Has Changed: New Tools, Skills, and Benchmarks.* Paper presented at the CCRC forum, 84th Annual American Association of Community Colleges Convention, Minneapolis, Minnesota, April 27.

Carifio, J., I. Jackson, and L. Dagostino. 2001. Effects of Diagnostic and Prescriptive Comments on the Revising Behaviors of Community College Students. *Community College Journal of Research and Practice,* 25(2), 109–122.

Carnevale, A. P., and Desrochers, D. M. 2001. *Help Wanted . . . Credentials Required: Community Colleges in the Knowledge Economy.* Princeton, N.J.: Educational Testing Service Press.

Carnevale, A. P., N. C. Johnson, and A. R. Edwards. 1998. Performance-Based Appropriations: Fad or Wave of the Future? *Chronicle of Higher Education,* 44(31), B6–7.

Carnevale, D. 2004. Distance Education: Keeping Up With Exploding Demand. *Chronicle of Higher Education,* 50(21), B8.

Carroll, J. M. 1990. *The Nurnberg Funnel: Designing Minimalist Instruction for Practical Computer Skill.* Cambridge, Mass.: MIT Press.

Casazza, M. E. 1999. Who Are We and Where Did We Come From? *Journal of Developmental Education,* 23(1), 12–14.

Clark, B. R. 1960a. The "Cooling-Out" Function in Higher Education. *American Journal of Sociology,* 65(6), 569–576.

Clark, B. R. 1960b. *The Open Door College: A Case Study.* New York: McGraw-Hill.

Clark, R. W. 2001. *Dual Credit: A Report of Progress and Policies That Offer High School Students College Credits* (executive summary). Philadelphia: Pew Charitable Trusts.

Coalition for Evidence-Based Policy. 2003. *Identifying and Implementing Educational Practices Supported by Rigorous Evidence: A User-Friendly Guide.* Washington, D.C.: U.S. Department of Education, Institute of Education Sciences, National Center for Education Evaluation and Regional Assistance.

Cochran, S. 2005. Office of Academic Affairs, City University of New York. Personal communication with the authors, April 8.

Cohen, A. M., and F. B. Brawer. 1982. *The American Community College,* 1st ed. San Francisco: Jossey-Bass.

Cohen, A. M., and F. B. Brawer. 2003. *The American Community College,* 4th ed. San Francisco: Jossey-Bass.

Cohen, D. K., S. W. Raudenbush, and D. L. Ball. 2003. Resources, Instruction, and Research. *Educational Evaluation and Policy Analysis,* 25(2), 119–142.

Coll, K. M., and R. M. House. 1991. Empirical Implications for the Training and Professional Development of Community College Counselors. *Community College Review,* 19 (fall), 43–52.

College Entrance Examination Board. 2004. *Trends in College Pricing, 2004.* Washington, D.C.: College Entrance Examination Board.

Collins, R. 1979. *The Credential Society: An Historical Sociology of Education and Stratification.* New York: Academic Press.

Commander, N. E., and B. D. Smith. 1995. Developing Adjunct Reading and Learning Courses That Work. *Journal of Reading,* 38, 362–370.

CSAW (Commission on the Skills of the American Workforce). 1990. *America's Choice: High Skills or Low Wages!* Washington, D.C.: National Center on Education and the Economy.

Conley, D. 2004. Connecting Measures for Success in High School and College. In R. Kazis, J. Vargas, and N. Hoffman, eds., *Double the Numbers: Increasing Postsecondary Credentials for Underrepresented Youth.* Cambridge, Mass.: Harvard Education Press.

Council for Advancement of Adult Literacy. 2005. *To Ensure America's Future: Building a National Opportunity System for Adults.* New York: Council for Advancement of Adult Literacy.

CHEA (Council for Higher Education Accreditation) and the Institute for Higher Education Policy. 2000. *Distance Learning in Higher Education: CHEA Update Number 3.* Washington, D.C.: Council for Higher Education Accreditation.

Cox, R. 2004. Navigating Community College Demands: Contradictory Goals, Expectations, and Outcomes in Composition. Doctoral dissertation, University of California, Berkeley.

Crespin, J. L. 2004. *Keeping Student Success on the Front Burner.* Phoenix: League for Innovation in the Community College.

Crowe, E. 1998. *Statewide Remedial Education Policies: State Strategies That Support Successful Student Transitions from Secondary to Postsecondary Education: Technical Report.* Boulder, Col.: State Higher Education Executive Officers.

Cuban, L. 2001. *Oversold and Underused: Computers in the Classroom.* Cambridge, Mass.: Harvard University Press.

Deegan, W. L., and D. Tillery. 1985. The Evolution of Two-Year Colleges through Four Generations. In W. L. Deegan and D. Tillery, eds., *Renewing the American Community College: Priorities and Strategies for Effective Leadership,* pp. 3–33. San Francisco: Jossey-Bass.

Deil-Amen, R. 2005. *Do Traditional Models of College Dropout Apply to Non-Traditional Students at Non-Traditional Colleges?* Paper presented to the 2005 Annual Meetings of the American Sociological Association, Philadelphia, August 13–16.

Deil-Amen, R., and J. Rosenbaum. 2003a. Charter-Building at Low-Status Colleges: Charters as Mechanisms of Labor-Market Access for Two-Year College Students. Unpublished manuscript.

Deil-Amen, R., and J. Rosenbaum. 2003b. The Social Prerequisites of Success: Can College Structure Reduce the Need for Social Know-How? In J. Jacobs and K. Shaw, eds., *Annals of the American Academy of Political and Social Science*, 586, 120–143.

DiMaggio, P. J., and W. W. Powell. 1991. The Iron Cage Revisited: Institutional Isomorphism and Collective Rationality in Organization Fields. In W. W. Powell and P. J. DiMaggio, eds., *The New Institutionalism in Organizational Analysis*, pp. 63–82. Chicago: University Of Chicago Press.

Dougherty, K. J. 1994. *The Contradictory College: The Conflicting Origins, Impacts, and Futures of the Community College.* Albany, N.Y.: State University of New York Press.

Dougherty, K. J. 2002. The Evolving Role of the Community College: Policy Issues and Research Questions. In J. C. Smart and W. G. Tierney, eds. *Higher Education: Handbook of Theory and Research*, Vol. 18: 295–348. New York: Agathon Press.

Dougherty, K. J. 2004. *The Political Sources of the Origins (and Sometimes Demise) of State-Level Performance Funding for Higher Education.* Paper presented to the 2004 annual meeting of the American Educational Research Association. San Diego, California, April 12–16.

Dougherty, K. J., and M. F. Bakia. 2000. Community Colleges and Contract Training: Content, Origins, and Impact. *Teachers College Record*, 102(1), 197–243.

Dougherty, K.J. and E. Hong. 2005. *State Systems of Performance Accountability for Community Colleges: Impacts and Lessons for Policy Makers.* An Achieving the Dream Policy Brief. Boston: Jobs for the Future.

Dowd, A. 2003. From Access to Equity: Revitalizing the Democratic Mission of the Community College. *Annals of the American Academy of Political and Social Science*, 586, 92–119.

Dynarski, S. 2002. The Behavioral and Distributional Implications of Aid for College. *American Economic Review*, 92(2), 279–285.

Education Commission of the States. 2000. *State Funding for Community Colleges: A 50-State Survey.* Denver: Education Commission of the States.

Elder, L. and R. Paul. 2002. Critical Thinking: Teaching Students How to Study and Learn (Part II). *Journal of Developmental Education*, 26 (2), 34–35.

Ellwood, D. T., and T. J. Kane. 2000. Who Is Getting a College Education? Family Background and the Growing Gaps in Enrollment. In S. Danziger and J. Waldfogel, eds., *Securing the Future: Investing in Children from Birth to College.* New York: Russell Sage Foundation.

Evelyn, J. 2002a. City Colleges of Chicago Is Accused of Plan to Eliminate Academic Counselors. *Chronicle of Higher Education.* Retrieved February 1, 2006 from http://chronicle.com/daily/2002/02/2002022705n.htm.

Evelyn, J. 2002b. A Community College Tests the Limits of Outsourcing. *Chronicle of Higher Education*, 48(31), A30.

Evelyn, J. 2004. Community Colleges at a Crossroads. *Chronicle of Higher Education*, April 30, 50(34), A27.

Ewell, P. T. 2004. An Accountability System for "Doubling the Numbers." In R. Kazis, J. Vargas, and N. Hoffman, eds., *Double the Numbers: Increasing Postsecondary Credentials for Underrepresented Youth, pp. 101–112.* Cambridge, Mass.: Harvard Education Press.

Ewell, P. T., P. R. Schild, and K. Paulson. 2003. *Following the Mobile Student: Can We Develop the Capacity for a Comprehensive Database to Assess Student Progression?* Indianapolis: Lumina Foundation for Education.

Ewell, P. T., and J. Wellman. 1997. *Refashioning Accountability: Toward a "Coordinated" System of Quality Assurance for Higher Education.* Policy Papers on Higher Education PS 97–1. Denver: Education Commission of the States. ERIC ED 410812.

Featherstone, L. 1998. The Half-Price Diploma. *Rolling Stone, 797,* 87–90.

Field, K. 2005. Proposed Student-Data System Can Be Made Secure, Report Says. *Chronicle of Higher Education,* 51(30), A1.

Fischer, K. 2006. "State Spending on Colleges Bounces Back" *Chronicle of Higher Education,* 52 (19), A1.

Fix, Sybil. 1996. Legislators OK College Funding Bill. *Charleston Post and Courier,* May 10.

Fleming, B. 2004. Public Colleges Raise Tuition Sharply, But Not As Much As in Recent Years. *Chronicle of Higher Education,* 51(3), A22.

Florida Community College System. 1998. *The Florida Community College Accountability Plan at Year Four: A Report for South Florida Community College.* Tallahassee: Florida Community College System.

Florida Community College System. 2000. *Accountability in the Year 2000.* Tallahassee: Florida Community College System.

Florida Community College System. 2001. *The Fact Book: Report for the Florida Community College System February 2001.* Tallahassee: Florida Community College System.

Florida Community College System. 2002. *The Fact Book: Report for the Florida Community College System February 2002.* Tallahassee: Florida Community College System.

Florida Department of Education. 2003a. *2001–02 Associate of Science by Program.* Tallahassee: Florida Department of Education. Retrieved September 2005, from www.firn.edu/doe/ weois/fetpip/pdf/0001pdf/0102pdf/cc0102as.pdf

Florida Department of Education. 2003b. *2001–02 Associate in Applied Science Degree.* Tallahassee: Florida Department of Education.

Florida Department of Education. 2003c. *2001–02 Postsecondary Vocational Certificates by Program.* Tallahassee: Florida Department of Education.

Florida Department of Education. 2003d. *2001–02 Postsecondary Adult Vocational by Programs.* Tallahassee: Florida Department of Education.

Florida Department of Education. 2004a. *The Fact Book: Report for the Florida Community College System.* Tallahassee: Florida Department of Education.

Florida Department of Education. 2004b. *Impact of dual enrollment on high performing students* (Data Trend No. 26). Tallahassee: Florida Department of Education.

Florida Department of Education. 2004c. *K-20 Education Performance Accountability: Progress and Recommendations.* Tallahassee: Florida Department of Education.

Florida State Division of Colleges and Universities. 2001. *1994–2001 State University System Factbook.* Tallahassee: Florida State Division of Colleges and Universities.

Floyd, D. L., M. L. Skolnik, and K. P. Walker. 2005. *The Community College Baccalaureate: Emerging Trends and Policy Issues.* Sterling, VA: Stylus Publishing.

Flynn, William. 2002. More Than a Matter of Degrees. *American Community College Journal,* 72(6), 16–21.

Foorman, B., ed. 2003. *Preventing and Remediating Reading Difficulties: Bringing Science to Scale.* Timonium, MD: York Press.

Fuhrman, S.H., ed. 2001. *From the Capitol to the Classroom: Standards-Based Reform in the States.* Yearbook of the National Society for the Study of Education, Volume 100, Issue 2. Chicago: University of Chicago Press.

Futures Project 2000. *A Briefing on For-Profit Higher Education.* Providence, R.I.: Futures Project, Brown University.

Gabelnick, F., J. MacGregor, R. S. Matthews, and B. L. Smith. 1990. *Learning Communities: Creating Connections among Students, Faculty, and Disciplines. New Directions for Teaching and Learning, p. 41.* San Francisco: Jossey-Bass.

Gaither, G., B. P. Nedwek, and J. E. Neal, eds. 1994. *Measuring Up.* ASHE/ERIC series. San Francisco: Jossey-Bass.

Gandara, P., and J. Moreno. 2002. The Puente Project: Issues and Perspectives in Preparing Latino Youth for Higher Education. *Journal of Educational Policy,* 16(4), 463–473.

Garofoli, E., and J. Woodell. 2003. Faculty Development and the Diffusion of innovations. *Syllabus: Technology for Higher Education,* January.

Garrison, D. R. 1997. Self-Directed Learning: Toward a Comprehensive Model. *Adult Education Quarterly,* 48, 18–34.

Gittell, M., and T. Steffy. 2000. *Community Colleges Addressing Students' Needs: A Case Study of LaGuardia Community College.* New York: Howard Samuels State Management and Policy Center, City University of New York.

Gordon, V., W. Habley, and Associates. 2000. *Academic Advising: A Comprehensive Handbook.* San Francisco: Jossey-Bass.

Grubb, W. N. 1996. *Working in the Middle: Strengthening Education and Training for the Mid-Skilled Labor Force.* San Francisco: Jossey-Bass.

Grubb, W. N. 2001a. *From Black Box to Pandora's Box: Evaluating Remedial/Developmental Education.* New York: Community College Research Center, Teachers College, Columbia University.

Grubb, W. N. 2001b. "Getting into the World": Career Counseling in Community Colleges. Occasional paper, Community College Research Center, Teachers College, Columbia University.

Grubb, W. N. 2002a. Learning and Earning in the Middle. Part 1. National Studies of Pre-Baccalaureate Education. *Economics of Education Review,* 21(4), 299–321.

Grubb, W. N. 2002b. Who I Am: The Inadequacy of Career Information in the Information Age. Prepared for the OECD Career Guidance Policy Review, Paris.

Grubb, W. N., and N. Badway. 1998. *Linking School-Based and Work-Based Learning: The Implications of LaGuardia's Co-op Seminars for School-to-Work Programs.* (MDS 1046). Berkeley, Calif.: National Center for Research in Vocational Education.

Grubb, W. N., and J. Badway. 1999. *Performance Measures for Improving California Community Colleges: Issues and Options.* Berkeley: University of California, School of Education.

Grubb, W. N., and N. Badway. 2004. *From Compliance to Improvement: Accountability and Assessment in California Community Colleges.* Stockton, Calif.: Higher Education Evaluation and Research Group, for the California Community Colleges Chancellor's Office.

Grubb, W. N., N. Badway, D. Bell, D. Bragg, and M. Russman. 1997. *Workforce, Economic, and*

Community Development: The Changing Landscape of the Entrepreneurial Community College. Phoenix: League for Innovation in the Community College/Berkeley, Calif.: National Center for Research in Vocational Education/Columbus: National Council for Occupational Education.

Grubb, W. N., N. Badway, D. Bell, and E. Kraskouskas. 1996. *Community College Innovations in Workforce Preparation: Curriculum Integration and Tech-Prep.* Berkeley: University of California, School of Education, League for Innovation in the Community College, National Center for Research in Vocational Education, and National Council for Occupational Education.

Grubb, W.N., C. Lara, and S. Valdez. 2002. Counselor, Coordinator, Monitor, Mom: The Roles of Counselors in the Puente Program. *Journal of Educational Policy,* 16(4), 547–571.

Grubb, W. N., and M. Lazerson. 2004 *The Education Gospel: The Economic Power of Schooling.* Cambridge, Mass.: Harvard University Press.

Grubb, W.N., and J. Tuma. 1991. Who Gets Student Aid? Variation in Access to Aid. *Review of Higher Education,* 14(3), 358–382.

Grubb, W. N, and C. Watson. 2002. Engagement and Motivation in High Schools: The multiple Roles of Guidance and Counseling. Unpublished paper, prepared for the National Research Council Committee for Increasing High School Students' Engagement and Motivation to Learn.

Grubb, W. N., H. Worthen, B. Byrd, E. Webb, N. Badway, C. Case, S. Goto, and J. C. Villeneuve. 1999. *Honored but Invisible: An Inside Look at Teaching in Community Colleges.* New York: Routledge.

Hagedorn, L. 2005. Transcript Mining: Dealing with Diverse Student Records. Workshop presentation to faculty and administration at Valencia Community College, Orlando, Florida, January 2.

Haimson, J., and L. Hulsey. 1999. *Making Joint Commitments: Roles of Schools, Employers, and Students in Implementing National Skill Standards.* (MPR reference no. 8466–400). Princeton, N.J.: Mathematica Policy Research.

Haimson, J., and M. Van Noy. 2004. *Developing the IT Workforce: Certification Programs, Participants, and Outcomes in High Schools and Two-Year Colleges: Final Report.* Princeton, N.J.: Mathematica Policy Research.

Hammons, J., and J. Barnsley. 1996. The Elusive Search to Define the Effective Community College Teacher. *Community College Journal of Research and Practice,* 20, 311–323.

Harrell, P. E., and W. S. Forney. 2003. Ready or Not, Here We Come: Retaining Hispanic and First-Generation Students in Postsecondary Education. *Community College Journal of Research and Practice,* 27, 147–156.

Hart, E. R., and D. L. Speece. 1998. Reciprocal Learning Goes to College: Effects for Postsecondary Students at Risk for Academic Failure. *Journal of Educational Psychology,* 90, 670–681.

Hatch, T., R. Bass, T. Iiyoshi, and D. P. Mace. 2004. Building Knowledge for Teaching and Learning. *Change Magazine,* 36(5), 42–49.

Hauptman, A.M. 2004. Using Institutional Incentives to Improve Student Performance. In R. Kazis, J. Vargas, and N. Hoffman, eds., *Double the Numbers: Increasing Postsecondary Credentials for Underrepresented Youth,* pp. 123–133. Cambridge, Mass.: Harvard Education Press.

Hawkins, M. R. 2004. Researching English Language and Literacy Development in Schools. *Educational Researcher*, 33 (3), 14–25.

Hayward, G. C., D. P. Jones, A. C. McGuinness, Jr., and A. Timar. 2004. *Ensuring Access with Quality to California's Community Colleges.* San Jose, Calif.: National Center for Public Policy and Higher Education.

Healy, C. C., and K. Reilly. 1989. Career Needs of Community College Students: Implications for Services and Theory. *Journal of College Student Development*, 30(6), 541–545.

Hearns, J., and J. Holdsworth. 2004. Federal Student Aid: The Shift from Grants to Loans. In E. St. John and M. Parsons, eds., *Public Funding of Higher Education: Changing Contexts and New Rationales*, pp. 40–59. Baltimore: Johns Hopkins University Press.

Hebel, S. 1999. Community College of Denver Wins Fans with Ability to Tackle Tough Issues. *Chronicle of Higher Education*, 45(35), A37–38.

Hebel, S. 2003. Unequal Impact: Community Colleges Face Disproportionate Cuts in State Budgets. *Chronicle of Higher Education*, 49(38), A21.

Herr, E., and S. Cramer. 1992. *Career Guidance and Counseling through the Life Span: Systematic Approaches*, 4th ed. New York: HarperCollins.

Hershey, A., M. Silverberg, J. Haimson, P. Hudis, and R. Jackson. 1998. *Expanding Options for Students: Report to Congress on the National Evaluation of School-to-Work Implementation.* Princeton, N.J.: Mathematica Policy Research.

Hillocks, G. 1999. *Ways of Thinking, Ways of Teaching.* New York: Teachers College Press.

Hoachlander, G., A. C. Sikora, and L. Horn. 2003. *Community College Students: Goals, Academic Preparation, and Outcomes.* NCES 2003–164. Washington, D.C.: U.S. Department of Education, National Center for Education Statistics.

Hoffman, N. 2005. *Add and Subtract? Dual Enrollment as a State Strategy to Increase Postsecondary Success for Underrepresented Students.* Boston: Jobs for the Future.

Horn, L., and C. D. Carroll. 1996. *Nontraditional undergraduates: Trends in enrollment from 1986 to 1992 and persistence and attainment among 1989–90 beginning postsecondary students.* Washington, D.C.: U.S. Department of Education, National Center for Education Statistics.

Howard, J., and W. S. Obetz. 1996. Using the NALS to Characterize the Literacy of Community College Graduates. *Journal of Adolescent and Adult Literacy*, 39 (6), 462–467.

Hoyt, J. E., and C. T. Sorensen. 2001. High School Preparation, Placement Testing, and College Remediation. *Journal of Developmental Education*, 25 (2), 26–33.

Hudgins, J. L., and J. Mahaffey. 1997. When Institutional Effectiveness and Performance Funding Co-exist. *Journal of Applied Research in the Community College*, 5(1), 21–28.

Hughes, K. L., and M. M. Karp. 2006. *Strengthening Transitions by Encouraging Career Pathways: A Look at State Policies and Practices.* Washington, D.C.: American Association of Community Colleges/Phoenix, AZ: League for Innovation in the Community College.

Hughes, K. L., M. M. Karp, B. J. Fermin, and T. R. Bailey. 2005. *Pathways to College Access and Success.* Washington, D.C.: U.S. Department of Education, Office of Vocational and Adult Education.

Hull, G., M. Rose, K. L. Fraser, and M. Castelano. 1991. Remediation as Social Construct: Perspectives from an Analysis of Classroom Discourse. *College Composition and Communication*, 42(3), 299–329.

Hull, G., and J. Zacher. 2002. *New Literacies, New Selves, and Second Chances: Exploring Possibilities for Self-Representation through writing and Multi-Media in a Community Technology Center.* Paper presented at the meeting of the American Educational Research Association, New Orleans, LA, April 1–5.

Illich, P.A., C. Hagan, and L. McCallister. 2004. Performance in College-Level Courses among Students Concurrently Enrolled in Remedial Courses: Policy Implications. *Community College Journal of Research and Practice,* 28, 435–453.

Illinois Board of Higher Education. 2002. *Establishing Performance Indicators to Assess Progress toward Meeting the Goals of the Illinois Commitment: Status Report.* Board item 8, June 4, 2002. Springfield: Illinois Board of Higher Education.

Illinois Board of Higher Education. 2003. *Assessing Progress toward Meeting the Goals of the Illinois Commitment: Performance Indicators. 2003 Annual Report.* Springfield: Illinois Board of Higher Education.

Illinois Community College Board. 1998. *Report of the Advisory Committee on a Performance-Based Incentive System.* Springfield: Illinois Community College Board.

Illinois Community College Board. 1999. *Illinois Community College System Results Report: Fiscal Year 1999.* Springfield: Illinois Community College Board.

Illinois Community College Board. 2000a. *Accountability and Productivity in the Illinois Community College System.* Springfield: Illinois Community College Board.

Illinois Community College Board. 2000b. *Promise for Illinois.* Springfield: Illinois Community College Board.

Illinois Community College Board. 2002a. *Accountability and Productivity in the Community College System, October 2002.* Springfield: Illinois Community College Board.

Illinois Community College Board. 2002b. *Data and Characteristics of the Illinois Community College System, August 2002.* Springfield: Illinois Community College Board.

Illinois Community College Board. 2003. *Illinois Community College System Results Report 2003. Part 2: Report on Performance Indicators for Higher Education.* Springfield: Illinois Community College Board.

Illinois Community College Board. 2004a. *Measure 4M7: Remedial Credits Earned versus Attempted by College, Fiscal Years 2000–2003.* Springfield: Illinois Community College Board.

Illinois Community College Board. 2004b. *Measure 5M3: Summary of Transfer Rates by College, Fiscal Years 2001–2004.* Springfield: Illinois Community College Board.

Illinois Community College Board. 2004c. *Performance Measure IS3: Annual Number of Pre-Baccalaureate Graduates by Broad Field of Study. Total Academic Program Graduates. Fiscal Years 1996 through 2003.* Springfield: Illinois Community College Board.

Illinois Community College Board. 2004d. *Performance Report for Fiscal Year 2004.* Springfield: Illinois Community College Board.

Illinois Community College Board. 2004e. *Student Enrollments and Completions in the Illinois Community College System, Fiscal Year 2003.* Springfield: Illinois Community College Board.

Immerwahr, J. 2002. *Meeting the Competition: College and University Presidents, Faculty, and State Legislators View the New Competitive Academic Arena.* New York: Public Agenda.

Information Technology Association of American. 2001. Jobs, Skills, and the Continuing Demand for IT Workers. *Community College Journal,* 73(2), 32–35.

Jacobs, J., and R. Teahen. 1997. Shadow College and NCA Accreditation: A Conceptual Framework. *NCA Quarterly*, 71 (4) 472–78.

Jacobson, L., R. Lalonde, and D. Sullivan. 2005. *Industrial and Labor Relations Review*, 58 (April), pp. 298–415.

Jenkins, D. & Boswell, K. 2002. *State Policies on Community College Remedial Education: Findings from a National Survey.* Technical report no. CC-0201. Denver, CO: Education Commission of the States, Center for Community College Policy.

Jetton, T. L., and J. Dole, eds. 2004. *Adolescent Literacy Research and Practice.* New York: Guilford Press.

Jobs for the Future, 2004. *The Early College High School Initiative at a Glance.* Boston: Jobs for the Future.

Johns, A. M. 1985. Summary Protocols of "Unprepared" and "Adept" University Students: Replications and Distortions of the Original. *Language Learning*, 35, 495–517.

Johnson, L. F. 1996. Developmental Performance as a Predictor of Academic Success in Entry-Level Mathematics. *Community College Journal of Research and Practice*, 20, 333–344.

Johnstone, D. B., and B. Del Genio. 2001. *College-Level Learning in High School: Purposes, Policies, and Practical Implications.* Washington, D.C.: Association of American Colleges and Universities.

Jonassen, D.H., T. Mayes, and R. McAlesse. 1993. A Manifesto for a Constructivist Approach to Use of Technology in Higher Education. In T. M. Duffy, J. Lowyck, D. H. Jonassen, and T. M. Walsh, eds., *Designing Environments for Constructivist Learning*, pp. 230–248. New York: Springer-Verlag.

Kane, T. J. 1994. College Attendance by Blacks since 1970: The Role of College Cost, Family Background, and the Returns to Education. *Journal of Political Economy*, 102(5), 878–911.

Kane, T. J. 1995. *Rising Public College Tuition and College Entry: How Well Do Public Subsidies Promote Access to College?* NBER Working Paper no. 5164. Cambridge, Mass.: National Bureau of Economic Research.

Kane, T. J. 2004. College-Going and Inequality. In K. M. Neckerman, ed., *Social Inequality*, pp. 319–354. New York: Russell Sage Foundation.

Kane, M.A., C. Beals, E. Valeau, and M. J. Johnson. 2004. Fostering Success among Traditionally Underrepresented Student Groups: Hartnell College's Approach to Implementation of the Math, Engineering, and Science Achievement (MESA) Program. *Community College Journal of Research and Practice*, 28, 17–26.

Kane, T. J., P. R. Orszag, and D. L. Gunter. 2003. *State Fiscal Constraints and Higher Education Spending: The Role of Medicaid and the Business Cycle.* TPC Discussion Paper No. 11. Washington, D.C.: The Urban Institute.

Kane, T. J., and C. E. Rouse. 1995. Labor Market Returns to Two- and Four-Year Colleges: Is a Credit a Credit and Do Degrees Matter? *American Economic Review*, 85(3), 600–614.

Kane, T. J., and C. E. Rouse. 1999. The Community College: Educating Students at the Margin between College and Work. *Journal of Economic Perspectives*, 13(1), 63–84.

Karp, M. M., T. R. Bailey, K. L. Hughes, and B. J. Fermin. 2005. *State Dual Enrollment Policies: Addressing Access and Quality.* CCRC Brief no. 26. New York: Community College Research Center, Teachers College, Columbia University.

Kazis, R., J. Vargas, and N. Hoffman. 2004. *Double the Numbers: Increasing Postsecondary Credentials for Underrepresented Youth.* Cambridge, Mass.: Harvard Education Press.

Keim, M. C. 1988. Two-Year College Counselors: Who Are They and What Do They Do? *Community College Review,* 16 (summer), 39–46.

Kienzl, G. 2004. The Triple Helix of Education and Earnings: The Effect of Schooling, Work, and Pathways on the Economic Outcomes of Community College Students. Doctoral dissertation, Columbia University.

Kim, J. 2003. Returns to College Education: An Analysis of Hispanic Workers. *Journal of Hispanic Higher Education,* 2, 276–291.

Kimmel, I., and J. R. Davis. 1996. Moving to the Center: Students' Strategies for College Survival. *Research and Teaching in Developmental Education,* 12 (2), 71–79.

Kinney, D. P. 2001. A Comparison of Computer-Mediated and Lecture Classes in Developmental Mathematics. *Research and Teaching in Developmental Education (RTDE),* 18(1), 32–40.

Kirst, M. W. 2004. Using a K-12 Assessment for College Placement. In R. Kazis, J. Vargas, and N. Hoffman, eds. *Double the Numbers: Increasing Postsecondary Credentials for Underrepresented Youth,* pp 155–160. Cambridge, Mass.: Harvard Education Press.

Kleiman, N. S. 2001. *Building a Highway to Higher Ed: How Collaborative Efforts are Changing Education in America.* New York: Center for an Urban Future.

Kleiner, B., and L. Lewis. 2005. *Dual Enrollment of High School Students at Postsecondary Institutions: 2002–2003.* NCES 2005–008. Washington, D.C.: U.S. Department of Education, National Center for Education Statistics.

Krei, M. S., and J. E. Rosenbaum. 2001. Career and College Advice to the Forgotten Half: What Do Counselors and Teachers Advise? *Teachers College Record,* 103 (5), 823–842.

Laanan, F. S. 2001. Accountability in Community Colleges: Looking toward the 21st Century. In Barbara K. Townsend and Susan B. Twombly, eds., *Community Colleges: Policy in the Future Context,* pp. 57–76. Westport, Conn.: Ablex.

Labaree, D. F. 1997. *How to Succeed in School without Really Learning: The Credentials Race in American Education.* New Haven, Conn.: Yale University Press.

Layzell, D. 1999. Linking Performance to Funding Outcomes at the State Level. *Research in Higher Education,* 40, 233–246.

Lee, T. W. 1998. *Using Qualitative Methods in Organizational Research.* Thousand Oaks, Calif.: Sage.

Leigh, D. E., and A. M. Gill. 2003. Do Community Colleges Really Divert Students from Earning Bachelor's Degrees? *Economics of Education Review,* 22(1), 23–30.

Leigh, D. E., and A. M. Gill. 2004. The Effect of Community Colleges on Changing Students' Educational Aspirations. *Economics of Education Review,* 23(1), 95–102.

Leonhardt, D. 2005. The College Dropout Boom: Working Class and Staying that Way. *New York Times,* May 24, pp. A1, A15.

Levin, J. S. 2001. *Globalizing the Community College: Strategies for Change in the Twenty-First Century.* New York: Palgrave.

Levine, A. 1997. How the Academic Profession is Changing. *Daedalus,* 126(4), 1–20.

Liff, S. B. 2003. Social and Emotional Intelligence: Applications for Developmental Education. *Journal of Developmental Education,* 26 (3), 28–34.

Little, J. W. 1996. The Emotional Contours and Career Trajectories of (Disappointed) Reform Enthusiasts. *Cambridge Journal of Education*, 26 (3), 345–359.

Long, B. T. 2005. *State Financial Aid: Policies to Enhance Articulation and Transfer.* Boulder Col.: Western Interstate Commission for Higher Education.

Longanecker, D. A. 2004. Financing Tied to Postsecondary Outcomes: Examples from States. In R. Kazis, J. Vargas, and N. Hoffman, eds., *Double the Numbers: Increasing Postsecondary Credentials for Underrepresented Youth,* pp. 113–122. Cambridge, Mass.: Harvard Education Press.

L'Orange, H. P. 2004. Data and Accountability Systems: From Kindergarten through College. In R. Kazis, J. Vargas, and N. Hoffman, eds., *Double the Numbers: Increasing Postsecondary Credentials for Underrepresented Youth, Chapter 13.* Cambridge, Mass.: Harvard Education Press.

Lords, E. 2000. New Efforts at Community Colleges Focus on Underachieving Teens. *Chronicle of Higher Education,* 46(43), A45–46.

Lumina Foundation for Higher Education. 2004. *Achieving the Dream: Colleges Count.* Indianapolis: Lumina Foundation for Higher Education.

Lundell, D. B., and J. L. Higbee, eds. 2000. *Proceedings of the First International Meeting on Future Directions in Developmental Education* (October 5–6, 1999). Minneapolis: Center for Research on Developmental and Urban Literacy, General College, University of Minnesota.

Lundell, D. B., and J. L. Higbee, eds. 2002. *Proceedings of the Second Meeting on Future Directions in Developmental Education.* (April 5–6, 2001). Minneapolis: Center for Research on Developmental and Urban Literacy, General College, University of Minnesota.

Manski, C. 1989. Schooling as Experimentation: A Reappraisal of the College Dropout Phenomenon. *Economics of Education Review,* 8(4), 305–312.

Marcotte, D. E., T. R. Bailey, C. Borkoski, and G. S. Kienzl. 2005. The Returns of a Community College Education: Evidence from the National Education Longitudinal Study. *Educational Evaluation and Policy Analysis,* 27(2), 157–175.

Marklein, M. B. 2003. Two-Year Schools Aim High: They're Giving Honors Students a Boost to Big-Name Colleges. *USA Today,* June 10, 10D.

Martinez, M., and J. Bray. 2002. *All Over the Map: State Policies to Improve the High School.* Washington, D.C.: The Institute of Education Leadership.

Matthews. R. S. 1994. Enriching Teaching and Learning through Learning Communities. In T. O'Banion and Associates, *Teaching and Learning in the Community College,* pp 179–200. Washington, D.C.: American Association of Community Colleges.

Matus-Grossman, L., and S. Gooden. 2002. *Opening Doors: Students' Perspectives on Juggling Work, Family, and College.* New York: Manpower Demonstration Research Corp.

Mayor's Advisory Task Force on the City University of New York. 1999. *City University of New York: An Institution Adrift.* New York: Mayor's Advisory Task Force on the City University of New York.

McCabe, R. H. 2000. *No One to Waste: A Report to Public Decision-Makers and Community College Leaders.* Washington, D.C.: Community College Press.

McCabe, R. H. 2003. *Yes We Can! A Community College Guide for Developing America's Underprepared.* Phoenix: League for Innovation in the Community College and American Association of Community Colleges.

McCabe, R. H., and P. R. Day, Jr., eds. 1998. *Developmental Education: A Twenty-First Century Social and Economic Imperative.* Mission Viejo, Calif.: League for Innovation in the Community College.

McClenney, B. N., and R. M. Flores. 1998. Community College of Denver Developmental Education. In R. H. McCabe and P. R. Day, Jr., eds. *Developmental Education: A Twenty-First-Century Social and Economic Imperative,* pp. 45–52. Mission Viejo, Calif.: League for Innovation in the Community College.

McCusker, M. 1999. ERIC Review: Effective Elements of Developmental Reading and Writing Programs. *Community College Review,* 27(2), 93–105.

McGrath, D., and M. B. Spear. 1991. *The Academic Crisis of the Community College.* Albany, N.Y.: State University of New York Press.

McKeown-Moak, M. P. 2000. *Financing Higher Education in the New Century: The Second Annual Report from the States.* Denver: State Higher Education Executive Officers.

McPherson, M. S., and M. O. Schapiro. 1991. Does Student Aid Affect College Enrollment? New Evidence on a Persistent Controversy. *American Economic Review,* 81(1), 309–318.

Merisotis, J., and R. Phipps. 2000. Remedial Education in Colleges and Universities: What's Really Going On? *Review of Higher Education,* 24(1), 67–86.

Meyer, J. W., and B. Rowan. 1977. Institutionalized Organizations: Formal Structure as Myth and Ceremony. *American Journal of Sociology,* 83(2), 340–363. Revised version reprinted in W. D. Powell and Paul J. DiMaggio, eds., *The New Institutionalism in Organizational Analysis,* pp. 41–62. Chicago: University of Chicago Press, 1991.

Meyer, K. A. 2002. Quality in Distance Education: Focus on On-Line Learning. *ASHE-ERIC Higher Education Report,* 29(4).

Michelau, D. K. 2001. *Postsecondary Enrollment Options Programs.* NCSL State Legislative Report, 26(4), pp. 1–8. Denver: National Conference of State Legislatures.

Miller, L. 1999. Reframing Teacher Burnout in the Context of School Reform and Teacher Development in the United States. In R. Vandenberghe and M. Huberman, eds., *Understanding and Preventing Teacher Burnout: A Sourcebook of International Research and Practice.* Cambridge, Mass.: Cambridge University Press.

Minkler, J. E. 2002. ERIC Review: Learning Communities at the Community College. *Community College Review,* 30(3), 46–63.

Minnesota State Legislature. 1985. Postsecondary Enrollment Options Act, §123.3514.

Moden, G. O. and A. M. Williford. 2002. Ohio's Challenge: A Clash of Performance Funding and Base Budgeting. In Joseph C. Burke and Associates, *Funding Public Colleges and Universities for Performance,* pp. 169–194. Albany, N.Y.: Rockefeller Institute.

Mohr, K. A. J. 2002. Planning for Productive College-Level Work: Using the Course Assignment Framework. *Community College Journal of Research and Practice,* 26, 469–477.

Morest, V. S. 2004. The Role of Community Colleges in State Adult Education Systems: A National Analysis. Working Paper 3. New York: Council for Advancement of Adult Literacy.

Morest, V. S. In press. *Institutional Research at Community Colleges.* New York: Teachers College, Columbia University, Community College Research Center.

MPR Associates. 1996. *Skill Standards: Concepts and Practices in State and Local Education.* Berkeley, CA: MPR Associates for OVAE, U.S. Department of Education.

Muraskin, L. 1997. *"Best Practices" in Student Support Services: A Study of Five Exemplary Sites.*

Rockville, MD: Westat/Washington, D.C.: SMB Economic Research for the Planning and Evaluation Service, U.S. Department of Education.

NASSGAP (National Association of State Student Grant and Aid Programs). 2005. *35th Annual Survey Report on State-Sponsored Student Financial Aid, 2003–2004 Academic Year.* Springfield, Ill.: National Association of State Student Grant and Aid Programs.

National Center for Public Policy and Higher Education. 2004. *Measuring Up 2004: The National Report Card on Higher Education.* San Jose, Calif.: National Center for Public Policy and Higher Education.

National Commission on Accountability in Higher Education. 2005. *Accountability for Better Results: A National Imperative for Higher Education.* Denver, Col.: State Higher Education Executive Officers.

National Commission on the High School Senior Year. 2001. *Raising Our Sights: No High School Senior Left Behind.* Princeton, N.J.: Woodrow Wilson National Fellowship Foundation.

NCOE-NCEET (National Council on Occupational Education and National Council for Continuing Education and Training). 2001. *New Forms of Certification.* Atlanta, GA: NCOE/Carlsbad, CA: NCEET.

National Governors Association 2005. *Getting It Done: Ten Steps to a State Action Agenda.* Washington, D.C.: National Governors Association.

National Information Center for Higher Education Policymaking and Analysis. 2004. *Completion: Retention Rates: First-Time College Freshmen Returning Their Second Year.* Boulder, Col.: National Information Center for Higher Education Policymaking and Analysis.

Newman, F. 2000. Saving Higher Education's Soul. *Change,* September/October, pp. 16–23.

Newman, F. 2001 *Interesting Times: The End of the Status Quo and the Rise of the Market in Higher Education.* Providence, R.I.: Futures Project, Brown University.

Newman, F., L. Couturier, and J. Scurry. 2004. *The Future of Higher Education: Rhetoric, Reality, and the Risks of the Market.* San Francisco: Jossey-Bass.

Nissenson, B. 2003. Performance Measures Funding: The Journey of One Washington Community College. Doctoral dissertation, Oregon State University.

Nist, S. L., and J. L. Holschuh. 2000. Comprehension Strategies at the College Level. In R.F. Flippo and D. C. Caverly, eds. *Handbook of College Reading and Study Strategy Research, pp. 75–104.* Mahwah, NJ: Erlbaum.

Nist, S. L., and M. L. Simpson. 2000. College Studying. In M. Kamil, P. Mosenthal, P. D. Pearson, and R. Barr, eds. *Handbook of Reading Research,* Vol.3, pp. 645–666. Mahwah, N.J.: Erlbaum.

O'Banion, T. 1994. Teaching and Learning: A Mandate for the 90s. *Community College Journal,* 64, 21–25.

Olson, L. 2001. "Overboard on Testing?" In *Education Week: Quality Counts 2001,* pp. 23–30. Bethesda, Md.: L. Olson.

Oudenhoven, B. 2002. Remediation at the Community College: Pressing Issues, Uncertain Solutions. *New Directions for Community Colleges,* 117, 35–44.

Palattella, J. 2001. May the Course Be with You. *Lingua Franca: The Review of Academic Life,* 11(2), 50–57.

Parsons, F. 1909. *Choosing a Vocation.* Boston: Houghton Mifflin.

Pascarella, E. T. and P. T. Terenzini 2005. Educational Attainment and Persistence. In *How*

College Affects Students: A Third Decade of Research, Vol. 2, pp. 373–444. San Francisco: Jossey-Bass.

Perin, D. 2001. Academic-Occupational Integration as a Reform Strategy for the Community College: Classroom Perspectives. *Teachers College Record,* 103, 303–335.

Perin, D. 2002. The Location of Developmental Education in Community Colleges: A Discussion of the Merits of Mainstreaming vs. Centralization. *Community College Review,* 30(1), 27–44.

Perin, D. 2004. Remediation beyond Developmental Education: The Use of Learning Assistance Centers to Increase Academic Preparedness in Community Colleges. *Community College Journal of Research and Practice,* 28 (7), 559–582.

Perin, D. 2006. Can Community Colleges Protect Both Access and Standards? The Problem of Remediation. *Teachers College Record,* 108 (3), 339–373.

Perin, D., A. Keselman, and M. Monopoli. 2003. Effects of Text, Domain, and Learner Variables on the Academic Writing of Developmental Reading Students. *Higher Education,* 45(1), 19–42.

Petrides, L. A. 2002. Organizational Learning and the Case for Knowledge-Based Systems. *New Directions for Institutional Research* 113 (spring), 69–84.

Pfeffer, J., and G. R. Salancik. 1978. *The External Control of Organizations: A Resource Dependence Perspective.* New York: Harper and Row.

Phillippe, K. A., ed. 2000. *National Profile of Community Colleges: Trends and Statistics,* 3rd ed. Washington, D.C.: Community College Press.

Phillippe, K. A., and M. J. Valiga. 2000. *Faces of the Future: 1999 Survey Results.* Washington, D.C.: American Association of Community Colleges.

Phipps, R. 1998. *College Remediation: What It Is, What It Costs, What's at Stake.* Washington, D.C.: Institute for Higher Education Policy.

Powell, A. G., E. Farrar, and D. K. Cohen. 1985. *The Shopping Mall High School: Winners and Losers in the Educational Marketplace.* Boston: Houghton Mifflin.

President's Commission on Higher Education. 1947. *Higher Education for American Democracy: A Report of the President's Commission on Higher Education.* Washington, D.C.: Government Publication Office.

Prince, D., and D. Jenkins. 2005. *Building Pathways to Success for Low-Skill Adult Students: Lessons for Community College Policy and Practice from a Statewide Longitudinal Tracking Study.* New York: Community College Research Center, Teachers College, Columbia University.

QSR International. 2000. N5 [computer software]. Melbourne, Australia: QSR International Pty. Ltd.

QSR International. 1998–1999. NVivo 1.1 [computer software]. Melbourne, Australia: QSR International Pty. Ltd.

Raftery, S., and R. VanWagoner. 2002. Using Learning Communities to Develop Basic Skills. *Learning Abstracts,* 5(9). Phoenix: League for Innovation in the Community College.

Reay, D., and S. J. Ball. 1997. "Spoilt for Choice": The Working Classes and Educational Markets. *Oxford Review of Education,* 23(1), 89–101.

Reder, S. 2000. Adult Literacy and Postsecondary Education Students: Overlapping Populations and Learning Trajectories. In J. Comings, B. Garner, and C. Smith, eds., *The Annual Review of Adult Learning and Literacy,* Vol. 1, pp. 111–157. San Francisco: Jossey-Bass.

Regional Technology Strategies, and Technology Institute, Copenhagen. 2004. Comparison of ICT Educational Preparation in the United States and Denmark. Chapel Hill, N.C.: Research Technology Strategies.

Reuters. 2004. Rise in Hispanics and Asian-Americans Is Predicted. *New York Times*, March 18, p. A20.

Reynolds, T., and P. Bruch. 2002. Curriculum and Affect: A Participatory Developmental Writing Approach. *Journal of Developmental Education*, 26, 12–20.

Richardson, R. C., and D. B. Elliot. 1994. Improving Opportunities for Underprepared Students. In T. O'Banion, ed., *Teaching and Learning in the Community College*, pp 97–115. Washington, D.C.: Community College Press.

Rochford, R. A. 2003. Assessing Learning Styles to Improve the Quality of Performance of Community College Students in Developmental Writing Programs: A Pilot Study. *Community College Journal of Research and Practice*, 27, 665–677.

Rogers, E. M. 1962. *Diffusion of Innovations*. New York: Free Press of Glencoe.

Rosenbaum, J. E. 2001. *Beyond College for All: Career Paths for the Forgotten Half*. New York: Russell Sage Foundation.

Rothwell, W. J., P. E. Gerity, and E. A. Gaertner. 2004. *Linking Training to Performance: A Guide for Workforce Development Professionals*. Washington, D.C.: Community College Press.

Roueche, J. E. 1968. *Salvage, Redirection, or Custody? Remedial Education in the Community Junior College*. Washington, D.C.: American Association of Community Colleges.

Roueche, J. E., E. E. Ely, and S. D. Roueche. 2001. *In Pursuit of Excellence: The Community College of Denver*. Washington, D.C.: Community College Press.

Roueche, J. E., and S. D. Roueche. 1993. *Between a Rock and a Hard Place*. Washington, D.C.: American Association of Community Colleges.

Roueche, J. E., and S. D. Roueche. 1999. *High Stakes, High Performance: Making Remedial Education Work*. Washington, D.C.: Community College Press.

Rouse, C. E. 1995. Democratization or Diversion? The Effect of Community Colleges on Educational Attainment. *Journal of Business and Economic Statistics*, 13(2), 217–224.

Ruppert, S. 1995. Roots and Realities of State-Level Performance Indicator Systems. *New Directions for Higher Education*, 91, 11–23.

Ruppert, S. 2001. *Where We Go from Here: State Legislative Views on Higher Education in the New Millennium: Results of the 2001 Higher Education Issues Survey*. Littleton, Col.: Educational Systems Research.

Schneider, B., and D. Stevenson. 1999. *The Ambitious Generation: America's Teenagers, Motivated but Directionless*. New Haven, Conn.: Yale University Press.

Scott, M., T. R. Bailey, and G. Kienzl. 2006. Relative Success? Determinants of College Graduation Rates in Public and Private Colleges in the US. *Research in Higher Education*, 47 (3), 247–277.

Scott, W. R. 1998. *Organizations: Rational, Natural, and Open Systems*, 4th ed. Upper Saddle River, N.J.: Prentice Hall.

Secretary's Commission for Achieving Necessary Skills. 1991. *What Work Requires of Schools: A SCANS Report for America 2000*. Washington, D.C.: U.S. Department of Labor.

Selinger, B. M. 1995. Summarizing Text: Developmental Students Demonstrate a Successful Method. *Journal of Developmental Education*, 19, 14–16, 18, 20.

Selingo, J. 1999. For-Profit Colleges Aim to Take a Share of State Financial-Aid Funds. *Chronicle of Higher Education,* 46 (5), A41–42.

Sener, J. 2004. Escaping the comparison trap: Evaluating online learning on its own terms. *Innovate,* 1 (2). Retrieved December 3, 2004, from http://www.innovateonline.info/index .php?view=article&id=11.

Shults, C. 2000. *Institutional Policies and Practices in Remedial Education: A National Study of Community Colleges.* Washington, D.C.: American Association of Community Colleges.

Simpson, M. L., C. R. Hynd, S. L. Nist, and K. I. Burrell. 1997. College Academic Assistance Programs and Practices. *Educational Psychology Review,* 9, 39–87.

Simpson, M. L., and S. L. Nist. 2001. Encouraging Active Reading at the College Level. In C. C. Block and M. Pressley, eds., *Comprehension Instruction: Research-Based Best Practices,* pp. 365–381. New York: Guilford Press.

Slaughter, S., and L. L. Leslie. 1997. *Academic Capitalism: Politics, Policies, and the Entrepreneurial University.* Baltimore: Johns Hopkins University Press.

Smith, B. 1991. Taking Structure Seriously: The Learning Community Model. *Liberal Education,* 77(2), 42–48.

Smittle, P. 2003. Principles for Effective Teaching in Developmental Education. *Journal of Developmental Education,* 26, 10–16.

Snyder, V. 2002. The Effects of Course-Based Reading Strategy Training on the Reading Comprehension of Developmental College Students. *Research and Teaching in Developmental Education,* 18(2), 37–41.

Spann, M. G., Jr. 2000. *Remediation: A Must for the 21st-Century Learning Society.* Denver: Education Commission of the States, Center for Community College Policy.

St. John, E. P. 2003. *Refinancing the College Dream: Access, Equal Opportunity, and Justice for Taxpayers.* Baltimore: Johns Hopkins University Press.

St. John, E. P., and M. D. Parsons, eds. 2004. *Public Funding of Higher Education: Changing Contexts and New Rationales.* Baltimore: Johns Hopkins University Press.

Stanley, P. 2000. Credentialing Success Story for Maryland Community Colleges. *Workplace,* 13(2), 12–13, 34.

State Higher Education Executive Officers. 2003. *Student Success: Statewide P–16 Systems.* Boulder, Col.: State Higher Education Executive Officers.

State University of New York. 1998. *Intra-SUNY Transfer Enrollments by Sending Institution and by Academic Program Area of Students at the Receiving Institution.* Statistical Release 371. Albany, N.Y.: State University of New York Press.

State University of New York. 2003. *Retention of All First-Time, Full-Time Students in an Associate Degree Program, Initial Cohorts of Fall 1992 through Fall 2002 Followed for Four Semesters.* Albany, N.Y.: State University of New York Press.

State University of New York. 2004. *Trends in Degrees and Other Formal Awards Granted by Institution and Award Level, 1994–1995 through 2003–2004.* Albany, N.Y.: State University of New York Press.

State University of New York at Buffalo. 2001. *Intra-SUNY Transfer Enrollments.* Statistical Release 397. Buffalo, N.Y.: State University of New York at Buffalo.

Stein, R. B. 2002. Integrating Budget, Assessment, and Accountability Policies: Missouri's Experiment with Performance Funding. In J. C. Burke and Associates, eds., *Funding Public*

Colleges and Universities for Performance: Popularity, Problems, and Prospects, pp. 107–135. Albany, N.Y.: Rockfeller Institute Press.

Stern, D. 1999. Improving Pathways in the United States from High School to College and Career. In *Preparing Youth for the 21st Century: The Transition from Education to the Labour Market.* Paris: OECD.

Strosnider, K. 1998. For-Profit Higher Education Sees Booming Enrollments and Revenues. *Chronicle of Higher Education,* 44(20), A36–38.

Stull, W. J. 2003. School-to-Work in Schools: An overview. In W. J. Stull and N. M. Sanders, eds., *The School-to-Work Movement: Origins and Destinations,* pp. 3–25. Westport, Conn.: Praeger.

Texas Higher Education Coordinating Board. 1998. *Strategic Plan for Texas Public Community Colleges.* Austin: Texas Higher Education Coordinating Board.

Texas Higher Education Coordinating Board. 1999a. *Data Resources for the 1999 LBB Performance Measures: Texas Community and Technical Colleges.* Austin: Texas Higher Education Coordinating Board.

Texas Higher Education Coordinating Board 1999b. *The Effectiveness of Developmental Education at Texas Public Institutions of Higher Education.* Austin: Texas Higher Education Coordinating Board.

Texas Higher Education Coordinating Board. 2000a. *Closing the Gaps: The Texas Higher Education Plan.* Austin: Texas Higher Education Coordinating Board.

Texas Higher Education Coordinating Board. 2000b. *Data Resources for the 2000 LBB Performance Measures: Texas Community and Technical Colleges.* Austin: Texas Higher Education Coordinating Board.

Texas Higher Education Coordinating Board. 2000c. *State-Level Institutional Effectiveness Process for Texas Community and Technical Colleges.* Austin: Texas Higher Education Coordinating Board.

Texas Higher Education Coordinating Board. 2001a. *Data Resources for the 2001 LBB Performance Measures: Texas Community and Technical Colleges.* Austin, TX: Author.

Texas Higher Education Coordinating Board. 2001b. *Guidelines for Instructional Programs in Workforce Education.* Austin: Texas Higher Education Coordinating Board.

Texas Higher Education Coordinating Board. 2002a. *2002 Annual Data Profile: Community and Technical Colleges Statewide Summary.* Austin: Texas Higher Education Coordinating Board.

Texas Higher Education Coordinating Board. 2002b. *Skill Development Fund Evaluation Instrument for Texas Community and Technical Colleges.* Austin: Texas Higher Education Coordinating Board.

Texas Higher Education Coordinating Board, and Community and Technical College Division. 2002c. *2002 Statewide Annual Licensure Report.* Austin: Texas Higher Education Coordinating Board.

Texas Higher Education Coordinating Board. 2002d. *Appropriations for Developmental Education in Texas Public Institutions of Higher Education.* Austin: Texas Higher Education Coordinating Board.

Texas Higher Education Coordinating Board. 2002e. *A Report Evaluating the Effectiveness of the Developmental Education Accountability Pilot Programs.* Austin: Texas Higher Education Coordinating Board.

Texas Higher Education Coordinating Board. 2004a. *Data Resources for Institutional Effectiveness Measures and Standards, 2003–2004.* Austin: Texas Higher Education Coordinating Board.

Texas Higher Education Coordinating Board. 2004b. *Data Resources for the 2004 LBB Performance Measures: Texas Community and Technical Colleges.* Austin: Texas Higher Education Coordinating Board.

Texas Legislative Budget Board. 2002. *Public Community/Junior Colleges Performance Measure Definitions.* Austin: Texas Legislative Budget Board.

Thompson, J. D. 1967. *Organizations in Action : Social Science Bases of Administrative Theory.* New York: McGraw-Hill.

Tinto, V. 1997. Classrooms as Communities: Exploring the Educational Character of Student Persistence. *Journal of Higher Education, 68*(6), 599–623.

Tinto, V., and A. Goodsell-Love. 1995. *A Longitudinal Study of Learning Communities at La-Guardia Community College.* ERIC Document No. ED 380 178. Washington, D.C.: National Center on Postsecondary Teaching, Learning, and Assessment, Office of Educational Research and Improvement, U.S. Department of Education.

Tinto, V., A. Goodsell-Love, and P. Russo. 1994. *Building Learning Communities for New College Students: A Summary of Research Findings of the Collaborative Learning Project.* Washington, D.C.: National Center on Postsecondary Teaching, Learning, and Assessment, Office of Educational Research and Improvement, U.S. Department of Education.

Tinto, V., P. Russo, and S. Kadel. 1994. Constructing Educational Communities: Increasing Retention in Challenging Circumstances. *AACC Journal, 64*(4), 26–29.

Tokina, K. 1993. Long-Term and Recent Student Outcomes of Freshman Interest Groups. *Journal of the Freshman Year Experience, 5*(2), 7–28.

Townsend, B. 2005. A Cautionary View. In D. L. Floyd, M. L. Skolnik, and K. P. Walker, eds., *The Community College Baccalaureate: Emerging Trends and Policy Issues,* pp. *179–190.* Sterling, VA: Stylus Publishing.

Townsend, B. K., J. Donaldson, and T. Wilson. 2004. *Marginal or Monumental? Visibility of Community Colleges in Selected Higher Education Journals.* Paper presented at Annual Meeting of Council for the Study of Community Colleges, Minneapolis, Minnesota, April.

Trow, M. 2000. *Some Consequences of the New Information and Communication Technologies for Higher Education.* CSHE Research and Occasional Paper Series No. 5.00. Berkeley: Center for Studies in Higher Education, University of California.

Turner, R. H. 1960. Sponsored and Contest Mobility and the School System. *American Sociological Review, 25*(6), 855–867.

Twigg, C. A. 2002. The Impact of the Changing Economy on Four-Year Institutions of Higher Education: The Importance of the Internet. In P. A. Graham and N. G. Stacey, eds., *The Knowledge Economy and Postsecondary Education: Report of a Workshop,* pp. 77–104. Washington, D.C.: National Academies Press.

U.S. Department of Education. 1990. *Integrated Postsecondary Education Data System (IPEDS), Fall 1990.* Washington DC: U.S. Department of Education, National Center for Education Statistics.

U.S. Department of Education. 1992. *Integrated Postsecondary Education Data System (IPEDS), Fall 1992.* Washington DC: U.S. Department of Education, National Center for Education Statistics.

U.S. Department of Education. 1993. *Integrated Postsecondary Education Data System (IPEDS), Fall 1993*. Washington DC: U.S. Department of Education, National Center for Education Statistics.

U.S. Department of Education. 1993. *National Assessment of Vocational Education.* Washington, DC: National Center for Education Statistics.

U.S. Department of Education. 1994. *National Assessment of Vocational Education: Final Report to Congress, Volume 1, Summary and Recommendations.* Washington D.C. U.S. Department or Education, Office of Educational Research and Improvement. Retrieved January 20, 2006, from http://eric.ed.gov/ERICDocs/data/ericdocs2/content_storage_01/0000000b/80/26/cc/a4.pdf.

U.S. Department of Education. 1995. *Digest of Educational Statistics, 1995,* Table 171. Washington DC: U.S. Department of Education, National Center for Education Statistics.

U.S. Department of Education. 1996. *Statistical Analysis Report: Remedial Education at Higher Education Institutions in Fall 1995: Postsecondary Education Quick Information System (PEQIS).* Technical Report NCES 97–584. Washington, D.C.: U.S. Department of Education, National Center for Education Statistics.

U.S. Department of Education. 2000a. *Common Core of Data, Public Elementary/Secondary School Universe Survey, 2000–01.* Washington, D.C.: U.S. Department of Education, National Center for Education Statistics.

U.S. Department of Education. 2000b. *Integrated Postsecondary Education Data System (IPEDS), Fall 2000.* Washington DC: U.S. Department of Education, National Center for Education Statistics.

U.S. Department of Education. 2001. *Integrated Postsecondary Education Data System (IPEDS), Fall 2001.* Washington DC: U.S. Department of Education, National Center for Education Statistics.

U.S. Department of Education. 2002a. *Adult Education and Lifelong Learning Survey 1999, National Household Education Survey (AELL-NHES:1999).* NCES 2002-005 [Data CD-ROM]. Washington, DC: U.S. Department of Education, National Center for Education Statistics.

U.S. Department of Education. 2002b. *Integrated Postsecondary Education Data System (IPEDS), Fall 2002.* Washington DC: U.S. Department of Education, National Center for Education Statistics.

U.S. Department of Education. 2002c. *Interim Report to Congress.* Executive summary. Washington, D.C.: U.S. Department of Education, National Assessment of Vocational Education.

U.S. Department of Education. 2002d. *Teaching with Technology: Use of Telecommunications Technology by Postsecondary Instructional Faculty and Staff in Fall 1998.* Technical Report NCES 2002–161, by E. C. Warburton, X. Chen, and E. M. Bradburn, Project Office: L. J. Zimbler. Washington, D.C.: U.S. Department of Education, National Center for Education Statistics.

U.S. Department of Education. 2003a. *The Condition of Education, 2003,* Appendix 1 Supplemental Tables, p.117, Table 7.1. Washington DC: U.S. Department of Education, National Center for Education Statistics. Retrieved January 20, 2006, from http://nces.ed.gov/programs/coe/2005/section1/table.asp?tableID=238.

U.S. Department of Education. 2003b. *The Condition of Education 2003,* p.81 (Indicator 42).

Washington DC: U.S. Department of Education, National Center for Education Statistics. Retrieved January 20, 2006, from http://nces.ed.gov/pubs2003/2003067_6.pdf.

U.S. Department of Education. 2003c. *Digest of Educational Statistics, 2002,* Tables 173 and 178. Washington DC: U.S. Department of Education, National Center for Education Statistics.

U.S. Department of Education. 2003d. *Integrated Postsecondary Education Data System [Data Files].* Washington DC: U.S. Department of Education, National Center for Education Statistics.

U.S. Department of Education. 2003e. *NELS: 88/2000 Postsecondary Education Transcript Study (PETS: 2000).* NCES 2003–402 [Data CD-ROM]. Washington DC: U.S. Department of Education, National Center for Education Statistics.

U.S. Department of Education. 2003f. *1995–96 Beginning Postsecondary Students Longitudinal Study, second follow-up (BPS: 96/01).* NCES 2003–160 [Data CD-ROM]. Washington, DC: U.S. Department of Education, National Center for Education Statistics.

U.S. Department of Education. 2003g. *Remedial Education at Degree-Granting Postsecondary Institutions in Fall 2000: Statistical Analysis Report.* Technical Report NCES 2004–0101. Washington, D.C.: U.S. Department of Education, Institute of Education Science.

U.S. Department of Education. 2003h. *The Secondary and Technical Education Excellence Act of 2003: Summary of Major Provisions.* Washington, D.C.: U.S. Department of Education, Office of Vocational and Adult Education.

U.S. Department of Education. 2004. *National Postsecondary Student Aid Study, 2004 (Data Analysis System).* Washington, DC: U.S. Department of Education, National Center for Education Statistics.

U.S. Department of Education. 2005a. *Digest of Educational Statistics, 2004.* Washington DC: U.S. Department of Education, National Center for Education Statistics, Chapter 3, Table 315. Retrieved January 20, 2006, from http://nces.ed.gov/programs/digest/d04/tables/dt04_315.asp.

U.S. Department of Education. 2005b. *Digest of Educational Statistics, 2004.* Washington DC: U.S. Department of Education, National Center for Education Statistics, Chapter 3, Table 333. Retrieved January 20, 2006, from http://nces.ed.gov/programs/digest/d04/tables/dt04_333.asp.

U.S. Department of Education. 2005c. *Digest of Educational Statistics, 2004.* Washington DC: U.S. Department of Education, National Center for Education Statistics, Chapter 3, Tables 347–349. Retrieved January 20, 2006, from http://nces.ed.gov/programs/digest/d04/tables/dt04_347.asp.

Villeneuve, J. C., and W. N. Grubb. 1996. *Indigenous School-to-Work Programs: Lessons from Cincinnati's Co-op Education.* Berkeley, Calif.: National Center for Research in Vocational Education.

Waits, T., J. C. Setzer, and L. Lewis. 2005. *Dual Credit and Exam-Based Courses in U.S. Public High Schools, 2002–03.* NCES No. 2005009. Washington, D.C.: U.S. Department of Education, National Center for Education Statistics.

Warford, L. J. 2002. Funding Lifelong Learning: A National Priority. *Community College Journal,* 72 (3), 15–18.

Washington State Board for Community and Technical Colleges. 1994. *The Progress of Students*

Who Enroll in Developmental Studies Courses in Washington Community Colleges. Research report no. 94–1. Olympia: Washington State Board for Community and Technical Colleges.

Washington State Board for Community and Technical Colleges. 1997. *Performance Funding for Improvement in Washington Community Colleges.* Olympia: Washington State Board for Community and Technical Colleges.

Washington State Board for Community and Technical Colleges. 1998a. *Washington Community and Technical Colleges 1998–99 Performance Funding Allocation $2.05 Million Assigned to Demonstrated Performance.* Olympia: Washington State Board for Community and Technical Colleges.

Washington State Board for Community and Technical Colleges. 1998b. *Patterns Underlying the Current and Future Trends in Transfers from Community Colleges to Four-Year Public and Independent Institutions.* Research Report No. 98–7. Olympia: Washington State Board for Community and Technical Colleges.

Washington State Board for Community and Technical Colleges. 1998c. *1997–98 Academic Year Report.* Olympia: Washington State Board for Community and Technical Colleges.

Washington State Board for Community and Technical Colleges. 2000a. *Status Report to the Legislature: Community and Technical College Performance Measures.* Olympia: Washington State Board for Community and Technical Colleges.

Washington State Board for Community and Technical Colleges. 2000b. *Washington Community and Technical Colleges Performance Reporting Plan.* Olympia: Washington State Board for Community and Technical Colleges.

Washington State Board for Community and Technical Colleges. 2001a. *District Performance Results.* Olympia: Washington State Board for Community and Technical Colleges.

Washington State Board for Community and Technical Colleges. 2001b. *Running Start: 2000–01 Annual Progress Report.* Olympia: Washington State Board for Community and Technical Colleges.

Washington State Board for Community and Technical Colleges. 2002. *Mid-Biennium District Performance Reporting: Academic Year 2001–02.* Olympia: Washington State Board for Community and Technical Colleges.

Washington State Board for Community and Technical Colleges. 2003a. *Washington Community and Technical Colleges Performance Reporting Plan 2003–2005 Biennium Targets.* Olympia: Washington State Board for Community and Technical Colleges.

Washington State Board for Community and Technical Colleges. 2003b. *State Board Study Session Agenda.* Olympia: Washington State Board for Community and Technical Colleges.

Washington State Board for Community and Technical Colleges. 2004a. *Academic Year Report: 2003–04.* Olympia: Washington State Board for Community and Technical Colleges.

Washington State Board for Community and Technical Colleges. 2004b. *Making Important Performance Connections: How This Budget Request Links to the Priorities of Government Process.* Olympia: Washington State Board for Community and Technical Colleges.

Washington State Higher Education Coordinating Board. 2001. *Higher Education Statistics. State of Washington.* Olympia, WA: Washington State Higher Education Coordinating Board.

Washington State Higher Education Coordinating Board. 2004. *Higher Education Statistics: State of Washington.* Olympia: Washington State Higher Education Coordinating Board.

Weick, K. E. 2001. Sensemaking in Organizations: Small Structures with Large Consequences. In K. E. Weick, ed., *Making Sense of the Organization*, pp. 5–31. Malden, Mass.: Blackwell Publishing.

Weiner, E. J. 2002. Beyond Remediation: Ideological Literacies of Learning in Developmental Classrooms. *Journal of Adolescent and Adult Literacy*, 462(2), 150–168.

Wellman, J. V. 2002. *State Policy and Community College–Baccalaureate Transfer*. San Jose, Calif.: National Center for Public Policy and Higher Education and the Institute for Higher Education Policy.

White House. 2004. Fact Sheet: Job Training for the 21st Century Economy. Press release August 10.

Wills, J. L. 1993. *Industry-Driven Skill Standards Systems in the United States*, Vol. 3. Washington, D.C.: Institute for Educational Leadership, Center for Workforce Development.

Windham, P. 2003–2005. Private communication with the authors.

Winerip, M. 2004. Good Teachers + Small Classes = Quality Education. *New York Times*, May 26, p. B7.

Winter, G. 2002. Junior Colleges Try Niche as Cheap Path To Top Universities. *New York Times*, December 15, Section 1, p. 1.

Woodlief, B., C. Thomas, and G. Orozco. 2003. *California's Gold: Claiming the Promise of Diversity in our Community Colleges*. Edited by C. Dowell. Oakland, Calif.: California Tomorrow.

Wright, D. L., P. H. Dallet, and J. C. Copa. 2002. Ready, Fire, Aim: Performance Funding Policies for Postsecondary Education in Florida. In J. C. Burke and Associates, eds., *Funding Public Colleges and Universities for Performance: Popularity, Problems, and Prospects*, pp. 137–168. Albany, N.Y.: Rockfeller Institute Press.

Yin, R. K. 1984. *Case Study Research: Design and Methods*. Beverly Hills, Calif.: Sage.

Young, J. R. 2004. When Good Technology Means Bad Teaching: Giving Professors Gadgets without Training Can Do More Harm Than Good in the Classroom, Students Say. *Chronicle of Higher Education*, 51(12), A31.

Zeiss, T. 1998. The Realities of Competition: Will Our Students Become Theirs? *Community College Journal*, 68(6), 8–13.

Zeitlin, A. N., and T. C. Markus. 1996. Should Remediation Be Mandatory in the Community College? *Community Review*, 14, 27 33.

Zemsky, R., and W. F. Massy. 2004a. *Thwarted Innovation: What Happened to e-Learning and Why*. West Chester: Learning Alliance for Higher Education at the University of Pennsylvania.

Zemsky, R., and W. F. Massy. 2004b. Why the e-Learning Boom Went Bust. *Chronicle of Higher Education*, 50(44), B6.

Zumeta, W. 2001. Public Policy and Accountability in Higher Education: Lessons from the Past and Present for the New Millennium. In D. E. Heller, ed., *The States and Public Higher Education Policy: Affordability, Access, and Accountability*, pp. 155–197. Baltimore: Johns Hopkins University Press.

Zumeta, W. 2004. State Higher Education Financing. In E. P. St. John and M. D. Parsons, eds., *Public Funding of Higher Education: Changing Contexts and New Rationales*, pp. 79–107. Baltimore: Johns Hopkins University Press.